# Pioneer Girl Perspectives

THE PIONEER GIRL PROJECT

The Pioneer Girl Project is a research and publishing program of the South Dakota State Historical Society, working since 2010 to create a comprehensive edition of Laura Ingalls Wilder's *Pioneer Girl* and books dedicated to exploring her life and works.

PUBLICATIONS OF THE PIONEER GIRL PROJECT

*Pioneer Girl: The Annotated Autobiography*,
edited by Pamela Smith Hill

*Pioneer Girl Perspectives: Exploring Laura Ingalls Wilder*,
edited by Nancy Tystad Koupal

# Pioneer Girl Perspectives

*Exploring Laura Ingalls Wilder*

NANCY TYSTAD KOUPAL, editor

*A publication of the Pioneer Girl Project*

SOUTH DAKOTA HISTORICAL SOCIETY PRESS

Pierre

© 2017 South Dakota Historical Society Press. All rights reserved.

"Speech for the Detroit Book Fair" by Laura Ingalls Wilder
© 1937 Little House Heritage Trust. All rights reserved.

The quotations from the writings of Laura Ingalls Wilder,
Rose Wilder Lane, and Roger Lea MacBride are used with permission of
Little House Heritage Trust, the copyright owner.

This book or portions thereof in any form whatsoever may not be reproduced
without the express written approval of the South Dakota Historical Society Press,
900 Governors Drive, Pierre, S.Dak. 57501.

This publication is funded, in part, by the
Great Plains Education Foundation, Inc., Aberdeen, S.Dak.

Library of Congress Cataloging-in-Publication Data is available.

The paper in this book meets the guidelines for permanence and
durability of the committee on Production Guidelines for Book Longevity
of the Council on Library Resources.

Cover image: *Summer Fields* © 2016 Judy Thompson

Frontispiece: Laura Ingalls Wilder, 1937.
*Laura Ingalls Wilder Historic Home and Museum, Mansfield, Mo.*

Text and cover design by Rich Hendel

Typeset in Bulmer

Please visit the Pioneer Girl Project website at www.pioneergirlproject.org.

Printed in Canada

21  20  19  18  17    1  2  3  4  5

# Contents

Introduction
Exploring Laura Ingalls Wilder / 1
NANCY TYSTAD KOUPAL

## *Working Writers*

1. Speech for the Detroit Book Fair, 1937 / 9
LAURA INGALLS WILDER

2. The Strange Case of the Bloody Benders:
Laura Ingalls Wilder, Rose Wilder Lane, and Yellow Journalism / 20
CAROLINE FRASER

3. "Raise a Loud Yell":
Rose Wilder Lane, Working Writer / 52
AMY MATTSON LAUTERS

## *Beginnings and Misdirections*

4. *Pioneer Girl*: Its Roundabout Path into Print / 79
WILLIAM ANDERSON

5. Little Myths on the Prairie / 103
MICHAEL PATRICK HEARN

6. Her Stories Take You with Her:
The Lasting Appeal of the Little House Books / 135
NOEL L. SILVERMAN

## *Wilder's Place and Time*

7. Laura Ingalls Wilder as a Midwestern Pioneer Girl / 145
JOHN E. MILLER

8. Women's Place: Family, Home, and Farm / 177
PAULA M. NELSON

*Enduring Tales and Childhood Myths*

9. Fairy Tale, Folklore, and the Little House in the Deep Dark Woods / 209
   SALLIE KETCHAM

10. The Myth of Happy Childhood (and Other Myths about Frontiers, Families, and Growing Up) / 231
    ELIZABETH JAMESON

11. Frontier Families and the Little House Where Nobody Dies / 264
    ANN ROMINES

Contributors / 301

Index / 305

# Introduction
## *Exploring Laura Ingalls Wilder*
### NANCY TYSTAD KOUPAL

*"The mowing machine's whirring sounded cheerfully from the old buffalo wallow south of the claim shanty, where bluestem grass stood thick and tall and Pa was cutting it for hay."*
LAURA INGALLS WILDER, *The Long Winter*

Sitting in front of the class, my fifth-grade teacher in Mitchell, South Dakota, read these opening words from *The Long Winter*, Wilder's sixth novel. My classmates and I had just trudged through snow and wind, parked our rubber boots and snow-crusted winter coats and scarves in the cloakroom, and taken our seats in the warm classroom. The sunny haying scene that unfolded immediately grabbed our attention. As the hard winter of 1880–1881 outlasted our own, it made us proud that Laura Ingalls was a South Dakota pioneer—De Smet was just a few miles up the road. Even before the teacher had finished *The Long Winter*, I had visited the Carnegie Library downtown and borrowed all the Wilder books in the original edition with the Helen Sewell and Mildred Boyle illustrations. I was embarked on what would become a lifelong exploration of the life and career of Laura Ingalls Wilder. That endeavor would reach a high point in November 2014, when the South Dakota Historical Society Press released Wilder's *Pioneer Girl: The Annotated Autobiography*, with Pamela Smith Hill as editor.

My professional interest in Wilder had started back in the 1980s. As editor of *South Dakota History*, I got to know William Anderson, then a graduate student at South Dakota State University. While editing his article, "The Literary Apprenticeship of Laura Ingalls Wilder" in 1983, I first encountered the richness and complexities of Wilder scholarship. The following year, my appreciation grew when Nancy DeHamer published a research guide for the Rose Wilder Lane Papers at the Herbert Hoover Presidential Library in *South Dakota History*.[1] In the 1990s, the Laura Ingalls Wilder Memorial Society in De Smet asked me to join its board as the members continued their

---

1. Anderson, "The Literary Apprenticeship of Laura Ingalls Wilder," *South Dakota History* 13 (Winter 1983): 285–331; DeHamer, "The Rose Wilder Lane Papers at the Her-

ongoing stewardship of the Surveyors' House and the Ingalls Home. In 2005, as director of the South Dakota Historical Society Press, I commissioned a biography of Laura Ingalls Wilder as a part of our South Dakota Biography Series,[2] and once again, I found myself steeped in Wilder scholarship, adding to the file cabinets of research material that line my office.

Perhaps the single most impressive moment in my exploration of Wilder came in November 2011, when Hill and I became the first researchers in over thirty years to see the original, handwritten "Pioneer Girl" manuscript. The trip to Mansfield, Missouri, was the culmination of months of negotiation and preparation. The South Dakota Historical Society Press had earned the right to publish the manuscript from the Little House Heritage Trust in 2010, but no one outside of the staff and board members of the Laura Ingalls Wilder Home and Museum in Mansfield had seen the original manuscript in decades. It was an exciting moment. Museum director Jean Coday opened the vaults and brought out the aging tablets that contain the handwritten story of the young Laura Ingalls. The lined pages of those inexpensive pads of paper had toned over the years and become brittle. They had been treated for acidity, but they remained fragile. I pulled on white gloves and touched them carefully. The transcription, annotation, and publication of the material in those tablets would take another three years.

Back in 2009, when the South Dakota Historical Society Press first contemplated publishing Laura Ingalls Wilder's autobiography, we speculated that we might be able to sell five thousand copies. We had in mind a scholarly exploration of Wilder's work, based on meticulous documentation and scrupulous attention to historical detail, a comparative study of preliminary texts and finished works. But we also knew we needed to make it readable and accessible to those who had loved the Little House books through the years. As a publisher, readability combined with scholarship had always been our hallmark, and it was that combination that we intended to bring, with the help of editor Hill, to the Wilder memoir. But imagine our surprise in 2014 when fifteen thousand copies of *Pioneer Girl: The Annotated Autobiography* made their way off the press just before Thanksgiving and sold out within three weeks. Thousands of readers snatched it up, talked about it, and before we knew it, the book was on bestseller lists. It went through eight printings

---

bert Hoover Presidential Library," ibid. 14 (Winter 1984): 335–48. *See also* Anderson, "Laura Ingalls Wilder and Rose Wilder Lane: The Continuing Collaboration," ibid. 16 (Summer 1986): 89–143.

2. Pamela Smith Hill, *Laura Ingalls Wilder: A Writer's Life* (Pierre: South Dakota Historical Society Press, 2007).

Wilder wrote *Pioneer Girl* on these inexpensive tablets.
*South Dakota Historical Society Press*

in the first year as more than a hundred fifty thousand copies found their way around the world. Once again, Laura Ingalls Wilder had proven just how relevant she was to another generation.

Bemused, reporters and critics asked, what was the appeal? What were readers hoping to find in this massive, encyclopedic volume? What made Wilder and her books resonate with so many people in so many countries? As we contemplated these questions, I also began to wonder, what did *Pioneer Girl: The Annotated Autobiography* itself contribute to the general understanding and scholarly appreciation of Wilder's life and work? These questions were the genesis of this book. And I decided to ask them of a variety of people with various perspectives on Wilder—those who had already written about her and those who had not but who studied children's literature or women's history more broadly. I also wanted some answers to questions that had not been resolved in *Pioneer Girl: The Annotated Autobiography*. Why, for example, was Laura Ingalls not a supporter of women's rights and suffrage—what was she thinking? Even as I asked the authors in this book to comment on the appeal, relevance, and thinking of Wilder, I set them each "free to take the discussion in any direction that you deem appropriate."[3] And they did.

---

3. Koupal to Ann Romines, Dec. 17, 2015. This line appears in each of the invitation letters to the authors in this book.

In the serendipitous way of such things, the resulting book is both diverse and cohesive, a rich sourcebook for those who wish to explore and learn about Wilder. I have grouped the essays into four categories, "Working Writers," "Beginnings and Misdirections," "Wilder's Place and Time," and "Enduring Fairy Tales and Childhood Myths." While the essays in each section relate to each other in some direct way, the arrangement is arbitrary, and all the essays complement the others in one way or another, sometimes quite unexpectedly. For example, Michael Patrick Hearn in the second section of the book asked a rhetorical question about a song that Sallie Ketcham suggested an answer for in the fourth section.

"Working Writers" opens with an essay by Wilder herself, in which she offered her own perspective on her life and her work at the midpoint of her Little House series. In 1937, she had completed her first four novels. To my knowledge, Wilder only wrote about her working life in one other essay, which she wrote a year earlier and also gave as a speech, called "My Work."[4] Of the two, the speech presented here, which she wrote for a book fair in Detroit, is longer and more reflective, and it is the one that scholars most often cite. In it, Wilder shared her personal understanding of her motives and concepts but also interjected material that brings into question her ideas of truth and fact. Caroline Fraser took on those questions directly in her essay, "The Strange Case of the Bloody Benders." In the process, Fraser also showcased the working relationship of Wilder and Rose Wilder Lane, her daughter, during the formative years when Lane was learning her trade from the masters of yellow journalism. Closing the section on "Working Writers" is Amy Mattson Lauters, with an essay on the writing career of Lane. No book about Wilder can be complete without serious consideration of her daughter and editor, and Lauters provided insight into the motivations and craftsmanship of Lane during her long career as a working writer.

The next section jumps from a consideration of writers at work to the results of their labors—*Pioneer Girl* and the Little House books. William Anderson opens "Beginnings and Misdirections" with a history of *Pioneer Girl* as only he can tell it. When Wilder and Lane completed their work with the handwritten manuscript and its multiple typescript versions, they filed these documents away in drawers and cabinets in their homes until Wilder's death in 1957. As one of the first people to become aware of the neglected autobiography and the clues it presented for Wilder scholars, Anderson went back into his own extensive research files to reconstruct the path the

---

4. Wilder, "My Work," printed in Wilder and Rose Wilder Lane, *A Little House Sampler*, ed. William Anderson (Lincoln: University of Nebraska Press, 1988), pp. 174–80.

manuscript took in finding its way into print. Michael Patrick Hearn, who has studied such classic children's authors as L. Frank Baum, Mark Twain, and Charles Dickens, utilized his knowledge of the field to discuss the myths that cloud Wilder research and affect her reputation. For many years, the idea that Wilder was a sort of Grandma Moses of literature has obscured a true understanding of the genius of the Little House books. Finally, Noel L. Silverman, counsel for the Little House Heritage Trust, shared his appreciation of *Pioneer Girl: The Annotated Autobiography* in an interview, offering insights about Wilder gained during almost fifty years of guarding her legacy. In the process, he suggested some new directions for understanding Wilder and corrected some misunderstandings.

Stepping back, the authors in "Wilder's Place and Time" addressed questions of geographical location and societal values as they relate to Wilder. John E. Miller looked at Wilder's identity as a midwestern pioneer, comparing her with such other prominent artists of the region as Willa Cather and Harvey Dunn. Historian Paula M. Nelson tackled my questions about Wilder's stance on women's rights. In reading Dakota Territory newspapers for the annotations in *Pioneer Girl: The Annotated Autobiography*, I observed that prominent members of the De Smet community were actively involved in the struggle for woman suffrage in the 1880s. Wilder could hardly have missed the literary debates, traveling speakers, and opinion columns on the issue, and yet, she never mentioned the topic in her autobiography. At the same time, she was unwilling to promise to "obey" her husband during her 1885 marriage ceremony, as recorded both in her memoir and in *These Happy Golden Years*.[5] That unwillingness to bend to her husband's will had always impressed me as feisty and modern, and I remember hunting up the marriage vows before my own wedding to be sure that the onerous promise was not a part of my ceremony (writing one's own vows was not then in vogue). To me, Wilder's indifference to women's rights and her objection to vowing obedience to her husband always seemed contradictory, so I asked Nelson to shed some light on women's issues during Wilder's lifetime.

In the final section, "Enduring Fairy Tales and Childhood Myths," attention focuses on the ongoing critical study of Wilder's works and addresses the role of storytelling and the significance of family and childhood in her novels. Selecting the author's first book, *Little House in the Big Woods*, Sallie Ketcham examined the fairy-tale elements of the woods and the little house.

---

5. Wilder, *Pioneer Girl: The Annotated Autobiography*, ed. Pamela Smith Hill (Pierre: South Dakota Historical Society Press, 2014), p. 322; Wilder, *These Happy Golden Years* (New York: Harper & Row, 1953), p. 269.

She also looked at Wilder's affinity for fairy tales expressed in her nonfiction writings. In her essay, Elizabeth Jameson turned the issue of childhood myths back on itself and took a hard look at Wilder's childhood in the West. In the process, she also illuminated the role of women on the Turnerian frontier. Bringing both the section and the book to a close is Ann Romines, the only author in this volume who actually met Laura Ingalls Wilder. With years of immersion in Wilder studies, she brought her expertise to bear on the ongoing value of a family and home where no one grows old and no one dies.

While these essays do not, either individually or collectively, answer all questions about Wilder's life and career, together they go a long way toward explaining some of the universal appeal of Wilder's novels. The various authors' perspectives on *Pioneer Girl* and its role in Wilder's and Lane's careers also lead us naturally into further exploration of Laura Ingalls Wilder and her works.

# Working Writers

# { 1 }
# Speech for the Detroit Book Fair, 1937

## LAURA INGALLS WILDER

*Editor' Note:* Laura Ingalls Wilder seldom spoke publicly about herself or her writing career. A major exception occurred in the speech she presented in Detroit on October 16, 1937, preserved as a handwritten document at the Herbert Hoover Presidential Library.[1] In its pages, Wilder shared with her audience some of her motivation—preserving her father's stories—but most importantly, she gave an overview of her completed and future novels as she conceived of them. At midpoint in her series, she indicated that she had a clear vision of what she was doing creatively and, among other things, outlined her understanding of the frontier and what it meant in her writing.

Wilder delivered her speech during "A Week of Authors"—sponsored by the J. L. Hudson Company, a department store in Detroit, Michigan. The program billed it as the company's "Fourth Annual Book Fair—intended as an informal get-together of those who write books, those who read them, and those who publish them." Each afternoon, from Monday through Saturday, an adult session at 2:30 and a juvenile program at 4:00 showcased authors and their publishing representatives.[2] Louise Raymond, who headed the Juvenile Department at Harper & Brothers, and her featured author Laura Ingalls Wilder were the final speakers of the event. Wilder spent the week in Detroit and likely participated in the lavish luncheons and other parties for presenters.[3]

---

1. Box 13, file 197, Laura Ingalls Wilder Series, Rose Wilder Lane Papers, Herbert Hoover Presidential Library, West Branch, Iowa. This transcription is as close as possible to the original. Corrections in punctuation or spelling have been made in brackets, allowing the reader to see any changes made. While Wilder did not underline her book titles, we have rendered them in italics.

2. *The Book Fair: "A Week of Authors"* (Detroit: J. L. Hudson Co., 1937), p. 3.

3. Ibid., pp. 18–19; "Visiting Writers Complimented at Luncheons Preceding Program of Afternoon Talks," *Detroit Free Press*, Oct. 12, 1937, p. 12.

The nineteen-page program for the Detroit book fair contained daily schedules and introduced each speaker participating in the week-long event.
*Burton Historical Collection, Detroit Public Library*

The program of events, which quoted Rose Wilder Lane, informed the audience that Wilder had been "born in the log house described in 'Little House in the Big Woods'" and that her "earliest memories are of life in the Indian Territory, where her father was a pioneer hunter, trapper and Indian fighter. Later they traveled west. . . . My mother is now about seventy, small, dresses more in the mode than I do. Reads 'Adventure' magazine, makes gingerbread famous throughout the county." Lane also summarized her mother's nonfiction writing career, emphasized her job at the Federal Farm Loan Bank, and described her duties as farm wife, "expert cook, dairy-maid and poultry raiser." The person who put the program together concluded that Wilder was "surely a woman who has stepped most gracefully from one generation to another, using the experience of her pioneer past to solve the problems of the present day."[4]

Lane, who was then in New York, had coached her mother by letter on what to wear, whom to talk with, what to tell them, and how to deliver her message, but she had not participated in the writing of the speech itself.[5] When she received a copy in late October, she wrote to her mother: "Detroit talk came and it is *fine*. No wonder you made a great hit. Those stories are marvelous."[6] The speech contains anecdotes and tall tales of the prairie, including one of the most problematical of all Wilder's stories—her account of the Bender murders in Kansas. What often gets overlooked in considering this speech, however, are the ways in which it showcases Wilder's command of her material and the trajectory of her novels. The ending is also noteworthy. Just as she had in her novels, Wilder underscored the pluck and courage of the pioneers with snippets of song.[7] We can only wonder, did she sing them to her listeners?

Many years ago, in the Little House in the Big Woods, Sister Mary and I listened to father[']s stories.

There was no radio to amuse us then, no moving pictures to go see, so when the day's work was done, we sat in the twilight or by the evening lamp and listened to Pa's stories and the music of his violin. Our little family must be self sufficient for its own entertainment as well as its livelihood and there was no lack in either.

---

4. *Book Fair*, p. 19. Other children's authors/illustrators were (in order of appearance) May Lamberton Becker, Bertha L. Gunterman, Eloise Lownsbery, Marie Emilie Gilchrist, Ralph Henry Barbour, Sidney Corbett, William Heyliger, Dorothy Bryan, Munro Leaf, Kurt Wiese, Elizabeth Foreman Lewis, Majorie Flack, Eleanor Rawlinson, Will Rannells, Ruth Sawyer, Alice Dalgliesh, and Paul Brown.

5. Lane to Wilder, Oct. 11, 1937, Box 13, file 193, Lane Papers.

6. Lane to Wilder, postscript, [late Oct.], ibid.

7. As here, the last words of four of her novels are verses or lines from songs (*Little House on the Prairie*, *By the Shores of Silver Lake*, *These Happy Golden Years*, *The First Four Years*). Two more conclude with Pa's fiddle in the background (*Little House in the Big Woods*, *On the Banks of Plum Creek*), and one (*The Long Winter*) ends with family and friends singing.

Wilder composed her own speech for the book fair, writing in a neat, deliberate hand.
*Herbert Hoover Presidential Library and Museum*

Mother was descended from an old Scotch family and inherited the Scotch thriftiness which helped with the livelihood.

Altho born and raised on the frontier she was an educated, cultured woman. She was very quiet and gentle, but proud and particular in all matters of good breeding.

Father's ancestors arrived in America on the Mayflower and he was born in N. Y. State[.] But he also was raised on the frontier. He was always jolly, inclined to be reckless and loved his violin.

So Ma taught us books and trained us in our manners, while Pa taught us other things and entertained us.

We had a busy, happy childhood, but of it all, Sister Mary and I loved Pa's stories best. We never forgot them and I have always felt they were to[o] good to be altogether lost. Children to day could not have a childhood like mine in the Big Woods of Wisconsin but they could learn of it and hear the stories that Pa used to tell.

But I put off writing them from year to year and was past 60 when I wrote my first book, *The Little House in the Big Woods*.

When to my surprise the book made such a success and children from all over the U. S. wrote to me begging for more stories, I began to think what a wonderful childhood I had had. How I had seen the whole frontier, the woods, the Indian country of the great plains, the frontier towns, the building of railroads in wild, unsettled country, homesteading and farmers coming in to take possession.

I realized that I had seen and lived it all—all the successive phases of the frontier, first the frontiersman then the pioneer, then the farmers and the towns.[8]

Then I understood that in my own life I represented a whole period of American history. That the frontier was gone and agricultural settlements had taken its place when I married a farmer.

It seemed to me that my childhood had been much richer and more interesting than that of children to-day even with all the modern inventions and improvements.

I wanted the children now to understand more about the begin[n]ing of things[,] to know what is behind the things they see—what it is that made America as they know it.

Then I thought of writing the story of my childhood in several volumes—a seven volume historical novel for children covering every aspect of the American frontier.

After the work was well started, I was told that such a thing had never been done before; that a novel of several volumes was only for grown-ups.

---

8. These concepts echo those of Frederick Jackson Turner's famous essay "The Significance of the Frontier in American History," in Turner, *The Frontier in American History* (New York: Henry Holt & Co., 1920), pp. 1–38. For more on Wilder and the frontier thesis, *see* Elizabeth Jameson's "The Myth of Happy Childhood (and Other Myths about Frontiers, Families, and Growing Up)" in this volume.

When I told my daughter, R. W. L.[,] about it she said it would be unique, that a seven volume novel for children had never been written.[9]

I hesitated. Perhaps my idea was all wrong.

But letters kept coming from children—individuals, whole classes in schools, Mothers of children to[o] small to write letters—all wanted to know what happened next, wanted me to go on with the story.

I decided to do so. Someone has to do a thing first. I would be the first to write a seven volume novel for children.

So I wrote the second volume, *Farmer Boy*. This is the story of a farm boy in the east before he went west. It is the story of the childhood of my husband on his father[']s farm near Malone N. Y.

The old house is still standing just as it was when his mother sat at her spinning wheel in the attic chamber.

We got some wintergreen plants from the old place, a few years ago, to set out on our Ozark farm.

Almanzo still loves horses as well as when he was that Farmer Boy, but he doesn't drive them now. He drives our new Chrysler sedan instead, at least he holds the wheel. Of course I do the driving with my tongue.

You may wonder that the name Almanzo, of Central-Asian origin as it is, should have been given to a Yankee farmer boy.

The name Almanzo comes from El Mansur and was brought into England from Asia during the crusades[,] and from England to America by the Wilders when they came to Plymouth in 1631.

The third volume of my seven volume childrens' [sic] novel goes back again to Laura in *The Little House on the Prairie* and in the fourth volume, *On the Banks of Plum Creek*, just published.

9. During the years 1933–1934, Lane outlined an adult "American novel in many volumes, an enormous canvas, covering horizontally a continent, vertically all classes" (Lane, Journal [1933–1934], Jan. 11, 1933, Box 23, item #51, Lane Papers). Her novel *Let the Hurricane Roar* was "the prelude" (ibid., n.d.). One wonders who influenced whom— mother or daughter—in the desire to craft a multi-volume novel about American history. Wilder published her second book (about Almanzo) in 1933 and had returned to her own childhood to create a chronological bridge between the events in her first and third books. The idea of completing her life story in seven volumes may have occurred to her during this process and then prompted Lane, who was using her mother's material at this point, to outline her own adult version. In any case, there is little thematic connection between the two concepts. Lane's outline painted a bleak picture of American life and of the pioneer, who was "typically the poor man, of obscure or debased birth, without ability to rise from the mass, and his westward movement was largely escape. Beyond regions of established law, he was irresponsible, always lawless in point of view, often dishonest in practice" (ibid., n.d.).

Almanzo, the Farmer Boy appears again in the fifth volume on which I am now working. He goes with Laura the rest of the way through the two more volumes it will take to make the seven and complete the novel. But these are still to be written so I'll not give any details now.[10]

You haven't yet had time to read the fourth volume, *On the Banks of Plum Creek*.

It shows Laura and her family in Western Minnesota where Ma thought they were all safe in a civilized country where nothing could happen to them. When you read the book you will see how wrong she was. There were runaways and fires and storms—such terrible storms—and the grasshoppers—the grasshopper plague of 1874, the worst ever known since the plagues of Egypt.

I read recently of a grasshopper invasion where, so the author said, the grasshoppers' breaths smelled strongly of onions from eating so many of those vegetables.

Now I never smelled a grasshopper's breath, but I have lived among uncounted millions of them. I have seen clouds of them darken the noo[n]day sun. I saw their bodies choke the waters of Plum Creek, I saw them destroy every green thing on the face of the earth, so far as a child would know. There are unforget[t]able pictures of those grasshoppers in my mind that I have tried to draw plainly in *On the Banks of Plum Creek*.

Even so Plum Creek was to[o] civilized for Pa and we went west again to Dakota Ter. where Almanzo was homesteading, where he helped save Laura, and the other people of the new settlement, from starving during the Hard Winter. And where he and Laura thought zero weather fine for sleighing and decided 40 below was just a little to[o] cold.

But that will all be told in the sixth and seventh volumes of my children['s] novel which ends happily as all good novels should when Laura of the Little Houses and Almanzo of *Farmer Boy* were married.[11]

Every story in this novel, all the circumstances, each incident are true[.]

All I have told is true but it is not the whole truth. There were some stories

---

10. Wisely, Wilder did not disclose details, for she originally planned only one book, which she tentatively titled "Prairie Girl," to follow *The Long Winter*. In the end, she had enough material for a total of eight volumes. Wilder, "Prairie Girl" (outline), Box 16, file 243, Lane Papers.

11. In 1936, Wilder wrote: "Rose insists that I must carry the story on until Laura married Farmer Boy. And so I suppose I will" (Wilder to Louise Raymond, Oct. 26, 1936, in Wilder, *The Selected Letters of Laura Ingalls Wilder*, ed. William Anderson [New York: HarperCollins, 2016], p. 100).

I wanted to tell but would not be ~~response~~ responsible for putting in a book for children, even though I knew them as a child.

There was the story of the Bender family that belonged in the third volume, *The Little House on the Prairie*[.] The Benders lived half way between it and Independence Kansas. We stopped there, on our way in to the Little house, while Pa watered the horses and brought us all a drink from the well near the door of the house. I saw Kate Bender standing in the doorway, we did not go in because we could not afford to stop at a tavern.[12]

On his trip to Independence to sell his furs, Pa stopped again for water, but did not go in for the same reason as before.

There were Kate Bender and two men, her brothers, in the family and their tavern was the only place for travelers to stop on the road south from Independence.

People disappeared on that road. Leaving Independence and going south they were never heard of again. It was thought they were killed by Indians but no bodies were ever found.

Then it was noticed that the Bender's garden was always freshly plowed but never planted. People wondered. And then a man came from the east looking for his brother who was missing.

He made up a party in Independence and they followed the road south, but when they came to the Bender place there was no one there. There were signs of hurried departure and the[y] searched the place.

The front room was divided by a calico curtain against which the dining table stood. On the curtain back of the table were stains about as high as the head of a man when seated. Behind the curtain was a trap door in the floor and beside it lay a heavy hammer.

In the cellar underneath was the body of a man whose head had been crushed by the hammer. It appeared that he had been seated at the table back to the curtain and had been struck from behind it.

A grave was partly dug in the garden with a shovel close by. The possie [*sic*] searched the garden and dug up human bones and bodies[.] One body was that of a little girl who had been buried alive with her murdered parents. The garden was truly a grave-yard kept plowed so it would show no signs.

The night of the day the bodies were found a neighbor rode up to our

---

12. *See* Caroline Fraser's "The Strange Case of the Bloody Benders: Laura Ingalls Wilder, Rose Wilder Lane, and Yellow Journalism" in this volume. This episode is also recounted in the Bye version of *Pioneer Girl*. *See* Wilder, *Pioneer Girl: The Annotated Autobiography*, ed. Pamela Smith Hill (Pierre: South Dakota Historical Society Press, 2014), App. B, "The Benders of Kansas," pp. 353-56.

house and talked earnestly with Pa. Pa took his rifle down from its place over the door and said to Ma[,] "The vigelents [sic] are called out." Then he saddled a horse and rode away with the neighbor.

It was late the next day when he came back and he never told us where he had been.

For several years there was more or less of a hunt for the Benders and a reports that they had been seen here or there[.] At such times Pa always said in a strange tone of finality, "They will never be found."

They never were found and later I formed my own conclusions why.

You will agree it is not a fit story for a childrens' book. But it shows there were other dangers on the frontier besides wild Indians.

Then there was the family of children frozen in the terrible blizzard on Plum Creek. I couldn't tell that either.[13]

Sister Mary and I knew of these things but someway were shielded from the full terror of them. Although we knew them true they seemed unreal to us for Ma was always there serene and quiet and Pa with his fiddle and his songs.

The spirit of the frontier was one of humor and cheerfulness no matter what happened and whether the joke was on oneself or the other fellow. Strangers coming west possessed or acquired this spirit if they survived as westerners.

There was the man from the east who knew nothing of Dakota mirages.

The first morning after stopping at a little frontier town, he saw from the hotel a large lake and trees nearby. He said to the hotel keeper, "I always like a short walk before breakfast. I am going to the lake. Will breakfast be ready when I come back?"

The hotel man looked at the lake that appeared so near and knew it was a mirage and that the real lake was over forty miles distant.

He said[,] "Your breakfast will be ready by the time you get back," and watched the stranger walk away.

At noon a teamster coming in met the easterner away out on the prairie on the bank of a tiny creek. He had taken off all his clothes and was rolling them into a tight bundle.

13. Wilder had told children just such a story in *On the Banks of Plum Creek* (New York: Harper & Row, 1937, 1953), where Pa says: "I heard of some folks that went to town and a blizzard came up so quickly they couldn't get back. Their children at home burned all the furniture, but they froze stark stiff before the blizzard cleared up enough so the folks could get home" (p. 281). She also mentioned this event in *Pioneer Girl*, p. 69, but in her speech, she may have had in mind the more graphic tale from her autobiography of the children who left their house after the wind destroyed their stovepipe, pp. 139-40.

"What in the world are you doing?" the teamster asked.

Looking up from his bundle the man answered[,] "I don't want to get my clothes wet and I'm going to carry them on my head when I swim across this water." And seeing how astonished the teamster looked he added[,] "Oh I know it looks only a step across, but judging from how near the lake looked this morning and how far I have walked without finding it there is no telling how far I will have to swim before I get to the other bank of this creek.["]

Then there was the settler leaving the country after one of its periodic drouths. All his worldly goods were in the covered wagon with the family. A cow was tied behind and several scrawny colts and horses followed. The kind of horses that in that place at that time sold for $1 a head[.]

He stopped at a little wind-blown town to water his horses before camping on the prairie beyond.

The hotel keeper at that place had a great curiosity and was noted all over that country for asking questions.

He asked the traveler where he was from and then, "Own a farm out there?["]

"Yes!" the man answered.

"How much land?" the hotel man wanted to know.

"160 acres," the man told him.

"And what did you do with it?" the hotel man asked.

The man turned on the wagon seat and pointed to the poorest, most worthless colt among the horses.

"See that colt back there?" he asked. "Well I traded 80 acres of the land for that colt."

The hotel keeper looked at the colt but he wasn't satisfied.

"What did you do with the other 80?" he persisted[.]

"Oh!" was the reply, "The man I traded with was a poor, ignorant fellow from the east. I slipped the other 80 in on the deed and he never noticed it."

My parents possessed this frontier spirit to a marked degree. It shines through all the seven volumes of my childrens' novel.

Whether it was the Indian troubles in the Little House on the Prairie or the terrible storms and the ~~grassh~~ grasshoppers on Plum Creek, once past they refused to dwell on them but looked ahead to better things.

When times were hard the fiddle and Pa sang —

"Oh drive dull car[e] away
For weeping is but sorrow.
If things are wrong today
There's another day tomorrow.

"So drive dull care away
And do the best you can
Put your shoulder to the wheel
Is the mottoe [sic] for every man."[14]

If our fare was scanty at times[,] still it never lacked variety for as Pa and the fiddle sang

"One day we had greens
And a dish full of bacon.
The next we had bacon
And a dish full of greens."[15]

---

14. Wilder also quoted these verses from "A Motto for Every Man," by Harry Clifton (1832–1872), in *By the Shores of Silver Lake* (New York: Harper & Row, 1953), p. 265. *See* Dale Cockrell, ed., *The Ingalls Wilder Family Songbook* (Middleton, Wis.: A-R Editions, 2011), pp. 120–23.

15. The lyrics to this song, called "Bacon and Greens," can be found in T. Maclagan, *Maclagan's Musical Age Songster* (London: Music-Publishing Co., 1864), p. 30, which uses "plateful" rather than Wilder's "dish full." While Wilder did not use this song in any of her books, Lane had suggested it to her for *On the Banks of Plum Creek*. She asked, "Do you remember the words of 'Bacon and Greens' if it had any?" (Lane to Wilder, June 13, 1936, Folder 19, Laura Ingalls Wilder Papers, Laura Ingalls Wilder Home Association, Mansfield, Mo., Microfilm ed., University of Missouri Western Historical Manuscript Collection & State Historical Society of Missouri).

# { 2 }
# The Strange Case of the Bloody Benders
## *Laura Ingalls Wilder, Rose Wilder Lane, and Yellow Journalism*

### CAROLINE FRASER

In 1915, in one of the most momentous trips she would ever take, Laura Ingalls Wilder traveled by train, alone, to San Francisco, California. She was forty-eight. She had never been to the West Coast, had never seen an ocean, had never visited a major city outside the Midwest. She was missing her twenty-eight-year-old daughter, Rose Wilder Lane, living and working in the big city, whom she had not seen for several years. Like her father before her, she yearned to see the Pacific and touch the farthest reaches of the American continent. She hungered as well to take in the giddy and glorious attractions of that year's world's fair, the Panama-Pacific International Exposition, celebrating the completion of the Panama Canal and the renaissance of the city after the 1906 earthquake and fires. But even as she reveled in views of sagebrush, Rocky Mountain ramparts, and the Great Salt Lake unspooling out the train windows, Wilder had more in mind than mere tourism. She undertook the journey with an overriding professional ambition. She saw the trip as an opportunity, a chance to apprentice herself to her daughter, a fledgling newspaper writer.

That apprenticeship was well underway. Beginning in 1908, Rose Wilder had briefly served as a freelancer for the *San Francisco Call*. After marrying an itinerant salesman, Claire Gillette Lane, the following year, she wrote a few pieces for the *Kansas City Post* and perhaps other papers. As soon as she began dabbling in the trade, she urged her mother to do likewise and write for local papers or farm journals to bridge the family's income gap.[1] Wilder assiduously followed her daughter's advice. Between 1910 and her trip to San Francisco, she published a handful of articles, beginning with humble topics

---

1. *See* fragments of correspondence from Rose Wilder Lane to Laura Ingalls Wilder, 1911–1915, Box 13, file 182, and Box 14, file 202, Laura Ingalls Wilder Series, Rose Wilder Lane Papers (hereafter cited as Lane Papers), Herbert Hoover Presidential Library, West Branch, Iowa.

—"Profits of the Good Fat Hen" in the *Coffeyville* (Kansas) *Daily Journal*, for example—before tackling more substantial fare.[2]

Wilder's first major essay, "The Small Farm Home," was delivered at a homemakers' conference during Farm Week at the University of Missouri's College of Agriculture in 1911. Reprinted in a newly expanded regional journal, the *Missouri Ruralist*, it compared the stress and pollution of city life to the "freer, healthier, happier life" of smallholders, celebrating the fresh air and "green slopes" of rural living, along with wondrous new conveniences from oil stoves to cream separators that made quick work of heavy labor. Its sunny, optimistic portrait of farming impressed the *Ruralist*'s editor, sitting in the Farm Week audience, and it launched Wilder's career as a columnist.[3] Critically, however, her essay glossed over the difficulties, reversals, and failures that were the farmer's lot, something its author knew only too well.

At its core, Wilder's writing sprang from a desire to capture her early childhood, but economic necessity was also a compelling factor. She and her husband, Almanzo, had never been able to achieve steady financial security on the farm. In Dakota Territory, where they had married in 1885, they had been forced off their land after several disastrous years. Relocating to the Ozarks in 1894, they struggled as well on Rocky Ridge Farm, their acreage outside of Mansfield, Missouri, and let the land after only a few years. To eke out a living, they relocated to town, working at a series of jobs: making deliveries, balancing accounts for a local fuel company, renting out rooms, and cooking meals for boarders. Even after moving back to Rocky Ridge in 1910, their orchards and egg-and-dairy operation produced sporadic and limited income at best.[4]

Almanzo Wilder's disability exacerbated the precariousness of their posi-

---

2. "Profits of the Good Fat Hen," *Coffeyville* (Kans.) *Daily Journal*, Sept. 12, 1910. This early article apparently excerpted Mrs. A. J. Wilder's counsel from the *Woman's National Daily*, a short-lived newspaper published in Saint Louis.

3. Wilder's talk was delivered in absentia and published as Mrs. A. J. Wilder, "The Small Farm Home," in *Forty-third Annual Report of the Missouri State Board of Agriculture: A Record of the Work for the Year 1910* (Jefferson City, Mo.: Hugh Stephens Printing Co., 1911), pp. 252–57. The article was reprinted as "Favors the Small Farm Home" in the *Missouri Ruralist*, Feb. 18, 1911, and in *Laura Ingalls Wilder, Farm Journalist: Writings from the Ozarks*, ed. Stephen W. Hines (Columbia: University of Missouri Press, 2007), pp. 13–16. For its affect on her career, *see* William Anderson, *Laura Ingalls Wilder: A Biography* (New York: HarperCollins, 1992), p. 176.

4. Various biographies record these years. *See*, for example, John E. Miller, *Becoming Laura Ingalls Wilder: The Woman behind the Legend* (Columbia: University of Missouri Press, 1998), chap. 4.

tion. Affected by a stroke in 1888 after contracting diphtheria, he never regained full strength in his feet and legs, walking with a pronounced limp. The fear that he might become fully disabled must have heightened his wife's and daughter's need to supplement the family income.

Lane expressed her frustration with farm economics in the summer of 1914, writing to her aunt Eliza Jane Wilder Thayer. She had been hoping to have her parents visit San Francisco for the past four years, she said, but disappointing harvests and her own financial worries interfered: "There have been three very dry years in Missouri . . . when the crops were nearly complete failures, and now this year, when they get a fair crop, it is impossible to sell anything at a profitable price." Whatever money the farm made, she admitted, was plowed right back into the land.[5] Thus the long-planned 1915 trip exerted financial strain on all involved. The Wilders and their daughter could not afford train fare for both parents, along with wages for a hired man to care for the livestock in their absence, so Almanzo Wilder stayed home. "I am being as careful as I can," Wilder wrote from the city, "and I am not for a minute losing sight of the difficulties at home or what I came for."[6] What she came for was a start in a new career and the money it might bring.

Lane had been hired earlier that year by her friend and former roommate Bessie Beatty at the *San Francisco Bulletin* for $12.50 a week, raised to $30 by the time her mother arrived. Prior to that, the Lanes, working in real estate, had been so hard up that they had borrowed $250 from her parents. The couple may have split before Wilder arrived, keeping the news quiet for appearances' sake.[7] While both were preoccupied with financial worries, Wilder and her daughter nonetheless exhibited sharply divergent attitudes toward debt. Acknowledging that there were still "notes and mortgages" on the farm, Lane bubbled with youthful optimism and a certain frivolity, assuring her mother, "there are only the debts to clear off and you will have a self-supporting home and can use the little extra sums—the bunches of money, like from the apples or strawberries—that come in, to play with."[8] Her mother's more anxious

---

5. Lane to Eliza Jane and Wilder Thayer, Oct. 3, 1914, Box 11, file 11, Dorothy Smith Collection, Almanzo and Laura Ingalls Wilder Association, Malone, N.Y.

6. Wilder to Almanzo Wilder, Sept. 21, 1915, in *West from Home: Letters of Laura Ingalls Wilder to Almanzo Wilder, San Francisco 1915*, ed. Roger Lea MacBride (New York: Harper & Row, 1974), p. 67.

7. William Holtz, *The Ghost in the Little House: A Life of Rose Wilder Lane* (Columbia: University of Missouri Press, 1993), pp. 59, 61, 65; Wilder to Almanzo Wilder, Aug. 29, Sept. 23, 1915, in *West from Home*, pp. 32–33, 74. Lane later recalled leaving her husband in January 1915.

8. Lane to Wilder, [Spring 1915], in *West from Home*, p. 5.

William Randolph Hearst sought out the sensational in order to build a newspaper empire. *Library of Congress*

calculations, by contrast, were grounded in practicality. Writing privately to her husband, she shared Gillette Lane's extravagant promise not only to pay them back but to "lift" their $500 mortgage if he found a job, but her hopes were carefully hedged.[9]

Wilder's letters to Almanzo—collected posthumously in *West from Home: Letters of Laura Ingalls Wilder to Almanzo Wilder, San Francisco, 1915*—were full of the delights of the city. She described sightseeing, fair-going, and her intense enjoyment of the Pacific Coast and ferry rides. She shadowed her daughter as she went about her *Bulletin* duties, hoping to move beyond the farm market. "Rose and I are blocking out a story of the Ozarks for me to finish when I get home," she told her husband. "If I can only make it sell, it ought to help a lot and besides, I am learning so that I can write others for the magazines. If I can only get started at that, it will sell for a good deal more than farm stuff." On occasion, she was doing the housework, she said, to free her daughter "so that she will have time to help me with my learning to

9. Wilder to Almanzo Wilder, Sept. 21, 23, 1915, ibid., pp. 66–67, 74.

write."[10] The problem with this casual instruction, however, was that Wilder would be learning from someone who was herself a novice. What is more, Lane was not only a beginner, she was absorbing tactics and methods that fell far outside the realm of conventional reporting. In the city that sparked William Randolph Hearst's yellow-journalism empire, Lane was learning how to lie for a living.

Yellow journalism rose from the rivalry between newspaper titans Joseph Pulitzer and William Randolph Hearst. Dubious reporting practices had long existed but achieved startling new lows during their rancorous competition. The most intense phase of their battle lasted fifteen years, from 1895 to 1910, playing out in New York City, where Hearst set his *New York Journal* against Pulitzer's *New York World* in a circulation war that gave rise to Sunday color comics and near-hysterical feats of sensationalism. But Hearst's initial immersion began in the same city where Rose Wilder commenced her freelance career, San Francisco.

Son of a United States senator and heir to a mining fortune, Hearst was born in the city by the bay in 1863. Sent to Harvard, he flunked out, remembered chiefly for keeping a pet alligator and sending personalized chamber pots to his professors. Back home, at the age of twenty-four, he began managing the *San Francisco Examiner* in 1887, bought by his father to support his own political ambitions. Inspired by the *New York World*, which he read at Harvard, Hearst transformed the paper by aping Pulitzer's hyperbolic crime coverage and shouting headlines, running populist reports of corporate and civic malfeasance. He paid top dollar to talented columnists and writers, including Ambrose Bierce, Mark Twain, and Bret Harte, printing fictional serials by H. Rider Haggard and Jules Verne on the front page. He promoted women reporters, called "sob sisters," for their emotive, heart-tugging exposés.[11] Every newspaper in the city, including the *San Francisco Call* and the *Bulletin*—for which Rose Wilder Lane would write—felt the pressure of the *Examiner*'s competitive rise. Reporter Will Irwin, who worked for its chief competitor, the *Chronicle*, later acknowledged in a pioneering study of yellow journalism that all the city's newspapers "fell universally" to Hearst's influence.[12]

---

10. Ibid., Sept. 21, 1915, p. 67.

11. David Nasaw, *The Chief: The Life of William Randolph Hearst* (Boston: Houghton Mifflin Co., 2000), pp. 40, 43, 52–54, 69–73, 76.

12. Will Irwin, "The American Newspaper: A Study of Journalism in Its Relation to the Public," Part 4, "The Spread and Decline of Yellow Journalism," *Collier's* 46 (Mar. 4, 1911): 18.

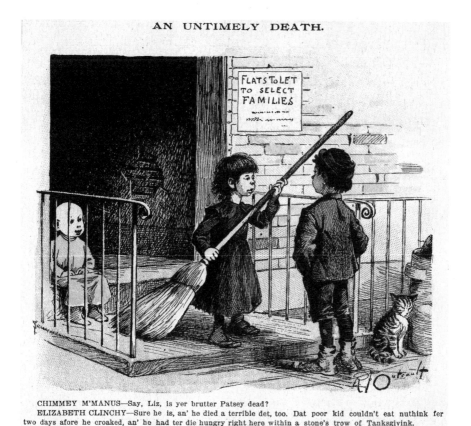

The "Yellow Kid," featured at far left in this comic from the November 24, 1895, issue of the *New York World*, gave rise to the term "yellow journalism." *San Francisco Academy of Comic Art Collection*

Less than a decade after taking over the *Examiner*, Hearst bought a "penny paper" in New York in 1895 called the *Journal* and launched his assault on Pulitzer, importing his best San Francisco editors, managers, and cartoonists to the East Coast. His aggressive tactics pushed Pulitzer to follow his lead, adopting ever-more extreme topics and methods. Observers struggled to find a name for the phenomenon, first calling it "the new journalism." But the name that stuck grew out of Hearst's and Pulitzer's tussle over possession of the popular colorized "Yellow Kid" comic character, who debuted in the *World* only to be appropriated by the *Journal* when Hearst hired away the cartoonist. Speaking truth to power, the Kid was a bald, barefoot, and nearly-inarticulate working-class ghetto child, head shaved for lice and body clad in a grimy yellow nightgown. The character would eventually appear in both papers at the same time, thanks to copyright issues, appealing to the working-class audience the warring dailies sought to win and lending the name "yellow kid journalism" to the papers.[13]

Shortened to yellow journalism, the term became synonymous with sensationalism but also referred to a range of technological advances, typographical and photographic experimentation, and various forms of journalistic license. According to scholars, yellow journals' distinguishing characteristics included:

- dramatic use of graphics and typography
- vivid exploitation of photography and illustration
- Sunday color supplements
- self-promotion, touting an identification with the working class
- emphasis on muckraking investigatory series, exposing corruption and covering murders and scandals
- opening the front page to a wide variety of topics, presenting celebrity news, sports, and social features alongside weightier political or economic news
- devious tactics in reporting and interviewing, including the use of anonymous sources and "faked" or fraudulent interviews
- subjective fictional techniques, including re-creation of dialogue, composite or imaginary characters, and a lack of distinction between factual and fabricated material.[14]

In spite of its extravagance, the movement was not wholly without merit. "A notably impertinent genre," as one historian called it, yellow journalism nonetheless paved the way for newspapers to appeal to a broader variety of readers, seeking both to entertain as well as inform.[15] It played a critical—and sometimes legitimate—role in the evolution of muckraking investigations, lending impetus to the Progressive era's reform-minded reporting on corporate monopolies such as Standard Oil, corrupt politicians, sweat shop and child labor, and even yellow journalism itself. Egregious though their excesses were, the *Journal* and the *World* popularized the news, providing readers with papers that were "brighter, more aggressive, more colorful, and on the whole far more interesting than their conservative rivals." Then as

---

13. W. Joseph Campbell, *Yellow Journalism: Puncturing the Myths, Defining the Legacies* (Westport, Conn.: Praeger, 2001), pp. 25–26. *See also* David R. Spencer, *The Yellow Journalism: The Press and America's Emergence as a World Power* (Evanston, Ill.: Northwestern University Press, 2007), pp. 214–15.

14. Campbell, *Yellow Journalism*, pp. 7–8. *See also* Frank Luther Mott, *American Journalism: A History, 1690–1960*, 3rd ed. (New York: Macmillan Co., 1962), p. 539.

15. Campbell, *Yellow Journalism*, p. 12.

now, their serious competition included the staid and respectable *New York Times*, said to be the "*antithesis* of yellow journalism," and the *Washington Post*. The *Times* foreswore banner headlines, gaudy illustrations, and ostentatious self-promotion, although it allowed the use of anonymous sources (something for which it is still criticized today).[16]

In its heyday, the shamelessness of the yellow press knew no bounds. Stirring sports coverage was tremendously popular, and the Ingalls clan demonstrated their proclivity for colorful prose when former Kansas senator John J. Ingalls, distant cousin of Wilder and her father, Charles Ingalls, contributed a front-page account to the *New York Journal* of a heavyweight bout—"The Great Fight Described by Ingalls"—including a "Realistic Picture of the Terrible Knock-Out Blow" and the victor's "Fiendish Smile."[17] Other popular features relied on "impostures and frauds of various kinds," often inspired by pseudoscience or the supernatural.[18] Messages from Mars were revealed, and the antics of sea serpents were closely covered.[19] In Kansas City, Rose Wilder Lane penned a contribution to this genre about a hen laying an egg in the shape of Halley's Comet.[20] "Faked" interviews were cobbled together out of whole cloth, such as the *Journal*'s 1897 discovery of "Pontius Pilate's Interview with Christ" and an equally astounding "last will and testament of Job."[21]

Yellow journalism would become most closely associated with Hearst's campaign of outrage over the sinking of the USS *Maine* in Havana Harbor in 1898, during Cuba's war of independence from Spain. Both the *Journal* and the *World* whipped up public sentiment, triggering the three-month Spanish-American War later that year. While the tale of Hearst's reputed message to an artist—"You furnish the pictures, and I'll furnish the war"—was probably apocryphal, his inflammatory coverage nonetheless tied him so firmly to the

---

16. Ibid., pp. 36, 163 (italics in the original). *See also* p. 152. Debate still rages over the ethics and reliability of anonymous sources, the most notable recent case involving the widely discredited reporting of Judith Miller for the *New York Times* on weapons of mass destruction in the run-up to the Iraq War.

17. *See* Campbell, *Yellow Journalism*, between pp. 51–52, for a photographic reproduction of the front page of the *New York Journal,* Mar. 18, 1897. For more on Ingalls (1833–1900), *see* "John James Ingalls," *Kansapedia*, Kansas Historical Society, kshs.org/kansapedia/john-james-ingalls/12095.

18. Mott, *American Journalism*, p. 539.

19. Campbell, *Yellow Journalism*, p. 37.

20. Lane, "Mount Washington Hen Lays Comet Egg; 'Tail' 10 Inches Long," *Kansas City Post,* May 20, 1910, clipping, Box 40, file 524, Lane Papers.

21. These articles appeared in the *New York Journal*'s Sunday supplements, Mar. 14, Nov. 7, 1897.

outcome that it became known as "Mr. Hearst's War."[22] But the most notorious incident traced to yellow journalism (however wrongly) was the assassination of President William McKinley, shot by an anarchist in 1901. The conservative press and Hearst critics fingered a satirical verse by *Examiner* columnist Ambrose Bierce published months earlier as the instigation for the shooting, although the assassin could not read English. Hearst got a sharp taste of his own medicine when a backlash broke out, with protestors (and perhaps competitors) burning copies of Hearst papers in the streets.[23]

Journalistic ethics had been subject to debate for decades, but these incidents pushed institutions to adopt moral codes in the manner of the medical and legal fields, a movement that was well underway by the time Lane came to learn the trade. Institutions in the Midwest took the lead. In 1904, the University of Illinois instituted a four-year journalism degree, and a few years later, the University of Missouri at Columbia, one hundred fifty miles from Wilder's home in Mansfield, opened the first dedicated school of journalism. In 1910, a group of editors in Kansas devised a written series of principles, the Kansas Newspaper Code of Ethics. As editors sought to put the brakes on the outrages of yellow journalism, the competition between the titans waned. Aging and remorseful over his role in cheapening the news, Pulitzer donated millions to Columbia University in 1912 to found a school of journalism, and Hearst's attention turned to a political career.[24]

But by then, their influence was pervasive. Bogus news and forged sources became commonplace, along with the use of anonymous sources. Over time, some tactics became more mainstream and harder to spot, and far from disappearing, yellow methods were widely copied, disseminated, and diffused throughout American media culture. Adapted in many forms, some more reputable than others, many of its practices would live on in newspapers across the country, especially in cities where Hearst or Pulitzer owned dailies, including Boston, Chicago, Denver, Saint Louis (home of Pulitzer's *Post-Dispatch*), and San Francisco.[25]

Yellow journalism had drawn whole new demographics into the fold, em-

---

22. Campbell, *Yellow Journalism*, p. 2. Campbell devotes a chapter to debunking Hearst's purported quotation; *see* Chap. 3, "Not Likely Sent: The Remington-Hearst 'Telegrams,'" pp. 71–95.

23. Nasaw, *Chief*, pp. 156–57; Dan Schreiber, "For the Past 150 Years, The Examiner Has Recorded Life in the City," *San Francisco Examiner*, June 11, 2015, sfexaminer.com.

24. Details in this paragraph are drawn from Lee Anne Peck, "Ethics," in *Encyclopedia of American Journalism*, ed. Stephen L. Vaughn (New York: Routledge, 2008), pp. 155–61.

25. Campbell, *Yellow Journalism*, argues that some journalistic practices that evolved

ploying women reporters, including Ida Tarbell and Nellie Bly. Will Irwin, the San Francisco reporter who explored the topic in 1911, wrote, "The yellows had created new bodies of newspaper readers; first, women, then just entering the new era of feminine development."[26] Among those eager readers was a young telegrapher who arrived in San Francisco from the Midwest in 1908. Yellow journalism may have been receding, but the dubious practices it spawned would become her forte. Rose Wilder Lane cut her teeth in what would be called the "Journalistic Kindergarten" of the yellow press.[27] From her arrival in San Francisco to her departure a decade later, she would be schooled in the tactics Hearst had developed, specializing in celebrity interviews that were inflated, padded, manufactured, and sold to the reader as "autobiographies." Her inventions may not have been quite as outrageous as Pontius Pilate's interview with Christ, but they were close.

From the beginning, Lane's work was steeped in specious details. She studded the handful of features she produced in 1908 and 1909 for the *San Francisco Call* with the lively dialogue prized by the yellow press. Dramatizing the subculture of messenger boys, she reproduced their Artful Dodger working-class vernacular.[28] Her theatrical account of the night on Russian Hill when a telegraph operator broke the trans-Pacific record by receiving a message from Hawaii emphasized unlikely sound effects: "With a deafening roar, a blinding glare, the electric spark leaped out. Crash! crash! crash!" Its melodrama stands out against a more factual report that ran on the front page of the same newspaper the previous month.[29] During the period in Kansas City, she covered the Halley's Comet egg, as well as the return of a missing stenographer involved in a "sensational fake slugging episode," and the price of bread and milk, said to be so steep that only the "extremely rich" could afford it.[30] All were tabloid fare appealing to the down-market sensibilities of working-class readers.

during the yellow era were adapted or diffused over time; *see* "Part II: Defining the Legacies," p. 151–75.

26. Irwin, "Spread and Decline of Yellow Journalism," p. 20.

27. Campbell, *Yellow Journalism*, p. 20n81. The phrase appeared first in an article for a trade journal, "Journalistic Kindergarten," *Fourth Estate* (May 5, 1900): 6.

28. Rose Wilder [Lane], "Ups and Downs of Modern Mercury," *San Francisco Call*, Sept. 20, 1908.

29. [Lane], "The Constantly Increasing Wonders of the New Field of Wireless," ibid., Nov. 22, 1908. *See also* "Gap to Hawaii is Bridged by Wireless Men," Oct. 12, 1908.

30. "Bower of Roses Is to Greet Return of Anna Lee Owen," *Kansas City Post*, May 4, 1910, and "'Bread and Milk' May Become High Luxury in Future," ibid., 5 May 1910, clippings, Box 40, file 524, Lane Papers.

The inscription on the back of this photograph of Lane and a companion identified as Wright, reads "working hard on a Swope Park assignment for Kansas City Journal, 1910."
*Herbert Hoover Presidential Library and Museum.*

Back in San Francisco, after her real-estate period, Lane eagerly accepted the offer in 1915 to assist in producing the *Bulletin*'s woman's page, entitled "On the Margin of Life." Given the tenor of her subsequent work, its subhead was ironic: "Truth is seldom on the written page—We must search the margins and read between the lines."[31] Touted in promotional copy as "a brilliant member of The Bulletin staff," Lane first wrote fiction. One of her early contributions was a serial, "A Jitney Romance: The Heart-Moving Story of a Country Girl's Struggle with Life in San Francisco."[32] Later that year, her mother's light verse began appearing in the newspaper in the "Tuck 'Em in Corner Poems" slot.[33]

The man who made it all possible was Fremont Older, the *Bulletin*'s storied editor, a cigar-smoking California character with a handlebar mustache

31. *See*, for example, "On the Margin of Life," *San Francisco Bulletin*, Mar. 27, 1915.

32. "Watch for 'A Jitney Romance,'" ibid., Mar. 1, 1915. The serial ran from Mar. 4 to Apr. 13, 1915.

33. Several of the poems featuring Wilder's byline can be found in Box 40, file 523, Lane Papers. They have also been published as *Laura Ingalls Wilder's Fairy Poems*, ed. Stephen W. Hines (New York: Doubleday, 1998).

and the populist touch. He would become an important friend and mentor. Twenty years earlier, he had revived the sleepy paper, hiring cartoonist Rube Goldberg and Robert Ripley (of "Ripley's Believe It or Not") and raising circulation within a year to the largest in the West. A crusading muckraker, he was anything but impartial, engaging in decades-long partisan campaigns against graft and wrongful prosecution. When he left the *Bulletin* in 1918 (inspiring Lane to quit in sympathy), Hearst would hire him to edit the *Call*. His wife, Cora Older, would become Hearst's official biographer.[34]

When Rose Wilder Lane began working at Older's *Bulletin*, its eye-popping headlines, splashy photographs, and creative use of typefaces established its yellow credentials. She joined the ranks of scores of young men, many of them college graduates, whom newspapers had recruited for low pay in exchange for experience, much like unpaid interns of today. Lane herself had virtually no training before she began churning out copy, and she may have had less experience and respect for institutions than those who had gone to college. Ill-paid, ill-taught, and something of a loose cannon, she exhibited an overweening self-confidence, a characteristic evident from her earliest years and polished, perhaps, by recent experience in real-estate sales. Her rival in salesmanship, Claire Gillette Lane, seemed, at times, little better than a confidence man: he had once encouraged her participation in a scam defrauding the railroad.[35]

Unlike Hearst's "sob sisters," who concentrated on exposing the perils of the weak and downtrodden in hospitals and mental institutions, Lane was drawn toward figures of fame and power. If she could not find them, she fabricated them. "Ed Monroe, Man-Hunter: The Life Story of a Real Detective" was an early effort, embroidering heavily on its sources. Ed Monroe (not his real name) was based on a real person, a reformed burglar retailing whoppers about his exploits from a sinecure in the newspaper's circulation department. But in Lane's hands, he was transformed into a wholly different character: a heroic "real detective," a crime fighter with twenty years of experience on the police force who had witnessed dramatic incidents such as the day when "Three-Fingered Doolan," released from San Quentin, pumped a "stool pigeon" full of lead. Told in the first person, said to be "edited" by Rose Wilder Lane, the serial was illustrated with crude line drawings, and its invented dia-

34. John C. Ralston, "Fremont Older: Newsman, Statesman, Thinker," in *Encyclopedia of San Francisco*, San Francisco Museum & Historical Society, sfhistoryencyclopedia.com/articles/o/olderFremont.html; Mrs. Fremont Older, *William Randolph Hearst, American* (New York: D. Appleton-Century Co., 1936). Cora Older is described as Hearst's "handpicked biographer" in Nasaw, *Chief*, p. 43.

35. Campbell, *Yellow Journalism*, p. 20n81; Holtz, *Ghost*, p. 53.

logue and cartoonish theatrics lent it the air of a dime novel in miniature. Yet, it was advertised not simply as a "fine tale of adventure" but as one bearing "the authority of TRUTH, the power of REALITY."[36]

The "Ed Monroe" serial in thirty-one installments began appearing in mid-August 1915, only days before Wilder arrived in San Francisco.[37] Lane continued working on the project while her mother was there. Among the highlights of Wilder's visit was a dinner with her daughter and "Ed," who may have been an ex-convict named Jack Black.[38] Neither Wilder nor her daughter saw anything wrong with the liberties that had been taken with his life story, nor did they blanch at the presentation of fictionalized interviews as autobiography. In a passage that would reveal much about the women's attitudes toward fact and fiction, Wilder wrote to her husband to assure him that "all the stories" in the articles, "although incidents, are true, and *actually happened*. 'Ed Monroe' came to dinner with us and told Rose those stories for her to use until after midnight." She then acknowledged the inventions:

> Instead of being an old detective, he is an old crook who has served time more than once. He was a burglar who did the high-class work, jewelry robberies, etc. He is straight now and working in the circulation department. He is very interesting and of course his name is not the one used in the story. He strung Rose's pearls for her, the ones I brought her, you know. He said it was his old trade, the restringing and resetting of jewels—when he had stolen them, I suppose.[39]

Wilder's interpretation shows just how elastic the concept of "true stories" was at the time and to her personally. In years to come, she and Lane would cling to the notion of "truth," which reflected not objective reality but something closer to felt experience.

---

36. "Real Detective to Tell Story: 'Ed Monroe, Man-Hunter,'" *San Francisco Bulletin*, Aug. 5, 1915 (promotional copy announcing the serial's launch).

37. "Ed Monroe, Man-Hunter" ran in the *Bulletin* from Aug. 11 through Sept. 15, 1915. Wilder arrived in San Francisco sometime on Aug. 27 or 28, 1915. Wilder to Almanzo Wilder, Aug. 29, 1915, p. 25.

38. Holtz, *Ghost,* p. 66, theorizes that "Ed Monroe" was Jack Black, an ex-convict that Fremont Older had befriended. Black's 1926 memoir, *You Can't Win*, was dedicated to Older, and the author mentions working in the *Bulletin*'s circulation department and later as librarian for the *Call*. Black, *You Can't Win* (New York: Macmillan Co., 1926), pp. [v], 368, 390–91. If Black was the source of Lane's "Ed Monroe," it is notable that the material in his memoir differs markedly from that in her serial.

39. Wilder to Almanzo Wilder, Sept. 11, 1915, in *West from Home*, pp. 47–48 (emphasis in original).

Prior to Wilder's arrival, Lane had concocted two previous first-person "autobiographies" for the *Bulletin*, the first of the stunt-flyer Art Smith and then a memoir of Charlie Chaplin, based on interviews. Both serials were heavily promoted in the hyperbolic yellow fashion—"Charlie Chaplin to Tell You Story of His Life in Bulletin"—and would soon appear between covers, launching Lane's book-publishing career.[40] The *Bulletin* brought out the "autobiography" of Art Smith as a souvenir booklet, selling it for twenty-five cents during the exposition.[41] As fast as she finished one, Lane was on to another. While Wilder was in San Francisco, she waited ashore as her daughter interviewed Henry Ford on board a battleship. Yet another serial and book would be spun from that encounter.[42]

That Fremont Older chose the unseasoned Lane to interview Chaplin and Ford, two of the most famous men in the world, suggests the *Bulletin*'s cavalier approach to celebrity journalism. While her subjects paid little attention to newspaper serials, Lane's inexperience caused havoc when she sought to reach a wider, more legitimate market. In 1916, after she had sold the Chaplin articles in book form—a deal brokered by Associated Press reporter Guy Moyston, with whom she would later be involved romantically—the transaction blew up. The Chaplin book had already gone to print when the actor discovered it, and it quickly became clear that Lane had hoodwinked both her mark and her publisher.[43] The copyright page included a duplicitous note, "The subject of this biography takes great pleasure in expressing his

---

40. "Charlie Chaplin to Tell You Story of His Life in Bulletin," *San Francisco Bulletin*, June 30, 1915. "How I Learned To Fly," attributed to Art Smith, appeared in the *Bulletin* from May 19 to June 21, 1915; "Charlie Chaplin's Story: The Life History of the Funniest Man in Filmland, Told by Himself," appeared in twenty-nine installments from July 3 to Aug. 5, 1915.

41. Lane, ed., *Art Smith's Story: The Autobiography of the Boy Aviator Which Appeared as a Serial in The Bulletin* (San Francisco: The Bulletin, 1915). *See also* Rachel Sherwood Roberts, *Art Smith: Pioneer Aviator* (Jefferson, N.C.: McFarland & Co., 2003), pp. 78–79. Roberts takes the *Bulletin* serial as true autobiography, but Lane's authorial fingerprints may be seen in such language as that describing Smith's mother. Compare "Mother was a little, quick woman, all nerve and energy" on p. 9 of *Art Smith's Story* with Lane's description of her own mother's "surface quickness and sparkle" in a sketch reprinted in *A Little House Reader: A Collection of Writings by Laura Ingalls Wilder*, ed. William Anderson (New York: HarperCollins, 1998), p. 171.

42. Wilder to Almanzo Wilder, Oct. 22, 1915, in *West From Home*, p. 115. "Henry Ford's Story" appeared in the *Bulletin* in thirty installments from Nov. 2 to Dec. 6, 1915.

43. David Robinson, *Chaplin: His Life and Art* (New York: McGraw-Hill, 1985), pp. 181, 184. Robinson misspelled Moyston as Mayston, a typographical error derived from a telegram from the publisher to Chaplin.

obligations and his thanks to Mrs. Rose Wilder Lane for invaluable editorial assistance."[44] Chaplin took no such pleasure: he had not known of the book's existence and was so disgusted by her portrayal of his father as a "drunken sot" that he threatened the publisher, Bobbs-Merrill, with a lawsuit.[45]

Far from apologizing, Lane scolded the actor for expecting a pay-off, an astonishing act of impertinence. "I don't believe you realize how very well that story was written," she told Chaplin.[46] The book was withdrawn. A few copies would circulate in decades to come (Stan Laurel had one), causing rumor and speculation.[47] Contemporary scholars have described the work, reprinted in 1985, as a "flagrant autobiographical fake."[48] If Lane learned anything from the episode, it was only the need to cover her tracks. In contrast to the Chaplin autobiography, she wrote her hagiography of Ford in the third-person, with a byline reading "*As Told To* Rose Wilder Lane." It too would be repudiated by its subject for inaccuracy.[49]

Desperate for copy to fill the *Bulletin*'s columns, Lane turned next to her mother's biography, pumping her for information while she was still in San Francisco. Lane attached tidbits of Wilder's recollections of life in Dakota Territory to "Behind the Headlight," a first-person serialized "memoir" of an unnamed and remarkably articulate railway engineer who waxes on about the "magnificent courage" that drove the settlers. Recounting anecdotes that would reappear in *Pioneer Girl* and Wilder's later fiction, the engineer describes an Indian wrapped in a blanket predicting "'BIG snows'" and the dramatic perils of the Hard Winter.[50] Detached from the context of Wilder's

44. Chaplin, *Charlie Chaplin's Own Story: Being the Faithful Recital of a Romantic Career, Beginning with Early Recollections of Boyhood in London and Closing with the Signing of His Latest Motion-Picture Contract* (Indianapolis: Bobbs-Merrill Co., 1916), copyright page.

45. Robinson, *Chaplin*, p. 182. Robinson concluded, "Bobbs Merrill had acted in good faith, believing that Chaplin had authorized what Mrs. Lane wrote."

46. Lane to Chaplin, Oct. 6, 1916, reprinted ibid., p. 183.

47. Robinson, *Chaplin*, p. 185.

48. David Robinson, "An Imposture Revived," review of reprint of *Charlie Chaplin's Own Story*, ed. Harry M. Geduld, in *Times Literary Supplement*, June 27, 1986, p. 716.

49. "As Told to Rose Wilder Lane" appears on the title page of *Henry Ford's Own Story: How a Farmer Boy Rose to the Power That Goes with Many Millions Yet Never Lost Touch with Humanity* (Forest Hills, N.Y.: Ellis O. Jones, 1917). Her name also appears on the Foreword. For Ford's reaction to the book, see Holtz, *Ghost*, p. 394n14.

50. "Behind the Headlight," chaps. 2 and 3, *San Francisco Bulletin*, Oct. 11–12, 1915. The serial appeared in fourteen installments, Oct. 9–Nov. 5, 1915. *See also* Wilder, *Pioneer Girl: The Annotated Autobiography*, ed. Pamela Smith Hill (Pierre: South Dakota Historical Society Press, 2014), p. 203.

experience, the details float free of emotional import; yet, Wilder again assured her husband that "every incident . . . is true."[51] Lane's account, however, veered far from both Wilder's own blizzard experiences, as well as from the grim stories her mother may have heard about the "children's blizzard" of 1888.[52]

Lane had still not absorbed any appreciation of ethics and standards in journalism. Jack London died suddenly on November 22, 1916, and less than six months later, she began importuning his widow, Charmian London, for permission to write a serialized biography for *Sunset* magazine. Against her better judgment, London acquiesced out of pity for Lane, who had told her that the opportunity was her "first chance to break into the magazines, and . . . they have given me an advance, and I have spent it!"[53] Lane's tactics over the course of writing, editing, and publishing "Life and Jack London," an eight-part monthly serial beginning in October 1917, established a pattern of unscrupulous professional behavior. William Holtz, Lane's own biographer, condemned her "subtle and continuing calculation," her skirting of outright lies as she cajoled, argued, and played on the sympathies of the bereaved woman.[54] While admitting that "the whole [serial] is fictionized," she assured London in the same breath that she had "verified as carefully as I possibly could, in a wilderness of conflicting reports, all the facts," an assertion that was not only contradictory but patently untrue.[55] At one point, she tried to excuse her erroneous account of Charmian London's miscarriage by telling her, "My own two babies died."[56] (Records indicate that Lane delivered one stillborn child.)[57]

---

51. Wilder to Almanzo Wilder, Oct. 22, 1915, p. 115.

52. "Behind the Headlight," chap. 3. Compare to the corresponding material in Wilder, *Pioneer Girl*, pp. 207, 315, 315–16n90–91.

53. Lane to London, May 31, 1917, Box 13, file 14, Jack and Charmian London Correspondence and Papers, 1894–1953 (hereafter cited as London Correspondence), Utah State University Special Collections and Archives, Logan.

54. Holtz, *Ghost*, p. 69.

55. Lane to London, Sept. 22, 1917, Box 13, file 14, London Correspondence.

56. Ibid., May 2, 1918. For information on Charmian London's miscarriage, *see* Earle Labor, *Jack London: An American Life* (New York: Farrar, Straus & Giroux, 2013), pp. 326–27.

57. Holtz, *Ghost*, p. 51; Sallie Ketcham, *Laura Ingalls Wilder: American Writer on the Prairie* (New York: Routledge, 2015), pp. 91, 93n41. Ketcham describes a premature birth, but the Utah death certificate lists it as "still born" (Utah State Archives, archives.utah.gov/indexes/data/81448/2229322/2229322_0000278.jpg). What Lane was referring to in claiming that she had "two babies" who died remains unknown.

Responding to London's "violent objections," as the widow termed them,[58] Lane offered a misleading reprise of her own career, saying that she had "never done newspaper work" because she held herself above it, although she defended the *Bulletin* for having "a conscience." Echoing her response to Chaplin, she cast the *Sunset* serial in a self-justifying light, claiming that she had "much more conscience about LIFE AND JACK LONDON than, I think, you quite realize." She directly raised the specter of Hearst and his practices, saying, "Surely, you can appreciate that I tried not to be 'yellow.'"[59] Swiftly, London replied, "YOU FAILED TO DO WHAT YOU TRIED TO DO." In the end, London denounced the *Sunset* serial as fiction.[60] Scholars, too, have found "little value" in it, noting that it relied on "devices of imagined conversations, impressionistic descriptions, and tailored atmosphere . . . based on skimpy evidence."[61] Yet, even as London was venting her anger and disappointment, Lane continued to press for permission to publish the serial as a book. At that point, London, like Chaplin, threatened to sue. Without regard for the widow's wishes, Lane would eventually take her approach to its logical conclusion, publishing her revised life of London as a novel.[62]

For her last biography, of Herbert Hoover, Lane again employed the third person. In the *Sunset* serial, she drew on the magazine editor's collegiate relationship with Hoover and conducted interviews with family.[63] Her research may have been somewhat more substantial, but her portrayal was again a novelization, recreating gauzy interior scenes from the life of young "Bertie," emphasizing his boyhood musings on the Iowa prairie, where he suffered through long church services and encountered Indians (parallels between this work and the Little House books). Lane and Will Irwin would be the authors of the first and second biographies of Hoover, respectively, but

---

58. London to Lane, Apr. 28, 1918, Box 10, file 5, London Correspondence.

59. Lane to London, May 2, 1918.

60. London to Lane, May 6, 1918, Box 10, file 5, London Correspondence. *See also* London to Lane, Sept. 19, 1917, Box 25, Papers of Jack London, 1866–1977, Huntington Library, San Moreno, Calif.

61. Richard W. Etulain, "The Lives of Jack London," *Western American Literature* 11 (Summer 1976): 152.

62. London to Lane, May 6, 1918; Lane, *He Was A Man* (New York: Harper & Bros., 1925).

63. Holtz, *Ghost*, p. 90. Charles Kellogg Field, editor of *Sunset*, coauthored the Hoover serial with Lane. "The Making of Herbert Hoover" ran in six installments, from April to September 1920. Field and Hoover were members of Stanford's first graduating class. Kevin Starr, "Sunset Magazine and the Phenomenon of the Far West," web.stanford.edu/dept/SUL/library/ sunset-magazine/html/influences_1.html.

a comparison of their work reveals distinct differences. While Lane fictionalized, Irwin constructed a fact-based account, identifying both his sources and areas where he engaged in conjecture.[64]

After completing her Hoover biography, Lane went abroad, reporting for a Red Cross newsletter and abandoning biography for fiction. But her work in the genre, flowing out of her period at the *Bulletin*, reveals that everything she learned about journalism she learned from the yellow press. Her technique involved spinning a few thin strands of raw material gleaned from brief interviews into fictional gold, bright, alluring, and false. These were the techniques she would bring to bear on her mother's manuscript when Wilder, fifteen years after her trip to San Francisco, sat down to write her own life story.

Wilder began writing "Pioneer Girl" sometime in 1929 or 1930, intending to sell it as an autobiographical serial about her childhood. She had completed it by May of 1930. Published posthumously in 2014 as *Pioneer Girl: The Annotated Autobiography*, the manuscript from its first words introduced a note of ambiguity about its factual basis. Wilder opened in the timeless fashion of a fairy tale—"Once upon a time"—but then added a time element, "years and years ago."[65] Invoking both fable and memoir, she appeared to want to have it both ways. Drawing on memories of an intense childhood, studded with life-and-death incidents, Wilder included occasional asides to her daughter, recounting things she intended to omit, such as an anecdote about her father's encounter with wolves that she considered implausible and reference to an embarrassing bout of lice or scabies. Her notes reveal that she intended Lane to be her first audience as well as her editor. While she would maintain a flexible attitude toward her material in her later novels, freely adding fictional characters and incidents and altering the chronology of her life, the autobiography, by contrast, appears largely factual.[66]

The initial typescript of *Pioneer Girl*—a largely faithful copy prepared by Lane and submitted to her agent Carl Brandt—failed to elicit interest in New York. At that juncture, the daughter's first instinct was to take liberties with her mother's life story. She quickly edited and revised second and third versions that included in their first ten pages a fictionalized narrative so mark-

---

64. Will Irwin, *Herbert Hoover: A Reminiscent Biography* (New York: Century Co., 1928).

65. Wilder, *Pioneer Girl*, p. 1.

66. Ibid., pp. 8, 83. One possible exception may be Wilder's lengthy anecdote about the grim fate of the "Robbins" children, left home alone during a blizzard near Walnut Grove. *See* ibid., p. 139. The editors found no records of a family by that name in the area; local newspapers did not cover the incident. This anecdote may have been one that Wilder heard or read and then transposed into her life story.

edly salacious—and so revealing of Lane's propensities—that the editors of the annotated *Pioneer Girl* excerpted it in an appendix entitled "The Benders of Kansas."[67] Like the Ingalls family, the Benders were real people struggling through hard times, surviving on odd jobs. Their jobs, however, were odder than most. They were serial killers. During a brief but notorious career, four adults under that name took up residence on a plot of land northeast of Independence. Perhaps masquerading as a family, the older man and woman, John Bender, Sr., and his wife, German immigrants who spoke heavily accented English, portrayed themselves as the parents of two younger adults, John and Kate Bender. Much attention would focus on the allure of Kate, said to be around twenty-four and "well formed."[68]

Land records are scarce, but it appears that, sometime in 1870 or 1871, the Benders opened an inn and store for travelers in Labette County, Kansas.[69] Taking advantage of the isolation of the prairie, they soon began murdering customers, stealing money and livestock from victims, and surreptitiously burying the bodies around the property. Rumors of missing persons soon spread but remained mysterious, for accidents or attacks on settlers were hardly unknown. The Ingalls family left nearby Montgomery County sometime in early 1871, and it is unlikely that they had anything to do with their murderous neighbors to the northeast.

67. For description and chronology of the "Brandt Revised" and "Bye" versions, *see* Hill, "The *Pioneer Girl* Manuscripts," in Wilder, *Pioneer Girl*, p. lxii. *See also* "Appendix B," pp. 353–56, for a transcription of the "Bye" version of the Bender tale.

68. Kansas, Governor's Proclamation, May 17, 1873, printed as "Governor's Proclamation," *Atchison* (Kans.) *Daily Champion*, May 23, 1873.

69. Most historical accounts place the Benders in Labette County in late 1870 or early 1871. Several sources offer a legal description for John Bender's land, giving it as Township 31, Section 13, Range 17 (Osage Township, Labette County, Kansas). *See* John T. James, *The Benders in Kansas* (Wichita: Kan-Okla Publishing Co., 1913), p. 15; Fern Morrow Wood, *The Benders: Keepers of the Devil's Inn* (Cherryvale, Kans.: By the Author, 1992), p. 7; Phyllis de la Garza, *Death for Dinner: The Benders of (Old) Kansas* (Honolulu: Talei Publishers, 2003), p. 6. Documentation, however, appears to be lacking. The National Archives reports that tract books for the State of Kansas contain no land entry transactions for a John Bender on that property or for a neighboring property, Township 31, Section 12, Range 17, said to be associated with John Bender, Jr. Records covering land transactions at the Labette County Register of Deeds do not survive prior to July 1871. Likewise, Labette County plat maps do not extend back to the 1870s. A plat map has been reconstructed but may be based on speculation. Wood claims that the Benders filed in the town of Humboldt in Allen County, Kansas, because "there was no land office closer" (Wood, *Benders*, p. 7). Yet, Allen County's land records, which stretch back to the 1860s, contain no Bender transactions.

The Benders continued in these activities for some months, until early in 1873, when they killed the wrong man, William York, a notable doctor from Independence and the brother of a state legislator. On news of the doctor's disappearance, his relatives mounted an intensive search, reported in newspapers in late March. On May 5 or 6, hearing that the Benders' inn had been abandoned several weeks earlier and their team left hitched outside a railroad depot in Thayer, Kansas, a search party investigated the property, finding starving livestock abandoned in the barn. The party then made a number of grisly discoveries, including the body of the doctor in a shallow grave. Eventually, the remains of ten or so additional victims were unearthed, among them widower George Newton Longcor and his eighteen-month-old daughter. Longcor, whose name appears variously as Loncher or Lunker, may have been a near neighbor of Charles Ingalls and his family. The name "G. N. Lunker" directly follows that of Wilder's infant sister, Carrie Ingalls (misspelled "Ingles"), in the 1870 federal census of Rutland Township, Montgomery County, Kansas. After the death of his wife, Mary Jane, Longcor was apparently traveling to relatives in Iowa in late 1872, when he stopped at the Bender property.[70]

Evidence at the scene suggested that the Benders preyed on unsuspecting customers when they were seated at a table for a meal. One of the family was said to attack from behind a curtain, striking the victim in the head with a shoe hammer. Through a trap door, the body was then tipped into a squalid cellar below, where it was stripped of valuables and concealed until it could be buried in the orchard or fields. Highlighting Americans' worst fears about the perils of the remote West, the murders would remain the most infamous unsolved mystery in Kansas until Truman Capote investigated the Herbert Clutter slayings for his book *In Cold Blood* (1966).

Events surrounding the Bender crimes passed into legend, leaving few verifiable details. The true identities of the Benders were never established, and their relationships to each other never explained. They were never found or brought to trial.[71] The only credible physical descriptions may have been

---

70. "Discovery of Wm. York's Body" *Emporia* (Kans.) *Weekly News*, May 9, 1873; "Bloody Benders," *Topeka Daily Capital*, Nov. 15, 1889; "George Longcor" (family tree), person.ancestry.com/tree/7238777/person/-1136027707/facts; U.S., Department of the Interior, Census Office, *Ninth Census, 1870*, Rutland Township, Montgomery County, Kans., National Archives Microfilm Publication M593, roll 439. Extensive Civil War service records tend to support the identification of "G. N. Lunker" as Longcor, born in 1842 in Lee County, Iowa. *See* "George Longcor," fold3.com/image/236994666.

71. Two Michigan women were arrested and brought to trial in Labette County in 1889, but they were released the following year when it was determined that it was a case

those included in the Kansas Governor's Proclamation, issued on May 17, 1873, offering a two-thousand-dollar reward—five hundred dollars for each member of the family.[72] A railway clerk recalled persons matching that description buying tickets out of town. The trail was days if not weeks cold by the time the bodies were found, and contemporaneous reports did not describe pursuit of the murderers by vigilantes or posses on horseback.[73] They made reference only to an unfortunate German neighbor, said to have been nearly lynched by the "excited people" of nearby Cherryvale, convinced that he knew something.[74]

Lack of information created a vacuum that the nascent yellow press was happy to fill. Dubbed the "Bloody Benders," their inn refashioned as "the Devil's Kitchen," the family became a hot property for newspapers, which fanned the hellish flames of their macabre raw material, elaborating on reports that Kate Bender had been a spiritualistic medium.[75] Inevitably, her satanic dealings and witchlike "spells" featured prominently in Bender cover-

---

of mistaken identity. *See* James, *Benders in Kansas*, pp. 63–116. More recently, de la Garza has advanced a theory regarding their identities, suggesting that Joseph and Katie Bender, a married couple buried in a Glenwood Springs, Colorado, cemetery, may match the description of the two younger Benders, while offering little hard evidence to support it. *See* Phyllis de la Garza, "History Mystery Solved?" Hiding in Plain Sight," *True West*, Sept. 3, 2012, www.truewestmagazine.com.

72. Kansas, Governor's Proclamation.

73. The "vigilante" tales may be a later accretion to the Bender mythology because few early accounts mention pursuers. *See* "The Bender Murders," *Harper's Weekly* 27 (June 7, 1873): 484, 485, for example. A search of two newspaper archives, the National Archives' "Chronicling America" and the commercial website, newspapers.com, for such terms as "Bender and vigilante" or "Bender and posse" turned up no relevant hits in 1873 through 1876. In 1877, a couple dozen relevant articles appear. More would follow in the last years of the nineteenth century and the early decades of the twentieth.

74. "A Murderers' Den Explored: Eight Mangled Bodies Unearthed," *Lawrence* (Kans.) *Daily Journal*, May 8, 1873. Suspicion would later focus again on Rudolph Brockman, whose property apparently adjoined the Benders'. He was convicted in 1897 of the first-degree murder of his teenaged daughter. *See* "Said to Know of Bender Murders: Rudolph Brockman Pardoned by Governor Hodges," *Wichita* (Kans.) *Beacon*, Feb. 25, 1913; de la Garza, *Death for Dinner*, pp. 189–90.

75. For more on the spiritualist angle, *see* Edith Connelley Ross, "The Bloody Benders," *Kansas State Historical Society Collections* 17 (1928): 468. Ross quotes a "notice" (perhaps a newspaper advertisement) placed by "Prof. Miss Katie Bender," claiming her prowess in healing "all sorts of Diseases . . . Blindness, Fits, Deafness and . . . Dumbness." Ross's article cites no sources but appears to be drawn from contemporary newspaper accounts.

# Governor's Proclamation.

# $2,000 REWARD

### State of Kansas, Executive Department.

WHEREAS, several atrocious murders have been recently committed in Labette County, Kansas, under circumstances which fasten, beyond doubt, the commissions of these crimes upon a family known as the "Bender family," consisting of

JOHN BENDER, about 60 years of age, five feet eight or nine inches in height, German, speaks but little English, dark complexion, no whiskers, and sparely built;

MRS. BENDER, about 50 years of age, rather heavy set, blue eyes, brown hair, German, speaks broken English;

JOHN BENDER, Jr., alias John Gebardt, five feet eight or nine inches in height, slightly built, gray eyes with brownish tint, brown hair, light moustache, no whiskers, about 27 years of age, speaks English with German accent;

KATE BENDER, about 24 years of age, dark hair and eyes, good looking, well formed, rather bold in appearance, fluent talker, speaks good English with very little German accent:

AND WHEREAS, said persons are at large and fugitives from justice, now therefore, I, Thomas A. Osborn, Governor of the State of Kansas, in pursuance of law, do hereby offer a **REWARD OF FIVE HUNDRED DOLLARS** for the apprehension and delivery to the Sheriff of Labette County, Kansas, of each of the persons above named.

In Testimony Whereof, I have hereunto subscribed my name, and caused the Great Seal of the State to be affixed.

[L. S.] Done at Topeka, this 17th day of May, 1873.

**THOMAS A. OSBORN,**
Governor.

By the Governor:
**W. H. SMALLWOOD,**
Secretary of State.

The 1873 proclamation from the governor of Kansas did little to bring the notorious Bender family to justice.
*Kansas State Historical Society*

age, drawing out the latent sexual subtext of the female temptress. Her physical attributes grew more exaggerated, and she acquired green eyes, a head of "coppery . . . red-gold" hair, and "very red" lips.[76] In one extensive elaboration, Kate Bender writhes like a demon when caught. Practically foaming at the mouth, "She spoke like some fiend that had never known a human sentiment . . . laughed devilishly and spit at her captors." In this tale, Kate bragged about doing all the throat-cutting herself, "having killed one hundred persons" because "she LIKED TO SEE THE BLOOD."[77]

Scores of such articles appeared over the years, as well as books devoted wholly or in part to the Bender saga. Among the more outlandish stories was a seaman's yarn, attributed to someone named "Fritz," who spun a tale of the Benders fleeing across the Gulf of Mexico in a hot-air balloon fueled by natural gas siphoned from a Kansas swamp. The balloon having burst, the Benders fell from a clear blue sky, their bodies crashing onto a passing vessel. The younger male, mortally wounded, survived a few hours to deliver a deathbed confession. Corpses were conveniently lost at sea.[78] Another source reported that in 1873 the *New York Ledger* published a "very gratifying narrative" claiming that all the Benders were shot to death, a report said to be have been republished across the country.[79] The *Ledger*, however, was not a newspaper; it was a weekly magazine publishing serialized fiction. As a child working in the Masters Hotel in Walnut Grove, Minnesota, Laura Ingalls avidly consumed its wares. "Great stories they were of beautiful ladies and brave, handsome men," she recalled, "of dwarfs and villians [sic] of jewels and secret caverns."[80] Whatever the *Ledger*'s contribution to the Bender mythology, it was probably not factual.

76. Ibid., p. 466.
77. "The Benders," *Columbus* (Ind.) *Republican*, May 10, 1877.
78. "The Benders," *Fort Scott* (Kans.) *Daily Monitor*, Aug. 7, 1877.
79. James, *Benders in Kansas*, p. 8. A search of two online newspaper archives—the National Archives "Chronicling America" and the commercial site, newspapers.com—did not yield syndicated accounts in 1873 that match James's description of the *Ledger* piece.
80. Wilder, *Pioneer Girl*, p. 123. Wilder may have continued to appreciate the *Ledger* as an adult. Her library at Rocky Ridge contains a copy of an 1894 biography of the *Ledger*'s pioneering woman columnist Fanny Fern, the pen name of Sara Willis Parton, perhaps a model for Wilder's own moralizing farm columns. Fern published another work that may have held meaning for Wilder, a bestselling 1854 autobiographical novel, *Ruth Hall*, and was notable for being a cofounder of the Sorosis clubs for women. It was at a Sorosis meeting in Mountain Grove, Missouri, that Wilder gave a speech on "My Work" in the mid-1930s, reprinted in Laura Ingalls Wilder, *The Little House Books*, ed. Caroline Fraser, 2 vols. (New York: Library of America, 2012), 1:581–84.

The most persistent elaboration on the murderers' fate involved their righteous execution at the hands of vigilantes, an Old West-style posse, Indians, or outlaws. These avenging angels were said to have pursued the murderers, caught them, and delivered on the spot a rough form of frontier justice. Attributed to eyewitnesses or deathbed confessions, a flood of such accounts appeared nationally in 1877, perhaps consumed by the Ingalls family.[81] Rose Wilder, too, may have read them, for versions continued to be published in Kansas City newspapers for years, including during the time she worked there as a young telegrapher. In May 1907, for example, the *Kansas City Star* published "He Knew the Bender Family," quoting a man claiming to have accompanied the search party, although he incorrectly identified the county where the murders took place. In his version, "outlaws" in Indian Territory killed the Benders. "'They will never be found,'" the informant said, knowingly.[82] Lane echoed that language when she patched together her revisions of the *Pioneer Girl* manuscript. In her last version, Charles Ingalls makes the same veiled reference to a posse administering frontier justice that appeared in the *Star* (and widely in syndication), "'They'll never find Kate Bender anywhere.'"[83]

As was often the case, Lane was working under intense financial pressure, embarking on her labors during a stupefying heat wave in the early summer of 1930. Her hasty work suggests a transparently commercial motive: connecting her mother's earliest childhood to a notorious murder case. But she was not content merely to take advantage of the glancing proximity of the Ingalls family to a crime scene. (Surely, she did not know that Longcor may have been a neighbor). Instead, she injected them bodily into the story, claiming that Charles Ingalls had stopped for a drink at the Benders, nearly entering

81. The 1877 vigilante tales may have derived from or, alternately, may have inspired the account of the Benders that appeared in J. H. Beadle, *Western Wilds, and the Men Who Redeem Them* (Cincinnati: Jones Bros. & Co., 1880, ©1877), pp. 434–37. Earlier news reports had promised details on "The Pursuit of the Fiends" but failed to deliver details; *see*, for example, "Death's Wayside Inn," *San Francisco Chronicle*, May 27, 1873. The persistence of the vigilante tales continues to the present day. Residents of Cherryvale, Parsons, and Oswego, Kansas, whose ties extend back to that era, often recall tales told by grandfathers or other relations who claimed to have pursued the Benders.

82. "He Knew the Bender Family," reprinted in James, *Benders in Kansas*, pp. 148–49. This piece appeared widely in syndication, for example, as "Story of the Bendeys [*sic*]" *Independence* (Kans.) *Evening Star*, June 9, 1907, and "Knew The Bender Family," *Freeport* (Ill.) *Journal-Standard*, July 1, 1907. Lane's presence in Kansas City in June 1907 can be inferred from Holtz, *Ghost*, p. 48. He suggests that she likely remained in the city until the Commercial Telegraphers Union strike, which began in August of 1907.

83. Wilder, *Pioneer Girl*, p. 355.

the house at Kate Bender's invitation. She had him riding out as one of the "vigilantes" who chased, caught, and executed them. She elaborated on a particularly lurid detail, involving the child buried with her father, much gory speculation having extrapolated that the girl had been buried alive. In her version, Charles Ingalls tells his wife, in his children's hearing: "They found a little girl, no bigger than Laura. They'd thrown her in on top of her father and mother and tramped the ground down on them, while the little girl was still alive." Hearing this, the fictional Laura begins to scream.[84]

Lane's image of the Benders racing across the prairie in a wagon pursued by men on horseback matches versions published in newspapers. Her avenging furies probably derive from the initial 1877 outburst of "vigilante" reports in the *Chicago Times*, the *Columbus* (Indiana) *Republican*, and other papers, which described "horsemen" following the Benders' trail away from the inn "at full speed," just after the discovery of the bodies.[85] Pure yellow, its histrionic scenes of gunplay and capture supply the satisfying and definitive conclusion that real life could never deliver.

Within a few years, Wilder herself experimented with the Benders. One of her original manuscripts of *Little House on the Prairie* preserves the intriguing evidence. Pages from the end, as the family leaves Indian Territory, she scrawled lines describing her father's return from a trip to sell their cow and calf "at a place half way to Independence, the only house on the way there." Her father goes on to remark on the eerie feeling he had, finding "something queer about the place. They seemed in a mighty hurry to get rid of me." He wonders why they were planting a garden past planting time. Wilder's stab at the Benders was far more tentative than Lane's, and she must have deemed it unconvincing, inappropriate, or in poor taste. The scene does not arise again in two additional handwritten manuscripts of the novel. Nowhere else in the works based on her life does she mention her father or family stopping at strangers' properties, only those of neighbors or friends. Before she was finished with the manuscript, she deleted the entire passage in the same pencil she wrote it in.[86]

---

84. Ibid., p. 354.

85. "The Benders," *Columbus Republican*, May 10, 1877. This piece is signed "Kaw." Above the dateline is a parenthetical note: "(Special Correspondence of the Chicago Times)."

86. Wilder, "Little House on the Prairie" (fragmentary draft), unpaginated, Laura Ingalls Wilder Papers, Laura Ingalls Wilder Home Association, Mansfield, Mo., Microfilm ed., University of Missouri Western Historical Manuscript Collection & State Historical Society of Missouri, Folder 14, image 211.

That conscious deletion marks an intriguing moment in the editorial struggle between Wilder and her daughter. More and more, their literary collaboration would become a competition between varied styles, the mother's plain, unadorned, fact-based, the daughter's polished, fictionalized, and dramatic. The competition between them—which often took the form of truth versus fiction—would become an argument over the portrayal and interpretation of Wilder's life. Lane would often add the emotion her mother had left out, while Wilder would resist, arguing for the "stoicism" that comprised so much of the settlers' response to misfortune or tragedy.[87] "God's Altar needs not our polishings" was the creed promulgated by the original New England neighbors of the Ingallses, Puritans all, and Wilder would cling to the plain style as to a moral lifeline.[88]

Lane soon revisited the Benders in promoting the forthcoming *Little House on the Prairie*. In December 1934, she wrote a letter to Isabel Paterson. The two women, who shared similar childhood experiences on the Great Plains, may have met during their early careers in San Francisco. Since 1924, Paterson, a successful novelist, had been writing a regular book-review column for the *New York Herald Tribune*, "Turns with a Bookworm." One of her acolytes was a young Ayn Rand, and Paterson would eventually serve as an influential mentor to both Rand and Lane, who subscribed to the *Herald Tribune* book section when she lived at Rocky Ridge.[89] (In later years, Lane and Paterson would be near neighbors in Connecticut). Sometime in 1934,

---

87. Wilder to Lane, Mar. 7, 1938, Box 14, file 194, Lane Papers.

88. *The Bay Psalm Book: Being a Facsimile Reprint of the First Edition, Printed by Stephen Daye at Cambridge, in New England in 1640* (New York: Dodd, Mead & Co., 1903), preface. Often said to be the first book printed in the New World, *The Bay Psalm Book* would have been familiar to generations of Ingallses descended from the family's original forebear on this continent, Edmund Ingalls, who arrived in Salem, Massachusetts, in 1628.

89. Paterson's biographer believes Lane and Paterson may have met as early as 1917 or 1918; *see* Stephen Cox, *The Woman and the Dynamo: Isabel Paterson and the Idea of America* (New Brunswick, N.J.: Transaction Publishers, 2004), p. 216. Lane was reading the *New York Herald Tribune Books* section assiduously, from at least the late 1920s on. Living in Albania, she thanked Clarence Day for a gift subscription in 1927; *see* Lane to Clarence Day, July 10, 1927, Box 5, Lane Papers. She mentioned another gift subscription to the publication in Lane to Virginia Brastow, Feb. 13, 1935, Subject Titles, Box 61, file 16, William Holtz Papers, Herbert Hoover Presidential Library, West Branch, Iowa. She also thanked Brastow for sending copies of the review. Years later, she quarreled with Paterson over who had paid for the subscription; *see* Lane to Paterson, Mar. 26, 1942, Box 3, file 6, Lane Papers. This letter is misdated as 1932, but it originated from McAllen, Texas, where Lane stayed briefly in 1942.

Paterson had referred to the Benders in a column, and Lane wrote to correct her. The columnist obligingly reprinted her remarks, quoting at length from the letter, which repeated all of Lane's favorite fabrications:

> "I beg your pardon," [Lane] says, "the Bender family did not commit their murders in a tent. Or at least did not earn their deserved reputation in that way. Kate Bender lived in an ordinary house of the times, midway between Independence, Kan., and my grandfather's log cabin on the Verdigris in Indian territory. My grandfather often stopped there, but though he had a good team, a wagon and (on the return trip) a load of supplies amply justifying his murder, he never could afford to buy a meal from the Benders, but frugally ate by his own campfire. The Bender house, completely conventional, had a canvas curtain across the middle, dividing sleeping and living quarters. A bench stood against this curtain, and a table before the bench. Prosperous travelers who could afford to pay for Kate Bender's good home cooking sat on the bench to eat it. . . . My grandfather was one of the volunteer posse that pursued the fleeing Benders. Darkly, he said little about what happened. . . . The ultimate fate of the Bender family is usually reported as shrouded in mystery. . . . But there really was no tent. Kate Bender was the dominant force in that family, and was there ever a woman who would live in a tent if she could help it?"[90]

Lane's audacity in presenting herself as an authority, while peddling outright lies, is remarkable. More than that, she seemed to find something irresistibly appealing about the Benders. Certainly, there was the lurid, sensational element, which she believed might raise the commercial profile of her mother's work. But deeper than that may have been something fundamental. The Benders, after all, represented the dark side of everything about her mother's past. Like the Ingallses, they were a family, isolated, impoverished, and fending for themselves. While Wilder's work celebrated the struggles and satisfactions of survival by means of an essential American value—self-reliance—the Benders exposed a different side to that supposed virtue, revealing a deranged and terrifying exceptionalism. Perhaps a subconscious desire to probe or expose that darker side compelled Lane—and her mother—to return to the story again and again.

---

90. Quoted in Paterson, "Turns with a Bookworm," *New York Herald Tribune Books*, Dec. 23, 1934. Ellipses appear in the original column; the letter itself apparently does not survive.

Having fabricated in the name of fact-checking, Lane was not satisfied to leave it there. She plugged her mother's book while she was at it (*Little House on the Prairie* would not be published until the fall of 1935):

> "This letter was begun as a disinterested service to pure truth; it strikes me suddenly . . . that I am wasting a publicity note. My mother's new juvenile will not be out till next year. It is all about that log cabin on the Verdigris, and the publicity angle would be that it does NOT contain any reference to the Benders. She wouldn't put that in—too gory for her readers of tender age, though I told her they'd love it."[91]

"I told her they'd love it." That was Lane's testimony (for what it was worth) that Wilder had refused her entreaties to write the Benders into *Little House on the Prairie*. Both women were willing to fictionalize, but Lane's offhand comment—"she wouldn't put that in"—suggests that there was a line that her mother was unwilling to cross.

What are we to make of the Bloody Benders in the context of Wilder's work? From Lane's perspective, the commercial and fictional possibilities seem clear. Introducing the Benders transformed the character of Charles Ingalls from a relatively passive father, driven from Kansas by soldiers, into an active hero who rides out to avenge the murder of innocents. It hitched his personality to archetypal frontiersmen of the Old West, from Davy Crockett and Daniel Boone to Wyatt Earp. Subconsciously, Lane may even have been tantalized by the sexual demonization of Kate Bender. As a daughter who struggled to separate from her mother, trying and failing to establish an independent and autonomous life, she often sought to distinguish herself by emphasizing her bohemian nature, set against what she took to be her mother's prudery.[92]

Wilder, on the other hand, deleted the Benders from her fiction and then inserted them in a fact-based essay. Like the frontier ghosts they had become, they rose up in her Detroit Book Fair speech in 1937. Invited to a "Week of Authors" celebration at the J. L. Hudson Department Store, a massive landmark in the Motor City, Wilder was promoting the publication of her fourth book, *On the Banks of Plum Creek*, which was just appearing in bookstores.

---

91. Ibid.

92. Tension between Wilder and Lane over how to address sexual issues in fiction can be seen in their debate over the manuscript of *By the Shores of Silver Lake*; *see*, for example, Wilder to Lane, Jan. 25, 1938, Box 14, file194, Lane Papers. The topic also crops up in Lane's letters to others; *see* Lane to Guy Moyston, May 30, 1925, Box 9, file 127, ibid., for Lane's description of her mother's distaste for the racy content in her Jack London novel.

In a speech written without assistance from her daughter (who was then in New York City), she spoke of her plans for a "seven-volume historical novel for children covering every aspect of the American frontier," emphasizing that her books were fiction and sketching out volumes to come.[93] While the speech would come to be seen as a central statement of her artistic vision, she never sought to publish it.

After laying out her fictional plans, her remarks took a turn in a different direction, emphasizing the "truth" of her work: "Every story in this novel, all the circumstances, each incident are true. All I have told is true but it is not the whole truth. There were some stories I wanted to tell but would not be responsible for putting in a book for children, even though I knew them as a child." The "whole truth" she "wanted to tell" was that of the Bloody Benders. The fact that there were children in the audience in Detroit did not deter her. Like her father swapping stories in the hardware store, she embroidered freely, giving Kate Bender two brothers and placing the inn "halfway" between her own little house and Independence. She did not spare her wide-eyed juvenile audience the girl buried alive "with her murdered parents." She included her father's participation in a vigilante posse. She wrote herself into the tale, saying that the family had stopped outside the Benders' on their way to find their own property. "I saw Kate Bender standing in the doorway," she said. She concluded by saying, "You will agree it is not a fit story for a children's book."[94]

She evoked the courtroom oath—"the truth, the whole truth, and nothing but the truth"—in telling a story she knew to be false, echoing Lane's insistence that *she* was motivated by "a disinterested service to pure truth." Judging by this tale, however, the truth, in Wilder's mind, was whatever she made of it. Her truth was drawn from and determined by her memories, feelings, and convictions. Her work was based on facts but was not factual; it was historical fiction, not history. Its chronology, along with certain incidents and characters, were invented, altered, and fictionalized. Of course, she had just acknowledged that she was writing fiction. Yet, emblazoned on the pale yellow covers of the books she was selling in Detroit, above the title and the cover image of Mary and Laura wading in Plum Creek, appeared these words:

---

93. Wilder, Speech, Detroit Book Fair, Oct. 16, 1937, reprinted in Wilder, *The Little House Books*, 1:586. This speech is also reprinted in this volume.

94. Ibid., pp. 588–89. Note that Wilder repeats Lane's erroneous version, claiming that the murdered child was thrown in the grave with both parents. Contemporaneous accounts describe George Longcor as a widower, found buried with his daughter.

"The True Story of an American Pioneer Family."[95] The tagline had come into being the year before, when Wilder had pressed her editor at Harper & Brothers, Ida Louise Raymond, to emphasize the autobiographical nature of her books. Raymond had immediately assented: "I think you are quite right in saying we have not sufficiently stressed the fact that these stories are true. We shall do so in the future."[96]

That ambiguous relationship to the truth enabled Wilder to transform her family's lifelong struggles into a sterling portrait of indomitability, security, and success, things she never knew as a child. The freedom she took with facts was the creative act of a novelist, enabling her to achieve something beyond the relatively constrained and more purely autobiographical *Pioneer Girl*. Her falsifications in the Detroit speech take away nothing from the artistic achievement of the Little House books, classics of American frontier literature. But her fictional freedom jibed oddly with her insistence that "all the circumstances, each incident" were true. Privately, to adults and friends, she would acknowledge the extent of her fictionalizing. Publicly, and to children, she hewed to a different line. She seemed ever more invested in presenting her idealized view of her parents as factual, fulfilling a deep longing within herself not only to preserve their memory—something she spoke of repeatedly in Detroit and elsewhere—but to elevate their legacy, elevating herself in the process. She wanted to have it both ways, claiming what her daughter once called "the authority of TRUTH, the power of REALITY" as well as the emotional depth of fiction.[97]

Wilder's attitude toward the "truth" of her work would cause considerable confusion, first for editors and later for readers and scholars. In one of their first communications, Virginia Kirkus, the Harper & Brothers editor who published *Little House in the Big Woods*, gently remarked that she was "a little in the dark as to the exact source of your material," asking Wilder to clarify its foundation: "I had understood when your manuscript was given to me to read, that it was autobiographical and that these were your own childhood experiences of frontier life. Your letter makes me feel that perhaps we were wrong in this understanding." She asked Wilder to supply a brief sketch of her life, the reply to which has been lost.[98] Kirkus's decision to publish the books as novels—while taking the unusual step of using the real names of

---

95. *See* the dust jacket of the original edition of Wilder's *On the Banks of Plum Creek* (New York: Harper & Bros., 1937).

96. Raymond to Wilder, Dec. 22, 1936, Box 13, file 192, Lane Papers.

97. "Real Detective to Tell Story: 'Ed Monroe, Man-Hunter.'"

98. Kirkus to Wilder, Dec. 15, 1931, Box 13, file 189, Lane Papers.

real people—suggests their genre-bending nature. Lane would later describe them as "autobiography in the third person," a designation more fitting to experimental modernism than to stories for children.[99]

After her mother's death, Lane would play a critical role in further muddying these waters. To scholars inquiring about chronological inconsistencies, she took a fundamentalist line, insisting that everything in the books was "the truth, and only the truth"[100] and that her mother was not "a liar."[101] Her mother may not have been, but Lane, schooled in the ways of the yellow press, exhibited a pattern of deceptive behavior throughout her career. For material gain, she lied to *Bulletin* readers; she lied to her publisher about Charlie Chaplin; she lied to Charmian London. For no good reason, she lied to Isabel Paterson, her friend, in print. She lied to everyone about her mother's work, consistently concealing to her own agents, was well as to editors, readers, and scholars the extent of her editing and fictionalizing. Eventually, the weight of Lane's remarks about truth and lies would constitute an unconscious gesture to a bad conscience. As the lies came to light, they would sully her mother's reputation, leading to exaggerated charges of "ghostwriting."[102] Her defensiveness would play into the mythology growing up around the Little House books, whose autobiographical authority deepened the influence of these chronicles of pioneer triumph.

Indeed, it was the books' secondary role as spur to the widely popular and internationally distributed television show that, more than anything else, established them as a commodity representing a nebulous American idea of family values, pegged to the frontier era. Inaccurate as it was, that interpretation has extended the reach of Wilder's influence beyond that of most children's classics. It has made her books a politically tinged touchstone for everyone from a narcissistic television actor, Michael Landon, to a charismatic film-star president, Ronald Reagan, and a populist Yellow Kid come to life, Sarah Palin.[103] There is great irony in the fact that Wilder's publisher,

---

99. Lane to Jasper Crane, Mar. 20, 1962, in *The Lady and the Tycoon: The Letters of Rose Wilder Lane and Jasper Crane*, ed. Roger Lea MacBride (Caldwell, Idaho: Caxton Printers, 1973), p. 288.

100. Quoted in Louise Hovde Mortensen, "Idea Inventory," *Elementary English* 41 (Apr. 1964): 428-29.

101. Lane to William T. Anderson, June 30, 1966, quoted in Anderson, "The Literary Apprenticeship of Laura Ingalls Wilder," *South Dakota History* 13 (Winter 1983): 288.

102. *See* Caroline Fraser, "The Prairie Queen," *New York Review of Books* 41 (Dec. 22, 1994): 38, 40-45.

103. For more on Wilder's influence on Landon, Reagan, and Palin, *see* Caroline Fraser, "Laura Ingalls Wilder and the Wolves," *Los Angeles Review of Books*, Oct. 10, 2012.

HarperCollins, is owned by the Hearst of our day, the figure most closely associated with the latest effulgence of yellow journalism, Rupert Murdoch.

Late in life, Wilder would counsel readers that it was "best to be honest and truthful."[104] But that simple maxim concealed telling omissions: the debts, deaths, and failures present in *Pioneer Girl* and the historical record but elided in the Little House books. Wilder's moral authority rested uneasily on her personal history but also upon conflicted feelings about her past, feelings that found expression in the Bender embellishments and the ennobling of her father. She grappled constantly with the desire not only to preserve the memory of her parents but to obscure the lifelong economic insecurity with which they struggled, much as she had obscured the difficulties of farming in her first essay. Leaning on her daughter's apprenticeship in yellow journalism, Laura Ingalls Wilder felt free to meld genres, molding fact into fiction in ways she did not acknowledge even to herself, attesting to her novels' "truth" while providing the succor of a fictitious happy ending. That was a feature, she said, of "all good novels."[105] It is a testament to the moral complexity of her art that we are still wrestling, decades after the fact, to separate truth from fiction.

---

104. "'Dear Children': A Letter from Laura Ingalls Wilder," reprinted in Wilder, *The Little House Books*, 2:802.

105. Wilder, Speech, Detroit Book Fair, 1:587.

# { 3 }
# "Raise a Loud Yell"
## *Rose Wilder Lane, Working Writer*

### AMY MATTSON LAUTERS

When I first read the *Pioneer Girl* manuscript, I was seated in the Herbert Hoover Presidential Library, finally going through the Rose Wilder Lane Papers, and incredibly excited to see the work in its first form. I have been a fan of the Little House books since I was small, and as I grew to become a journalist and a women's historian in my own right, I became fascinated by the real women behind those books. At first, Wilder held my attention, and a great deal of my own research has focused not only on her but on the history of American farm women and their engagements with mass media in general.[1] But as I grew into my understanding of the works, I realized I personally related much better to Wilder's daughter, Rose Wilder Lane. It was she whose memory had called me to the Hoover library, where reading Wilder's autobiography put Lane's life and career trajectory into perspective for me. *Pioneer Girl* delivers a portrait of Wilder's early life that clearly influenced the way she raised her daughter. The pioneer experience fostered self-reliance, independence, and individualism. Charity, when needed, came at the hands of neighbors; poverty inspired creativity and ingenuity. At the same time, I was struck by the fact that the Little House series itself would not exist without the professional connections and writing savvy of Lane. However, Lane's own drive and ideological perspectives were heavily influenced by her mother.

Rose Wilder Lane represents a conundrum for the true Wilder fan. In some circles, she is nearly vilified for her perceived lack of tact and theft of her mother's memoirs for her personal work; in others, she is praised as the only true writer in the family and credited for the actual writing of the Little House books. The truth about Lane can be difficult to ascribe. As she was personally prone to exaggeration for greater effect in her storytelling, sorting

---

1. *See* Amy Mattson Lauters, *More than a Farmer's Wife: Voices of American Farm Women, 1910–1960* (Columbia: University of Missouri Press, 2009).

out her truth, even in searching among her personal artifacts, represents a nearly Herculean effort. In all of our arguing about Lane's perceived lack of gentility and the liberties she took in her own work, we often fail to recognize that Lane blazed a different kind of trail for women, rooted firmly in the twentieth century, and one that her mother encouraged. Wilder allowed her daughter to grow into a tenacious, independent, fierce professional woman in a period when such drive in women was frowned upon. Wilder raised a woman who firmly believed that it was her duty to, as Lane told J. Edgar Hoover in 1943, "raise a loud yell" in the face of authority when necessary. *Pioneer Girl* shows us how Wilder's own experiences could have allowed her to raise such a daughter.

In other works, I have made strong arguments for the inclusion of Rose Wilder Lane in the existing canon of literary journalists—those writers who embrace literary style for telling factual stories.[2] I personally think her most successful writing does this effectively. But Lane wrote a variety of pieces for a variety of publications in a variety of styles. In that sense, she defies any niche writing category we could place her into. Lane was simply a working writer. Whatever we think of Lane as fans, we must acknowledge that without her aggressive approach to her own writing and to writing as a career, fostered in the cradle of the pioneer experience, it is likely we would not have the Little House series of books. Lane worked hard at her craft, and she was successful with her approach. By the end of her nearly sixty-year career as a writer, she had an impressive list of works to her credit, and they ranged from ad copy to news to literary nonfiction to political commentary, as well as to fiction. Lane wrote for a living; she wrote for advocacy; and she wrote for the sheer pleasure of doing so.

We need first to understand, and underscore, the fact that women writers in general were scarce when Lane decided on this career. The kinds of jobs available to women between 1904, when Rose Wilder graduated from high school, and 1909, when she married Claire Gillette Lane, were limited. Women helped run or outright ran farms, but in town, jobs for unmarried women were largely limited to heavily chaperoned teaching positions. In larger urban environments, women could and did work in large factories as laborers, working with machinery that required a delicate touch and smaller hands. Writing as a profession for women existed somewhat outside the boundaries of conventional Victorian ideals. In choosing telegraphy as an

2. Amy Mattson Lauters, "From Her Own Point of View: Rediscovering Rose Wilder Lane, Literary Journalist," *American Journalism* 24 (Winter 2007): 7–33; Amy Mattson Lauters, ed., *The Rediscovered Writings of Rose Wilder Lane, Literary Journalist* (Columbia: University of Missouri Press, 2007).

occupation right after high school, Lane stumbled upon one of the new careers open to young unmarried women that relied on new communications technology. In marrying the man she called Gillette, the avenue of writing appeared, too, with significantly greater appeal.

When Lane and Gillette married, he had been working as a reporter for the *San Francisco Bulletin*. Sources disagree about when Lane met her only husband. Some suggest they met when Lane was a telegrapher in Kansas City, and it was his influence that led her to take a transfer to San Francisco. Regardless, we do know that Claire Gillette Lane lived in the same apartment building as his future wife in San Francisco. Rose Wilder roomed with Bessie Beatty, who also worked for the *San Francisco Bulletin*. Rose Wilder married Claire Gillette Lane in March 1909, and with their marriage, the pair decided to sell real estate in California and other spots along the West Coast, looking to build a nest egg for themselves. Not much has been written about this period in Lane's life; her diaries only occasionally reflect upon these years. Some sources suggest that her first novel, *Diverging Roads* (1919), is autobiographical and reflective of this time. It tells of the growing despair of a young wife who, having achieved the goal of marriage, did not know quite what to do with herself, but relying on the man she married was becoming increasingly difficult. Gillette Lane apparently spent freely and earned slowly, a troubling situation that must have been heightened when their only child, a boy, was stillborn in a Salt Lake City hospital at six months gestation in November 1909. The couple was traveling, still trying to make money in land sales. Lane was seriously ill afterwards, and she recuperated with her parents back at Rocky Ridge Farm while Gillette looked for work nearby. He fell back on reporting.[3]

Lane probably knew at this point that she would have no more children, and I can imagine, with the hormonal aftereffects of childbirth as well as the burgeoning depression that would claim her off and on over the course of her life, she spent a great deal of time in reflection. What would Lane do with her life now that parenthood would apparently elude her? Was there nothing more? She, too, picked up a reporter's notebook. Her reasons have not been put down on paper, but they are not hard to guess. The Lanes needed money. She needed something to do. The couple both wrote for newspapers

---

3. William Holtz, *The Ghost in the Little House: A Life of Rose Wilder Lane* (Columbia: University of Missouri Press, 1993), pp. 46, 49, 51, 54; Sallie Ketcham, *Laura Ingalls Wilder: American Writer on the Prairie* (New York: Routledge, 2015), pp. 90–91; Utah, State Board of Health, Death Certificate, File no. 1713, Utah State Archives, archives.utah.gov/indexes/data/81448/ 2229322/2229322_ 0000278.jpg. Infant Lane, stillborn on Nov. 23, 1909, is buried in Mount Olivet Cemetery, Salt Lake City, Utah.

in Kansas City, and articles attributed to Lane show up in the *Kansas City Post* beginning in 1910. They include standard fare for a cub reporter: business, crime, farm news, and particularly women's news. The couple worked their way east, taking jobs in New York and in Maine, before ultimately going back to San Francisco.[4] There, Lane renewed her acquaintance with Bessie Beatty and joined her on staff at the *San Francisco Bulletin* in 1915, a move that truly launched Lane's writing career. Once she decided she would be a writer, she threw herself into the vocation wholeheartedly. Her diaries list books on craft and style, and her notes reflect on the same.[5] Her first salaried writing job in San Francisco tossed her into the cutthroat world of yellow journalism in an era known for its sometimes-literal muckraking and at a time when the "girl reporter" was starting to make her mark on the profession.

The first comprehensive history of women in journalism appeared in 1936, written by former New York reporter Ishbel Ross. At that time, Ross estimated that nearly twelve thousand women editors, feature writers, and reporters were at work in the country, but they had "not made much impression in the front-page field." Ross pointed out that the real work and contribution of women in journalism came through the "old standbys": women's pages, clubs, and social news. Readers can detect her sarcasm as she outlined the requirements of a female reporter, many of which seem nigh unattainable. She listed traits of a paragon of virtue who remains untouched by the abuse heaped upon her by others in the profession, even as she works to a capacity beyond reproach and demonstrates talent far beyond her male peers. "Where is this paragon to be found?" Ross queried. "No editor believes that she exists. She probably doesn't. And if she did, she would not have much chance to prove it, for although women have hit the sky in feature writing, they still have a long way to go to establish themselves as first-string news reporters."[6]

Ross named one of Lane's closest friends, Dorothy Thompson, as an exception to the rule, while Lane herself she identified as one of the profession but not a hard-hitting reporter. According to Ross, Lane's *Bulletin* editor, Fremont Older, groomed her for pictorial writing rather than crusading journalism. He gave her serial and feature-story assignments that encouraged her

---

4. Holtz, *Ghost*, pp. 51–53. Lane's clipping files can be found in Box 40, Rose Wilder Lane Papers (hereafter cited as Lane Papers), Herbert Hoover Presidential Library, West Branch, Iowa.

5. Lane's diaries, journals, and notebooks are also held in the Lane Papers at the Hoover. *See*, for example, her Sausalito Diary, 1918, July 29, 1918, Box 19, Item #1, and her Notes and Analysis—Books Read, 1928–1933, Box 21, Item #35.

6. Ishbel Ross, *Ladies of the Press* (New York: Harper & Row, 1936), pp. 2–4.

to describe conditions and people. "And she tramped the countryside with the energy and perceptions of a pioneer," Ross wrote. "Since then Mrs. Lane has traveled far, worked hard, and become well known for her fiction."[7]

What emerges from Ross's work and that of others is the fact that a woman who wanted to write professionally had a fairly set career trajectory. She started by writing for women's pages and branched out from there. Lane's successes with the women's page at the *Bulletin* encouraged her to freelance for other publications, and some of her best literary journalism came out of the period immediately following her divorce from Gillette and her separation from the *Bulletin*. Her diary entry of July 12, 1918, reads: "Independence Day. Left the Bulletin." She recorded that Older's last day at the newspaper was July 16, commenting: "The old crowd disintegrates. . . . The Bulletin is dead. Funeral early in 1919. No flowers. Only members of the family will be present at the interment." In August, Lane declined an offer to resume work at the *Bulletin* and proclaimed, "Am now really starting a free-lance career." By mid-September, she had begun freelance work for Older, who had moved to the Hearst newspaper, the *San Francisco Call*.[8]

During this time in her career, Lane's diaries and correspondence offer insight into her study of writing as a craft. In a letter to Charles Caldwell Dobie, another writer, Lane thanked him for an earlier critique of her work and added: "I wish I knew something about writing. All I know a little about is living, and life is so chuck-full of false leads!"[9] Lane listed numerous titles of handbooks on writing in her diaries, adding her own observations and reflections about the works. She explored how writing itself worked as she engaged with and discussed the craft, ultimately concluding, "The writer does not construct a mosaic of definite particles; he tries to paint in clear lines with a rainbow."[10]

Lane accepted a job offer to write from Europe in the immediate aftermath of the First World War, and she lived and worked out of Paris in the 1920s. Her correspondence with friends at this time shows the depth and breadth of the work she was attempting to complete even as she forged connections and friendships among the American expatriates who were also working in Paris, including Ernest Hemingway, Sinclair Lewis, and two women who would become lifelong friends, Dorothy Thompson and Helen Boylston. She was managing to support herself and the free-spirited lifestyle to which she was

---

7. Ibid., pp. 580–81.
8. Lane, Sausalito Diary, July 12, 20, Aug. 6, 14, Sept. 24, 1918.
9. Lane to Charles Caldwell Dobie, Apr. 17, 1918; Box 5, file 58a, Lane Papers.
10. Lane, Sausalito Diary, July 29, 1918.

becoming accustomed, but it was a struggle. "I am so broke that I must write and write and write," she wrote her friend Berta Hoerner Hader in November 1920.[11]

For Lane, writing was first and foremost a profession that enabled her to earn a living and enjoy her life. She knew herself and her own motivations fairly well on that front, too. In a piece she wrote for a trade magazine called *The Writer* in 1928, Lane explained her process with regard to writing a short piece of original fiction called "Yarbwoman," which had made the list of best short stories of 1927. She began by telling her readers that she herself would not have included the story in such a collection. "It is to me merely a good job of carpentry, not the best even of my own stories," she confided. "But it does illustrate my method of producing a story which has for its first motive the necessity of paying the rent." Lane explained that she had gone through her idea notebooks until she found something that caught her attention, developed a bit of a plot, and then let her mind brood on the scene until she imagined herself there, able to describe and tell the story. Along the way, she made editorial choices, such as setting the scene in a swamp in the Ozarks when she was not sure there was a swamp in the Ozarks, which she shrugged off with a laissez-faire nod to the ignorance of the general reader. "This is indefensible," Lane wrote. "Had I been in the States I would have verified this point, but in Albania I couldn't; there was not time; I needed the check."[12]

In short, Lane knew how to scope out the market, and she knew what would sell. She kept her finger on the pulse of the audiences for the national magazines she targeted and deliberately wrote for those audiences. She sold pieces to *Sunset* literary magazine in California, *Ladies' Home Journal, Good Housekeeping,* and *Harper's,* among others. Her goal? To support her newly single self as well as her parents, if possible, and to enjoy the kind of "fun" she liked to have as she made her way across Europe. To that end, she wrote anything that would sell—fiction and commercial nonfiction alike. So much of Lane's career can be underscored with the final phrase of that line in *The Writer*: "I needed the check."

For someone who had thus finally managed to gain a positive reputation as an internationally known writer and therefore a degree of job security, the stock market crash in 1929 came as a shock. Lane panicked when her nest egg, invested along with her parents' money, disappeared into the economic morass that became the Great Depression. With few choices left to her, she returned to the Ozarks and fought deep personal depression to settle into writ-

---

11. Lane to Hader, Nov. 30, 1920, Box 5, file 64, Lane Papers.
12. Lane, "How I Wrote 'Yarbwoman,'" *The Writer* 40 (May 1928): 143.

ing to recoup their losses.[13] When Wilder's *Pioneer Girl* manuscript brought her new source material, Lane somewhat coldly used it to give her personal writing career a boost, ultimately rationalizing her actions. Arguably, her two most famous pieces of fiction came out of her reading of her mother's autobiography: *Let the Hurricane Roar* (1933) and *Free Land* (1938). Despite the friction her actions caused with her mother, the success of those two works helped Lane settle down.[14] Her mother's commercial success, and the work Lane did to help her edit and polish the Little House series, also went a long way toward easing the stranglehold that paying assignments had on Lane. But she did not turn them down.

Instead, Lane developed a hugely profitable relationship with *Woman's Day* magazine, one she maintained for a little over thirty years. In the 1930s, the A & P supermarket chain, in an attempt to help the depression-era homemaker find good recipes for economical meals, began putting out a free flier that featured menus and recipes for its regular shoppers. Few were taken, and the chain decided that in order to continue this perk, it needed to charge for it. At two cents a copy beginning in 1937, the flier sold out, and *Woman's Day* magazine was born.[15] At the time of its inception, Lane was working from New York, where her contacts provided her with a steady source of assignments, and she continued to churn out copy at a staggering rate. She wrote primarily for magazines that targeted a decidedly middle-class audience, placing pieces with *Saturday Evening Post*, *Country Gentleman*, *McCall's*, *Good Housekeeping*, and others.

When A & P decided to make its flier into a magazine, Lane was in on the ground floor. As a friend of the new editor, Eileen Tighe, she was able to write nearly anything she liked. In her letters to industrialist Jasper Crane, Lane decisively said that charging for the fledgling publication made it immediately popular. "I, or any sensible person, could have told them that anybody values a purchase higher than a give-away, but I guess they were listening to 'public relations' experts," Lane wrote Crane.[16] In the magazine's earliest years, Lane wrote a number of opinion pieces, all from her ideological point of view that

---

13. Holtz, *Ghost*, p. 218.

14. The strained relationship between Lane and Wilder is explored in Pamela Smith Hill, Introduction to Laura Ingalls Wilder, *Pioneer Girl: The Annotated Autobiography*, ed. Hill (Pierre: South Dakota Historical Society Press, 2014), pp. l–li.

15. "A Brief History of *Woman's Day*," handout distributed by *Woman's Day*, 2001. *See also* Stuart Elliott, "*Woman's Day* Turns 75 While Looking Forward," *New York Times*, Sept. 16, 2012, nytimes.com. The original price of the magazine is variously reported at two, five, or ten cents per copy.

16. Lane to Crane, Nov. 7, 1963, reprinted in *The Lady and the Tycoon: The Letters of*

capitalism and individualism were the cornerstones of Americanism; "freedom" meant freedom from government interference in the everyday lives of Americans. Lane also wrote varied features and slice-of-life vignettes in the 1940s.[17] As *Woman's Day* garnered an ever-widening audience, Lane's reach, and that of her political ideology, was likewise extended.

In the 1940s, Lane also tapped into her increasingly large network of friends and acquaintances to advocate for her particular brand of Americanism, even as she finished work on her political treatise, *The Discovery of Freedom*, published in 1943. It is perhaps not a coincidence that one of her letters also brought her national attention in the same year. In March, at the height of the Second World War, the United States Department of Justice received a note from Albert P. Walsh, the postmaster for Danbury, Connecticut, where Lane then lived:

> "My dear Sir: -
> I am sending for your attention, the wording which appeared on a Post Card and mailed by a rural patron of this office, by giving same to Rural Mail Carrier. The message is as follows:
>
>> If schoolteachers say to German children, "We believe in social security" the children will ask, "Then why did you fight Germany?" All these "social security" laws are German, instituted by Bismark [*sic*] and expanded by Hitler. Americans believe in freedom, not in being taxed for their own good and bossed by bureaucrats."
>
> This card was addressed to [Samuel Grafton], WOR, New York City.
> This card was allowed to pass through the mails and no doubt will be received by the addressee.[18]

The postmaster's note caused a bit of a stir. A state trooper was dispatched to confirm the identity of the writer, which appeared to be a "Mrs. C. G. Lang."[19]

When the trooper arrived at the return address in Danbury, however, he

---

*Rose Wilder Lane and Jasper Crane*, ed. Roger Lea MacBride (Caldwell, Idaho: Caxton Printers, 1973), p. 340.

17. Lauters, "From Her Own Point of View," pp. 22–25; Lauters, *Rediscovered Writings*, chaps. 6–7.

18. Walsh to U.S. Department of Justice, Mar. 15, 1943, Box 5, file 58d, Lane Papers. Grafton's name was blacked out but is supplied from other sources. Unless otherwise specified, all original documents referenced in this discussion can be found in this FBI file (58d) in the Lane Papers.

19. J. R. Mumford to Mr. Ladd, FBI, Aug. 9, 1943.

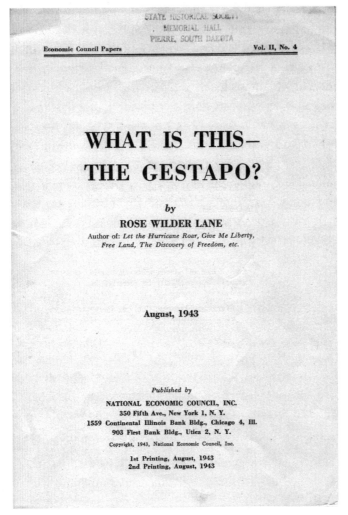

Lane protested the FBI surveillance of writers and other citizens, publicizing her own experience in this 1943 pamphlet. *South Dakota Historical Society Press*

found Mrs. C. G. Lane—otherwise known as writer Rose Wilder Lane—who freely admitted writing the note. She also took issue with the investigation, believing it to be a thinly veiled attempt to control freedom of speech. Subsequently, Lane widely publicized the event by writing a story about the incident and, working with the National Economic Council, having it printed into a pamphlet titled "What Is This—The Gestapo?"[20] It went into three printings, the last in January 1944. In a different year, it might not have caused the same ruckus. But in 1943, the Federal Bureau of Investigation (FBI), under the direction of J. Edgar Hoover, tasked itself with surveillance on the

20. Lane, "What Is This—The Gestapo?" *Economic Council Papers* 2, no. 4 (Aug. 1943).

population in an effort to both curb Communism and unmask espionage during wartime. As an organization, the FBI showed a distinct aggression toward creative writers and kept surveillance files on a wide number of them, including Sinclair Lewis, Theodore Dreiser, Upton Sinclair, Pearl Buck, and William Faulkner. As historian Rhodri Jeffreys-Jones wrote, "it would seem that virtually every significant interwar fiction author came under surveillance."[21]

Under Hoover's direction, the bureau took a hard stance against left-wing politics, politicians, and creative forces. Hoover was especially unhappy with Eleanor Roosevelt, who not only leaned left but criticized the bureau and campaigned for civil rights for black citizens. Roosevelt drew a comparison between the Gestapo and the FBI's efforts to investigate civic organizations that had left-leaning members. Hoover, for his part, kept extensive files on Roosevelt that included surveillance on her private relationships. But high-profile citizens were not the only ones vulnerable to such treatment. An incident in 1940 during which the FBI had swept through homes in Detroit to arrest several people on charges of recruitment for the Abraham Lincoln Brigade particularly drew ire. The agents searched homes without warrants and held prisoners without allowing them to contact lawyers, but in the end, no one was charged. When news came from Europe in 1942 about Nazi genocide and Gestapo raids, some critics, including Eleanor Roosevelt, drew parallels between the Gestapo and the FBI.[22]

By 1943, the FBI's actions and investigations into the lives of United States citizens had thus reached a point of public concern, and such high-profile discussions about its secret policing methods meant that the FBI director had reason to worry about the organization's public image. Recent scholarship has documented Hoover's attempts to control and manipulate the press, especially in an effort to maintain a positive public image for the bureau despite its behind-the-scenes abuses of power.[23] Lane's pamphlet, however, skirted established media outlets and went straight to the public, eliminating the possibility that anyone within the FBI could interfere in its publication or its message.

Despite the fact that a number of her known acquaintances and fellow writers already had FBI files, Lane herself did not have a surveillance file prior to 1943. It is possible that she escaped scrutiny because of her virulent anti-

---

21. Jeffreys-Jones, *The FBI: A History* (New Haven, Conn.: Yale University Press, 2007), p. 130.

22. Ibid., pp. 132–33, 138, 140.

23. *See* Matthew Cecil, *Hoover's FBI and the Fourth Estate: The Campaign to Control the Press and the Bureau's Image* (Lawrence: University Press of Kansas, 2014).

Communist sentiments. It is also possible that she was not seen as important or influential enough to undergo the scrutiny her fellow writers seemed to endure. However, the FBI made up for the lack once she put her postcard to Samuel Grafton at Radio WOR, protesting Social Security and making an explicit comparison to Germany, in the mail. In response to the postmaster's report, the FBI, as represented by Special Agent in Charge R. H. Simons, issued a request to the Danbury Police Department on March 23, 1943, to investigate Lane. The letter included a list of things to be investigated, the text of which was in a lighter typeface than the original query at the top of the letter, suggesting that it was a standard request for background investigation on a possible threat to national security. The rest of the letter specified how the sources of information should be documented and noted that, if at any time it was discovered that the writer of the note was a member of the armed forces or an employee of the federal government, the investigation should be turned immediately back over to the FBI. Special Agent Simons included a self-addressed envelope for the return report.[24]

The Danbury police identified the address given for the sender of the postcard—still erroneously identified as Mrs. C. G. Lang—as a rural address and turned it over to the Connecticut State Police for investigation. The State Police issued the report to Simons on May 20, 1943, noting that Mrs. C. G. Lang was actually Rose Wilder Lane and describing her as five foot, six inches, "150 lbs., grey hair—grey eyes, age about 50, wears white gold-rimmed glasses." She had no criminal history, was a writer with "a national reputation," native born, with good credit and no links to any organizations with un-American sympathies.[25]

The trooper (name redacted) who talked to Lane during the investigation reported that she had sent the postcard in question to Samuel Grafton at radio station WOR in New York City "in response to his radio talks and requests for letters." She had signed the card "Mrs. C. G. Lane" because "she did not want any publicity, which she would probably receive if she signed the card 'Rose Wilder Lane.'" Obviously, "someone copied the name Lane wrong and made it Lang," the trooper noted. He concluded: "It is evident that Mrs. Lane is not in sympathy with our social security laws and was merely expressing her opinions on the card to Mr. Grafton. From my conversation with her and from my investigation at the home of her neighbors I have no reason to believe that she is connected in any manner with any subversive

24. Special Agent in Charge R. H. Simons to Danbury Police, Mar. 23, 1943.
25. Connecticut Department of State Police, Report on Rose Wilder Lane, May 17, 1943.

Lane is pictured here in 1942, not long before her confrontation with the Connecticut state trooper over her "subversive" postcard.
*Herbert Hoover Presidential Library and Museum*

activity. Mrs. Lane has two adopted sons in the armed services."[26] This report might have been the end of the entire incident, but it was not. And I sincerely doubt that Lane "did not want any publicity."

Instead of letting the incident go, Lane seized the opportunity to call attention to one of her favorite causes—freedom from government interference in the lives of everyday Americans. Working in concert with Lowell Thomas and the National Economic Council, Lane wrote a story about her experience, setting forth her account of the meeting with the state trooper. Writ-

26. Ibid.

ing in third person, she described herself as a woman listening to a radio broadcast by Samuel Grafton from her Connecticut farm. Grafton, she wrote, extolled the virtues of "Social Security" and advocated sending American school teachers to "teach Germans democracy after the war." Lane jotted her response to the broadcast on a postcard and sent it to him in care of the radio station. Two weeks later, she "was digging dandelions from her lawn, when a State Police car stopped at her gate," Lane wrote. "A State Trooper, uniformed and armed, walked up to her. He said that he was investigating subversive activities for the F.B.I., and asked whether anyone in her house had sent a postcard to Samuel Grafton." Lane replied that she had.[27]

The trooper produced a copy of the wording on the postcard and asked her again "sternly" if she had written it. The next part of the text needs to be read in its original form:

> She said, "Yes, I wrote that. What have the State Police to do with any opinion that an American citizen wants to express?"
>
> The trooper said, more sternly, "I do not like your attitude."
>
> A furious American rose to her full height. "*You* do not like *my* attitude! I am an American citizen. I hire you, I pay you. And you have the insolence to question *my* attitude? The point is that *I* don't like *your* attitude. What is this—the Gestapo?"
>
> The young State Trooper said hastily, "Oh, no, nothing like that. I was not trying to frighten you."
>
> "You know perfectly well that your uniform and your tone would frighten a great many Americans in this neighborhood who remember the police methods in Europe. You know, or you should know, that any investigation of opinions by the American police is outrageous!"
>
> "Oh, come now," the trooper protested. "At least give me credit for coming to you, instead of going around among your neighbors and gathering gossip about you. I only want to know whether you wrote that postcard."
>
> "Is that a subversive activity?" she demanded.
>
> Somewhat confused, the trooper answered, "Yes."
>
> "Then I'm subversive as all hell!" she told him.[28]

Lane continued to explain to the trooper why she was against Social Security, reiterating that she was going to express her opinions as loudly as she wanted, wherever she wanted, and that he was free to report that to his su-

---

27. Lane, "What Is This—The Gestapo?" p. [3].
28. Ibid., pp. [3–4].

periors. The trooper backed off a bit, then told Lane he would report that she was a writer. "'If you'd signed your professional name to that postcard, I wouldn't've bothered you,'" the trooper allegedly said. "'Of course, if you're a writer, it's all right; you can say what you want to.'" Lane continued the story: "She refused this special immunity; she insisted that he report her as an American citizen; she declared again that every American citizen has a right to say what he wants to say." The last paragraph of the pamphlet raised questions about who had reported the postcard, asked whether Grafton had actually gotten it, and wondered whether American mail was being censored or controlled. "Precisely what is happening?" she queried.[29]

The pamphlet circulated widely, catching the attention of numerous newspapers. The Associated Press picked up the story, and various agents and concerned people reported the pamphlet to Hoover at least six times, according to Lane's FBI file. As late as February 1944, United States Attorney General Francis Biddle asked Hoover, "Are we doing anything about this?"[30] The FBI was, of course, investigating. Agents began by verifying that Lane's assertion was true—a Social Security system had been in play under the German chancellor Bismarck. The investigation then looked into Lane's potential Communist ties and revealed her participation on a 1938 committee for the defense of labor worker and accused murderer Fred E. Beal. It also referenced her participation in an Industrial Workers of the World "propaganda" arm called the Finnish Singing Society in 1919. Finally, it noted that Grafton had found the card among his correspondence—eventually.[31]

In a letter to Hoover in August 1943, "RE: ROSE WILDER LANE SECURITY MATTER," Special Agent in Charge D. K. Brown wrote that a number of smaller stories about the pamphlet had sprung up around the country, and he noted that Hoover needed to be concerned about the negative publicity. He advised the director that the bureau needed to do a better job of reigning in local law enforcement officers charged with conducting investigations on behalf of the FBI. "It appears to me," he wrote, "that the Lane woman is a sensationalist and publicity seeker, who seized upon a minor and unimportant incident to gain nation-wide publicity. I believe that all of us recognized the danger of such an incident occurring and have warned police officers to whom cases are assigned that they must use the utmost discretion in handling the investigations." Brown emphasized that it was much too late to fix the

---

29. Ibid., p. [4].

30. Office of the Attorney General, handwritten note on memo cover sheet, to J. Edgar Hoover, Feb. 13, 1944.

31. FBI Memorandum, Aug. 14, 1943.

problem now, but he also pointed out that the incident itself would not have gotten publicity without Lane. "As a matter of fact, the Lane incident would not have come to the attention of anyone except Rose Wilder Lane had she not seen fit to make a great to do in the public press," Brown wrote.[32]

The director of the American Civil Liberties Union, Roger N. Baldwin, got involved, too, writing a letter of protest to Hoover, who responded by outlining the facts of the case as he knew them. "I, of course, do not know what the trooper said, and I am not in a position to comment on the statements attributed to him," Hoover wrote. "I do know that such statements would not have been made by a Special Agent of this Bureau, and certainly such statements do not meet with my approval." However, Hoover told Baldwin, the bureau had a duty to identify "Mrs. C. G. Lang," but "I do disavow any statements to the effect that the writing of the card was 'a subversive activity.'" He also claimed that Lane had personally known the trooper who interviewed her.[33] In further correspondence, Hoover remained frustrated by the continued press coverage. He told Baldwin that Lane should have contacted the FBI directly after the incident with her concerns rather than air them publicly.[34]

A copy of Hoover's first letter to Baldwin made its way to Lane from Baldwin himself. Lane responded that Hoover's original informant was unreliable and should be reported as such. She reiterated her story as told in the pamphlet, pointed out witnesses to the altercation that could be questioned, and stated her belief that the trooper in question would corroborate her story. Moreover, Lane said, Hoover missed the point of the pamphlet. "I protest again that no American official should make a distinction between American citizens. If an opinion requires an investigation when held by Mrs. C. G. Lane, it requires an investigation when held by Rose Wilder Lane. A distinction between persons warrants a question: What is this—the Gestapo? So does an investigation of a statement of historical fact and of an opinion obviously patriotic, though at variance with an Administration measure." Lane added that she had received letters since the pamphlet was published that expressed the writers' fears of reprisals for anti-administration opinions and that the public needed to be aware of these issues. She expressed concern that Hoover had a policy of holding a "secret police strictly within the limitation of American principles."[35]

Lane wrote Hoover the same day to ensure she was understood. She as-

32. Brown to Hoover, Aug. 16, 1943.
33. Hoover to Baldwin, Aug. 19, 1943. *See also* ibid., Aug. 17, 1943.
34. Ibid., Sept. 3, 1943.
35. Lane to Baldwin, Sept. 9, 1943.

serted that a secret police "always holds a potential danger to individual freedom and human rights" and the FBI should be aware of this danger. "To this end, whenever a policeman or an investigator puts so much as the toe of his boot across the line protecting any American citizen's right to free thought and free speech, I regard it as that citizen's duty to refuse to permit this, and to **raise a loud yell**," Lane wrote. She closed by telling Hoover that she had expressed to reporters "my admiration and gratitude and loyal support of the splendid work that the FBI is doing" but her comments to that effect had not been reported.[36]

Lane remained on the FBI radar in the postwar period. Even though she increasingly let other writing assignments go, she continued her work with *Woman's Day*, and she grieved for her parents. Almanzo died in 1949; Wilder herself died in 1957. Lane safeguarded the legacies of the Little Houses, but she also ensured that her own voice was heard. This twilight period of her life showed a working writer who knew how to use her typewriter to advocate for her beliefs and how to be sneaky about it. While her best-known works are fiction, she also infused her ideological advocacy into a bestseller found in many working American homes: *Woman's Day Book of American Needlework*.[37]

From the beginning, *Woman's Day* magazine focused on the needs of the homemaker, making itself a key publication to which American women could turn for advice and information about a wide variety of topics. While it continued to feature menus and recipes, it grew to encapsulate women's fashion, homemaking tips, crafting patterns and discussion, and political commentary. Still published today, the magazine also offered a community forum for its readers, which now takes form in its interactive web site. The community of readers in Lane's time contributed their thoughts on a wide variety of issues, and Lane's voice was not the only notable one recognized within its pages. Other women writers, including such notables as Pearl S. Buck, contributed material to *Woman's Day*. Because of its status as a woman's magazine, it often flew under the radar of larger corporate and elite America because its content was geared to a middle-class, feminine audience. Magazine editorial staff campaigned tirelessly to have the magazine content included in the *Reader's Guide to Periodical Literature;* their efforts failed, mostly, as one staffer put it, because *Woman's Day* is "just a woman's magazine."[38] However,

36. Lane to Hoover, Sept. 9, 1943 (emphasis added).

37. Lane, *Woman's Day Book of American Needlework* (New York: Simon & Schuster, 1963).

38. Suzan Schaefer, reprint editor, *Woman's Day*, personal email to author, Mar. 8, 2004, when I was seeking out Lane's writings.

this public ignorance of the political commentary the magazine offered allowed women writers an uninhibited space in which to forward their agendas and beliefs.

Lane certainly took advantage of that opportunity. As the United States entered the tense domestic-containment era of the 1950s, when the happy and traditional American home became part of the bulwark against Communism, Lane and *Woman's Day* partnered to create an American needlework series. Lane wrote the historical and political commentary that accompanied the patterns and instructions; *Woman's Day* editorial staff scoured the country looking for photographic examples of pieces to go with the commentaries. Originally published in the magazine, the articles were collected and printed as the *Woman's Day Book of American Needlework* in 1963. The book went into several printings, and it can still be found readily available in used bookstores.[39] It also exceeded all of Lane's expectations. She told Crane that the response to the magazine series had been "tremendous," resulting in "an avalanche, tens of thousands of reader letters; very nearly ALL overflowing gratitude for the *Americanism*. Orders for patterns, etc., engulfed the business department too, but the patriotic, individualistic, anti-Welfare State response overwhelmed the editorial staff so that twelve more typists had to be added to the Answers-to-Readers department. And seven publishers asked for the series in book." Lane also noted that the circulation of *Woman's Day* at the time was eight million and that the deal with Simon and Schuster obliged the publisher to meet all the demand for the book.[40]

The popularity of the text suggests that it did strike a chord for its readers. The combination of historical commentary, written from Lane's right-wing point of view, full-color photographs of American women's needlework, and instructions for basic patterns in each form of needlecraft appeared to fill a need for the women who purchased the book. It was clearly more popular than her 1943 political magnum opus, *The Discovery of Freedom,* and reached a wider audience. The writer, whose main motivation had been earning a living with her work, had finally found a platform that allowed her to be paid for her advocacy.

In her new role as writer-advocate, Lane opened with a central theme to which she adhered in all the commentary that followed. "Needlework," she

---

39. When researching this piece, I mentioned the book in passing to my mother, who pointed out that she owned a first edition that my grandmother had given her and that I likely read it as a child. My mother, Linnea Mattson, is a fibers artist.

40. Lane to Crane, Nov. 7, 1963, in *Lady and the Tycoon*, p. 341 (emphasis in the original).

Lane's ideas on individualism and self-reliance accompanied the patterns collected in the *Woman's Day Book of American Needlework*.

have chosen and American flowers and birds are in the designs, but the cushion top and the chair seat are primly conventional, made for the parlor that was opened only when company came. The gentlemen's needlepoint slippers and braces (Americans called them suspenders) were Christmas or wedding gifts, to be worn only on Sundays.

Needlepoint is not necessary. It isn't thrifty. It has no utility; its value is beauty alone. And three generations of the Old World's emigrants, at last free, worked and saved for a long century before they abolished the hungry poverty in which their ancestors lived for six thousand years. The nineteenth century was growing old before homekeeping women in all the thirty-five States could afford to create an art purely for its own sake.

Our grandmothers began to make American needlepoint, and few examples of it are in museums yet. Many more are in homes, and countless numbers are in embroidery frames. Recently scores of such artists as the late Mrs. Theodore Roosevelt, Jr. have been working original American designs and hundreds are making them now. The characteristic American freshness, originality, freedom, are in them. If you are not working one yourself, you see them in your friends' homes and you can find in libraries a few books showing pictures of this new American art.

The first needlepoint that I saw may have been an early example of it. My mother

BELOW: *Chair cushion with a shell motif, one of ten embroidered by Martha Washington at the age of 69.* [MOUNT VERNON LADIES' ASSOCIATION, MOUNT VERNON, VA.]

*Swatches, surprisingly modern in design although embroidered over a century ago, found in a work basket at Sunnyside, home of Washington Irving.* [SLEEPY HOLLOW RESTORATIONS]

wrote, "is the art that tells the truth about the real life of people in their time and place." She continued:

> The great arts, music, sculpture, painting, literature, are the work of a few unique persons whom lesser men emulate, often for generations. Needlework is anonymous; the people create it. Each piece is the work of a woman who is thinking only of making for her child, her friend, her home or herself a bit of beauty that pleases her.
>
> So her needlework expresses what she is, more clearly than her handwriting does. It expresses everything that makes her an individual unlike any other person—her character, her mind and her spirit, her experience in living. It expresses, too, her country's history and cul-

ture, the traditions, the philosophy, the way of living that she takes for granted.[41]

It was a simple message: American needlework expresses the values of the women who create it more clearly than any "great" art of any other country can. Lane's voice asserted authority as it stated that Americans lived in the only classless society, a theme echoed elsewhere. In this section, and in each subsequent section, Lane interweaved historical anecdotes and verifiable but unsourced facts with that same voice of authority, starting in her introduction with the tale of Betsy Ross, who, she asserted, created the American flag using American patchwork techniques. "In the tradition of American patchwork she made the flag that stands today, with its fifty stars, for the inalienable liberty and human rights of every human being, the flag of the Revolution that already has carried the New World far around this earth and some day will help banish the last tyranny and free all mankind" (p. 15). In other places, Lane talked about traditions linked to women's needlecrafts, but she framed all in terms of American history as she perceived it.

In this sense, Lane began her work in validating women's pursuits, bolstering the hobbies of needlecraft, and building up women's confidence in their important contributions to American culture. The themes to which Lane returned repeatedly were (1) individualism as a strength of American culture, reflected in American women's needlework; (2) poverty and self-reliance as shapers of individualist philosophy, again reflected in American women's needlework; and (3) freedom from government interference in women's arts as essential to the creativity and progress of those arts. Overall, Lane used her commentary to reinforce the idea that American women were critical to founding American culture and that American women themselves held special and important places in American history.

Lane sent a clear message throughout the book: American needlework was unique because it was created by women who had been freed from the bonds of communal thought and could, therefore, adapt old patterns or create new ones of their own. She strongly advocated individualism, a theme introduced before the first needlework style was even mentioned. "Just as individual freedom suddenly released the terrific human energy that swept the Old World's Great Powers from this hemisphere and wholly transformed North America in a third of the time that those Old World Powers had held it, so this reversal of meaning gives American needlework an almost explosive energy," Lane

---

41. Lane, *Book of American Needlework*, p. 10. Hereafter, page numbers for this book can be found in the text.

wrote in the Introduction. "No other needlework is so alive" (p. 12). This message, that the individualism and freedom that American women enjoyed fostered independent creative expression through their needlework, permeated each of the subsequent commentaries. In the section prefacing embroidery, Lane discussed the anti-American sentiment in the crafts industry that led to the introduction of hideous patterns that American women refused to buy. She testified that, when she contacted a company manager to protest the crudely drawn designs, she was told that the country "isn't Europe; most Americans have the minds of twelve-year-olds." But Americans "did not buy that trash," Lane shared with her readers, adding: "Still we embroidered. We copied good designs in museums or drew new ones" (p. 23).

In discussing crewel work, Lane defined it first in the "old" way as "embroidery solidly done with crewel wools." However, "in America," she continued, "the women no more followed the old way with a needle than men and women followed the old way of reverent subjection to rulers" (p. 41). She noted the American innovation of using linen thread rather than wool yarn. In discussing needlepoint, an art that used a costly, specialized fabric, Lane referred to it as the preferred craft of Queen Elizabeth I and her ladies in England (p. 65), but she added at the end, "American women are creating American needlepoint, now. . . . It is all original, individual, homemade, and it is wonderful" (p. 71).

In discussing American appliqué, Lane returned to the idea that American women created their own brand of needlework by going their own way with the materials; that individual spirit transformed old appliqué into something beautiful, unique, and different. "You don't know half the joy of needlework," she wrote, "until you create something wholly yours. . . . It will not be original because nothing is; it will be unique because you are" (p. 92). Talking about the art of quilting, Lane asserted that American women became innovators in separating the art of quilting from the art of patchwork, making intricate patterns with small stitches on whole cloth. "It is the most experimental, the most individually creative needlework," she wrote, "so it is the most endlessly fascinating to do. And, we Americans being what we are [individuals interested in fast forward progress], we do it swiftly" (p. 118).

In the commentary about hooked work, Lane asserted the importance of American women's individualism to the country. In talking about hooked rugs, in particular, she stated that American colonial women invented them. She lamented that the art had been neglected and nearly lost at the hands of "dominant American thinkers" in the nineteenth century who claimed that Americans had no culture and that all culture was European, and she gloried in the revival of rug-hooking as interest in American culture rose in the wake of the First World War. "The making of so many hooked rugs" she said, "is part of the revival of personal independence and self-reliance, of individual self-expression in American life" (pp. 126–27). She added that women should really continue to create their own patterns because "a woman who copies a hooked rug is wasting an opportunity to express and truly satisfy herself" (p. 132). In the section about crochet, Lane proclaimed, "the true art of crochet is the American lace," which required only a little skill, a hook, and some thread. "And the whole range of human imagination, of individual creativeness, . . . makes this new lace in the air" (p. 152).

The continual repetitiveness of this theme, asserted in each of the historical commentaries, underscored for women the idea that their arts—particularly as they require no patterns but those women can create for themselves—are as individual and unique as they are, and that American values foster such individualism. The book reinforced the notion in the patterns included with each commentary, which demonstrated the techniques, and included a library of stitches used in their creation. The book did not contain a variety of patterns to copy but left its readers to create their own. In that sense, the work acted to foster individualism. Lane repeatedly told her readers that creating their own patterns was a strength of American needlework; she underscored the idea that, in continuing to practice their craft in their own ways, they took part in an exclusively American tradition that made their work unique.

Lane included the theme of self-reliance most frequently in historic anecdotes interwoven in the introductions to each type of needlecraft. She used the history to draw a connection between Americanism as a time-honored past and the ways in which the needlework under discussion fit into that past, often repeating the idea that the original settlers of the American colonies and of the American West had no political or economic support on which to rely in their struggles to live and live well under dangerous and strenuous conditions. In this context, Lane asserted, the practical function of much needlecraft was to make needed fabric items for the settlers' homes, and poverty, of necessity, forced invention. It is hard not to see the ghost of Wilder's hand in these stories.

In talking about rug-making, for example, Lane discussed the hardships the original colonists had faced and the difficulty women found in keeping floors clean and stopping drafts. "Slowly, year by year," she said, "they improved their way of living, and they made a great discovery. . . . They learned that living in freedom is not easy because a free person must rely on himself, but free men make living easier, cleaner, better for everyone." When it came to rugs, the women had nothing to use but rags, "so dire poverty inspired their invention," she wrote. "Yet today, when free persons in this classless society have abolished the ancient wretchedness and every worker here is richer than King George was, our rugmaking is flourishing as never before" (p. 201). Particularly regarding hooked rugs, Lane celebrated the use of remnants and leftover pieces of fabric in creating something useful and beautiful. She reminded readers that at one time, poverty determined that only those small pieces were left to use and that every piece would be used or wasted. The women used those small pieces in patterns they created for the purpose. "The quiet self-reliance," Lane wrote, "with which generations of forgotten men and women created our country is expressed in these rugs" (p. 132). Patchwork, Lane told her readers, also began with the abject poverty in which people were forced to live in the Old World, and it proved useful for the colonists and settlers, too, as they faced the first hardships and poverty of the New World. "Women created this rich needlework art who had not a penny to spend or a half-inch bit of cloth to waste," Lane said. "I sing no praise of poverty—I have had plenty of it and I thoroughly detest it—but no one can deny that, in freedom, poverty is stimulating" (p. 78).

In discussing crewel work, Lane drew again on colonial history to tell readers that more than two thousand men, women, and children reached Massachusetts Bay in the 1630s, learning quickly that man "must, in fact, earn his bread; each must survive by his own effort or perish" (p. 41). In such an environment, women raised flax and, with backbreaking work, turned it into linen fabric and threads, which they then used to clothe the body and to indulge the spirit with the arts of crewel and embroidery. "In dire want [the woman settler] had learned to be self-reliant and inventive," Lane continued, "and probably she did not own a tambour needle. Certainly she did not cover the beautiful linen with monotonous loops of yarn" (p. 43). Lane returned to the colonists in talking about weaving, saying, "They starved until in utmost desperation they learned that God gives every person, with life, the responsibility for it" (p. 180). Only in discussing needlepoint did Lane relax her theme about poverty and self-reliance fostering invention. Noting that the craft itself is not necessary, nor thrifty, "its value is beauty alone," she swiftly added that three generations of emigrants had to work and save for a century before the "hungry poverty" that had kept many from pursuing such an expensive hobby was abolished. "The nineteenth century was growing old before homekeeping women in all the thirty-five States could afford to create an art purely for its own sake" (p. 69).

Despite her emphasis on self-reliance in the face of poverty, Lane recognized the need for compassion. In discussing patchwork, she stressed the concept of "neighborliness" in lieu of forced charity at the hands of the government, particularly as she discussed the uses of the Friendship Quilt, given by neighbors to couples and families undergoing hard times. "Neighborliness is not love, not friendship; it may be less than liking," she wrote. "It is the mutual helpfulness of human beings to each other, an unforced, voluntary co-operation springing from a sense of equality in common humanity and human needs" (p. 98). The idea that poverty fostered self-reliance and that together they fostered invention can be seen throughout the text. In this way, Lane celebrated the importance of self-reliance while making a point about the nature of poverty as a character-building experience. By building up the idea of self-reliance, she was tearing down the idea of reliance on government for poverty relief and obliquely making the point that people need to rely on themselves to get out of poverty. By focusing on neighborliness as opposed to charity, Lane made compassion toward others a choice and not a civic obligation. Again, the ghosts of *Pioneer Girl* made an appearance.

"It was women in America, quietly weaving, who began the world revolution for individual freedom," Lane stated in the introduction to the chapter about weaving. The statement simultaneously built up women's roles in the founding of the original Republic, stressed the demureness of the revolutionary act, and strengthened Lane's arguments about the importance of individual freedom—especially from government interference. The definition of freedom used by Lane in all her work focused on the idea of freedom from government interference in the lives of the governed, and her central argument here and elsewhere was that, without such freedom, humankind's creativity, self-reliance, and innovation would be destroyed. In the *Woman's Day Book of American Needlework*, Lane most particularly sent this message through the historical commentary that accompanied weaving and knitting, which are crafts that originated as professions. Lane created an archetype in the "American housewife," celebrating her thrift and determination, which laid the groundwork for revolution. In choosing to create her archetype in this way, Lane also stressed the importance of the *individual* in choosing defiance in the name of need and of self-reliance in the name of necessity.

The American Revolution, she argued, did not begin with muskets at Lexington but with women's needles in the decades leading up to that event. "She had only to be true to herself, trusting and relying on truth that she saw and knew, to express herself beautifully with needle and thread," Lane wrote, noting that women's innovations in the decades before the Revolution were a certain marker that it was coming. The American housewife was free to create her own crewel-work designs, and she did so for the betterment of the craft and the nation (p. 45). Lane's best example of this idea—that women's arts were the harbingers of Revolution and absolutely central to its success—was Betsy Ross's construction of the American flag for the American Revolution, which she mentioned in her Introduction and returned to in the discussion of patchwork. A woman created that symbol using the materials she had on hand. "That standard was a patchwork pattern of thirteen stripes, red and white, and a blue patch that once held thirteen stars and now holds fifty," she wrote, adding: "So let us treasure as part of American culture the inexhaustible variety of patterns in old patchwork that record gallant lives, and honor as culture bearers the thousands of women who are preserving and still enriching this heritage" (p. 85). All this innovation and revolution came about because, Lane argued, women refused to allow the government—in the form of King George III—to dictate what they would create in their own homes. Women thus became the standard-bearers, in both a figurative and a literal sense, for the patriotic cause and the trust-holders of Americanism.

In a decade—the fifties—when such standard-bearing was asked of all Americans, this thought likely expressed Lane's desire for women to take up the banner of patriotism in the form of that freedom from government interference in everyday life and to stand up against government that increasingly regulated matters that should have been left in the privacy of women's homes. She used needlework as the example, but the principle could have been applied in multiple ways. Read in one way, Lane's *Book of American Needlework* can be viewed as a call for women to campaign for their rights as individuals.

These values of individualism, self-reliance, and freedom, particularly from government interference in everyday life, resonated with a group of women who raised at least two generations of American voters. The shared culture unlocked through *Woman's Day* privileged an approach to life—and to political ideology—that emphasized the importance of relying on oneself, and not the government, for answers to problems such as poverty. It also praised innovation in the addressing of individual problems and fought collective action as anti-American. While this last point makes sense in the context of the Cold War, in which Americans were consistently bombarded with anti-Communist messages, the ways in which Lane and *Woman's Day* addressed the issue were subtle. They stressed the ideas of individualism, self-reliance, and freedom from government interference without stridently attacking Communism as a threat to American values. Instead, Lane let her examples of women's value to American history, and the value of women's arts to American culture, do that work. By reinforcing the concept of "neighborliness," Lane also turned the question of citizen-paid welfare on its head for an audience likely attuned to extending a helping hand by choice. Compassion was necessary, but whether to extend that compassion should be an individual choice and not a governmental mandate. In her book on needlework, Lane's ideology resonates with her mother's experiences related in *Pioneer Girl*.

The connections between the original *Pioneer Girl* manuscript and the writings of Rose Wilder Lane can easily be seen and not always in the most obvious ways. In Wilder's memoirs, we see hardship, poverty, self-reliance, and individualism manifested through her life story, one that influenced the way she raised her own child. Lane's own experiences as a working woman and a working woman writer, combined with her global travel, reinforced those early lessons. Both women agreed on the ideology that Lane espoused through her work, and Wilder allowed it to stand where it was written into the Little House books. More interestingly, as Lane's writing career took off, beginning in 1910, we see Wilder's writing career begin and soar, too. *Pioneer Girl* provided Wilder with the start to her Little House series; it provided Lane much-needed material to recoup financial losses for herself and her parents.

In the 1991 film *Soapdish*, actress Sally Field played an aging soap-opera star who justified her somewhat cagey personal actions throughout the course of the film by declaring that she was still "a working actress!" I imagine Lane could have related. Substitute the word "writer" for "actress," and we have Lane in a nutshell. In a period when working women professionals were scarce and fought significant challenges to making a living, Lane succeeded. She lived her life as a working writer, tucking her First Amendment rights close to her heart and raising that "loud yell" whenever necessary. Her final published piece for *Woman's Day*, "August in Vietnam," was rich in descriptive detail and in subtle political commentary, but it almost did not happen. State Department officials tried to refuse Lane's visa because of her age (seventy-eight). Lane, however, intended to go with or without their approval. They gave in.[42]

"Raise a loud yell," indeed.

---

42. Lane, "August in Vietnam," *Woman's Day* 29 (Dec. 1965): 33, 93–94. *See also* "Our Correspondent in Saigon," ibid., p. 3.

# Beginnings and Misdirections

# { 4 }
## *Pioneer Girl*
### Its Roundabout Path into Print

WILLIAM ANDERSON

In November 2014, I explored a preview copy of *Pioneer Girl: The Annotated Autobiography* published by the South Dakota Historical Society Press. My initial reaction was admiration. Although I was familiar with Laura Ingalls Wilder's unvarnished, never published "Pioneer Girl," I had not envisioned the handsome, hefty, 400-page volume which emerged from Wilder's penciled and typed drafts. Editor Pamela Smith Hill, project director Nancy Tystad Koupal, and the staff members involved with the Pioneer Girl Project created a monumental, encyclopedic volume from the Wilder manuscript no one had wanted in 1930. The media and publishing industry had repeatedly ignored the potential of Wilder's manuscript in the 1930s and would do so again in the 1980s. The South Dakota Historical Society Press had been tenacious in its belief that the historical and literary significance of Wilder's autobiography warranted book publication.

I waded through the detailed footnotes of *Pioneer Girl: The Annotated Autobiography.* I studied Hill's comprehensive history of Wilder's autobiography, the prelude to the subsequent Little House books. I re-read the *Pioneer Girl* manuscript itself, pored over maps and historic images—and realized that this book was what Wilder aficionados had craved ever since knowledge of the unpublished Wilder book manuscript became commonplace in the 1970s. It was not surprising that the first printing of *Pioneer Girl: The Annotated Autobiography* sold out immediately. The book became a runaway bestseller, appearing for several weeks on *The New York Times* bestseller list. Media coverage appeared globally. The book was a latter-day phenomenon from an author who died in 1957 and published her last book in 1943.

The sensational buzz created by Wilder's previously unpublished work was similar to the excitement aroused by Mark Twain's *Autobiography*, released by the University of California Press in Berkeley between 2010 and 2015. A decade earlier, the publication of Louisa May Alcott's long-shelved gothic, *A Long Fatal Love Chase,* indicated that long-dead classic American writers retained their staying power among readers. Throughout 2015, demand for *Pioneer Girl: The Annotated Autobiography* ran tandem with the release of another long-shelved first draft: Harper Lee's *Go Set a Watchman*, which had morphed into *To Kill a Mockingbird*. Both Wilder and Lee had devout worldwide audiences, avid for more of their written words.

As the remarkable news of *Pioneer Girl: The Annotated Autobiography*'s success continued to unfold, I recognized that I had been both participant and bystander, directly or indirectly, in the history of this Wilder manuscript. I read it when it was first available to scholars. I was engaged in preparing a version of it for publication that never happened in the 1980s. I observed varied uses of the informative manuscript through the years. I consulted it myself while writing several articles and books. Perhaps most meaningful for me, I was acquainted with the cast of characters who had significant connections with the *Pioneer Girl* manuscript through the years. There were those who had protected it to the point of suppression. Others comprehended its historical value and were willing to bring it to publication. I seemed to have known most of the principals in the *Pioneer Girl* saga, excepting only Laura Ingalls Wilder herself.

Pamela Smith Hill's introductory chapter in *Pioneer Girl: The Annotated Autobiography* provided the back story of how Wilder's autobiography evolved. Hill related how Wilder, the mistress of Rocky Ridge Farm in Mansfield, Missouri, gleaned any source of income she could to keep the semi-productive farm solvent ever since her family settled there in 1894. Likewise, her husband Almanzo and their daughter Rose multi-tasked to add to the family funds. Wilder sold butter and eggs and fruit, cooked for occasional boarders, and was secretary-treasurer of the Mansfield Farm Loan Association. More to her liking, she wrote articles and columns for the *Missouri Ruralist* from 1911 through 1924. That work gave her local and regional status as a writer.

Meanwhile, Rose Wilder Lane, the Wilders' only surviving child, ascended to national literary prominence as a journalist, ghostwriter, biographer, novelist, and short-story writer. Her lucrative career, enhanced by the media boom of the 1920s, made her the chief family bread-winner for her aging parents. She settled down in the family farmhouse in 1928, a visit that lasted eight years. Later that same year, she funded construction of a modern rock cottage for her parents on a remote ridge of the farm. Lane's literary output, mostly sold to mainstream magazines, supported both households. With the October 1929 stock market crash, the Wilder-Lane financial future appeared ominous. Probably as a result of dwindling income, as well as a rush of nostalgia, Wilder wrote *Pioneer Girl*, finishing it in 1930.[1]

---

1. Hill, Introduction to Wilder, *Pioneer Girl: The Annotated Autobiography*, pp. xv–lix.

From the inception, its intended audience was unclear. Wilder and Lane most likely saw the autobiography as a magazine serial, a one-shot money maker. Despite the efforts of Lane and New York literary agent George Bye, *Pioneer Girl* failed to sell. Wilder and Lane's revised plan was to modify her pioneer story as a children's book, and they successfully launched Wilder's Little House series in 1932 with *Little House in the Big Woods*. *Pioneer Girl* provided a chronological structure for seven books published between 1932 and 1943. (*Farmer Boy*, Almanzo Wilder's boyhood story, was the sole volume not based on happenings in *Pioneer Girl*.) Additionally, Lane mined incidents and story plots from the autobiography, using them as fodder for her lucrative magazine fiction published during the 1930s. Hefty chunks of *Pioneer Girl* also provided content for Lane's 1938 *Saturday Evening Post* serial "Free Land," a homesteading saga. The resulting book version was a bestseller. Following these uses, the manuscript versions of *Pioneer Girl* were stored away in Wilder's home on Rocky Ridge Farm and in Lane's permanent home in Danbury, Connecticut.

When Wilder died in 1957, Lane faced the necessity of disposing of the contents of her parents' home. With her cooperation, Mansfield citizens, who wished to preserve the Wilders' home and its contents, formed the Laura Ingalls Wilder Home Association. Lewis Lichty was the first president; his wife Irene was the secretary. Lane approved the association's goals and left the household essentially intact. Before she left Rocky Ridge for the last time, she conducted a cursory survey of her mother's papers. She burned some of them, but her selections for destruction appeared to have been random. The *Pioneer Girl* manuscript was left behind in a desk drawer. Later, Lane ruminated about what documentation she might have missed in her survey. She asked Irene Lichty to take charge of any papers and manuscripts still in the Wilder house, including the first drafts of Little House books. These included *Farmer Boy, Little House on the Prairie, On the Banks of Plum Creek, By the Shores of Silver Lake,* and *Pioneer Girl*, enfolded within which was also a version of *Little House in the Big Woods*.

The magnitude of the Wilder manuscript collection unfolded as the Lichtys inventoried the house contents. Lewis Lichty told me of the exciting moment when he unearthed Wilder's "The First Three Years and a Year of Grace" from the piles of papers. This manuscript later became *The First Four Years*, published posthumously by HarperCollins in 1971, fourteen years after Wilder's death. By default, *Pioneer Girl*, along with the other manuscripts, fell under the jurisdiction of the Laura Ingalls Wilder Home Association in 1957. The Wilder home was first opened to visitors in May of that year. Public curiosity focused on the house and its unique furnishings. No one thought

Irene Lichty and William Anderson pose next to the cornerstone of the museum of the Laura Ingalls Wilder Home Association in Mansfield, Missouri, in 1972. *William Anderson Collection*

of the manuscripts as more than literary curiosities on view in the showcases. As the Wilder home preservation project proceeded, volunteers made inventory lists of the household furnishings, including the manuscripts. The town librarian, Florence Williams, along with Irene Lichty, sorted through each piece of paper. Before starting, they had acquired a rubber stamp, with a magenta-colored stamp pad. "Property of Laura Ingalls Wilder Home Association" was boldly stamped on every letter, postcard, photograph, and manuscript, sometimes two or three times. These markings still emblazon the reams of vintage documentation, now in the Herbert Hoover Presidential Library.

As sporadic visitation to the Wilder home quickly evolved into a steady summer traffic, the Lichtys increasingly served as volunteers. They were native Kansans, "a couple of Jayhawkers" as Lewis Lichty said. People in Mansfield "didn't appreciate [Wilder] because she was a familiar face," Lichty explained. "Because we were not acquainted with her we saw her in a different light. We were aware she was an author, but we did not know her scope and standing in the world."² The Lichtys settled in Mansfield in 1946. Irene met Wilder at a church ladies' meeting and was immediately drawn to her. Their friendship grew slowly because Wilder was tending her husband, who was in failing health. After Almanzo Wilder's death in 1949, the Lichty-Wilder friendship intensified. Wilder was lonely and enjoyed dinner invitations, drives through the countryside, and visits from the Lichtys, who also met Rose Wilder Lane when she visited her mother on Rocky Ridge Farm.

The Lichtys were the first townspeople to champion the concept that the Wilder home had a future as a literary shrine. As realtors, they were familiar with the local properties and the impact of commerce on small communities. Tourism would enhance Mansfield. Harold Bell Wright's Ozark novel *Shepherd of the Hills* drew tourists to Branson, Missouri. Would Wilder's books not lure people to Mansfield? There was precedent; Little House readers from many states had stopped to meet Wilder beginning in the 1930s. Wilder herself was actually the first tour guide of her home, showing her callers through the unique rooms. While visiting Wilder once, Irene Lichty had suggested the possibility of preserving her home. Wilder replied neither pro nor con. She simply said that she had let the house get "shabby." Later, Lane confided to Lichty that the suggestion had greatly pleased her mother.³

By 1959, the Lichtys were officially installed as co-curators of the Laura Ingalls Wilder Home and Museum. They sold their house in Mansfield, settling on Rocky Ridge Farm to fulfill Lane's wish that the place have permanent supervision. They briefly lived in the upstairs of the Wilder home. For a time, a trailer home on the grounds served as their quarters. By 1963, at Lane's behest and with her financial support, a curators' residence was built within easy walking distance of the Wilder house. A routine developed. The Lichtys alternated giving tours, manning a small museum shop, filling mail orders, overseeing the buildings, and welcoming tourists. Their dedication was deep. For Lewis Lichty, the largely volunteer endeavor became a mission. His wife recalled: "It was L. D. Lichty who faced criticism and ridicule in his persistence and determination that this be done. . . . Often he remarked, 'Now we are paying for our space on earth which we have occupied for a long time.'"⁴

---

2. Lewis Lichty, quoted in Bill Snyder, "Memories of Mrs. Wilder Kept Alive at Mansfield," *Springfield* (Mo.) *News & Leader*, June 1971, clipping, author's collection.

3. [William Anderson], "The Story of the Laura Ingalls Wilder Home Association, 1957–2007," *The Rocky Ridge Review* (Summer 2007): 1.

4. Irene V. Lichty to William Anderson, n.d. [ca. 1980]. Unless otherwise stated, all letters cited in this article are in the author's collection.

The Lichtys' personal anecdotes of the Wilders added a homespun aura to the tours they gave through the farmhouse. They also remained intensely loyal to Lane, who, though absent, occupied a position of clout with the Wilder Home Association board. The Lichtys studied documentation in the farmhouse, ever keen to enhance their narrated tours. They also uncovered correspondence that indicated that Lane had assisted in editing and shaping the Little House books. Indeed, it was evident to them that mother and daughter had developed a family writing collaboration. Both Lichtys were also loyal to Wilder's public image—the notion that she had emerged as a late-blooming, consummate writer. The Lichtys were discreet, revealing nothing that indicated that Wilder did not act wholly independently while writing her books.

The *Pioneer Girl* manuscript, however, also defied the folklore that the Little House books were absolute autobiographical truth. Although the Lichtys skimmed it while inventorying the contents of the Wilder house, they did not tell visitors of the manuscript's existence. Their focus was to manage tours of the historic home, stressing the Wilders' work ethic, creativity, and independence. While comfortable with visitors, the Lichtys were sometimes uneasy with probing questions from a beginning groundswell of literary critics and researchers, who toured the home and were eager to analyze Wilder's work.

The first prairie fire the Lichtys attempted to quash involved questions about the date of the Ingalls family's move to Kansas. Although the dust-jacket copy of the 1953 edition of *Little House in the Big Woods* gave the setting of the book as Wisconsin in 1872, the reality was that the Ingalls family had already been to Kansas and had *returned* to their Wisconsin cabin by 1871; these facts did not square with the opening of *Little House on the Prairie*, which had the Ingalls moving to Kansas after the events in the first book. Wilder had stated these facts clearly in *Pioneer Girl*.

Ironically, this discrepancy had not disturbed Harper & Brothers, Wilder's publisher. Throughout the 1940s, the company distributed a four-page brochure about Wilder and her books that provided biographical information. The opening lines of the biographical sketch, penned anonymously by Lane, read: "Laura Ingalls Wilder was born in the log cabin described in *Little House in the Big Woods*. That is to say, the Big Woods of Wisconsin near Lake Pepin in the Mississippi. Her earliest memories are of a venture into the Indian Territory of Kansas. She was about three then."[5] Wilder herself sent out thousands of copies of this brochure to readers and friends, un-

---

5. "Laura Ingalls Wilder" (promotional brochure), Harper & Bros., [ca. 1942].

# Laura Ingalls Wilder

LAURA INGALLS WILDER was born in the log cabin described in *Little House in the Big Woods*. That is to say, the Big Woods of Wisconsin near Lake Pepin in the Mississippi. Her earliest memories are of a venture into the Indian Territory of Kansas. She was about three then, and Pa was a pioneer hunter, trapper and Indian fighter. However, he soon took his family back to Wisconsin, and at that point the story of *Little House in the Big Woods* begins. From Wisconsin the Ingalls traveled west by covered wagon, through Minnesota and Iowa to Dakota Territory, where Pa finally settled. For a year Pa was a railroad man and the family spent one winter by the shores of Silver Lake, sixty miles from the nearest neighbor. Pa hunted and trapped and guarded property of the Chicago-Northwestern, then building, from outlaws in the Black Hills. In the spring Pa put up the first building on the new town-site, founded the Congregational Church, served as Justice of the Peace for a while, and so was one of the founders of what later became De Smet, South Dakota. The Ingalls' first winter there was the remembered "Hard Winter" of 1880-81, when the tiny settlement of scarcely one hundred persons was cut off from all outside help. There were no trains from October to May. When all the supplies were used up and there was no light, food or fuel, Almanzo Wilder and another boy risked their lives to drive forty miles across the prairie to get a little seed wheat from a farmer known to have some; women ground it in coffee-mills and the people lived on small rations of it made into mush.

*The pamphlet Harper & Brothers distributed during the 1940s introduced some discrepancies between Wilder's life and her fiction.*
*South Dakota Historical Society Press*

fazed that the information clashed with the sequence of *Little House in the Big Woods* and *Little House on the Prairie*. Not until 1963 did the actual date of the Kansas sojourn of the Ingalls family command the attention of professional researchers.

Eileen Charbo, who worked at the Kansas State Historical Society library in Topeka, recalled the day that the head librarian passed her desk, vexed. A disturbing development had arisen in regard to *Little House on the Prairie*, one of the state's most cherished regional books. The librarian had received a letter from Harper & Row indicating that they were "deleting the word Kansas from the . . . Uniform Edition of the Little House books. A Colorado woman with charts and maps and facts has proved to their satisfaction that *Little House on the Prairie* was in Oklahoma, not Kansas."[6] Charbo disagreed with this theory. She requested an extension from Harper, long enough to conduct her own investigation. She contacted Lane, inquiring if she possessed any dates pinpointing the Ingalls family chronology throughout the 1860s and 1870s. Lane pled essential ignorance, but significantly, she typed a copy of the Ingalls family births and deaths direct from their Bible, which had been briefly in her possession. A birth entry provided the clue Charbo needed: "Caroline Celestia Ingalls born Wednesday, Aug. 3, 1870, Montgomery Co. Kansas."[7]

Charbo consulted the *Ninth United States Census* (1870) for Kansas and readily unearthed the Charles Ingalls family. Census taker Asa Hairgrove had misspelled the surname as "Ingles," but there they were: Charles, Caroline, Mary, Laura, and the infant Carrie. They were the ninetieth family (eighty-ninth dwelling) on Hairgrove's list, living in Rutland Township. Later, by matching neighbors' names mentioned in *Little House on the Prairie* and other clues, the vicinity of the Ingalls residence was established. A photocopy of the census record was sent to Harper & Row, satisfying the publisher that Kansas was the correct setting of *Little House on the Prairie*.[8] Even though she had helped in the process, such rumblings of research disconcerted Lane. She was in her seventies when hints emerged that her mother's books were being compared with historical accounts. By that time, she had assumed a rigid public amnesia regarding her role in developing the Little House books. Furthermore, knowing full well that *Pioneer Girl* stated autobiographical facts, she made no reference to its existence.

The first fledgling Wilder scholarship appeared in *Elementary English*, a publication of the National Council of Teachers of English. Louise Hovde Mortensen, editor of "Idea Inventory," a column in *Elementary English*, was an admirer of the Little House books. She also knew that thousands of elementary teachers across America were reading Wilder's books to their students. These teachers would be fascinated with emerging historical data on Wilder, she reasoned. From 1962 until 1965, Mortensen published articles on a wide gamut of Wilder topics, stopping only when her editor decided there

6. Quoted in Eileen Miles Charbo, "Letters from Laura's Daughter Rose Lane" (unpublished manuscript), [ca. 1987], author's collection.

7. Ibid. *See also* Eileen Charbo, "Kansas Proves Claim to Site of Beloved 'Little House' Book," *Kansas City Times*, Aug. 13, 1963.

8. Charbo, "Kansas Proves Claim."

had been a saturation of Wilder stories. The *Elementary English* articles still stand as a seminal body of early Wilder studies, produced by, as Nancy Tystad Koupal termed them, "the first of the diggers," the earliest generation to probe Wilder history.⁹

Mortensen, who corresponded with Lane, sent her copies of the Wilder articles. One, titled "The Ingalls of Kansas" in December 1963, reprinted a letter from Eileen Charbo regarding her research and the discrepancy it set up concerning the timing of the books. Mortensen had no agenda; she was not attempting to disprove the historical background of the books. But she hypothesized, "The fact must be that Mrs. Wilder, as an author, drew on her knowledge of those early days in Wisconsin from stories she heard her parents tell. As an artist working with her materials, Mrs. Wilder knew she could achieve a more artistic effect by altering the true facts occasionally."¹⁰

Lane promptly wrote Mortensen to obscure what the census record (and *Pioneer Girl*) had so solidly stated. In a letter, Lane asked for her "help in correcting an oversight of mine. I should have thought sooner of explaining to you the discrepancy in dates of events related in my mother's books.... I agree that my mother could have added to artistic effects by altering facts, but she did not write fiction. She did not want to. She wanted to set down the facts of her childhood as she knew them when she was a child. She wanted to save a record of them. I shall be most grateful, as I know she would be, if you can somehow give this explanation to your readers."¹¹

Lane later wrote to me in the same vein: "You know [my mother] said many times that every detail that she wrote was true, but that she did not write ALL the truth.... If my mother's books are not absolutely accurate, she will be discredited as a person and as a writer, since a great part of the value of her books is that they are '*true* stories.'"¹² It strikes me now that perhaps Lane had another concern. Her own conservative, libertarian values were embedded in the Little House books. These philosophies, stressing self-reliance, independent living, and anti-government feeling were stronger examples if practiced by actual historical people, as opposed to fictional ones. Lane possibly feared that if the books were labeled fiction, their philosophical impact would be diluted.

As a result of the *Elementary English* articles, Mortensen received mail from numerous readers. One letter came from Melbourne, Australia. The

---

9. Koupal, telephone conversation with Anderson, June 3, 2016.

10. Mortenson, "Idea Inventory," *Elementary English* 41 (Apr. 1964): 428.

11. Lane to Mortenson, Dec. 31, 1963, printed ibid., pp. 428–29.

12. Lane to William Anderson, July 13, 1966. Unless otherwise stated, all emphasis is in the original.

writer was Sheila Bignell, wife of Dr. Allan Bignell, and mother of four children. The entire Bignell family became enamored of the Little House books in 1963. Like many readers, they yearned to learn more about the Ingalls-Wilder families and their home sites. Mortensen forwarded a copy of Bignell's letter to all persons she knew who were engaged in Wilder activities. Bignell, who was writing an article on historical books for children, was instantly accepted into the informal Little House fellowship of the mid-1960s. Ultimately, Allan and Sheila Bignell planned a 1965 family vacation to America—a pilgrimage to the Little House home sites. Their children, Julia, Jonathan, Nicholas, and Anthony, ranged in age from eighteen to ten. The news of their coming electrified keepers of the Wilder flames in Pepin, Wisconsin, Independence, Kansas, Walnut Grove, Minnesota, De Smet, South Dakota, and Mansfield, Missouri. Visitors from "down under" were coming during winter blasts of December and January? No tourists visited the book sites at that time of year. But the timing was mandatory; our winter was school-vacation time for Australians.

Sheila Bignell hoped to conduct serious research during the family's journey. She initiated correspondence with Lane, but received a single peremptory response. Bignell's request to visit Lane in her new Texas home got no reply. After spending Christmas in California with Clara Webber, librarian and founder of the Laura Ingalls Wilder Room in the Pomona Public Library, the Bignells headed to the heartland and the towns where Wilder once lived. In each locale they visited, the Bignells experienced hearty midwestern welcomes. They met people who recalled the Ingalls family. Early pioneers in Wilder research, such as Aubrey Sherwood of the *De Smet News* and Charles Lantz of the *Walnut Grove Tribune*, entertained them. I was a beginner in the Wilder world during the Bignells' trip, but when they reached Chicago in January 1966, they contacted me, asking to visit my family in our Michigan home. We invited them to come ahead. Our friends, the Harry Myers family, were enlisted to help host the six Bignells. Jane Myers had already published a two-part account of her own family's vacation to the Little House sites in the October-November 1963 issues of *Elementary English*. We found our new friends just as the press in Independence, Kansas, had described them, "a handsome, healthy, sturdy family, poised and gracious. . . . They are all musical."[13]

Heavy snow, which was lacking when they visited De Smet, South Dakota, fell on Michigan during the Bignells' stay. The snowfall was a source of

---

13. Peggy Greene, "Australians Travel Thousands of Miles to follow the 'Little House' Books," *Midway*, Feb. 13, 1966, clipping, author's collection.

Allan and Sheila Bignell experienced a prairie-like winter at the Anderson home in January 1966. *William Anderson Collection*

amazement for the children, along with the new experience of sledding. We all engaged in almost nonstop Wilder discussion. We read and talked about a new find: a vintage copy of *The Horn Book* for September-October 1943, with Irene Smith's article "Laura Ingalls Wilder and the Little House Books." We pondered over Smith's statement: "It is interesting to know that all this personal history [of Wilder's life] was written first as matter-of-fact autobiography.... Later it was amplified and retold for children, beginning with a style appealing to the eight year olds."[14] The "matter-of-fact autobiography" was, of course, *Pioneer Girl*. (Acquaintance with the Bignell family evolved into an enduring friendship for the Anderson and Myers families. Continued contacts and numerous reunions ensued through the years. Whenever we met, the dialogue was lively, and Wilder-related conversation was inevitable.)

Following their Michigan visit, the Australians drove to Mansfield, Missouri, where Lewis and Irene Lichty awaited them at Rocky Ridge Farm. During that visit, Sheila Bignell was the first contemporary outsider to study *Pioneer Girl*. The occasion was groundbreaking for her—she could see that Lane was significantly linked to Wilder's writing and that fictional techniques had been utilized in creating the Little House books. While Bignell was among the first to discover these facts, they were destined to create covert and negative reverberations for her for decades to come. When William Holtz prepared to publish his 1993 biography of Lane, *The Ghost in the Little House*, his thesis went much further, suggesting that Lane had served as ghostwriter of her mother's books.[15] When I shared my prepublication understanding of Holtz's thesis with Bignell in 1992, she finally felt free to share her own *Pioneer Girl* experience.

In a retrospective letter, Bignell summarized the two days her family had spent at Rocky Ridge Farm, with emphasis on her critical reading of *Pioneer Girl*:

> "May I break 25 years of silence and give you [my thesis]? The Bignells visited Mansfield on 18 January 1966 and the next day I came to much the same conclusion as Holtz has now....
>
> My diary records that on 19 January Mrs. Lichty reluctantly conducted us into the unheated LIW "museum." In the few minutes before she hustled us out we noticed that the ms pages of [*Little House on the*

---

14. Irene Smith, "Laura Ingalls Wilder and the Little House Books," *The Horn Book* (Sept.-Oct. 1943): 296.

15. Holtz, *The Ghost in the Little House: A Life of Rose Wilder Lane* (Columbia: University of Missouri Press, 1993).

*Prairie, On the Banks of Plum Creek, By the Shores of Silver Lake* on display] did not tally at all with any pages of the published L. H. books. In the evening Mrs. Lichty gave me, to look at, a collection of writing pads that turned out to be Laura's autobiography—first person.... It had no grace nor style. Indeed little discrimination for a good story. Julia and I did more than glance at them. We read doggedly until about 10 p.m. Back at the motel we both wrote and wrote while our memories were fresh. Then we . . . "spent a long time discussing this amazing state of affairs" (Diary entry 19 Jan. 1966, S.B.), i.e., the fact that Laura's story was so raw, ill-written, ill-spelt (by the famous winner of spelling bees) and poorly shaped. All right, you will say, first drafts are often like that. So they are, I agree, up to a point....

Two days later it became clear to me that Mrs. L. had never before perused the notebooks she had handed to me until, puzzled by our avidity, she had belatedly done so after our departure on the 19th. Now, on the 21st, she was alarmed at her unwitting indiscretion and so she swore me to secrecy. I was never to make use of my new knowledge "without Mrs. Lane's permission." Upon receiving this assurance she gave me the last three pads to read.

Sometime later somebody else apparently wrote that the LH books were not entirely Laura's unaided efforts. . . . I, of course, got the blame for having spilt the beans—quite unjustly. I had not even breathed a word to you. Anyway, after an angry accusation Mrs. L. never wrote to me again....

My diary entry for 21 Jan. 1966 reads that the manuscripts I had been devouring "represent the stories that Laura wrote down and sent to Rose, upon the bones of which she [Rose] put some meat." Julia and Allan remember all this.

Laura's account [in *Pioneer Girl*] begins with the building of the little house on the prairie, i.e., as far back as her memory, supplemented by the family reminiscences, reached.[16]

Quite likely, Irene Lichty's concerned reaction focused on potential disclosure of the chronological discrepancy between *Little House in the Big Woods* and *Little House on the Prairie*. At the time, there was no precedent for allowing researchers access to the book manuscripts held by the Laura Ingalls Wilder Home Association. Later on, the staff displayed much original documentation on multiplex flip charts in the museum. Interested visitors

---

16. Bignell to Anderson, Dec. 15, 1992.

were welcome to read and make handwritten notes from that material. Perhaps Irene Lichty anticipated Lane's possible displeasure if she learned that the pages of *Pioneer Girl* had been viewed by a researcher.

Fifty years after the Bignells' interlude at Rocky Ridge Farm, daughter Julia vividly remembered the drama of reading *Pioneer Girl*: "My mother could see at first glance that [the exercise books] were quite different.... I think what really struck her was the quality of the writing.... This probably led her to look further into the possibility that Rose helped the wonderful story to be publishable." At some point, Julia recalled, her mother "voiced her surprise at how different the text was, and the Lichtys got rather alarmed and wouldn't give further access.... I have the feeling it was really my mother's deep knowledge of English literature and intuitive feeling for style that gave her the hunch of another hand at work." Julia said, "I wouldn't be surprised that my mother might have been the first scholarly person to have read at least part of the scripts properly, and to have made the deductions she did."[17] Sheila Bignell never publicly discussed her findings. Although she never lost her fascination with Wilder, she delved into other scholarly pursuits, researched classic art, architecture, and literature, and taught with flair. The Bignells maintained warm friendships with American friends, but the Lichty connection was ruptured. They never met again.

Three years after the Bignells' 1966 stopover at Rocky Ridge Farm, Barbara Muhs Walker wrote a travel story on the Little House sites for *The New York Times*. She alluded to ongoing conversation regarding the sequence of the books: "We were intrigued by [a] major conflict between official history and Laura's; by her own account she was several years older in 'Little House on the Prairie.' ... our guide [Margaret Clement] unfolded her theory: that the events of the first book actually occurred on the Ingalls family's *return* to Wisconsin in 1871 after their fruitless sojourn into Kansas Indian Territory."[18] Walker's travelogue generated major publicity for the book sites and led to her writing *The Little House Cookbook* for HarperCollins in 1979. But in spite of the increased publicity from the article, the Lichtys were unhappy that Margaret Clement of Independence, Kansas, had spoken publicly of the Ingalls family's return trip to Wisconsin and mentioned other facts that refuted what the Little House books said.[19]

17. Julia Breen to Anderson, Jan. 25, 2016.
18. Walker, "A Trail of History Refreshingly Free of Violence," *New York Times*, Sept. 21, 1969.
19. Margaret Clement and her husband John, merchants in Independence, Kansas, were heading the search for the Ingalls cabin site. While Wilder's book placed the site forty miles from town, the 1870 census data had made it clear that it was closer to thirteen

"I think it is time for people to quit 'digging' or the Little House books may be ruined for many children," Irene Lichty wrote to me. "Of course, Mrs. Wilder did not write everything that happened in her life and it is possible that not everything is in sequence, but I don't know how anyone can prove those things."[20] A few months later, Lichty wrote to tell me that she felt sure that Clement's remarks were "the result of Mrs. Bignell's talking to her." She worried that she might have to tell Roger Lea MacBride, Lane's heir, the whole story and "let him straighten it out."[21] But Sheila Bignell was not the source of the story. "The terrible secret I was supposed to have divulged ... seems to be common knowledge now," she wrote to me, "and it was not I who divulged it. It was the Ingalls return to Wisconsin in 1871, which I had hit on quite independently, and when I mentioned it *as a theory* to Mrs. L., she swore me to secrecy. . . . I think I only promised to tell you *after* consulting her. I thought that when Rose died it would be all right, because Rose seemed to be determined to maintain that every word her mother wrote was *literally* true."[22]

In 1970, the Lichtys themselves published a booklet to settle another Ingalls family mystery—the "missing years" between *On the Banks of Plum Creek* and *By the Shores of Silver Lake*. Wilder omitted the years 1875–1879 from her books but chronicled them in *Pioneer Girl*. During this era, the Ingalls family moved to Burr Oak, Iowa, for a year and then returned to Walnut Grove, Minnesota. In October 1968, the Lichtys had traveled to both towns to study the locales. Just days after their return, Irene Lichty wrote to inform me of Rose Wilder Lane's death on October 30. "We shall carry on here just as faithfully as we have and with even more determination for this to succeed," she wrote.[23]

The Lichtys published *The Ingalls Family from Plum Creek to Walnut Grove via Burr Oak, Iowa* in 1970. The booklet was a popular item in the souvenir shop on the grounds of the Wilder home. In covering the missing years, it paraphrased the museum's handwritten copy of *Pioneer Girl* in a simple narrative suited for youthful readers. The publication marked the first

---

miles. They would locate the Ingalls site in June 1974. Margaret Clement wrote: "On Father's Day we did some digging ... and we have found the foundation of The Little House on the Prairie. It is right where we thought it was" (Clement to Anderson, Sept. 9, 1974). *See also* Margaret Gray Clement, "Research on 'Little House on the Prairie'" (handout), [ca. 1975], Chamber of Commerce, Independence, Kans.

20. Lichty to Anderson, Mar. 5, 1969.
21. Ibid., Oct. 29, 1969.
22. Bignell to Anderson, Dec. 18, 1971.
23. Lichty to Anderson, Oct. 31, 1968.

public use of Wilder's autobiography as source material. The preface to the booklet contained a caveat: "Nothing in this story is intended to conflict with the facts in the Little House books. If any reader is led to feel there is a conflict, the truths in the Little House books are to be accepted rather than this story. The information in the booklet has come from visits with Mrs. Wilder, who was my friend, letters from Rose Wilder Lane, . . . some writings of Mrs. Wilder, and visits to the places told of in the booklet by my husband, L. D. Lichty and me."[24]

In 1974, *Little House on the Prairie* debuted on network television. Visitation at the Laura Ingalls Wilder Home and Museum increased, buoyed by the weekly series. In the midst of this renewed tourist boom, Lewis Lichty died suddenly. Despite this challenge, Irene continued the work she and her husband had wholeheartedly pioneered. With help from family members, employees, and volunteers, she remained sole curator of the historic Rocky Ridge Farm until 1988.

The popularity of television's *Little House on the Prairie* also prompted Donald Zochert, a *Chicago Daily News* writer, to pen the first full-length biography of Laura Ingalls Wilder. In 1975, Zochert visited Little House locales and delved into census and property records, investigating with a reporter's zeal. He asked Roger MacBride for permission to consult the Wilder papers in his possession. MacBride declined.[25] In a letter, he told me that he did not believe that a biography was needed. "In fact," he wrote, "I wonder just how much there is of significance to tell after Laura settled in Mansfield?"[26] Zochert also hoped to access primary material at the Laura Ingalls Wilder Home and Museum, but he was initially turned down. Later, in a surprising turnabout, Lichty offered him the opportunity to read the penciled manuscripts.[27] The *Pioneer Girl* manuscript was among the stacks of orange tablets in the Mansfield museum, and for Zochert, it was an astonishing literary discovery. Its impact on his project was paramount, essentially shaping his entire book, which was titled *Laura: The Life of Laura Ingalls Wilder*.[28]

In September 1976, Lichty and I discussed the recent publication and content of the Zochert biography. We were seated in the family room of the curators' home when Lichty explained that she had allowed Zochert to tran-

---

24. Irene V. Lichty, *The Ingalls Family from Plum Creek to Walnut Grove via Burr Oak, Iowa* (Mansfield, Mo.: By the Author, 1970), p. 1.

25. Zochert to Anderson, Aug. 28, 1975.

26. MacBride to Anderson, Apr. 10, 1975.

27. Zochert to Anderson, July 31, Aug. 28, 1975.

28. Zochert, *Laura: The Life of Laura Ingalls Wilder* (Chicago: Henry Regnery Co., 1976).

scribe the *Pioneer Girl* manuscript. She pointed to the spot where Wilder's first biographer set up his typewriter and doggedly typed from the yellowing pages. Possibly by mutual agreement between Lichty and Zochert, he never mentioned *Pioneer Girl* directly in his book, vaguely describing it as Wilder's "memoir." Zochert's book, which many readers assumed would relate the story of Wilder's adult life, evolved into a well-wrought pastiche of paraphrase and direct quotations from *Pioneer Girl*, which covered only sixteen years of Wilder's life. That portion of his biography comprised 207 pages of the 260-page book. Roger MacBride, who recognized the similarity between source and book, would later judge Zochert's biography harshly.[29] A month after the release of *Laura: The Life of Laura Ingalls Wilder*, he noted: "If the thrust of Zochert's book is to the effect that *Pioneer Girl* is largely true, and the nine later books are to the extent [that] they disagree fiction, he may be in trouble." MacBride, it turns out, had a typed copy of *Pioneer Girl*, and he knew that corrections had been made in later versions. At the same time, he also knew that Wilder had "certainly truncated some of her back and forth travels for the purpose of telling a [readable] story."[30]

MacBride also wondered how and where Zochert had utilized *Pioneer Girl*. He queried Irene Lichty, asking her "what Zochert may have seen in Mansfield that would add up to the 'memoir' he refers to." Irene apparently replied that there was "nothing in Mansfield that she would call a memoir" and did not know what Zochert was referencing. "Now I'm at sea," MacBride concluded.[31] For her part, Lichty wondered "where Roger came by typewritten copies of 'Pioneer Girl'? Mrs. Lane thought she gave *all* those manuscripts here. In fact, neither 'On the Way Home' nor 'First Four Years' would have been published if L. D. & I had done what *some* members of the Board wanted us to do—held on to them."[32]

As a skilled author and reporter, Zochert perceived that the level of writing skill in *Pioneer Girl* and the rough drafts of Wilder's books did not match the polished narratives of the Little House books. He delicately broached the topic in an essay, "The Truth of the Little House Books," appended to his book. "The artistic gulf," he wrote, "between the draft manuscript . . . and the final version . . . is too large to allow for anything less than an intermediate manuscript."[33] Within five years, the ability to substantiate Zochert's

---

29. MacBride to Anderson, June 3, 1992.
30. Ibid., Apr. 8, 1976.
31. Ibid., May 13, 1977.
32. Lichty to Anderson, Oct. 29, 1976.
33. Zochert, *Laura*, App. 2, p. 247.

cautious theory was possible. The Herbert Hoover Presidential Library in West Branch, Iowa, acquired the Wilder-Lane papers and opened them for scholarly study. This development was a monumental milestone in Wilder scholarship. At last, it was possible to understand the complex, sometimes dramatic literary partnership of Wilder and Lane.

I was a beginning teacher and a graduate student in June 1979 when I first visited the Hoover library. I stopped in West Branch on a whim while on route to De Smet, South Dakota, to spend another summer working with the Laura Ingalls Wilder Memorial Society during the tourist season. As I toured the exhibits pertaining to the thirty-first president, I wondered what the library staff knew of Lane's 1920 biography, *The Making of Herbert Hoover*. When I asked, I was ushered into the office of library director Thomas Thalken, who readily produced file folders of correspondence between Lane and Hoover. He also inquired whether Lane's papers were still extant. I replied affirmatively and mentioned that MacBride was considering placing them at the Library of Congress or the University of Virginia. I shared MacBride's contact information with Thalken.

Thalken soon made contact with MacBride who was impressed with the facilities at the library in West Branch. Six months after my visit, Thalken reported, "Our Senior Archivist, Dwight Miller, will be visiting Roger MacBride in April, and at that time he will pack up and ship the papers to the Library."[34] Transfer and gift of the Laura Ingalls Wilder-Rose Wilder Lane Papers to the Herbert Hoover Presidential Library transpired in 1980. By early 1981, the staff had sorted the material and prepared a finding aid. At the time, the collection amounted to thirty-one linear feet of archival boxes. I spent several days in the library reading room examining the contents of these boxes in March 1981. I had earlier examined portions of the papers but had never fully read *Pioneer Girl*. The most significant epiphany during my first study visit was the impact of *Pioneer Girl* for both its writing style and its content.

The Wilder-Lane holdings at the Hoover were destined to grow. In May of 1982, MacBride and archivist Dwight Miller made an unheralded visit to the Laura Ingalls Wilder Home and Museum in Mansfield. The purpose was to add what remained in storage at the Wilder home to the Hoover collection. MacBride had become aware of the disorganized and casually kept historical documents, photographs, and manuscript material kept in the upstairs rooms of the Wilder home. There, he found the letters Wilder wrote to her husband during her 1915 California trip (which he had previously edited for publica-

---

34. Thalken to Anderson, Nov. 26, 1979.

Roger MacBride, far right, visited Aubrey Sherwood,
editor of the De Smet newspaper, and his wife, Laura, in 1983.
*William Anderson Collection*

tion in *West from Home* (1974). MacBride, who was researching a nonfiction book about Wilder's Ozark years, had amassed copies of written material from many sources, including the Wilder home. Irene Lichty-Le Count graciously welcomed Miller and MacBride to the home and museum. MacBride told me that he simply said that he was there to collect his stored material and place it at the Hoover. During a long, extremely warm day in the stuffy upper rooms of the house, the men gathered up materials they found in closets, cupboards, and two niches under the eaves. Miller described finding photographs and negatives, "drafts of books and articles and the correspondence. . . . typed copies of LIW's original holograph manuscripts [which] contain the various changes and corrections of both RWL and LIW. They are, in essence, the definitive material about how the books began and arrived at final copy."[35]

The addition to the Wilder-Lane papers was dubbed the "Mansfield accretion." Over twelve hundred pages of Little House book manuscript material were included. There were more than seven hundred newspaper clip-

35. Miller to Anderson, June 2, 1982.

pings, articles, photographs, and postcards, plus a thousand photographs and five hundred postcards from Lane's travels throughout Europe and the Middle East.[36] The addition of these papers to those already at the library constituted an outstanding piece of the literary puzzle. Although the library did not announce the new material publicly, all Wilder-Lane researchers had reason to applaud the newly available documentation. Its importance was clear to me when I read the added materials before writing *Laura Ingalls Wilder: A Biography* (1992).

Not everyone was pleased with MacBride's action, however. He served on the board of the Laura Ingalls Wilder Home and Museum, where there was unrest among two fellow members regarding transfer of the collection to the Hoover. They called for the return of the papers to the Wilder home and ultimately left the board when their request went unheeded. MacBride's position as heir and executor of Wilder's and Lane's literary output was otherwise undisputed.

Later in the 1980s, the Wilder association board initiated two long-overdue preservation projects to conserve the Little House manuscripts that remained in their care. The manuscripts had deteriorated alarmingly. For fifteen years, they had been on display under harsh lighting in the Wilder house, which was unheated in winter and not cooled in summer. Their transfer to a new museum building in 1971 had improved somewhat the conditions of preservation, but the tablets demanded professional attention if they were to survive. The University of Missouri at Columbia offered to superintend microfilming of the brittle, yellowed school tablets. Next, the association board of directors enlisted the Northeast Document Conservation Center in Massachusetts to perform preservation work. The tablets were de-acidified, and the tablet covers were mended and stabilized. For the first time, researchers could consult the microfilmed manuscripts, including *Pioneer Girl*.[37] A welcome flurry of scholarship and publications ensued from writers and researchers with a variety of approaches. Tourists viewing the manuscripts through museum showcases saw evidence that their condition was much enhanced through the ministrations of the conservation center.

After reading and copying the *Pioneer Girl* manuscript at the Hoover, it had occurred to me that this nonfiction version of Wilder's life, spanning the late 1860s through 1885, might appeal to readers who welcomed each

---

36. Miller, inventory, n.d. (ca. 1982).

37. Laura Ingalls Wilder Papers, Laura Ingalls Wilder Home Association, Mansfield, Mo., Microfilm ed., University of Missouri Western Historical Manuscript Collection & State Historical Society of Missouri, Columbia.

periodic new installment of Wilder's words in book form. I shared the concept with MacBride, and he encouraged me to prepare a preliminary edited version of *Pioneer Girl* for publication. My idea was to incorporate unpublished anecdotes from Little House book manuscripts into the narrative with limited annotations. The working title of the 323-page first draft was "Pioneer Girl: More Stories from the Little Houses." This version was completed during the summer of 1983.

The editorial staff at the children's division at Harper & Row was excited and expectant at the possibility of another Wilder book, as they had been when *The First Four Years* and *West from Home* were announced. MacBride considered it unthinkable that Harper & Row would welcome the project with anything but exuberance. "I would be astounded if Harper weren't eager to bring it out," he commented.[38] From the onset, everyone involved envisioned *Pioneer Girl* as geared for children, to be published by the Harper & Row Junior Books Group. In retrospect, it is evident that this limited view, a product of then-current publishing concepts, was unworkable. MacBride wrote to Elizabeth Gordon, vice-president and publisher of Harper & Row Junior Books, with characteristic enthusiasm. "Are you ready to run screaming into the streets, crying out that Harper is eager to bring out an edited version of 'Pioneer Girl'?" he queried. "Or are you quietly going to let this marvelous opportunity pass to another firm?"[39]

At the time MacBride wrote, the methods of manuscript selection were changing at Harper & Row Junior Books. Previously, creative editorial autonomy had been the norm, allowing the dynamic department director Ursula Nordstrom and her editors to publish innovative books for children. By the 1980s, the sales and marketing department was exerting strong influence in manuscript purchases, page allocations, and financial considerations pertaining to new titles. In a lengthy letter to MacBride, Gordon cited the fear that publishing *Pioneer Girl* could be "detrimental to Laura's reputation." She told him that the staff had "thoroughly discussed it in a marketing meeting" at which probing questions had been asked: was it "a good story—on a par with the previous Little House books? . . . Will it be of interest to children?" The group concluded "that it would be a mistake to publish." Gordon rightly observed that the manuscript contained material "better left untold for children." She referred to some of the harsher, grimmer incidents of the Ingalls family's life, contrasting them with "an aura of warmth and security" in the

---

38. MacBride to Anderson, Feb. 8, 1983.
39. MacBride to Gordon, Sept. 15, 1983.

Little House books. Although she rejected MacBride's offer, she suggested alternatives, including a collection of Wilder's letters.[40]

MacBride was undaunted; he believed in *Pioneer Girl*. He studied fresh options for tweaking the manuscript during the next few years. An abbreviated version of the first working draft emerged, titled "Untold Tales from Laura Ingalls Wilder." I broached the possibility that *Pioneer Girl* was more suited to a university press, citing its suitability "for the historically-minded reader and just simply for scholarship."[41] But MacBride was confident that Harper would welcome the re-tooled version. On November 5, 1987, he announced the revised manuscript to Gordon. "What we've done," he wrote, "is mine the gold out of 'Pioneer Girl.'"[42] Harper & Row Junior Books remained unmoved by "Untold Tales from Laura Ingalls Wilder." Dial Press also passed on the opportunity to publish. MacBride then enlisted the William Morris Agency to locate a publisher. Literary agent Ned Leavitt, eerily echoing Lane's agent George Bye, reported that he found it charming and interesting," but was not "convinced I could put it across to a publisher."[43] In the end, the peregrinations of *Pioneer Girl* in its varied formats of the 1980s paralleled the long series of submissions and rejections the original manuscript encountered in 1930–1931.[44]

Once more, in 1990, MacBride discussed the subject of "Untold Tales" with HarperCollins, this time talking to Marilyn Kriney, Gordon's successor, and Eddie Bell, who oversaw HarperCollins for owner Rupert Murdoch. Kriney agreed to look it over again, but by this time, MacBride's emphasis had shifted to a new project, a series of novels that evolved into "The Rose Years," a spin-off series with Rose Wilder as the protagonist, growing up in turn of the century Mansfield. The books were published between 1993 and 1999.[45] During the same time period, the Harper children's division

40. Gordon to MacBride, Oct. 19, 1983. HarperCollins published *The Selected Letters of Laura Ingalls Wilder*, ed. William Anderson, early in 2016.

41. Anderson to MacBride, Aug. 3, 1985.

42. MacBride to Gordon, Nov. 7, 1987.

43. Ned Leavitt to MacBride, May 16, 1989. Lane's agent had written to her in this same vein in 1931. *See* Bye to Lane, Apr. 6, 1931, Box 13, file 189, Laura Ingalls Wilder Series, Rose Wilder Lane Papers, Herbert Hoover Presidential Library, West Branch, Iowa.

44. Hill, Introduction, pp. xxiii–ix, xxvii, xxxviii–xl, xliii.

45. MacBride to Anderson, May 21, 1990. The titles in the "Rose Years" series, by MacBride and published by HarperCollins, are *Little House on Rocky Ridge* (1993), *Little Farm in the Ozarks* (1994), *On the Other Side of the Hill* (1995), *In the Land of the Big Red Apple* (1995), *Little Town in the Ozarks* (1996), *New Dawn on Rocky Ridge* (1997), *On the Banks of the Bayou* (1998), and *Bachelor Girl* (1999).

launched a mammoth project called the Little House Publishing Program. It featured spin-off books, picture books, re-issues and novelties—calendars, photograph albums, baby books, board books, and address books. The plan called for one hundred fifty products to be released between 1994 and 1998.[46] Within Harper's wide-reaching merchandising blitz, it seemed that "Untold Tales from Laura Ingalls Wilder" might finally be included. It never happened. The manuscript drafts were filed away; notions of publication were quietly abandoned.

*Pioneer Girl*, however, was destined to have a third, and ultimately victorious, publication attempt. In late 2005, the South Dakota Historical Society Press commissioned author Pamela Smith Hill to write a biography of Wilder to inaugurate its South Dakota Biography Series and, in 2006, sponsored Hill's research trip to the Hoover library. While she was in West Branch researching *Laura Ingalls Wilder: A Writer's Life* (2007), Hill learned firsthand of the public curiosity about the manuscript. "I overheard a telephone conversation between an archivist and a Wilder fan, who wanted a copy of *Pioneer Girl*," she recalled. After he hung up, the archivist told her that the library "fielded dozens of calls" for the manuscript each year. "I did think there might be an unfulfilled *demand* for the book," Hill said. "That experience planted the seed, . . . and over time, it turned into a conviction that the best way to fill the demand was with an annotated version."[47]

On several occasions, Hill discussed the concept with Nancy Tystad Koupal, director of both the South Dakota Historical Society's Research and Publishing Program and its Press. Koupal, who held a long-time interest in Wilder and vast experience in editing writings about her and other authors, thought the idea had merit, "especially if it were researched thoroughly and produced attractively." She envisioned a work similar to annotated literary classics such as Mark Twain's *The Annotated Huckleberry Finn* (1981, revised 2001), edited by Michael Patrick Hearn, or Kenneth Grahame's *The Wind in the Willows: An Annotated Edition* (2009), edited by Seth Lerer. In 2009, she asked Hill to put her ideas on paper. Koupal then wrote an accompanying production concept and financial package and took it to the Little House Heritage Trust, the entity that had succeeded Roger MacBride following his death in 1995. Abigail MacBride and Noel Silverman, trustee and counsel of the trust, concurred that the time was ripe for publication of Wilder's autobiography. Once negotiations were complete late in 2010, Koupal set up the

---

46. I was serving as a consultant for HarperCollins during this time.

47. Hill to Anderson, Oct. 26, 2016. *See also* "The Beginning," May 18, 2012, www.pioneergirlproject.org.

Pioneer Girl Project, modeled loosely on the Mark Twain Project at the University of California, Berkeley, and she, her staff, and Hill began the research and preparation necessary to bring Wilder's seminal work to readers.[48]

A full four years ensued prior to the publication of *Pioneer Girl: The Annotated Autobiography*. In the fall of 2011, Hill and Koupal traveled to Mansfield. At the Laura Ingalls Wilder Home and Museum, director Jean Coday permitted them to examine Wilder's handwritten version of *Pioneer Girl*, the text on which the annotated edition would be based. With proper awe, the women paged through the cherished tablets, which had not been done since Zochert's transcription in 1975 and the conservation and microfilming of them in the 1980s. "I felt that, even though the tablets were fragile, it was absolutely imperative that we verify the manuscript's physical existence, examine its foibles, and thoroughly understand the document that we would spend so much time with," Koupal explained.[49] Years of transcription, research, mapmaking, and writing ensued, but in November 2014, *Pioneer Girl* at last made its roundabout way into print.

"Will it come to anything?" Rose Wilder Lane had wondered in 1930 at the onset of her writing partnership with Laura Ingalls Wilder.[50] It did. *Pioneer Girl* was the necessary first phase in the development of America's quintessential pioneer story, the Little House books. Over eighty years after Laura Ingalls Wilder wrote her autobiographical account, her legions of readers wholeheartedly welcomed *Pioneer Girl: The Annotated Autobiography* as a belated gift.

---

48. Koupal to Anderson, Dec. 5, 2016. *See also* Noel Silverman's "'Her Stories Take You with Her': The Lasting Appeal of Laura Ingalls Wilder" elsewhere in this volume.

49. Koupal, conversation with Anderson, Sept. 24, 2016, Brookings, S.Dak. *See also* Koupal, "Seeing the Original," June 19, 2012, www.pioneergirlproject.org.

50. Lane, Diary (1926–1930), Aug. 19, 1930, Box 21, item #25, Lane Papers.

# { 5 }
# Little Myths on the Prairie

## MICHAEL PATRICK HEARN

*"It can't beat us!" Pa said.*
*"Can't it, Pa?" Laura asked stupidly.*
*"No," said Pa. "It's got to quit sometime and we don't.*
*It can't lick us. We won't give up."*
LAURA INGALLS WILDER, *The Long Winter*

Once upon a time years and years ago, an old farm wife in Mansfield, Missouri, sat down at her writing desk, pulled out a cheap composition book, and began work on one of the greatest of American children's classics. Is that not a pretty fairy tale? Unfortunately, it is just one of the many myths concerning the composition and publication of the famous Little House books. The popular image of Laura Ingalls Wilder that persists today is that she was no more than the Grandma Moses of American juvenile literature. "Mrs. Wilder is now about 65, small, very pretty and modishly dressed with bobbed white hair," a Lansing, Michigan, newspaper reported in 1932. "Besides being a writer she is also an expert cook, dairy-maid and poultry raiser. Her gingerbread has already made her famous."[1]

Wilder did nothing to discourage this quaint picture of the elderly farmer's wife turned amateur author who somehow found the time between chores to become a celebrated chronicler of the Great American West. She did not even enjoy writing, or so she said. "It's hard work," she told a local newspaper reporter in 1949. "I wrote when I was doing everything else—my housework, taking care of chickens and cows. Writing is very tiring for me." The implication was that she found it much easier to look after livestock than sitting down and coming up with more stories to tell. She insisted that all she really wanted to do at first was to preserve her father's tales of pioneer life that became the

---

1. "'Little House in the Big Woods' Is April Choice of Junior Guild," *Lansing State Journal*, Mar. 26, 1932. This sketch of Wilder was undoubtedly supplied by her daughter Rose Wilder Lane through Harper & Brothers. It matches closely the profile of her mother that Lane submitted to the organizers of the book fair in Detroit in 1937. *See* the Editor's Note to Wilder's "Speech for the Detroit Book Fair, 1937" in this volume.

basis of *Little House in the Big Woods* (1932), but the public would not let her stop there.² She followed it in quick succession with seven more books in a sort of American agrarian *Remembrance of Things Past* (Marcel Proust, 1913–1927) for children: *Farmer Boy* (1933), her husband's childhood in Upstate New York; *Little House on the Prairie* (1935), homesteading in Indian Country; *On the Banks of Plum Creek* (1937), life in a dugout near Walnut Grove, Minnesota; *By the Shores of Silver Lake* (1939), early days in De Smet, Dakota Territory; *The Long Winter* (1940), one of the severest winters in American history; *Little Town on the Prairie* (1941), later years in De Smet; and finally, *These Happy Golden Years* (1943), the story of her courtship and marriage.³ The saga covered her life roughly from age five to eighteen.

"I was amazed" at the success of the first book, Wilder told Fred Kiewit of the *Kansas City Star* in 1955, "because I didn't know how to write. I went to little red schoolhouses all over the West and I never was graduated from anything." Of course, she was being disingenuous. She did earn a teacher's certificate in 1883 and taught three semesters in elementary schools before marrying farmer Almanzo Wilder in 1885. "The only reason I can think of for being able to write at all was that both Father and Mother were great readers and I read a lot at home with them," she told Kiewit. "I just had those stories to tell and I wrote them like I would tell them to you."⁴ The reality was that she was already a well-seasoned writer by the time the first Little House book appeared in 1932.

Another misconception that surfaced after her death is the idea that she did not even write the books but that they were "ghosted" by her daughter Rose Wilder Lane. Some have concluded that Lane played Galatea to Wilder's Pygmalion in transforming the autobiography *Pioneer Girl* into the famous Little House books. William V. Holtz, professor of English at the University of Missouri, revealed the literary collaboration of these two strong women in his incendiary biography of Lane, *The Ghost in the Little House: A Life of Rose Wilder Lane* (1993). Their sometimes contentious mother-daughter relationship has even been the basis for Susan Wittig Albert's novel *A Wilder Rose* (2013). Neither Wilder nor Lane nor the publisher ever publicly acknowledged the daughter's significant contribution to the evolution of the series; and some people have suspected something sinister and conspiratorial in keeping that secret. In his blurb for Albert's book, Holtz re-

2. "True Stories Brought Fame to Mrs. Wilder," *Springfield* (Mo.) *News and Leader*, May 22, 1949.

3. Page numbers will be given in the text from the 1953 Harper & Row uniform edition of the books.

4. Kiewit, "Stories That Had to be Told," *Kansas City Star*, May 22, 1955.

ferred to their silence as "a literary deception that has persisted for decades."[5] More cautious is the account offered in Pamela Smith Hill's recent biography, *Laura Ingalls Wilder: A Writer's Life* (2007).

As Hill corrected in her introduction to *Pioneer Girl: The Annotated Autobiography* (2014), Laura Ingalls Wilder was far from being a semi-literate country bumpkin, as she has been so popularly portrayed, hoodwinked by an overly ambitious daughter into perpetuating one the greatest of American literary frauds. "If you look at the original rough draft [of *Pioneer Girl*] you can see [Wilder] has a long way to go as a novelist," Hill admitted to a *New York Times* blogger in 2015, "but you can also see that the characters are there. The description is there. You can see whole chunks, especially of dialogue, that she lifted from 'Pioneer Girl' and placed into the Little House books. Her voice is there, too, and that's really one of the things that makes the books so special."[6] Wilder herself modestly informed the *Springfield News and Leader*, "all I did was write what had happened to me."[7] She was nobody's fool: Laura Ingalls Wilder was a gifted writer in her own right and a shrewd businesswoman—and not just on the farm. She knew exactly what she was doing. *Pioneer Girl* is a remarkable personal story and an important historical document. It is a wonder the original manuscript was never published in its entirety before.

Long before she first put pen to paper to record her life story, Mrs. A. J. Wilder wrote poultry articles for the *St. Louis Star Farmer* and contributed regular columns to the *Missouri Ruralist* from 1911 to 1924. These articles of agricultural domesticity were on the whole no more than ephemera, hackwork, no better and no worse than anything else then being published in America's countless farm journals. On occasion, Wilder peppered her brief sketches with anecdotes of her frontier girlhood. Through her daughter Rose Wilder Lane, then a nationally known professional writer, she was able to place a couple articles in at least two national magazines, *McCall's* and *Country Gentleman*. Both mother and daughter sold some verse to the children's department of the *San Francisco Bulletin*; and in 1919, Wilder wrote several children's stories (now lost) that she sent to her daughter for her opinion of their commercial value. Although the juvenile book business was booming now that World War I was over, Lane saw no potential in them. Except for *St. Nicholas* and *The Youth's Companion*, magazines aimed at young readers

5. Holtz, quoted on back cover of Albert's *A Wilder Rose* (Bertram, Tex.: Persevero Press, 2013).

6. Quoted in KJ Dell'Antonia, "The Book That Became the 'Little House' Books," Aug. 7, 2015, *Motherlode*, parenting.blogs.nytimes.com.

7. Wilder, quoted in "True Stories."

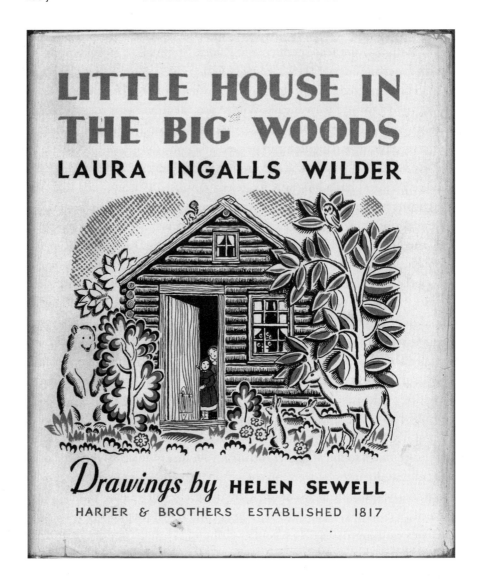

paid considerably less for freelance contributions than did the bigger adult publications, and staff writers provided most copy anyway. Lane bluntly informed her mother at the time, "there is no opportunity to make a name with children's stories."[8]

If true history is not the lives of great men but rather the stories of the common people, then the Little House books are great history. Laura Ingalls Wilder did nothing remarkable in her life, but she did witness the coming of

8. Lane, quoted in Hill, Introduction to Wilder, *Pioneer Girl: The Annotated Autobiography* (Pierre: South Dakota Historical Society Press, 2014), p. xxxv. For Wilder's newspaper columns, *see* Stephen W. Hines, *Laura Ingalls Wilder, Farm Journalist: Writings from the Ozarks* (Columbia: University of Missouri Press, 2007).

age of America. She also had the rare ability to write down exactly what she saw and felt as a child. Rose Wilder Lane believed that her mother had much to tell the world about those early pioneering days. As early as 1911, she tried to get her to sit down and record the story of her life. "As for that late start, you know I had my own family to take care of," Wilder told Kiewit in 1955. "Then when my daughter was grown and gone and my husband and I were taking things a little easier I used to think about the stories my father used to tell us four girls when we were little." Of course, Lane had been out of the house for years and was doing quite well on her own. It took two decades before Wilder got around to thinking about recording her frontier childhood.

So much of a book's success lies in the timing. *Little House in the Big Woods* came out just as America was reexamining its history. The story of the United States from its earliest days had been one of expansion. The doctrine of Manifest Destiny fueled as well as corrupted the pioneer spirit. It insisted that it was not just the right but the duty of Americans to claim what history demanded, what was preordained as theirs, no matter where it might be or who might stand in their way. This American dream swiftly evolved into the American nightmare for native people who were driven from their ancestral homes as the young nation expanded aggressively from coast to coast. When newspaper editor Horace Greeley declared in the *New York Tribune* in 1865, "Go West, young man, and grow up with the country," Charles Philip Ingalls and Caroline Lake Quiner Ingalls joined that great migration to grab a part of the American frontier as their rightful heritage. The Little House books merely perpetuated the popular myth of the Great American West—not how it was won but how it was settled. As she explained in a talk delivered at the book fair at the J. L. Hudson department store in Detroit in October 1937, Wilder had seen and lived it all in her childhood: "the whole frontier, the woods, the Indian country of the great plains, the frontier towns, the building of railroads in wild, unsettled country, homesteading and farmers coming in to take possession." Her life was not one of great heroic acts but of the everyday struggle to tame the land as a child witnessed it: "In my own life I represented a whole period of American history."[9] The title of one of the chapters in *The Long Winter* summarized the pioneer spirit as she knew it: "It Can't Beat Us" (pp. 309–13).

With the official closing of the American frontier in 1890, the myth of the West was ready for revision. While Owen Wister perpetuated the antiquated

---

9. Wilder, Speech, Detroit Book Fair, Oct. 16, 1937, pp. 2–3, Box 13, file 197, Laura Ingalls Wilder Series, Rose Wilder Lane Papers, Herbert Hoover Presidential Library, West Branch, Iowa.

notion of southern chivalry as the Code of the West in his bestselling novel *The Virginian* (1902), midwestern naturalist Hamlin Garland reported how the harsh, bleak landscape brutalized the people who dared to homestead on the prairie. This same devastating assessment can be found in the opening paragraphs of L. Frank Baum's great American fairy tale, *The Wonderful Wizard of Oz* (1900). The great gray Kansas prairie has made the people as gray as their surroundings. Uncle Henry never laughs, and Aunt Em screams and presses her heart whenever she hears her orphan niece laugh or even speak. No other picture of homesteading in any other work of American literature is more dismal than this one.[10]

At the turn of the century, Americans were reaching beyond the borders of continental North America to the Philippines and the Caribbean. They abandoned their rural society to join the vast influx of immigrants flocking to newly built metropolises. They believed that scientific progress rather than agricultural produce would make America the greatest country on Earth. Then the Yanks had to go fight in Europe. Once they returned from the War to End All Wars, an international disaster not of their own doing or choosing, Americans were perfectly content to stay out of the rest of the world's affairs. Did they not reject President Woodrow Wilson's grand dream of the League of Nations? New, more severe immigration laws were passed to keep out dangerous foreigners and their Bolshevism, anarchism, and other isms. While turning these undesirables and their politics away, Americans also rejected what they considered to be their old pernicious history. In so doing, Americans reclaimed their own myths and traditions, their own distinctive culture. Ironically, as technology was gaining its stranglehold on the country, a deeply felt nostalgia for America's long-lost agrarian past arose among the people. While many of the best and brightest were running off to live cheaply in London, Paris, Berlin, and elsewhere, those who stayed home went mad for American folk art, folklore, folk music, and folk heroes. The Great Depression encouraged Americans to become even more isolationist intellectually, economically, politically, and culturally. While refuting Europe's myths, they invented their own. And none was greater than the myth of the American West. It was within this cultural climate that *Little House in the Big Woods* was published in 1932. While hardly the only pioneer story on the market, it and its sequels proved to be the most enduring.

The Little House books were not fished out of the publisher's "slush pile" as some may have supposed, however. The first title in the series evolved

---

10. Baum, *The Annotated Wizard of Oz: Centennial Edition*, ed. and ann. Michael Patrick Hearn (New York: W. W. Norton & Co., 2000), pp. 18–20.

through a long, arduous, and sometimes painful process of rejection and revision. It began when the Wall Street Crash of 1929 devastated Lane and the Wilders just as it did the rest of the country. Lane's literary market was drying up along with her investments and savings. Many of the nation's periodicals were folding, and those that were just hanging on bought fewer and fewer original contributions. Lane knew there was great material in her mother's life story and urged her to commit it to paper. In late 1929 or early 1930, Wilder sat down to write her autobiography, tentatively titled "Pioneer Girl." On May 7, 1930, she showed the handwritten manuscript to Lane, who typed a copy while making only minor editorial changes. Being a well-seasoned professional, she offered it to Brandt & Brandt, her literary agency in New York. Carl Brandt returned it as unsalable at the end of June. Lane greatly reworked it into a tighter more focused narrative for adults. Ever mindful of new markets and apparently without her mother's knowledge, Lane also cobbled together a children's story, "When Grandma Was a Little Girl," of episodes from the unpublished manuscript. She also changed the narration from first to third person. A book for boys and girls was a natural because, due to the vast growth of the American children's library movement in the 1920s, nearly every publishing house was now developing a juvenile division.[11]

Because Brandt & Brandt was not willing to handle *Pioneer Girl*, Lane herself submitted it to *Ladies' Home Journal* and *Good Housekeeping*. No one was interested. Then, while visiting illustrators Berta and Elmer Hader, old friends living in Nyack, New York, she met Marion Fiery, the head of Alfred A. Knopf's Children's Book Department. Berta had already passed the children's version on to the editor, and Fiery liked what she read. However, she wanted its author to expand it into a novel for children of eight to ten years. It needed another fifteen thousand words.[12] "Daughter said they might be the basis of a picture book but nothing else," Wilder told Kiewit in 1955. "She told me to put some meat on the bones and then send the stories back and she would see what she could do." The point of view also had to be changed to conform to a prevailing myth of the American children's book trade. "For juveniles you can not use the first person," Lane wrote Wilder on February 16, 1931, "because the 'I' books do not sell well."[13] That, of course, was bunk. *Adventures of Huckleberry Finn* as narrated by the boy himself had been a bestseller for years; and the bulk of Hugh Lofting's popular Doctor Dolittle books were told in the first person.

---

11. Hill, Introduction, pp. xvii, xxix, xxiv–vi, xxxviii–xl.
12. Ibid., pp. xl–xli.
13. Lane to Wilder, Feb. 16, 1931, Box 13, file 189, Lane Papers.

Diligent Wilder did as she was instructed. Lane advised her on what other episodes from *Pioneer Girl* could be added to the children's story. Wilder gave greater shape to the novel as she fleshed out the details. "After I would write something I would set it back for a month or so and let it cool," Wilder told Kiewit. "Then I would read it back and maybe change it a little before I sent it in." During that cooling phase, Lane took a crack at the manuscript.

While pushing her mother's literary career, Lane also shamelessly exploited her by lifting names and events from her life and weaving them into two highly profitable novels, *Let the Hurricane Roar* (1933) and *Free Land* (1938), as well as some short stories. Although her parents approved the second book, a fictionalized account of Almanzo's early homesteading, Lane had not even told her mother what she was doing in the first one. Wilder was not amused. "My daughter's book, 'Let the Hurricane Roar' is fiction with a background of facts I told her many times when she was a child," she wrote a librarian in 1952. "The characters in the story have no connection with my family. Her choice of names was unfortunate and it creates confusion."[14] Wilder eventually got over her annoyance; and she and Almanzo generously provided their daughter with much valuable information for *Free Land*.

Fiery finally accepted *Little House in the Big Woods* and was ready to offer a three-book deal to Wilder. Lane also tried to sell Fiery on the adult autobiography but as a book for older children. Then Alfred A. Knopf decided to drop his children's book division and Fiery along with it. Lane offered her mother's book to a friend at Lippincott's, Ernestine Evans, who was in charge of juveniles there. Fiery on her own sent Wilder's manuscript to another children's book editor, Virginia Kirkus of Harper & Brothers, who agreed to publish it. Lane had recently changed literary agents, and George T. Bye became Wilder's agent as well, negotiating the terms for all her books with Harper & Brothers.[15]

Kirkus conceived of *Little House in the Big Woods* as a novel for nine and ten year olds, and Wilder and Lane readily complied. The particular style employed in the first book was certainly suited to this age, as evident in the following paragraph about butter churning from the chapter "Winter Days and Winter Nights":

When the cream was ready, Ma scalded the long wooden churn-dash, put it in the churn, and dropped the wooden churn-cover over it. The

---

14. Wilder to Clara J. Webber, Feb. 11, 1952, in Wilder, *The Selected Letters of Laura Ingalls Wilder*, ed. William Anderson (New York: HarperCollins, 2016), pp. 336–37. Unless otherwise noted, all quotations from Wilder's correspondence come from this source.

15. Hill, Introduction, pp. xliii–viii.

churn-cover had a little round hole in the middle, and Ma moved the dash up and down, up and down, through the hole. (p. 20)

Wilder chose simple declarative sentences in a bold, brief prose with a restricted vocabulary of words rarely more than two to three syllables long. Most of her young audience were just learning to read; and Wilder repeated certain unfamiliar but important words to make sure her readers remembered them. She described the Ingallses' humble house much as L. Frank Baum did Dorothy's on the great gray Kansas prairie in *The Wonderful Wizard of Oz* in what Gore Vidal called "the plain American style at its best"[16]:

> The house was a comfortable house. Upstairs there was a large attic, pleasant to play in when the rain drummed on the roof. Downstairs was the small bedroom, and the big room. The bedroom had a window that closed with a wooden shutter. The big room had two windows with glass in the panes, and it had two doors, a front door and a back door. (p. 4)

It is a clean, concrete, muscular English, almost Biblical in its cadences, Hemingwayesque in its clarity and precision. It is the journalistic style Wilder burnished all those years writing for the rural press. Ever aware of her young audience, Wilder was judicious in her use of adjectives and adverbs and other modifiers. She dispensed with the gratuitous.

The characters also speak in a surprisingly formal English throughout the series. (Laura Ingalls had been a school teacher after all.) Just as there is little local color in the descriptions, there is no dialect in the conversations. They use few contractions. They speak like characters in a novel rather than the way people speak in life. Laura Ingalls in *Little House in the Big Woods* is *not* Wisconsin's Huck Finn! Occasionally, colloquialisms slip in ("By Jinks!," "Plumb starved to death," "A man must keep everlasting at it," "You can't go but so fast no-how!"), but these are rare. Her parents rarely used them; and her father's strongest expletives were "gosh" or "darn." "But of course a lady like Ma would never use such expressions," Wilder informed Lane in 1931. "Her language was rather precise and a great deal better language than I have ever used."[17] Neither would she have said "young ones" and "I vow."

---

16. Vidal, "On Rereading the Oz Books," *The New York Review of Books* 24 (Oct. 13, 1977): 38. Baum wrote: "Their house was small, for the lumber to build it had to be carried by wagon many miles. There were four walls, a floor and a roof, which made one room; and this room contained a rusty looking cooking stove, a cupboard for the dishes, a table, three or four chairs, and the beds" (*Annotated Wizard of Oz*, p. 11).

17. Wilder to Lane, fragment, ca. 1931, p. 63.

However, Wilder did not concur when Fiery suggested changing "Ma" and "Pa" to "Mother" and "Father" throughout *Little House in the Big Woods*.[18]

Although neither galleys nor page proofs for the book survive, Wilder's story apparently went through only the most cursory of editing. During the process, there had been problems with the narrator in *Little House in the Big Woods*. "I had understood when your manuscript was given to me to read," Kirkus wrote Wilder, "that it was autobiographical and that these were your own childhood experiences of frontier life.... Won't you send us an autobiographical sketch so that we can see just how this material fits into your own background? Would you also place it for us geographically, as there seems to be a difference of opinion here as to the locale."[19] Evidently, the editor was baffled by the lack of transitions between Wilder's recollections and the tales Pa told throughout the manuscript. The confusion was easily rectified by clarifying the pronouns, adding titles to the stories within the story, and setting the episodes off with quotation marks. "We would not dream of making any changes that could in any way involve the very special setting of the story," Kirkus assured Wilder.[20]

Although the point of view of the book was from the child's perspective, Wilder clarified in 1949 that Pa's stories in *Little House in the Big Woods* were not merely his recollections of his own boyhood but also what he remembered of Laura's youngest days. "I had heard my father tell many stories of my very early childhood," she told the reporter, "and I decided to write them down, for I wanted them preserved."[21] Of course, there was a good dose of literary license in how she developed the narrative.

Much has been made of the theory that Rose Wilder Lane wrote the books and not her mother. It has become an urban myth much in the tradition that Shakespeare could not have written those plays. The problem with the ghostwriter theory is that none of the Little House books sounds like Lane. The narrator of *Little House on the Prairie* and all the others is *not* that of *Let the Hurricane Roar* and *Free Land*. It is the voice of *Pioneer Girl*. Lane's influence may be traced here and there of course, but the overall tone and drive of the multi-volumed novel are consistent, and they are Wilder's. What exactly Lane contributed to the stories may never be fully known. Some key links to the evolution of these books are missing. Neither letters between mother and daughter nor Lane's diaries fully clarify the exact nature of their collaboration, whether it was a true collaboration or Lane was merely editing Wilder's

18. Fiery to Wilder, Feb. 12, 1931, Box 13, file 189, Lane Papers.
19. Kirkus to Wilder, Dec. 15, 1931, ibid.
20. Ibid., Dec. 28, 1931.
21. Wilder, quoted in "True Stories."

text. Beyond Wilder's remarks about Lane's suggestion that she put meat on the bones of her story, the women did not comment publicly upon Lane's crucial role in the development of the books.

Fully aware that she was now writing for young readers in *Little House in the Big Woods*, Wilder shaped individual chapters as self-contained little moral tales that upheld good and right Puritan values. She left it to their mother to teach them good manners. "Ma never allowed them to play with their food at table," Wilder wrote; "they must always eat nicely everything that was set before them, leaving nothing on their plates" (p. 217). One can almost hear her chastising Laura and Mary at dinner. But Laura is a real girl who has the feelings of little girls everywhere. What other child would disagree that it is not quite fair that Laura must share her cookie with Baby Carrie (pp. 178–79)? Pa admonishes Laura for striking older sister Mary: "It is what I say that you must mind" (p. 183). When the pocket of Laura's dress tears from the weight of too many riverbank pebbles in the chapter "Going to Town," Ma provides the lesson of the story, "don't be so greedy" (p. 174). In the incident of Charley and the bees, a retelling of the old Aesop's fable of The Boy Who Cried Wolf, Pa offers the moral, "It served the little liar right" (p. 211).

The voice is crucial. Wilder always wrote from the child's vivid view. "Laura's strength was always her ability to see with the eye of wonder and to memorably communicate what she saw," admitted children's book writer and critic Eleanor Cameron in *The New York Times Book Review*.[22] Wilder once confessed in a letter to a friend that her favorite quotation was from Psalm 19, "The heavens declare the glory of God and the firmament sheweth his handiwork."[23] This childlike, wide-eyed optimism shines throughout the entire series. Using the third rather than the first person greatly liberated Wilder. Now she did not have to rely entirely on specific personal recollections. She infused her characters and incidents with more detailed descriptions and dialogue that recast them in greater relief. The conversations were probably all invented, for it is highly unlikely that Laura Ingalls could have recollected verbatim those speeches from her earliest days any more than Frank McCourt did in *Angela's Ashes* (1996).

Autobiographical works told in the third person by no means originated with Wilder. Surely the most famous American example in her day was *The Education of Henry Adams* (1918) that was published posthumously and

22. Cameron, review of *The First Four Years*, *New York Times Book Review*, Mar. 28, 1971.

23. Wilder to Suzanna, Sept. 29, 1952, p. 342.

awarded the Pulitzer Prize for Nonfiction the following year. The famous editor-in-chief of *The Ladies Home Journal* followed Adams's example in telling his own life story in the third person in *The Americanization of Edward Bok* (1920). It, too, won the Pulitzer Prize. Gertrude Stein produced a highly unorthodox bestseller, *The Autobiography of Alice B. Toklas* (1933), in which she could freely talk about herself in the voice of her long-time companion from San Francisco. Adherents of the "new journalism" of the 1960s and 1970s also employed the third person in autobiographical works, most notably Norman Mailer in *Armies of the Night: History as a Novel, the Novel as History* (1968). This seemingly novel genre of American journalism often applied fictional techniques to reporting. The "facts" were less important than "the truth." But of course there was nothing *new* about the new journalism. Wilder, and even Lane before her, used the same literary tricks decades before Mailer and the others.

Many of the popular biographies of the day were largely fictionalized accounts, and there was no greater master of this bastard form than Rose Wilder Lane. She saw no problem in inventing dialogue and events in the lives of prominent individuals, placing incidents out of sequence, combining characters, and creating others. It was all done in an attempt to tell a vivid story. But Henry Ford denounced her inaccurate biography of him. Chaplin threatened to sue Bobbs-Merrill if they sold the book based on her account in the *San Francisco Bulletin*, and the publisher capitulated by suppressing the edition. Jack London's widow and sister were also distressed by the liberties Lane took with the famous writer's life. This trend was perhaps even more true with the juvenile book trade. Perhaps the most infamous of fictionalized biographies for young readers was Bobbs-Merrill's Childhoods of Famous Americans, or the "orange biographies." Almost entirely fabricated, these tales rarely contained any more truth than did the legend of George Washington and his cherry tree. Yet, they sold like hot cakes, and nearly every children's library throughout the country stocked dozens of them. In some places, they were practically the only juvenile biographies on the shelf. They were all about exemplary characters even if they were not so in life.[24] By stressing the inherent virtues of prominent citizens in their earliest years, these books, like Lane's biographies, added considerably to the modern American mythology.

While Wilder's first book was in production, Kirkus suddenly left the firm.

---

24. Nancy Pate, "Publisher Gives Memorable 'Orange Biographies' an Update," *Athens Banker-Herald*, Oct. 21, 2003, onlineAthens.com. For more about Lane's writing, *see* Caroline Fraser's "The Strange Case of the Bloody Benders" elsewhere in this volume.

It was now the height of the Great Depression, and Harper & Brothers decided to cut down its juvenile department. Kirkus resigned to form her own successful reviewing service; and her assistant, Ida Louise Raymond, took over her list and became Wilder's editor. Replying to Raymond in March 1933, Wilder agreed to her "suggestion of adding incident and tightening up the plot" in her second novel, *Farmer Boy*.[25] Although no longer connected with the publisher, Kirkus continued to support the series as it developed. She gave some indication of what originally appealed to her about this "authentic picture of over sixty years ago" in her review of *Little House in the Big Woods*. "Until you read a book like this," she argued, "it is hard to realize that people lived in those days without access to a town, except at rare intervals, and that everything they ate, everything they wore, everything they used, had to be made right at home." She pointed out that Wilder "has a rare gift of making each fact take form and substance, and stamp itself upon the mind and the mind's eye.... And the knowledge that the material is drawn out of the storage of childhood memories of an actual woman living to-day, makes it seem even more worth while."[26]

Wilder immediately followed *Little House in the Big Woods* with quite a different story, *Farmer Boy*, about her husband Almanzo's growing up in New York State. It was longer and more complex than the earlier book, but it was just as well received by the public and reviewers as the previous one. *Kirkus Reviews* of October 1, 1933, favorably compared it to Gladys Hasty Carroll's bestseller *As the Earth Turns* (1933), an adult novel about a year on a farm in Maine. *Farmer Boy* did well, but the public was clamoring for more about Laura, Mary, Baby Carrie, and Ma and Pa Ingalls. Returning to *Pioneer Girl* for material, Wilder really came into her stride with *Little House on the Prairie*, the most famous of all her books. *Kirkus Reviews* gave the book a starred review on September 19, where the reviewer described it as "Good Americana—and a first rate tale. Personally, I liked it certainly as well, perhaps better than the other."[27] A *Los Angeles Times* reviewer pronounced it "as well woven and simple in style as a piece of homespun."[28]

*Pioneer Girl* provided plenty of material for all subsequent Little House books. But the series was by no means the first or only multi-volume fam-

---

25. Wilder to Raymond, Mar. 3, 1933, p. 65.

26. Kirkus, "The Book Nook," *The Home Quarterly Magazine* 35 [Oct.–Dec. 1935]: 6 (clipping), Box 14, file 215, Lane Papers.

27. Review of *Farmer Boy*, Oct. 1, 1933, and of *Little House on the Prairie*, Sept. 19, 1935, *Kirkus Reviews*, kirkusreviews.com.

28. I. S. A., "In the Wild West," *Los Angeles Times*, Nov. 17, 1935.

ily saga for children as both Wilder and Lane claimed. A likely model for Wilder's series, whether conscious or unconscious, was Louisa May Alcott's *Little Women* (1868–1869), the most popular of all American domestic stories. Alcott, like Wilder, freely drew on her own experiences and those of her three sisters during the Civil War and immediately after in composing her famous two-volume novel. But Wilder avoided the liberties her predecessor took with her life's story. Alcott, who never wed, conveniently married off her stand-in Jo at the end of the second volume of *Little Women*; and the husband, saintly Professor Bhaer, was merely a substitute for her own father, philosopher Bronson Alcott. The two sequels, *Little Men* (1871) and *Jo's Boys* (1886), were pure invention. Wilder could have drawn inspiration from many other girls' books, such as Margaret Sidney's insanely successful Five Little Peppers series and L. M. Montgomery's Canadian saga of Anne of Green Gables. She would have been familiar, too, with the American *Heidi*, Kate Douglas Wiggin's national bestseller *Rebecca of Sunnybrook Farm* (1903), another classic, rural-American coming-of-age story.

As the story of her life progressed and Laura grew older, Wilder employed a more advanced style of increasingly sophisticated concepts and language, just as J. K. Rowling did in her Harry Potter books as she met the changing needs of her maturing audience. Wilder never just put down the facts. "Good plain prose was precisely the prose Laura used but there was always a poet in her, an impressionist," Cameron observed in 1971. "And it is a curious fact, one that is true of most children's writers, that as long as Laura was re-creating her childhood years, she could keep the poetic vision, her impressionist's eye that never fails to kindle her 'good plain prose' in the series all the way up to 'These Happy Golden Years.'"[29]

By the time Wilder turned in the fourth title, *On the Banks of Plum Creek*, Lane had convinced her mother to carry the story of Laura several books further until her marriage to her first love just as she had in *Pioneer Girl*. In this way, *Farmer Boy* now fit neatly within the schema of the Little House books. Even so, Lane feared that the writing in the subsequent story, *By the Shores of Silver Lake* (1939), was too mature for young readers. However, it only made sense. Laura was growing up along with her audience, and her continuing saga had to reflect that reality. The publishers wisely altered the format of the books beginning with this title to make them look more adult, just as Laura herself was entering adolescence. Wilder immediately saw the shrewdness of their trying to cater to both juvenile and adult markets. "But it should be borne in mind," she warned her agent, "that all of the books are *one*

---

29. Cameron, review of *The First Four Years*.

*story* and some booksellers have intended selling them in sets when the story is completed. Because of this they should be made to look well together."[30]

As the series progressed, Lane seemed determined to mold her mother in her own image. (Wilder herself would have been the first to admit that her daughter was the better writer.) Lane could be blunt and brutal in her criticism. "Forget you are telling a story," she instructed Wilder in 1938; "you aren't, you are living Laura's experiences. Live every word and sentence and paragraph intensely enough, and you'll make them fit what you feel." She was particularly disappointed with the manuscript of *By the Shores of Silver Lake*, finding it marred by "deadwood, and clumsy spots and a lack of sufficient sharpness of identification with Laura—your point of view wavers." She continued to scold her mother: "Dialog should be used only to convey character and to keep the story moving. . . . Every paragraph must have its own shape . . . its shape and cadence and color must be suited to the tempo." She warned her that if she did not do as she said, "you'll lose your audience for future books, and cut your income, unless you work it over, and work it over by concentrating on every word and sentence until you know precisely what its values are, why you use it."[31]

As Wilder's letters to Lane attest, whenever these two strong-willed women did not see eye to eye on the manuscript, Wilder usually prevailed. She was not difficult. When Lane or an editor wanted her to shorten something, she freely suggested what might be cut without any harm to the narrative. But Wilder did refuse to rewrite *By the Shores of Silver Lake* completely to fit her daughter's standards. It was *her* life after all! It was *her* story! She promised to try harder with what became *The Long Winter*, which proved to be a harder book to write. But it surely must have been frustrating to capitulate to Lane's constant demands. "Change the beginning of the story if you want," mother finally wrote daughter about *By the Shores of Silver Lake*. "Do anything you please with the damn stuff if you will fix it up."[32]

Wilder's deep and sincere sympathy for the settlers (the good *and* the bad) elevates them above the hardships they must endure. She knew firsthand about their struggles in *The Long Winter*, while Lane did not really know nor understand the pioneers or what they were made of. This twentieth-century woman thought they must have been "monsters," but her mother corrected her. "You know a person cannot live at a high pitch of emotion, the feelings become dulled by a natural, unconscious effort at self-preservation," Wilder

30. Wilder to Bye, July 10, 1939, p. 209.
31. Lane to Wilder, Feb. 3, 1938, in Wilder, *Selected Letters*, pp. 160–61.
32. Wilder to Lane, n.d., p. 156.

explained. "Living with danger day after day people become accustomed to it. They take things as they come without much thought about it and no fuss, in a casual way." Pioneer boys and girls, too, were made of stronger stuff than modern ones, Wilder insisted in an earlier letter to Lane, "children weren't raised to be helpless cowards in those days."[33] It is not just enough to have sympathy. Empathy must be there, too. Wilder expressed both nobly in her children's books.

Wilder's perceptions of person, place, and period were extraordinarily acute. She recalled exactly how things were—how they looked, felt, sounded, smelled, and tasted. Since children are fascinated with what people eat, Wilder provided precise instructions for making cheese and butter, maple-sugar candy, hasty pudding, and johnny- or journey-cake. She explained what a deer lick is, the difference between store soap and home-made soap, and how to harvest grain and gather honey. As Cameron pointed out, Wilder maintained throughout the series this dependence on what Henry James in his famous essay "The Art of Fiction" called "the supreme virtue of the novel"—the "air of reality" or "solidity of specification." "What is unfailingly engrossing in the 'Little House' books," Cameron argued, "is the artistry with which Mrs. Wilder weaves one unforeseen event, one astonishment after another into all the fascinating 'solidities of specification' of frontier life in such a way that even a young child can understand the basics of how to build a log cabin, make a smoke house out of a hollow tree, make a button lamp, or solid fuel out of hay." The verisimilitude expressed through Wilder's "vibrantly felt spirit of place" provides the young reader with "the very feel and taste and smell and bite of being a settler's daughter in the brooding Wisconsin wilderness or in the midst of the endless prairie."[34]

Wilder knew her local history, too, and when her own memory faltered (as when she insisted she was fifteen when she began teaching when she was really sixteen), she sought someone else who could fill her in on the specifics. "Every story in this novel, all the circumstances, each incident are true," Wilder insisted in the talk she gave during the book fair in Detroit in 1937. "All I have told is true but it is not the whole truth. There were some stories I wanted to tell but would not be responsible for putting in a book for children, even though I knew them as a child."[35] Wilder did her research. In 1937 and 1938, she and Almanzo headed to South Dakota to refresh their impressions of the place, and she returned with her mind brimming with facts and memo-

---

33. Wilder to Lane, July 2, 1936, Mar. 7, 1937, pp. 89, 164.

34. Cameron, review of *The First Four Years*. For James's essay, *see* "The Art of Fiction," *Longman's Magazine* 4 (1884): 502-21, esp. p. 510.

35. Wilder, Speech, p. 8.

ries of the old life for *The Long Winter*, *Little House on the Prairie*, and *These Happy Golden Years*. This pilgrimage was much like Mark Twain's return to Missouri that fueled *Life on the Mississippi* (1883) and ultimately *Adventures of Huckleberry Finn* (1884). Wilder often turned to her husband, sisters, and others from her past to fill in details she only vaguely recalled.[36]

A great deal of the "filling out" of her stories, however, was a judicious welding of her memory with her imagination. Of course, myth is often as much a part of history as facts. "But the truth is that once [Wilder] adopted the form suggested by her publisher," argued British children's literature critic Dennis Butts, "she joined the company of Walter Scott and Fenimore Cooper, and became more a historical novelist than a historian."[37] Wilder never claimed otherwise. She did research but never said she was a scholar. She wrote about historical events without ever claiming to be a historian. "My series of stories, as you know, are literally true," she explained to a correspondent in 1943, "names, dates, places, every anecdote and much of the conversation are historically and actually true."[38] To Aubrey Sherwood of De Smet, she admitted, "Like the others, [*These Happy Golden Years*] is true to facts, with touches of fiction here and there to help the interest. Some names are fictitious for which you will see the reasons." She insisted to Congressman Clarence E. Kilburn of Malone, New York, in 1945, "the names, dates and circumstances of all the books are actually true—all true—written from my own and Almanzo's memories."[39] Of course, *truth* lies in the interpretation. She understood not only the events but the motivations of her characters in doing what they did to survive storm, fire, pestilence, death. She removed any suggestion made by her daughter that seemed to her to be "unnecessary . . . unnatural and untrue to the times."[40] She stayed true to her characters.

Wilder had her own peculiar method of composition, as she explained to Lane on August 17, 1938. She began with what she called "a skeleton outline" of each book, but she did not necessarily adhere to that original scheme. "The only way I can write," she wrote Lane, "is to wander along with the story, then rewrite and re-arrange and change it everywhere." Yet, she held such faith in her daughter that when she and Almanzo were heading back to De Smet

---

36. John E. Miller, *Becoming Laura Ingalls Wilder: The Woman behind the Legend* (Columbia: University of Missouri Press, 1998), pp. 226–27.

37. Dennis Butts and Peter Hunt, *How Did Long John Silver Lose his Leg? and Twenty-Six Other Mysteries of Children's Literature* (Cambridge, UK: Lutterworth Press, 2013), p. 116.

38. Wilder to Mrs. Phraner, May 10, 1943, p. 247.

39. Wilder to Sherwood, Feb. 23, 1943, p. 242, and to Kilburn, Mar. 9, 1945, p. 268.

40. Wilder to Lane, Aug. 17, 1938, p. 177.

for Old Settlers Day in June, 1939, she wrote Lane that she was sending the manuscript of what became *The Long Winter* and instructed her where to find her notes for the next volume, which were stored in her old writing desk. She added, "You could write the last book from them and finish the series if you had to do so."[41] Fortunately nothing happened to the Wilders, and she herself was able to complete what became the remaining two volumes, *Little Town on the Prairie* and *These Happy Golden Years*.

Wilder was well aware that she was writing historical fiction. She took judicious liberties with the facts when they aided the story. "The book is not a history," she said of *By the Shores of Silver Lake*, "but a true story founded on historical fact."[42] To Lane, she admitted, "I didn't write a day by day narrative of those days in [the railroad] camp. I only wrote of the interesting events that happened. . . . Otherwise the story would be too long."[43] Always a practical writer, she focused on the primary theme of the story, which was homesteading. From time to time, she had real people doing things they never did in real life. She invented the mob scene in "Pa's Bet" (pp. 233–38). Every act, every decision had to seem logical even if it was not always the literal truth of what occurred in the past. Everything had to be true to the times and the people she was writing about.

Some people were dropped from her life, and others were created for dramatic effect. The young family who stayed with the Ingallses during the Hard Winter was written out of *The Long Winter*. Wilder invented Mr. Edwards in *Little House on the Prairie* and used him later in the series whenever he suited her purpose. She combined three girls (Nellie Owens, Genevieve Masters, and Stella Gilbert) from different points in her childhood into the one odious Nellie Oleson.[44] "It pleases me," she slyly wrote her editor at Harper, "that you dislike Nellie Oleson so much, which I suppose is un-Christian, too. She was a hateful girl."[45] She thought nothing of transplanting her old nemesis to another town when the Ingallses moved there. She seemed quite pleased to report that the real Nellie Owens's husband was arrested for embezzlement and sent to prison and their marriage ended in divorce.[46] Laura Ingalls had her flaws, too; and Wilder did not whitewash them in the story of her childhood. She freely confessed to her daughter that the girl "had a temper and it didn't grow any less as she grew larger. . . . her big boy cousins

41. Ibid.; Wilder to Lane, June 3, 1939, p. 206.
42. Wilder to Aubrey Sherwood, Nov. 18, 1939, p. 211.
43. Wilder to Lane, Jan. 25, 1938, p. 148.
44. Wilder to Lane, Mar. 7, 15, 1938, pp. 164–69.
45. Wilder to Nordstrom, May 26, 1943, p. 251.
46. Ibid., Apr. 26, 1943, p. 245.

called her a wildcat because she bit and scratched and put up a good fight on occasion."[47]

Not everything ended up in the eight books. Most noticeable was the absence of any reference to the death of her baby brother Charles Frederick in 1876. Perhaps Wilder thought the introduction of still another child might just complicate the story unnecessarily. Or the loss may have been too painful to recall. She revealed to her audience at the book fair in Detroit that it would have been inappropriate to mention the notorious Bender family of Kansas in *Little House on the Prairie* or any other children's book. The Benders ran a little tavern not far from the Ingalls homestead. Wilder distinctly recalled seeing Kate Bender standing in the doorway while Pa watered the horses one afternoon. It was later discovered that the Benders murdered travelers who stopped there. Wilder recalled how her father joined the search party that turned into a lynch mob when they caught up with the fugitives. Wilder even described in detail the manner in which the Benders must have carried out their crimes. But her memory was playing tricks on her. Charles Ingalls probably never stopped at the Bender place and was surely not a member of the search party. Laura and her family were no longer living in the area when the murders were finally discovered. Memory creates its mirages. Of course, nothing prevented Lane from freely using the Bender story in *Free Land*.

Another period in her life Wilder conveniently left out was the family's time in Iowa in 1876 and 1877. "My family did live in Burr Oak for nearly two years," she confessed in a letter to editor L. Dale Ahern, which he published in his paper the *Decorah Public Opinion* in 1947, "but I fear my memories of that time will not be very interesting as they are more of the place than the people." She admitted to another correspondent in 1951, "The reason I did not put it in my stories was that it would bring too many characters. You know in writing a story the reader's interest must be held to the principal people, not scattered among so many."[48] She was first of all a storyteller, and the story was more important than just stringing together the facts. For example, she described in *By the Shores of Silver Lake* how Laura watches the building of the railroad. It never happened, she told Lane, because Charles Ingalls would never have taken her there.[49]

She did not hesitate to mention her older sister Mary's blindness at age fourteen brought on by spinal meningitis in *By the Shores of Silver Lake*, but she refused to dwell on it. She did not want the book to be, as she wrote Lane,

---

47. Wilder to Lane, Jan. 25, 1938, p. 147.
48. Wilder to Ahern, June 18, 1947, p, 286, and to Mrs. Weldon, Nov. 5, 1951, p. 334.
49. Wilder to Lane, n.d. [ca. Dec. 1937–Jan. 1938], Box 13, file 193, Lane Papers.

"a tale of sickness and failure and death."[50] Such sorrow was not unknown in children's books. Had not Alcott found the courage to recount the death of her sister Lizzie in *Little Women*? That may be why Wilder had her sister suffer like Beth March from scarlet fever (pp. 1–2) rather than from the real disease that did blind her. Mary's condition not only infused the story with some needed pathos but also supplied another admirable example of indomitable pioneer courage: "It Can't Beat Us." It was also important to show why Laura had to take the responsibility of replacing her older sister within their family.[51]

Because they were written for boys and girls, the Little House books had to be full of pictures. So Virginia Kirkus hired one of the most respected children's book illustrators of the time, Helen Sewell, to do the drawings. Despite her wide reputation, Sewell was an odd choice for this particular example of Americana. She was a modernist who worked in what was later called Art Deco. She provided vignettes that were more decorative than dramatic; and like the text, they were nebulous about any specific time and place. Her flat, stylized, geometric shapes and expressionless doll-like figures certainly had their charm, and her crosshatching and stipling suggested nineteenth-century engraving. Their *faux naif* manner betrayed more than just a hint of American folk art then being rediscovered and appreciated. At Kirkus's suggestion, Wilder provided some personal mementos to guide the illustrator in accurately depicting the people, place, and period of the story. These included an 1860 daguerreotype of Charles and Caroline Ingalls that Sewell copied for the half-title page in *Little House in the Big Woods*, but there was nothing particularly Victorian about her approach to the material. The benign jacket design was especially misleading; Laura and sister Mary at the front door of their cabin, surrounded by rabbit, deer, owl, squirrel, and bear, suggested they lived in Edward Hicks's *Peaceable Kingdom*. The illustrations supported the storybook nature of the narrative. Although Wilder was referring to a specific time and place in American history in her children's books, she was rather cavalier about dates and other specifics within the story. She was no longer writing an autobiography but rather a novel inspired by her biography.

Helen Sewell is nearly forgotten now, which is unjust. Although she never won the Caldecott Medal, she was an exceptional picture-book artist (even if her stories were weak). If remembered at all among bibliophiles and rare-book librarians, it is almost solely for her work on Laura Ingalls Wilder's

---

50. Wilder to Lane, Jan. 28, 1938, pp. 153–54.
51. Ibid., Jan. 26, 1938, p. 152.

Illustrator Helen Sewell based the half-title page of *Little House in the Big Woods* on a daguerreotype of Caroline and Charles Ingalls that Wilder had supplied.

books. Beginning with the fourth one, *On the Banks of Plum Creek* (1937), another artist, Mildred Boyle, joined Sewell in illustrating the series. They provided such a perfect marriage of styles that one can hardly tell where Sewell begins and Boyle ends. Illustrators had less clout then than they do now. Sewell was paid a flat fee of two hundred dollars for the pictures for *Little House in the Big Woods* and apparently did not retain copyright on any of her illustrations in the series. On the whole, Wilder approved the pictures in her books. On only one known occasion did she strongly object to a detail. She protested that Laura's cheeks were so overly be-rouged on Boyle's jacket of *Little Town on the Prairie* that they were dutifully toned down in the second printing of the book.[52] The author, who wore little to no makeup herself, must have thought the cover girl looked like a streetwalker.

Another popular assumption about the Little House books is that famed

---

52. Wilder to Raymond, Sept. 26, 1935, p. 80; Pamela Smith Hill, *Laura Ingalls Wilder: A Writer's Life* (Pierre: South Dakota Historical Society Press, 2007), p. 183.

Harper's children's book editor Ursula Nordstrom fashioned Laura Ingalls Wilder into the great writer she became. The truth was Nordstrom merely inherited Wilder when Ida Louise Raymond retired from Harper & Brothers in 1940. Of course, Nordstrom as editorial assistant read early drafts as they crossed Raymond's desk and wrote some jacket-flap copy, but she did not take charge of the series until the *sixth* book, *The Long Winter*. Nordstrom was as quirky as she was skillful. Although famous for "discovering" such important modern children's book writers and illustrators as Maurice Sendak, Tomi Ungerer, Louise Fitzhugh, and Shel Silverstein, she no more made Wilder an important children's book author than she did E. B. White. His first children's book, *Stuart Little* (1945), was literally dropped on her desk because she was head of the Department of Books for Boys and Girls at Harper's. (For every famous children's book author or illustrator she published, there must have been another dozen unremarkable ones.) Nordstrom's editing of Wilder, like that of White, was miniscule. One of the few significant suggestions she did make was changing the title "The Hard Winter" to the less bleak *The Long Winter*. "None of the [Wilder] manuscripts ever needed any editing," she later confessed. "Not any."[53] By this time, Wilder was so confident of her literary powers that she no longer relied on her daughter's editorial input, either.

Perhaps Nordstrom's most important contribution to the series was repackaging it with new illustrations by her pet illustrator Garth Williams. The English-born artist seemed as odd a choice as Sewell and Boyle for this great American saga, but he had already made a hit with his spirited pictures for White's *Stuart Little* in 1945. The Laura Ingalls Wilder uniform edition was the most ambitious project of his long career, and he was determined to get his drawings just right. To get every detail down exactly, he meticulously retraced the circuitous route of the Wilder family across the American frontier. He went to see Lane in Connecticut, and she urged him to visit her parents. (Neither Sewell nor Boyle ever met Wilder.) On arriving with his wife and daughter at Rocky Ridge Farm, near Mansfield, Missouri, in September 1947, he found Wilder weeding the garden and Almanzo off doing his chores. Williams sketched while they went over family photographs and discussed details of her life as a pioneer girl. "She understood the meaning

---

53. Nordstrom to Doris K. Stotz, Jan. 11, 1967, in *Dear Genius: The Letters of Ursula Nordstrom*, ed. Leonard Marcus (New York: HarperCollins, 1998), p. 234. *See also* Nordstrom to Wilder, Sept. 9, 1937, p. 3, and to Zena Sutherland, Nov. 18, 1969. For Nordstrom's suggestion of a title change for *The Long Winter*, *see* George Bye to Lane, n.d. [May 1940], James Oliver Brown Papers, Rare Book and Manuscript Library, Columbia University, New York, N.Y.

of hardship and struggle, of joy and work, of shyness and bravery," he said of Wilder after the new edition came out in 1953. "She was never overcome by drabness or squalor. She never glamorized anything; yet she saw the loveliness in everything."[54]

Wilder was equally impressed with the young artist. "When he visited here," she reported to Nordstrom, "he sat surrounded by old family photographs and while Mrs. Williams and I visited he was busy making drawings from the old pictures, so I am sure his illustrations will be authentic."[55] One thing she was adamant about: Jack the bulldog would have to look more like the real breed in Williams's pictures than he did in Sewell's. "I feel sure," she informed Nordstrom, "his illustrations of my stories will be beautiful."[56] He had to follow a similar approach to the material in his illustrations; there could be, he recalled, "no glamorizing for him either; no giving everyone a permanent wave."[57] The publisher's original intention was to print the pictures in color, but Williams settled on a homey, less ambitious style in his soft black-and-white pencil drawings rather than his usual crisp, clean pen-and-ink work. Despite their aim toward accuracy, they tended to romanticize that life as much as Wilder's words did.

Wilder could not quite comprehend why it took so many years for the new edition to be completed, but she could not have been happier when it finally came out in 1953. "The books are beautiful and I am so pleased with them," she wrote Nordstrom when *Little House in the Big Woods* and *On the Banks of Plum Creek* arrived in the mail. "The illustrations seem to bring the characters to life. Garth has done a grand job in these two books and I am impatient to see the others."[58] She happily supplied Nordstrom with a short-and-sweet endorsement of the project: "Mary, Laura and their folks live again in these illustrations."[59] There was only one problem: "I wish Laura's hair had always been shown in braids. She never wore it with a bow on top of her head or with a bang across her forehead."[60] Nevertheless, so many generations of children have grown up with the Garth Williams pictures that

---

54. Williams, "Illustrating the Little House Books," *The Horn Book* 29 (Dec. 1953): 422.

55. Wilder to Nordstrom, Mar. 14, 1953, p. 349.

56. Ibid., Nov. 3, 1947, p. 291.

57. Williams, "Illustrating the Little House Books," p. 422. For more on Williams's work on Wilder's books, *see* Elizabeth K. Wallace and James D. Wallace, *Garth Williams, American Illustrator: A Life* (New York: Beaufort Books, 2016), pp. 61–95.

58. Wilder to Nordstrom, June 6, 1953, p. 353.

59. Wilder, quoted by Anderson, *Selected Letters*, p. 355.

60. Wilder to Nordstrom, Nov. 22, 1952, p. 344.

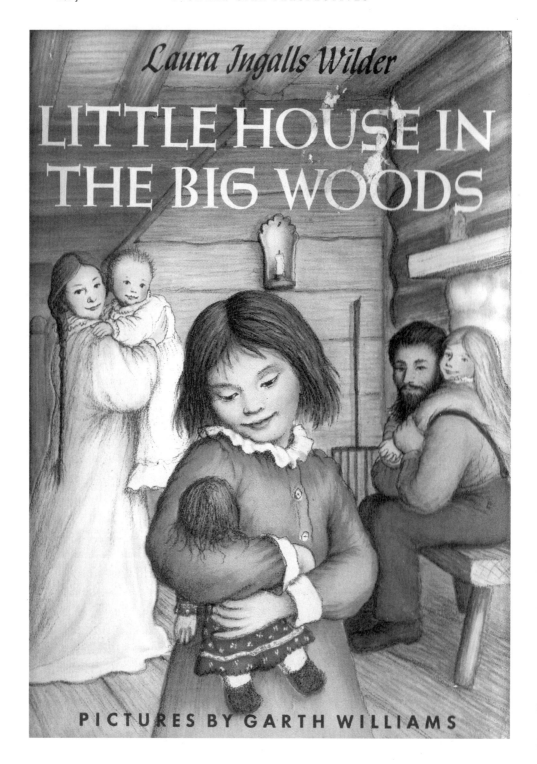

they are today indelibly linked to the books rather than the original ones by Sewell and Boyle. Most people have forgotten that they were ever illustrated by anyone else. The final result of Williams's diligent research was the production of one of the great illustrated classics of juvenile literature. Wilder and Williams were as perfect a match as Lewis Carroll and John Tenniel in the two Alice books, L. Frank Baum and W. W. Denslow in *The Wonderful Wizard of Oz*, and A. A. Milne and E. H. Shepard in the four Winnie the Pooh books.

As far as literary awards were concerned, Laura Ingalls Wilder was generally a bridesmaid but never the bride. Beginning with *On the Banks of Plum Creek*, the remaining five Little House books were all named runner-ups for the Newbery Medal by the American Library Association. (Runner-ups are now called Newbery Honor Books.) She lost to Kate Seredy's *The White Stag* (1937), James Daugherty's *Daniel Boone* (1939), Armstrong Sperry's *Call It Courage* (1940), Walter D. Edmonds's *The Matchlock Gun* (1941), and Esther Forbes's *Johnny Tremain* (1943)—works of dubious literary distinction and rarely read today. Perhaps the idea that each Wilder title was a part of an on-going series, then an anathema to librarians (even among the most fervent of her admirers), prevented her from winning the gold prize.[61]

This glaring injustice was finally corrected in 1954 when the American Library Association established the Laura Ingalls Wilder Award to be bestowed every five years for "a substantial and lasting contribution to literature for children."[62] (It was changed to three years and then two; it is currently presented annually.) Nordstrom felt that the reillustrated edition was largely responsible for the establishment of the award, and that Williams's new pictures in particular had an enormous influence on the decision. Appropriately, Laura Ingalls Wilder was the first to receive the Laura Ingalls Wilder Medal specially designed by (appropriately) Garth Williams. At one time, it could well have been nicknamed "The Overlooked Prize," for on occasion it recognized other American juvenile authors and illustrators who had long been slighted by the Newbery and Caldecott committees. Perhaps because *Charlotte's Web* lost in 1953 to a book hardly anyone reads any more (Ann Nolan Clark's *Secret of the Andes*), E. B. White got the medal in 1970. Illustrator/author Eric Carle, who has never been named for even a Caldecott Honor Book, was recognized in 2003. The only posthumous winner has been James Marshall in 2007, fifteen years after his death from AIDS. (His *Goldilocks*

---

61. "Newbery Medal and Honor Books, 1922–Present," Association for Library Services to Children, American Library Association, ala.org.

62. "About the Laura Ingalls Wilder Award," ibid.

*and the Three Bears* was named a runner-up in 1989, but he never won the Caldecott Medal.) Today, however, the Laura Ingalls Wilder Medal is often bestowed on those who have won almost every other prize possible.[63]

Sales of Wilder's books continued to soar as each new title created a demand for the backlist and new generations of children discovered them. With their emphasis on domestic chores, the Little House books were generally considered girls' books, but little boys liked them, too. Not only did librarians universally embrace the series, but teachers adopted them in school curricula around the country. Chapters were reprinted in textbooks, and Wilder approved editions in Braille. The State of Ohio alone ordered thirty-five hundred copies of a special edition of *Little House on the Prairie* for use in schools in 1941. And children, when introduced to just one of the titles, hunted up all the others to read. The publishers also arranged foreign translations of individual titles. "Though you are far away and speak a different language," Wilder wrote the children of Japan in 1948, "still the things worthwhile in life are the same for us all and the same as when I was a child so long ago."[64] Her good old solid American virtues were now being exported around the globe.

The success of Wilder's humble little books inspired what the *Charleston* (N.C.) *News and Courier* called "the plethora of pioneer stories,"[65] now almost all forgotten. Elizabeth Coatsworth, Alice Dalgliesh, Walter D. Edmonds, Elizabeth Enright, Rachel Field, Lois Lenski, Armstrong Sperry, and so many other once-admired children's book authors wrote an abundance of juvenile American historical fiction. Except perhaps for Carol Ryrie Brink's Newbery Medal winner *Caddie Woodlawn* (1936), only the Little House books are still read today. Their reputation as representative of the American spirit at its finest was legendary. "Like the work of her great contemporary, the late Willa Cather," as observed in a *Kansas City Times* editorial, "Mrs. Wilder's writing has the simplicity of a fine art. Each book is a small masterpiece of its kind and the cumulative effect of the whole series is greater than that of any of its parts."[66] The general consensus was that Wilder's books were perfect, that not a word could be changed. Written in artless and deceptively effortless prose, they were above criticism.

It made no difference what others said so long as the books sold. And

---

63. "Laura Ingalls Wilder Award, Past Winners," ibid.; Nordstrom to Garth Williams, in *Dear Genius*, pp. 74–76.

64. Wilder to Japanese Children, July 8, 1948, p. 301. *See also* p. 235.

65. *Charleston* (S.C.) *News and Courier*, Jan. 9, 1949.

66. "Child on the Frontier" (editorial), *Kansas City Times*, May 24, 1955.

they did. By 1939, the steady income from the series allowed the Wilders the luxury of being no longer dependent on their child's beneficence. As far as the publishing business was concerned, Wilder proved to be anything but a pushover. She was not a sweet old grandma sitting in her rocker, watching the world pass her by. She was a shrewd negotiator who instructed her agent to get her better deals with her publisher. Both mother and daughter were disappointed with the original terms, particularly for *Farmer Boy*, which earned a five-percent royalty. (She was earning about twelve hundred dollars a year in royalties by 1936, about the equivalent of twenty-one thousand dollars today.) She readily accepted whatever Harper & Brothers was offering her for *On the Banks of Plum Creek*, but terms began to improve with the next titles. Wilder urged Bye to get Harper to increase her royalty and refused to allow the publisher to take twenty-five percent of the motion-picture rights. Lane was now more interested in writing about politics than fiction; and so rapidly did her career decline that her mother generously arranged with her agent in 1949 to pay Lane ten percent of her royalties. This late acknowledgment, however, did not mean that her contribution to the development of the series should ever be made public. Until the day she died in 1968, Lane never revealed the secret, *their* secret.[67]

Laura Ingalls Wilder officially retired with the publication of *These Happy Golden Years* in 1943. "Mrs. Wilder is entitled to a rest," the *Kansas City Times* editor defended her decision in 1955. "She has earned it with eight volumes that have already taken a secure place in the literature of childhood."[68] No inducement, however lucrative, could make her return to writing. "I wrote all seven after the first one trying to stop and not being allowed," she told Kiewit of the *Kansas City Star* in 1955. "But now I'm 88 and I'm tired, and no one is going to get me to write any more." After her husband died at age ninety-two in 1949, Wilder sold the farmland and all the stock but retained the house and yard. "I'm not afraid to be living here, by myself, just cautious," she assured Kiewit. "You see, I have a little gun in a cabinet by the screen door. I've got a shotgun in my bedroom and I know how to use them both." On February 10, 1957, Laura Ingalls Wilder died from diabetes and cardiac problems at home, just days after her ninetieth birthday.[69]

Now considered modern classics by America's teachers and librarians, the Little House books became the keystone of the Harper backlist, along with

---

67. Anderson, quoting Lane, *Selected Letters*, pp. 97–98; Wilder to Bye, July 10, 1939, p. 209, June 21, 1940, p. 216, July 3, 15, 1941, pp. 229–30, and July 16, 1949, pp. 310–11.

68. "Child on the Frontier."

69. Anderson, *Selected Letters*, pp. 374–75.

Laura Ingalls Wilder at the Mansfield, Missouri, library in 1951.
*Laura Ingalls Wilder Memorial Society*

E. B. White's *Charlotte's Web* (1952) and Maurice Sendak's *Where the Wild Things Are* (1963). As early as 1955, Ursula Nordstrom was urging Wilder to get George Bye to sell the TV rights to the series. Westerns were all the rage on the three networks, but these oaters were all shoot-em-ups, and there seemed to be no real place at the time for a quiet little show about domestic frontier life. Everything changed in 1971 with the surprising success of *The Waltons,* set in the Virginia hills during the Great Depression and World War II. Every network now was hot for family entertainment. From 1974 to 1983, NBC produced a highly lucrative series only loosely based on the Little House books (and four made-for-television movies), all starring Michael Landon as "Pa." The show did much to keep the stories selling while further muddying the popular image of Laura Ingalls Wilder. It mattered little that clean-shaven Little Joe from *Bonanza* looked nothing like the real Charles Ingalls with his Smith Brothers beard. Historical accuracy was never a priority of the producers; and several episodes were more *Bonanza* than *Little House on the Prairie.*

The great success of the TV show in the more politically aware 1970s demanded a reevaluation of the content of the original books. What is not always apparent to young readers is the endemic racism of the times that is reflected in the series. While a black doctor does treat the Ingallses in *Little House on the Prairie*, the picture of the minstrel show complete with Pa in blackface (p. 258) in *Little Town on the Prairie* is especially alarming in the 2004 full-color edition. The treatment of the Indians in *Little House on the Prairie* is also problematical. It is never revealed in the books that Pa is actually trespassing on Osage land when he homesteads in Kansas. Of course, Wilder would not have known that when she was child. When two Osages enter the Ingalls home in *Little House on the Prairie*, Wilder described them as "two naked, wild men" in skunk skins with eyes "black and still and glittering, like snake's eyes" (p. 134). That may honestly be what she and other settlers felt at the time, but it is still a chilling comparison. "Land knows, they'd never do anything with this country themselves," Mrs. Scott complains to Ma about the Indians. "All they do is roam over it like wild animals. Treaties or no treaties, the land belongs to folks that'll farm it. That's only common sense and justice." The tension between native and settler that festers throughout the book apparently goes back to "the Minnesota massacre" (p. 211), now known as the Dakota War of 1862.

Wilder made a few editorial concessions as issues were brought to her attention. She dropped "Old Zip Coon" from the list of tunes Pa played on his fiddle in the Christmas chapter of *Little House in the Big Woods*. But what was the purpose of quoting "Uncle Ned ... gone where the good darkeys go"

(p. 100) in Chapter 5? Wilder and Nordstrom had pondered a similar song in *Little Town on the Prairie,* at which time Wilder wrote: "It is an old song and was sung as written. . . . It seems no one should be offended at the term 'darkies.'"[70] And yet some people were and are, although no one seemed to mind a particularly offensive slip of the pen in the opening of *Little House on the Prairie* until 1952: "There the wild animals wandered and fed as though they were in a pasture that stretched much farther than a man could see, and there were no people. Only Indians lived there."[71] The wording implied that Indians are not people, and Wilder was horrified when Nordstrom pointed it out to her, agreeing to replace "people" with "settlers."[72] Likewise, she readily changed the name of the lake in *Farmer Boy* from "Chatauqua" to "Chateaugay" when a distant relative of Almanzo's in Malone informed her of her error in 1951.[73]

Beginning with *The Birchbark House* in 1999, National Book Award-winner Louise Erdrich replied to the Little House books with her own multi-volume series, also published by HarperCollins. Drawing on her Ojibwa family history, Erdrich countered the false attitudes of Wilder's work toward American Indians by demonstrating that natives in the same parts of the country had as vital a story to tell as did any of the settlers. "I didn't start out that way," she explained, "but I'm awfully glad when people do read *The Birchbark House* and the rest of the books along with the Little House on the Prairie books, because one of the things about the Laura Ingalls Wilder books that always distresses me is Ma's racism. She's a terrible racist about native people." Erdrich viewed the "inherent racism in the structure of the Wilder books themselves" as "the simple acceptance of the fact that the Little House characters could just go along and take whatever they wanted and that the native people were apparently vanishing into the sunset. The natives were portrayed as vanishing people who were going to go away. And that's all that one could feel about them."[74]

Wilder herself recognized this injustice to the indigenous peoples of this country but not in the Little House books. She confessed in her diary of the 1894 trip from South Dakota to Missouri that became *On the Way Home* (1962), "If I had been the Indians I would have scalped more white folks

---

70. Wilder to Nordstrom, May 21, 1953, p. 352. *See also* the Christmas play list in Wilder, *Pioneer Girl,* p. 35.

71. Wilder, *Little House on the Prairie,* 1st ed. (New York: Harper & Bros., 1935), p. 1.

72. Wilder to Nordstrom, Oct. 4, 1952, p. 343; Hill, *Laura Ingalls Wilder,* pp. 190–91.

73. Wilder to Dorothy Smith, Jan. 31, 1951, p. 328.

74. Erdrich, quoted in "Louise Erdrich: In-depth Written Interview," Oct. 23, 2009, TeachingBooks.net, teachingbooks.net/interview.cgi?id=63&a=1.

before I ever would have left it [the land near the James River]."[75] Erdrich wanted to bring her own family alive for young readers and to correct the stereotypes still so widely promulgated in other American juvenile literature. Erdrich herself provided the illustrations in the manner of Garth Williams, and her series is often assigned side by side with Wilder's work. "The migration across Minnesota into the Dakotas, and the warmth of family life, is something that these books have in common with the Little House series," she told *The Horn Book* in 2012. "I am happy that they are being read together, as the Native experience of early western settlement is so often missing in middle-grade history classes."[76] Erdrich's saga fills in the blanks of this incomplete history of the American frontier.

But why have the Little House books endured while all the other contemporary children's books based on American history (and there were many) have disappeared? Their influence has been so vast that no American girl or boy can survive childhood without encountering little Laura and the rest of the Ingalls family sometime along the way. Wilder's books are primarily tales of personal survival. "I think what a man needs most is good straight common sense," Almanzo Wilder informed his daughter in 1939. "Our richest men did not have college education, they just had good common sense."[77] The structure of the books does not vary greatly from one title to the next, a year in the life of the Ingalls family revealed through the passing of the seasons. Was her life story really that different from that of thousands of others at the same time in American history? Plot is less important than verisimilitude. What does it matter if not every single incident is factually accurate? These books maintain, throughout eight volumes, the veneer of truth.

Not much really happens in the stories. Life is not a series of exciting adventures. Instead, the Little House books describe meticulously how things were done in the old days. "One of the things that I always liked about the Little House on the Prairie books," Erdrich admitted, "was the specificity of everything that the family made or used."[78] The books also propagate the old, basic American values. "This plain account focuses on ordinary lives, but that is why it is so thrilling and engrossing," Eden Ross Lipson, children's book editor of the *New York Times*, summarized. "The family's ordinary lives are so far from our own, unimaginably remote to today's children. But the

---

75. Wilder, *On the Way Home: The Diary of a Trip from South Dakota to Mansfield, Missouri, in 1894* (New York: Harper & Row, 1962), pp. 23–24.

76. Erdrich, quoted in Martha V. Parravano, "Five Questions for Louise Erdrich," *The Horn Book*, Sept. 12, 2012, hbook.com.

77. Almanzo Wilder to Lane, Jan. 15, 1939, in *Selected Letters*, p. 185.

78. Quoted in "Erdrich: In-Depth Written Interview."

lesson the books taught me, and still teach without comment, is that there is dignity, honor, and pleasure in work well done."[79] Famed children's book illustrator and writer Maurice Sendak brilliantly summed up the special appeal of these classic stories of pioneer life. "Calmly and clearly [Wilder] illustrates the courage necessary to live an ordinary life," he explained. "She is not concerned with fantasy heroics but with falling down and getting up, being ill and recovering. What is important, she says, is to continue. In persevering, you will discover triumphs." Wilder's books taught him, while recovering from a heart attack, "how to behave admirably in adversity."[80] And the message is revealed through the eyes of an American child as she grows up with the country.

Perhaps Wilder herself best defined the appeal of her work. "The Little House books are stories of long ago," she wrote the children of Chicago in 1947. "The way we live and your schools are much different now, so many changes have made living and learning easier. But the real things haven't changed. It is still best to be honest and truthful; to make the most of what we have; to be happy with simple pleasures and to be cheerful and have courage when things go wrong." Any young reader, whether girl or boy, can identify with Laura. And this sense of identification is international. This great American family saga has sold at last count over 60 million copies in thirty-three languages. "Things of real value do not change with the passing of years nor in going from one country to another," Wilder assured her Japanese readers in 1948 as she had the children of Chicago the year before. "These I am sure you have. It is always best to be honest and truthful; to make the most of what we have; to be happy with simple pleasures, to be cheerful in adversity and have courage in danger."[81] All these qualities she amply supplied in the tales of her childhood. Young readers still discover this great vast world with all its joys and dangers just as she did. The Great American Myth is safe with them.

79. Lipson, commentary on the Little House Books, in *Everything I Need to Know I Learned from a Children's Book: Life Lessons from Notable People from All Walks of Life*, ed. Anita Silvey (New York: Roaring Brook Press, 2009), p. 119.

80. Sendak, quoted in Katie Roiphe, *The Violet Hour: Great Writers at the End* (New York: Dial Press, 2016), p. 227.

81. Wilder, *Selected Letters,* pp. 284, 301.

# { 6 }
# Her Stories Take You with Her
## *The Lasting Appeal of Laura Ingalls Wilder*

NOEL L. SILVERMAN

*Editor's Note:* Just as Laura Ingalls Wilder's novels spoke to the imagination of readers during the Great Depression, her memoir, written in the same time period and published as *Pioneer Girl: The Annotated Autobiography* in 2014, awoke the interest of a new generation of readers even as it satisfied the curiosity of those who had read the novels in the 1950s or watched the television series in the 1970s and 1980s. Without the cooperation of the Little House Heritage Trust, however, *Pioneer Girl* would not have been published. And without the insightful comments of Noel Silverman, the representative of the Trust, the book would not be what it is. He served as Wilder's surrogate in the preparation of the autobiography for publication, sharing his ideas with the editorial team of the Pioneer Girl Project, suggesting avenues of research, and commenting on the editing and annotations. It was he who pointed out, for example, that Wilder failed to prepare her adult readers for the abrupt introduction of new siblings: "Did no one notice anything before they just found a new little baby had joined them, seemingly out of nowhere? A footnote?"[1] While Wilder grew up in an era when pregnancy was not openly discussed, the rest of us had not, and as Silverman suggested, the modern reader needed some context.[2]

To give a little context to the man himself, Noel Silverman is an attorney specializing in copyright and literary property. He began representing Roger MacBride, who had inherited the rights to Laura Ingalls Wilder's works as well as those of Rose Wilder Lane, shortly after Lane's death in 1968. Following MacBride's death in 1995, his daughter Abigail assigned all of the copyrighted literary property she had inherited from her father to the Little House Heritage Trust, which Silverman has represented since that time. Both he and Abigail MacBride have been and continue to be vital partners in the Pio-

---

1. Silverman to Nancy Tystad Koupal, Mar. 17, 2014.
2. *See* Wilder, *Pioneer Girl: The Annotated Autobiography*, ed. Pamela Smith Hill (Pierre: South Dakota Historical Society Press, 2014), p. 84n64.

neer Girl Project, which could not have proceeded without their approval. Here, in a retrospective interview, Silverman shared with me his thoughts about the publication of *Pioneer Girl: The Annotated Autobiography* and offered his perspectives on Wilder's writing, gained through nearly fifty years of close association with her works and those of Rose Wilder Lane.

NTK: The South Dakota Historical Society Press, with Pamela Smith Hill as editor, successfully presented its ideas to the Little House Heritage Trust and gained the right to publish Wilder's original handwritten autobiography. What convinced the Trust that what the Press and Hill proposed to do would work? Did you expect the final publication to be as popular as it is?

NS: The Trust believed that a scholarly treatment by a historical society press—with an offer to put the work into the hands of a Wilder scholar who was interested in annotating it—was a much better complement to the Little House books than a commercial publication, which would compete with its progeny and essentially depend on sales in an uncertain marketplace for its survival. I could not help but believe that an annotated autobiography would be joyfully received by scholars, lay readers, and fans of Little House books alike, each for their own reasons.

NTK: What was your reaction when you first read *Pioneer Girl: The Annotated Autobiography*? Was there any information that the book revealed about Wilder's life and the era in which she lived that surprised you?

NS: I think Pamela Smith Hill and the editors of the Pioneer Girl Project did a wonderful job in introducing and annotating Wilder's *Pioneer Girl*. There are many things I like about the book, but in particular, I think the maps and photographs lend a dimension and an immediacy to the Wilder story that I have not previously experienced.

*Pioneer Girl: The Annotated Autobiography* is a very fine work, full of valuable information about the underlying manuscript itself, the major works that were based upon it, its author, and the people—most notably Wilder's daughter Rose Wilder Lane—who shaped and guided the process. I have for years now considered myself reasonably knowledgeable about the world of Little House and, to a lesser extent, the world of Laura Ingalls Wilder—two substantially overlapping but nevertheless different worlds. Yet, after reading *The Annotated Autobiography* and reviewing yet again various portions of Wilder's other works, I cannot help but acknowledge how much I did not know, and still do not know.

NTK: The attention that *Pioneer Girl: The Annotated Autobiography* has received has raised a broader, historical awareness of Laura Ingalls Wilder's life and work, popularizing longstanding debates that have mostly been discussed by scholars and avid fans. What effect do you think this wider awareness has had on Wilder's legacy?

NS: The publication will, I think, over time prove an invaluable resource to anyone interested in understanding the transformation that occurred between the historical record that Wilder created in the writing of *Pioneer Girl* and the works of literature that she created in the writing of the Little House books. The book is also a valuable contribution to the history of the period and an even more valuable contribution to the context, which turns a childlike narrative into an important historical document.

I think the most dramatic revelation, at least for me, is the awareness that somewhere along the way Wilder changed from a scribe to an artist. I doubt very much that the change was conscious on her part; rather, it seems more an evolving realization that the description of a series of events needs to be tailored or fashioned for the audience for whom it is intended, and that effective storytelling changes from audience to audience. A great writer perhaps has the ability to reach a wider audience than do his or her less-distinguished colleagues, but the key to success still lies in knowing for whom your story is intended and finding a way to reach that audience.

NTK: Many literary critics have commented on Rose Wilder Lane's role in the success of the Little House books. What is your view of the Wilder-Lane collaboration?

NS: I think *Pioneer Girl: The Annotated Autobiography* sets to rest, if it needs setting to rest, the notion that the Little House books were really written by Laura's daughter Rose, based on raw material provided by Laura. It is not my intention to disparage Rose's contribution—most writers benefit greatly from the services of a good editor, and Rose was certainly that. Indeed, it is likely that the Little House books would never have appeared in print but for Rose's invaluable assistance and skills in organizing, focusing, and editing; in short, understanding her mother's objective and helping her to achieve it. For all of that, she deserves full credit. But that Laura wrote the books is beyond question, as *Pioneer Girl* helps to demonstrate. It is interesting, and ironic, that *Let the Hurricane Roar* and *Free Land*, both of which Rose wrote using her mother's recollections and recitation of the facts in her autobiography, are today little more than historical artifacts.

I think Laura's evolution came about as a result of her interaction with Rose and her realization of what Harper & Brothers was accepting for publication. Her original manuscript was intended for an older readership. When she realized that these readers were no longer her principal audience, her style changed in order to accommodate the new reality. Her relationship with Rose changed in the process. I do not want to suggest that I know more than I know. I do want to suggest that Laura was a talented writer from the outset, quick to understand the transition that was needed and able to accommodate the change. As I have said before, I neither dispute nor disparage Rose's contribution. It does not, at least for me, diminish or recast Laura's contribution. Rose deserves full credit as editor, and a very good one at that. Laura deserves full credit as author. Neither would have been the same without the other.

NTK: As you said earlier, you consider yourself "reasonably knowledgeable" about the Little House world, and I know you to be a thoughtful steward of the Wilder/Lane legacy. What have your many years of working with scholars and fans in safeguarding that legacy taught you about the reasons for Wilder's ongoing popularity?

NS: Laura is a classic underdog who began life with few material advantages apart from a close-knit loving family; who, growing up, faced natural hardships without end on a physical frontier that was as unforgiving as could be imagined; who had no one to depend on other than her immediate family (and they on her)—Laura's story is more one of interdependence than independence. She was small in stature, which limited her physical contributions. She was female, which, given the time and the place, limited her opportunities. Her family was poor, at least in terms of purchasing power, which meant that what she and they did not create for themselves they mostly went without.

Despite these seeming disadvantages, Laura triumphed not in a material sense (at least not prior to becoming a successful author in her sixties) but in a spiritual sense, which most readers quickly recognize as being of greater value. Her baby brother died in infancy. Her older sister became blind as the result of an illness. Her husband contracted diphtheria during an epidemic, leaving him seriously disabled. All these things mattered greatly, but none of them defeated her.

Laura experienced prairie fire, grasshopper infestation, and blizzard conditions, all of which seriously impeded her family's livelihood. There was little that nature did not send her way, if not to test her resolve, then at least to express its indifference to her welfare, let alone her comfort. And yet she persevered. As did her Pa and her Ma. And her sisters. And her husband. They were beset from all sides, and they extracted from all that adversity a sense of how lucky they were—how fortunate to have each other, to have an opportunity, to have an awareness that the glass was half full rather than half empty, to understand that, while no one owed them a

Laura stands barely a few inches above a friend's
young daughter at this gathering in Mansfield, Missouri, 1948.
*Laura Ingalls Wilder Memorial Society*

livelihood, they had every reason to be proud of the livelihood they made for themselves, and that they were still more fortunate than those who had less than they, little though that was.

It is not that failure was endemic to her lifestyle, although it often described the reality. It is not that she had easy answers. It is that she, and her Ma, and her Pa, and her sisters, and her husband, had durability, and sensitivity, and a sense of humor, and the ability not to take personally those things over which they had only ineffectual control at best. In spite of everything, they knew they had the ability to contribute to the control of their destinies.

All kinds of readers can relate to that attitude, draw strength from it, measure it against their own circumstances, reflect upon, cheer for, commiserate with, and, perhaps above all else, follow it with a sense of genuine interest, notwithstanding that most will never experience such obstacles. Laura and her family had no choice but to deal with each one, and each one was part of daily life in a setting that readers can only imagine, which

Laura Ingalls Wilder worked on her novels
at her writing desk in the Rocky Ridge farmhouse.
*Laura Ingalls Wilder Historic Home and Museum*

keeps one turning pages to see how they dealt with seemingly never-ending challenges, how they dealt with growth and the absence of growth, how they dealt with seasons and contingencies and death and new life.

Laura always came back for more, without always knowing what that "more" might be, and her readers and followers and casual observers and serious students also came back for more. And they continue to do so, to observe, compare, imagine, predict, empathize, criticize, and fantasize. And to wonder what they would do in her place.

NTK: Any final thoughts on why Wilder's work continues to resonate with today's readers?

NS: There is a thought that I'd like to come back to for a moment. I have suggested that this story is one of interdependence more than independence. The difference, I think, is crucial, and it creates a narrative somewhat different from the one that celebrates the idea of doing everything on one's own. It also attracts a somewhat different kind of readership, perhaps even a broader and more inclusive kind of readership.

This narrative says that I can build a better house, faster, if Mr. Edwards will help me, in return for which I will gladly help him build his house. It says that I can bring a child into this world if that kindly neighbor woman will help me through my labor, in return for which I will gladly do the same for her, or do whatever else it is she needs done. It says I can get along, sightless, if my sister will help me to "see," in return for which I will gladly help her with her lessons or her chores or whatever else she needs help with. It says Clarence and some of the other students in the class that I teach may be bigger and older than I am, but I can command their respect by respecting them, acknowledging their contribution to the common objective. It says those things many times, many ways. The message is always the same. We help ourselves when we help each other.

Wilder's ongoing popularity is largely a consequence of the message she conveyed, although it was more often than not conveyed subliminally. Her stories take you with her and deliver you to a place where, without having listened to a lecture, you recognize that you bear principal responsibility for the things over which you exercise control, and that you often have more influence over those things than you perhaps first imagined. Action is important. Decency is important. Perseverance works. Reciprocity works. Compassion works.

And if, with her pencils and notebooks, Wilder is able to capture the imaginations of emerging generations of young people, and innumerable others who happen upon her writings, and bring smiles of self-recognition to their faces at the end of an often-difficult journey, well, so much the better.

# Wilder's Place and Time

# { 7 }
# Laura Ingalls Wilder as a Midwestern Pioneer Girl

## JOHN E. MILLER

Laura Ingalls Wilder was many things, and her devoted readers and fans, as well as literary scholars, have thought about her in many different ways. Beyond being a much-beloved children's author, she can be seen as, among other things, a memoirist, a popularizer of history, a small-town nostalgist, a journalist, a moralist, a conservative political thinker, a writer who sought to bolster people's morale during the Great Depression, a representative woman, and a heroine to huge numbers of enthusiastic devotees. One of the most prominent ways to look at her is as a chronicler of the American frontier. She called the autobiography she completed in 1930 *Pioneer Girl*, and in a book-week speech in Detroit in 1937, she made one of the most revealing comments she ever made about her own literary career. While responding to letters written to her after the publication of her first novel, *Little House in the Big Woods* (1932), she said:

> I began to think what a wonderful childhood I had had. How I had seen the whole *frontier*, the woods, the Indian country of the great plains, the *frontier towns*, the building of railroads in wild, unsettled country, homesteading and farmers coming in to take possession.
>
> I realized that I had seen and lived it all—all the successive phases of the *frontier*, first the *frontiersman*[,] then the *pioneer*, then the farmers and the towns.
>
> Then I understood that in my own life I represented a whole period of American history.[1]

It is understandable that someone who had grown up on the frontier characterized herself as a pioneer girl. It is worthwhile to consider, however, that every place where Wilder lived as a child and as an adult, with the exception

---

1. Wilder, Speech, Detroit Book Fair, Oct. 16, 1937, Box 13, file 197, Laura Ingalls Wilder Series, Rose Wilder Lane Papers, Herbert Hoover Presidential Library, West Branch, Iowa (emphasis added). This speech is reprinted elsewhere in this volume.

Laura Ingalls Wilder at the age of seventeen in 1884 had already lived on several American frontiers. *Laura Ingalls Wilder Historic Home and Museum*

of a single year spent in Florida as a young married woman, was in what is now termed the Midwest or Middle West.

In considering people's life stories, place matters. The region in which a person resides often, if not always, constitutes a crucial part of that person's identity. In *The Power of Place*, journalist Winifred Gallagher noted: "Throughout history, people of all cultures have assumed that environment influences behavior. Now modern science is confirming that our actions, thoughts, and feelings are indeed shaped not just by our genes and neurochemistry, history and relationships, but also by our surroundings."[2] Of all the forces that motivate human behavior, one's surroundings and environment are among the most potent. But the way in which that influence works is by no means a simple or uncomplicated process. Place, Mark Vinz and Thom Tammaro have informed us, is something more than simply geographical landscape: "Rather, it is an emotional complex of associations, both genera-

2. Gallagher, *The Power of Place: How Our Surroundings Shape Our Thoughts, Emotions, and Actions* (New York: HarperPerennial, 1994), p. 12.

tive and restrictive; it is the human communities that inhabit landscapes—their attitudes and values, their particular (and sometimes peculiar) ways of arranging and expressing themselves and relating both to each other and 'the outside.'" Place derives in multiple ways from history, one's ancestry, interactions between individuals and the society around them, matters of the spirit, and inevitable change.³ In Laura Ingalls Wilder's case, place indeed mattered; region mattered. Her middle-western upbringing as a child and her residency in the region as an adult can help to explain both the kind of person that she became and the kind of writing that she did.⁴

After moving in 1894 at the age of twenty-seven with her husband, Almanzo, to Mansfield, Missouri, Wilder spent the last sixty-three years of her life in another portion of the region, the Ozarks. Although part of the Middle West, it presented a much different kind of cultural climate than Wilder had been accustomed to in the woods of Wisconsin; Walnut Grove, Minnesota; Burr Oak, Iowa; and De Smet, Dakota Territory. As a journalist writing bi-weekly columns for the *Missouri Ruralist* from the mid-1910s to the mid-1920s, Wilder chose to write about the people, activities, and institutions around her in southern Missouri, or the lower Midwest. But when it came time to write an autobiography intended for an adult magazine audience and then convert her memories of that period into children's novels, she decided to write about another sub-region—the upper Midwest—which emanated from a much different kind of culture.

---

3. Vinz and Tammaro, eds., Introduction to *Imagining Home: Writing from the Midwest* (Minneapolis: University of Minnesota Press, 1995), p. vii. In recent decades, developments ranging from transportation improvements, the rise of big-box retailers and multinational corporations, franchised food, educational standardization, pop culture, mass and electronic media, and urban sprawl have tended to smooth over differences in regional characteristics and engender a sense of "placelessness" in American society. *See*, for example, Joshua Meyrowitz, *No Sense of Place: The Impact of Electronic Media on Social Behavior* (New York: Oxford University Press, 1985), and James Howard Kunstler, *The Geography of Nowhere: The Rise and Decline of America's Man-Made Landscape* (New York: Simon & Schuster, 1993).

4. My claim here is rather modest but nonetheless significant. One's place of origin and residence have a major impact upon one's identity formation, but they are not the only factors. As historian Elizabeth Jameson observed: "Identity is a slippery business. We all have multiple identities, only some of which are rooted in where we live or the passports we carry" (Jameson, "Connecting the Women's Wests," in *One Step over the Line: Toward a History of Women in the North American Wests*, ed. Jameson and Sheila McManus [Edmonton and Athabasca, Can.: University of Alberta Press and Athabasca University Press, 2008], p. 22.

There was a time in American history when the study of regional distinctiveness mattered more than it has in recent decades as a means of explaining American history, culture, and current events. Early historians of the colonial period never failed to note the importance of regional, i.e., sectional, differences. Whether one lived in New England, the middle colonies, or the South had a crucial impact on who one was, what one thought, and how one behaved. Residents of the three major regions reacted differently to directives from the mother country, played different roles in the Revolution, took different stands on the Constitution, and followed different lines of development during the early national period. Sectional animosities, springing especially from divisions over slavery, precipitated a civil war in the 1860s that cost over six hundred thousand lives, and continued differences between North and South carried into the twentieth century, even as westward expansion created new and unfamiliar regions and sectional competition.

Efforts to overcome lingering sectional animosities achieved only partial success after the Civil War. Forces promoting nationalism, including imperialistic forays abroad, expanding world trade, participation in two world wars, and the Cold War, helped undermine enthusiasm for regionalist thinking as the twentieth century wore on. Frederick Jackson Turner's efforts and those of his successors to promote sectional history bore little fruit. A 1951 volume of essays, emerging out of a conference held on the subject at the University of Wisconsin, marked the apparent apex of interest in the approach. By the 1960s and 1970s, new trends in American history, from women's, African-American, and other minorities' histories to "history from the bottom up," quantitative, psycho-biography, and a bevy of "news"—new economic, labor, social, political, and so forth—all spoke to a younger generation of researchers. By then, even if southern history and the "new western history" were going concerns, the efforts of Turner and his disciples to nudge their fellow historians in the direction of some kind of comprehensive sectional history had clearly become passé. Meanwhile, as historian Jon K. Lauck pointed out, midwestern history fell far behind its regional counterparts in terms of interest, participation, institutional support, output, and impact.[5]

The recent revival of midwestern history in the form of a new organization (the Midwestern History Association), national conferences, print and electronic journals, increased book publishing, and other activities provides both an opportunity and a challenge for historians to use the lens of regional

---

5. Merrill Jensen, ed., *Regionalism in America* (Madison: University of Wisconsin Press, 1951); Jon K. Lauck, *The Lost Region: Toward a Revival of Midwestern History* (Iowa City: University of Iowa Press, 2013).

history to cast new light on old questions and issues.⁶ How the Midwest matters is always an empirical question, not something that can be presumed. The challenge for midwestern historians is to demonstrate just how place or location influenced people and events, in much the same way that historians have taken to using race, class, gender, occupation, religion, ethnicity, education, political views, intellectual trends, and other factors to help understand and explain people's ideas and behavior.

Talking about the Midwest also requires some background knowledge of how people's current understandings of the region came about. Public notions about the location of the region, for instance, have shifted considerably since the term first entered common parlance around the 1880s. During the period treated in Wilder's Little House novels—the late 1860s to 1885 (or 1889 if one includes *The First Four Years*)—neither Wilder nor most of her contemporaries possessed a notion of the Midwest, let alone thought of themselves as midwesterners. Terms that were commonly applied to areas of the region that the Ingalls family inhabited—Wisconsin, Minnesota, Iowa, and Dakota Territory—included the West, the Great West, the Northwest, and the Old Northwest to distinguish them from the East, New England, the Mid-Atlantic states, and the South. After being briefly applied to Tennessee and nearby states before the Civil War, the term Middle West began to be applied during the 1880s to Kansas and Nebraska to distinguish them from areas farther to the north, south, or west. The deep economic depression of the 1890s helped foster more of a sense of regional identity in the Middle West, and during the decade leading up to 1912, the locus of the region shifted farther east to include both the Old Northwest (Ohio, Indiana, Illinois, Michigan, and Wisconsin) and newer states to the west of it (Minnesota, Iowa, Missouri, North Dakota, South Dakota, Nebraska, and Kansas), with Chicago serving as the putative regional capital. By 1912, the generally accepted notion of the Middle West had solidified into these twelve states, with some observers extending its eastern boundaries to include parts of western Pennsylvania and New York. Alternative labels such as Central West or simply "the prairies" lost cachet.⁷

6. This revival coincides with a general renewal of interest in regionalism among historians. *See*, for example, Robert L. Dorman, *Hell of a Vision: Regionalism and the Modern American West* (Tucson: University of Arizona Press, 2012), and Michael C. Steiner, *Regionalists on the Left: Radical Voices from the American West* (Norman: University of Oklahoma Press, 2013).

7. James R. Shortridge, *The Middle West: Its Meaning in American Culture* (Lawrence: University Press of Kansas, 1989), pp. 3, 13–26. The boundaries of the Midwest continue to be a point of discussion. "Regions are subjective artistic devices," geographer John

The historical etymology of the phrase should not prevent us from thinking about Wilder as a midwesterner, however, even if the term did not solidify in usage and meaning until around 1912. While terminology evolved and the places that were considered to lie inside the Midwest underwent change, the experience of place was real for Wilder, her family, their friends, and their neighbors.[8] That experience became an integral part of their mindsets and filtered into their ways of thinking about themselves, the values they adopted, the behavioral habits they settled into, and the ideals and dreams they became attached to. Just because Wilder apparently never referred to herself (or thought of herself particularly) as a midwesterner does not detract from the fact that she *was* a midwesterner—one who had grown up in the region and who exemplified many habitual thought patterns and behaviors that have been attributed to people who live there. Historian Kathleen Neils Conzen observed that the central narrative that nineteenth-century midwesterners devised about themselves centered around the bringing of civilization to the wilderness as well as promoting progress and equality in the region. "It was

---

Fraser Hart reminded us. "There can be no standard definition of a region, and there are no universal rules for recognizing, delimiting, and describing regions. Far too much time can be wasted in the trivial exercise of trying to draw lines around 'regions'" (Hart, "The Highest Form of the Geographer's Art," *Annals of the Association of American Geographers* 72 [Mar. 1982]: 21–22). Some have contended that the geographical features and historical record of the area south of the Missouri River, which neatly divides Missouri into northern and southern halves, require assigning it to the South. Missouri was a slave state with many Civil War battles fought not too far from Mansfield, and lingering southern influences in the Ozarks have led others to argue that the area is an extension of the Greater Appalachian region and the Upland South. Woodard, *American Nations*, pp. 189–99, and D. W. Meinig, *The Shaping of America: A Geographical Perspective on 500 Years of History*, Vol. 2: *Continental America, 1800–1867* (New Haven: Yale University Press, 1993), pp. 226, 229, 233, 236, 273–79. A broader consensus of scholars, journalists, government officials, and laypeople, however, has had no trouble designating the entire state as part of the Midwest. See, for example, James H. Madison, ed., *Heartland: Comparative Histories of the Midwestern States* (Bloomington: Indiana University Press, 1988); J. L. Anderson, ed., *The Rural Midwest since World War II* (DeKalb, Ill.: Northern Illinois University Press, 2014); Lauck, *Lost Region*, p. 8; and Richard Sisson, Christian Zacher, and Andrew Cayton, eds., *The American Midwest: An Interpretive Encyclopedia* (Bloomington: Indiana University Press, 2007), p. xxiii.

8. It is worthwhile noting that Wilder gained her original writing experience producing bi-weekly columns for the *Missouri Ruralist*, which was published by Topeka-based Arthur Capper, who eventually owned a string of farm newspapers from Kansas to Pennsylvania. Capper, a former governor of Kansas and five-term United States senator, was a major voice for the Midwest.

irrelevant whether or not they all chose to call themselves Midwesterners or recognize a common regionality," she contended, for "those who told the same story about who they were, or had the same story told about them, were all Midwesterners together."[9]

The midwestern region may be the most difficult one to analyze and evaluate because it is allegedly so central, normal, undifferentiated, and nondistinct when compared to other regions. Situated in the middle of the country, it does not inhabit either of the coasts, and it is not part of the South, with that region's historical attachment to slavery and involvement in the race issue. But no region is uncomplicated. Healthy, dynamic regions "are constantly contesting the meanings of the imagined community, constantly struggling to define and redefine themselves," historian Andrew R. L. Cayton reminded us. He and others have noted how important it is to take account of the complexity and cultural diversity of the Midwest, which became more pronounced as the nineteenth century wore on. Midwesterners were by no means agreed among themselves on issues such as temperance, public education, civil liberties, and women's rights. Diversity, more than uniformity, characterized the region. Nevertheless, cultural observers attached labels and distinctive qualities to its residents and institutions—words and phrases such as responsibility, hard work, conventionality, normality, reliability, politeness, niceness, blandness, pleasantness, middle-of-the-road. Quoting Cayton again: "The Midwest, it would seem, is a place where, to paraphrase Gertrude Stein's famous line, there is no there, there."[10]

No matter how one wishes to define the Midwest, however, there can be little doubt that many residents have derived significance from their presence there. Former President Gerald Ford reflected in 1989, "Coming from the Midwest helped to keep my feet on the ground and head out of the clouds."[11] One of the region's most insightful interpreters, Scott Russell Sanders of Indiana, offered a short list of regional qualities that he had observed: "flatness, fertility, austerity, conformity, civility—and their opposites." None is unique to the Midwest, he noted, and all are qualities that one might ascribe to the nation as a whole.[12] Succinctly put, the problem for anyone writing about

---

9. Conzen, "Pi-ing the Type: Jane Grey Swisshelm and the Contest of Midwestern Regionality," in *The American Midwest: Essays on Regional History*, ed. Andrew R. L. Cayton and Susan E. Gray (Bloomington: Indiana University Press, 2001), p. 92.

10. Cayton, "The Anti-Region: Place and Identity in the History of the American Midwest," ibid., pp. 142, 144.

11. Ford, quoted in Editorial, *Omaha World-Herald*, Dec. 28, 2006.

12. Sanders, *Writing from the Center* (Bloomington: Indiana University Press, 1995), p. 49.

regional characteristics is that few things can be understood as unique to a region, and every region is so large that it necessarily entails considerable diversity and contradiction. Yet, these considerations should not block us from venturing limited generalizations that can help to illuminate the life and work of Wilder and other artists and writers.

While it is difficult to pin adjectives and broad generalizations on the Midwest and its people, a good starting place is to divide the region between "upper" and "lower" Midwests. The cultures, institutions, and populations of the northern and southern parts of the region overlap considerably, but they can also be separated from each other. The most important explanation for the distinctiveness of the southern parts of Missouri, Illinois, Indiana, and Ohio derives from migration patterns that brought the original white explorers, traders, and settlers to those places. Streams of migration emanating out of different cultural hearths along the East Coast and in Canada and Europe resulted in different kinds of people with a variety of recognizable habits, values, and traditions. The northern parts of Ohio, Indiana, and Illinois were settled by individuals and groups originating in New England and New York and, to a lesser degree, Pennsylvania and the Mid-Atlantic states. The earliest settlers living in the southern parts of those three midwestern states arrived largely from across the Ohio River, originating especially in Kentucky, Tennessee, Virginia, Maryland, and the Carolinas. This pattern carried farther west into Missouri, where the Ozark Mountains and other parts of the state south of the Missouri River were most heavily populated by people migrating from the same southern states. Arrivals from Europe and Canada as the century wore on further complicated the patterns that were developing.[13]

Common stereotypes attached to the northern and southern streams of migration were often misleading and exaggerated, fostering, for example, the notion that the northern Yankee migration was mostly tee-totaling and hard-working, while southern migrants were all hard-drinking and indolent. But the resulting cultures of the two sub-regions did display clearly recognizable variations. Northerners often traveled in groups and displayed more communitarian tendencies. Southerners tended to come as individuals and often

---

13. On the migratory patterns of midwestern settlers, *see* three of John C. Hudson's essays: "Yankeeland in the Middle West," *Journal of Geography* 85 (Sept.–Oct. 1986): 195–200; "North American Origins of Middlewestern Frontier Populations," *Annals of the Association of American Geographers* 78 (Sept. 1988): 395–413; and "Migration to an American Frontier," ibid. 66 (June 1976): 242–65. *See also* John Fraser Hart, "Facets of the Geography of Population in the Midwest," *Journal of Geography* 85 (Sept.–Oct. 1986): 201–11, and Colin Woodard, *American Nations: A History of the Eleven Rival Regional Cultures of North America* (New York: Viking, 2011), pp. 173–220.

shied away from town life. They jealously protected their independence, were more indifferent to schooling and more suspicious of governmental institutions. "The southerners feared the legendary Yankee sharp practices," wrote Richard Lingeman, while "the Yankees thought southerners irreligious, immoral, lazy, and dissolute."[14] The patterns of difference extended to disparities in foodways, architecture, speech patterns, and denominational membership. "Even the simple chore of milking the cows had cultural significance," observed historian Nicole Etcheson. "The nineteenth-century image of the two sections saw the Yankee as thrifty and industrious, and the Southerner as pleasure-loving, generous, and unaffected by monetary considerations."[15]

These distinctive migration patterns worked a pronounced effect upon the place that Laura and Almanzo Wilder discovered when they moved from De Smet, South Dakota, to Mansfield, Missouri. In their new home, they found themselves living primarily among individuals and families whose people had moved in from Kentucky, Tennessee, Virginia, and North Carolina. They possessed different speech patterns, different cultural practices, and, to a significant degree, different religious traditions. In Walnut Grove and De Smet, the Ingalls clan and the Wilders had been active in the Congregational church, which emerged straight out of Boston and New England. In Mansfield, the primary religious options available were Methodist, Baptist, and Cumberland Presbyterian. With no Congregational church present, the Wilders attended and were active in the Methodist church, but they never formally joined the congregation. They also continued active lodge membership with the Masons and the Eastern Star, which had local units in both sub-regions. Both husband and wife were heavily involved in supporting and helping lead the local agricultural fair group. Having departed the heavily Republican state of South Dakota, the Wilders discovered that they had settled in a predominately Republican area of a state that normally went Democratic at election time. Laura Wilder served in various official positions in the local Democratic Party in Mansfield, ran unsuccessfully for public office, and was a founder, director, and secretary-treasurer of the Mansfield branch of the Federal Farm Loan Association. She also participated in and promoted a bridge club and several women's study clubs.[16]

14. Lingeman, *Small Town America: A Narrative History, 1620–The Present* (New York: G. P. Putnam's Sons, 1980), p. 75.

15. Etcheson, *The Emerging Midwest: Upland Southerners and the Political Culture of the Old Northwest, 1787–1861* (Bloomington: Indiana University Press, 1996), pp. 4–5.

16. Teresa Lynn, *Little Lodges on the Prairie: Freemasonry & Laura Ingalls Wilder* (Georgetown, Tex.: Tranquility Press, 2014), pp. 76–78; John E. Miller, *Laura Ingalls Wilder and Rose Wilder Lane: Authorship, Place, Time, and Culture* (Columbia: Univer-

While both South Dakota and Missouri served as examples of French aristocrat Alexis de Tocqueville's observation that the United States was "a nation of joiners," the tone and practice of civic life in Missouri were in many ways different from what the Wilders had experienced earlier in South Dakota. Memories of the Civil War lingered on, and some courthouse squares sported statues of Confederate soldiers, something that would have been virtually blasphemous in South Dakota. The *Mansfield Mirror* sometimes ran cartoons and jokes that were overtly racist, and one can only imagine the kinds of things people said about blacks in private conversations and often in public. Southwestern Missouri and northwestern Arkansas had been hot spots during the Civil War, with battles and skirmishes in or near Springfield. After the war, night riders, vigilante groups, and racial supremacists made their presence felt. The lynching in 1894 of a black man in a town eighty miles west of Mansfield launched a series of racial episodes during the next several years that resulted in the ethnic cleansing of a large portion of the sub-region that Mansfield was part of. We cannot know to what degree the Wilders were willing to challenge the area's social mores or contest institutional racism, whether they accommodated themselves to the dominant culture or tried to undermine it in small ways.[17]

Wilder kept a list of favorite Bible verses close at hand and sometimes devoted all or part of her *Missouri Ruralist* column to the need for people to get along and treat each other benevolently in a Christian fashion. Although her particular religious beliefs and doctrinal positions cannot be known, we can speculate that her high degree of religiosity placed her in conformity with the conservative religious and political views of the majority of her neighbors. Springfield, the largest city in southwestern Missouri and located just fifty miles west of Mansfield, was a hotbed of old-time religion. Among other things, it became a center of gospel and country music, served as worldwide headquarters for Assemblies of God churches, and housed the regional offices of several other denominations. Southwest Missouri was also *Shepherd of the Hills* country. Harold Bell Wright's famous novel of life in the Ozarks reinforced religious notions that rural, small-town society operated at a higher moral level and was superior to the corrupting influences that tainted

---

sity of Missouri Press, 2008), p. 183, and *Becoming Laura Ingalls Wilder: The Woman behind the Legend* (Columbia: University of Missouri Press, 1998), pp. 99, 128, 134, 136, 163–64, 172, 179, 199, 233–34.

17. Miller, *Laura Ingalls Wilder and Rose Wilder Lane*, pp. 175–76; James W. Loewen, *Sundown Towns: A Hidden Dimension of American Racism* (New York: The New Press, 2005), pp. 67, 73–74, 90–91, 95–96.

city life.[18] Religious scholar Stanley Burgess observed, "Since pioneer days, religion has been a center of social life in the Ozarks."[19]

While a variety of differences distinguished residents of the upper Midwest from those in the lower Midwest, a number of qualities and characteristics have been attributed to residents living across the entire region that we can use to analyze Wilder's special connection to the Midwest and the influence that it exerted on her. These characteristics include (1) the prominence of the land in its residents' thinking and the centrality of agriculture in its way of life; (2) the Homestead Act and the frontier process as integral parts of its historical experience; (3) the crucial role that small towns played in its culture; and (4) the development and nurturing of specific values as a result of those cultural experiences that helped shape residents' special identities as Midwesterners.

The single feature of life in the Midwest that most prominently shaped its cultural outlook and its people's behavior was its agrarian character. Highly visible, as well as crucially implicated in residents' everyday lives, was the land, stretching out to the horizon in every direction, imposing itself on people's perceptions, feelings, and ways of thinking. Historical geographer James R. Shortridge identified "pastoralism," an evolving concept of rurality and advocacy for the agricultural way of life, as the most important identifying characteristic of the Midwest.[20] Other analysts have echoed that theme. "In most cases," wrote historian R. Douglas Hurt, "the rich, relatively cheap lands of the Midwest drew settlers who provided the foundation for regional identification."[21] Fellow historian Gilbert C. Fite concurred: "The most important influence that drew people to Dakota . . . was that age-old desire for land."[22] In occupying the land, these immigrants and native-born agrarians not only planted crops and tended livestock but also advanced the notion that hard work, self-reliance, and ownership of property would promote democracy, ensure liberty, and establish bonds of community. Extending back to the colonial period, writers and intellectuals such as Hector St. John de

---

18. Handwritten list of Wilder's favorite Bible verses, Laura Ingalls Wilder Home and Museum, Mansfield, Mo.; Wright, *The Shepherd of the Hills* (Chicago: Book Supply Co., 1907); Milton D. Rafferty, *Missouri: A Geography* (Boulder, Colo.: Westview Press, 1983), pp. 58–60, 185–88.

19. Stanley Burgess, "Perspectives on the Sacred: Religion in the Ozarks," *Ozarks Watch* 2 (Fall 1988): 5.

20. Shortridge, *Middle West*, pp. 1–2.

21. Hurt, "Midwestern Distinctiveness," in *American Midwest: Essays*, p. 165.

22. Fite, *The Farmers' Frontier, 1865–1900* (New York: Holt, Rinehart & Winston, 1966), p. 98.

Crevecoeur and Thomas Jefferson had lauded agrarianism, contributing to an "agrarian myth" that argued for the superiority of rural people and the rural way of life, a notion that only began to lose its hold on public opinion toward the end of the 1800s. The land and the unique features of the midwestern landscape, as much as anything else, are what set the Midwest apart from New England, the South, and the West, and Laura Ingalls Wilder joined her fellow midwesterners in promoting this mindset.[23]

As they ventured out into treeless expanses, leaving behind the wooded areas that dominated the eastern parts of the Midwest, agricultural pioneers confronted two major types of landscape: flat prairies seemingly as level as a table top, such as the Grand Prairie of Illinois, and rolling prairies, the undulations of which varied from gentle to extreme.[24] As the Ingalls family crossed the Mississippi River, leaving behind the Big Woods of Wisconsin, they encountered the gently rolling prairies of western Minnesota and eastern Dakota Territory, which were typical in their general lack of trees, their waving seas of grass, and the traces of Indian encampments and buffalo trails. After crossing the Big Sioux River west of Brookings, Wilder wrote in her autobiography, "we . . . were out on the broad prairie that looked like a big meadow as far as we could see in every direction. . . . and the wind was blowing, waving the tall prairie grass that had turned brown in the summer sun." Wilder was especially effective in capturing the beauty of the environment at sunset and sunrise:

> The sun sank lower and lower until, looking like a ball of pulsing, liquid light it sank gloriously in clouds of crimson and silver. Cold purple shadows rose in the east; crept slowly around the horizon, then gathered above in depth on depth of darkness from which the stars swung low and bright. The winds which all day had blown strongly, dropped low with the sun and went whispering among the tall grasses, where the earth lay breathing softly under the summer night falling softly over the prairie and tucking them gently in.[25]

The prairie, in Wilder's writings, was a place of wonder and delight, a rich storehouse of life that pleased the eye with luscious sights of wild flowers,

23. Richard Hofstadter, *The Age of Reform: From Bryan to F. D. R.* (New York: Alfred A. Knopf, 1955), chap. 1; Henry Nash Smith, *Virgin Land: The American West as Symbol and* Myth (Cambridge: Harvard University Press, 1950), pp. 140–46.

24. Allan G. Bogue, *From Prairie to Corn Belt: Farming on the Illinois and Iowa Prairies in the Nineteenth Century* (Chicago: University of Chicago Press, 1963), pp. 1–7.

25. Wilder, *Pioneer Girl: The Annotated Autobiography*, ed. Pamela Smith Hill (Pierre: South Dakota Historical Society Press, 2014), pp. 153, 155, 158.

tall grass, animal life, and water flowing in streams and contained in lakes. The land, providing sustenance for survival, was a place where her mother could garden and her father could hunt, trap, fish, and cultivate crops for food or for cash income. Kingsbury County, which was located near 97.5 degrees west longitude, sat on the edge of the midwestern corn belt, an area that was continually edging westward during the decades after the Civil War. Blessed by unusually wet seasons during the early 1880s, farmers in Dakota Territory enjoyed several good crop years, a pattern that quickly reversed itself during the latter half of the decade, when drought set in and farmers were in distress.[26] Thus, for a short period of time, Charles Ingalls could remain optimistic about the future, but eking out a living on the land proved no more successful for the family in Dakota Territory than it had on Indian lands in Kansas or grasshopper-infested fields in Minnesota. Purchasing horse-drawn farm equipment on credit at high interest rates, combined with the hazards of prairie fires, winter blizzards, volatile commodity prices, and exploitive railroad shipping rates, drove Charles Ingalls to abandon farming, build a house in town, and do carpentering and odd jobs to support himself, his wife, and their daughter Mary. Laura and Almanzo Wilder kicked around the area for nine more years after getting married in 1885, but they, too, gave up on farming in South Dakota to seek out more favorable circumstances in southern Missouri.

Wilder's *Pioneer Girl* and her subsequent Little House novels told one family's story, not the whole of the midwestern agricultural experience during the 1870s and 1880s, but other writers and artists have addressed many of the same themes. One of the most successful was illustrator/artist Harvey Dunn, whose closeness to Wilder in age and physical proximity makes him a suggestive counterpart. Dunn, born on March 8, 1884, grew up on a homestead about a dozen miles west and somewhat south of the Ingalls homestead. The marriage of his uncle Nathan Dow to Wilder's youngest sister, Grace, made Wilder and Dunn relatives by marriage. He grew up to be tall (6' 2"), strong, and handsome, hardened by miles of walking behind horses and oxen, manhandling plows and other implements. He received training in art at South Dakota Agricultural College in Brookings, the Art Institute of Chicago, and the studio of the famous illustrator Howard Pyle in Wilmington, Delaware. Talented, industrious, and ambitious, he rose quickly in the field of illustration and, during the years before World War I, found himself in high demand

---

26. Bogue, *From Prairie to Corn Belt*, p. 1; John C. Hudson, *Making the Corn Belt: A Geographical History of Middle-Western Agriculture* (Bloomington: Indiana University Press, 1994), pp. 1–2; Fite, *Farmers' Frontier*, pp. 94–110.

Harvey Dunn is shown here at work on his painting *Dakota Woman*.
South Dakota Art Museum

by magazines ranging from the *Saturday Evening Post* and *McCall's* to *Harper's* and *Century*. During the quarter-century or so after 1925, Dunn traveled frequently back to South Dakota to sketch and draw. Back in his studio in Tenafly, New Jersey, he converted the images into oil paintings portraying scenes of his childhood on the Dakota prairie during a slightly later era than the one Wilder described in her children's novels.[27]

Where Wilder described life in Dakota during the late 1800s in books for children, Dunn, in effect, told stories of life on the prairie in paintings. Both artists harbored positive outlooks on life, something that shone through in their writings and in their art. Both retained strong love for and attachment to the prairie. Both willingly acknowledged negative aspects of the prairie envi-

27. Robert F. Karolevitz, *Where Your Heart Is: The Story of Harvey Dunn, Artist* (Aberdeen, S.Dak.: North Plains Press, 1970); "Two Artists of the Prairie: Laura Ingalls Wilder and Harvey Dunn," in John E. Miller, *Laura Ingalls Wilder's Little Town: Where History and Literature Meet* (Lawrence: University Press of Kansas, 1994), chap. 10.

ronment in terms of challenges, threats, and, sometimes, people's bad behavior. By and large, however, they concentrated upon the positive features that they perceived there. Dunn liked to tell his art students, "Paint a little less of the facts, and a little more of the *spirit*."[28] While collaborating in the writing of the Little House novels, Wilder and her daughter were sticklers for getting the facts right, up to a point, but, like Dunn, they were willing to bend them when necessary and rely upon imagination to express the emotions they were trying to convey.

"Paint more with feeling than with thought," Dunn advised.[29] He and Wilder shared similar penchants for romanticism, sentimentality, and nostalgia. They relied upon memory and imagination to re-create times and places where spirit, will, determination, tenacity, and hard work assisted in overcoming the challenges and threats that the land regularly advanced. Dunn's career as an artist overlapped with the years Wilder spent writing her novels. Wilder and Lane explicitly viewed the work they were doing in the literary realm as a mode of assisting people in helping to overcome their fears and timidity in the face of economic depression and foreign military threat.[30] Dunn implicitly did much the same thing. He viewed his parents' generation as brave, bold, and tenacious people who had set a commendable example for individuals living in the mid-twentieth century. In his opinion, much could be learned from their achievements.[31]

Viewing Dunn's prairie paintings and reading Wilder's novels in tandem reveals many similarities in their characterization of the Middle West that they had grown up in. Both presented idealized, impressive, colorful portraits of the period and the place. In their artistic productions, they emphasized the enormity, the stillness, the grandeur, and the beauty of the landscape. Both illustrated how one's perceptions of people and places depend heavily upon

---

28. Dunn, *An Evening in the Classroom* (Tenafly, N.J.: Mario Cooper, 1934), reprinted in Walt Reed, *Harvey Dunn: Illustrator and Painter of the Pioneer West* (Santa Cruz, Calif.: Flesk, 2010), p. 245 (emphasis original).

29. Ibid.

30. Lane said that she wrote her novel *Let the Hurricane Roar* (1933) in response to pessimists during the Great Depression. Lane to Eleanor Hubbard Garst, printed in Garst, "New Books You'll Want," *Better Homes and Gardens* 12 (Dec. 1933): 19. Both Lane and her mother saw individual initiative as the better alternative to government intervention. Miller, *Laura Ingalls Wilder and Rose Wilder Lane*, pp. 183, 191–92.

31. Edgar M. Howell, "Harvey Dunn: The Searching Artist Who Came Home to His First Horizon," *Montana, the Magazine of Western History* (Winter 1966): 55; John Jellico, "Harvey Dunn, 1884–1952," *Artists of the Rockies and the Golden West* 8 (Fall 1981): 44.

This detail from Dunn's *After the Blizzard* dramatically communicates the impact of winter on the open prairie.
*South Dakota Art Museum*

one's social position and one's circumstances. Having grown up among and lived in the company of struggling farm families and ordinary town dwellers, Wilder developed natural empathy for common folks and understood their feelings and needs. In like fashion, although he married into wealth and lived an affluent lifestyle as an adult, Dunn never forgot his origins on a simple Dakota homestead and throughout his life retained a strong appreciation for the lives of common, ordinary people. On his visits back to South Dakota, he was able to re-experience the life he had known growing up on the prairie, often joining in to pitch hay, drive tractors, and work with threshing crews.[32] The prairie, in both artists' interpretation of it, presented two different faces: it was a place of beauty and fecundity, but it posed severe threats and dan-

32. Karolevitz, *Where Your Heart Is*, pp. 69, 97–101; William Henry Holaday III, "Harvey Dunn: Pioneer Painter of the Middle Border" (Ph.D. diss., Ohio State University, 1970), p. 30.

gers. Winter, especially, tested people's resourcefulness and survival skills. Wilder's *The Long Winter* and the relevant pages in *Pioneer Girl* constitute a quintessential survival story. She also wrote about the hazards of floods, drought, tornadoes, blizzards, and extremely cold weather in her autobiography.[33] In like fashion, Dunn's paintings *After the Blizzard, School Day's End*, and *30 Degrees below Zero* explored the hazards of extreme weather conditions on the prairie.

Though he was capable of depicting the domains of the wealthy and the elite, Dunn generally depicted "the majesty of simple things," i.e., the everyday, common, ordinary activities and artifacts of average people. Wilder's writing was directed at exactly the same things. Both of them appreciated sound as well as sight and loved poetry and music. Just as Dunn urged his students, "If you're going to make an illustration you must take poetry and song into it,"[34] Wilder filled her books with verses and song. Even though midwesterners vary in habit and thought, Dunn and Wilder were outstanding spokespersons who felt a close connection to the land and used their crafts to express the spirit of the region.

Both artist and writer, it must be said, fit comfortably into the spirit of the times, which assumed that white settlement of lands previously controlled by American Indians was both inevitable and just. It is difficult to infer much from Dunn's paintings or statements about his views of the original inhabitants of the land, but there is no reason to think that he had a quarrel with white occupation of Dakota and the rest of the Midwest. The implications of Manifest Destiny were also an accepted fact in the work of Laura Ingalls Wilder. Although there are some indications in *Little House on the Prairie* that she was not entirely comfortable with the dispossession of the Indians, she and her family certainly did nothing to try to prevent it. Her descriptions of midwestern lands as being empty of people before white settlers arrived reflected her unthinking naiveté rather than any malicious intent, but they have also earned her considerable criticism from several literary commentators and other supporters of Indian rights. Twentieth- and twenty-first-century critics see what operated as Manifest Destiny in the 1800s as a "legacy of conquest."[35]

33. Wilder, *Pioneer Girl*, pp. 69, 139, 201–25, 307, 315.
34. Dunn, quoted in Holaday, "Harvey Dunn," p. 247.
35. Patricia Nelson Limerick popularized the phrase "legacy of conquest" in *The Legacy of Conquest: The Unbroken Past of the American West* (New York: W. W. Norton & Co., 1987). For more on the new western historians' reassessment of the westward movement, *see* Limerick, Clyde A. Milner II, and Charles E. Rankin, eds., *Trails: Toward a New Western History* (Lawrence: University Press of Kansas, 1991), and William Cronon,

If the land and ideas about it, including pastoralism and the agrarian myth, have been integral parts of midwesterners' thinking about their region over a long period of time, a closely allied phenomenon was the process of homesteading, which continually moved the frontier line on the western edge of the region toward the Pacific Ocean. Beginning in the 1820s, agriculturalists advocated in Congress for making federally owned lands in the West available cheaply or even at no charge to would-be farmers. Declining prices for government land and the passage of the Preemption Act of 1841 moved a long way in that direction, but many wanted totally free homesteads. In 1862, the Homestead Act, one of the most significant pieces of legislation that Congress ever passed, accomplished just that. It was only after the Confederate states withdrew from the Union at the start of the Civil War that representatives from the Middle West could muster enough votes to secure passage of the law. The new Republican Party, whose major support and energy were to be found in the Midwest, led the campaign for free homesteads, and middle-western residents were in the forefront of taking advantage of them. Southerners, for their part, worried that the law would only benefit the North, encouraging rapid population expansion into the Northwest and shifting the political balance in Congress. New Englanders, meanwhile, feared that their region would lose more of its young people through out-migration. By the time the act passed in 1862, the frontier line was already poised on the eastern boundaries of Dakota Territory, and southern Dakota emerged as the chief beneficiary of the new legislation.[36]

The Homestead Act and the process of homesteading and acquiring land lie at the heart of any description of the Great Dakota Boom (1878–1889), which is one of the core events of South Dakota's history. For a short period of time during the early 1880s, the southern part of the territory stood out above other competitors in absorbing homesteaders and experiencing

---

George Miles, and Jay Gitlin, eds., *Under an Open Sky: Rethinking America's Western Past* (New York: W. W. Norton & Co., 1992). On Wilder's treatment of American Indians, *see* "'They Should Know When They're Licked': American Indians in Wilder's Fiction," in Miller, *Laura Ingalls Wilder and Rose Wilder Lane*, pp. 159–79.

36. Everett Dick, *The Lure of the Land: A Social History of the Public Lands from the Articles of Confederation to the New Deal* (Lincoln: University of Nebraska Press, 1970), pp. 135–36; Heather Cox Richardson, *The Greatest Nation of the Earth: Republican Economic Policies during the Civil War* (Cambridge, Mass.: Harvard University Press, 1997), pp. 140–49; Eric Foner, *Free Soil, Free Labor, Free Men: The Ideology of the Republican Party before the Civil War* (New York: Oxford University Press, 1970), pp. 27–29, 175; Ilia Murtazashvili, *The Political Economy of the American Frontier* (New York: Cambridge University Press, 2013), p. 186.

rapid population growth. In a single year near the height of the land boom, claimants filed on 22,061 homesteads and 11,199 timber claims in Dakota, constituting thirty-nine percent of all the new homesteads claimed in the United States that year and fifty-four percent of all the timber culture claims. Established in 1883, the land office at Huron was soon doing more business than any of its counterparts in the nation. In five years' time, between 1880 and 1885, the population of southern Dakota Territory jumped from about eighty-two thousand to almost a quarter million.[37]

Homesteading and the Great Dakota Boom connected the territory to what happened in the Middle West as a whole. Much of the story of midwestern history revolves around the continual westward movement of the frontier as farmers, ranchers, miners, lumbermen, manufacturers, retailers, and other people scrambled to better their economic prospects and, in the process, transformed the region. As the family began its move to De Smet in 1879, Wilder commented in *Pioneer Girl,* "we were on our way again and going in the direction *which always brought the happiest changes.*"[38] Throughout the history of the Middle West, the western frontier constituted a crucible for fashioning a new society, a new economy, and a new culture. Settlers often found themselves caught between efforts to achieve their individualistic goals while at the same time harboring a strong yearning for community and the pursuit of the common good. The Ingalls family, just like every other, was caught up in these contradictions. Hopeful of bettering his family's economic position, Charles Ingalls frequently moved them from place to place in the Midwest until the family finally settled down for the last time in De Smet.

Homesteading entailed a lot of hard work, and those who took part in it tended to develop a strong work ethic. Wilder addressed the energy required and skills needed to accomplish women's tasks on a farmstead in her *Missouri Ruralist* column of August 5, 1919:

> the farmer's wife must know her own business, which includes the greatest variety of trades and occupations ever combined in one all-around person. Think of them! Cook, baker, seamstress, laundrywoman, nurse, chambermaid, and nurse girl. She is a poultry keeper, and expert in dairy work, a specialist in canning, preserving and pickling, and besides all else she must be the mother of the family and a smiling hostess.[39]

---

37. Fite, *Farmers' Frontier*, pp. 98–99; Herbert S. Schell, *History of South Dakota*, 4th ed., rev. John E. Miller (Pierre: South Dakota Historical Society Press, 2004), p. 159.

38. Wilder, *Pioneer Girl*, p. 145 (emphasis added).

39. Wilder, "The Farm Home," Aug. 5, 1919, reprinted in *Laura Ingalls Wilder, Farm Journalist: Writings from the Ozarks*, ed. Stephen W. Hines (Columbia: University of

Much of the narrative of Wilder's *Pioneer Girl* revolved around the tasks of the pioneer mother, her husband, and the children. Work never seemed to end, and it began at an early age. By the time Wilder was eight or nine years old in Walnut Grove, she and her older sister were running errands, washing dishes, driving cows to pasture, and watching over their younger sister. As time went by, Wilder performed other chores, including bringing in wood, sweeping, dusting, baby-sitting, cooking, ironing, mending, making beds, milking cows, gardening, caring for chickens, and waiting on tables in a hotel. Wilder also took note of the compensations of living during the frontier period: wild flowers, singing birds, abundant wildlife, freedom, games to play, singing, wandering, and just enjoying oneself.[40]

The homesteading experience has been a quintessential part of the American national story and occupies a special place in the history of the Midwest. With regard to South Dakota history, I would suggest that it has been *the* most frequently told story of all, whether in textbooks, county history books, newspaper accounts, personal memoirs, television and radio programs, plays, movies, or any other medium. In some ways, the homestead experience *is* the quintessential South Dakota experience. And no one told it to more readers and listeners than Laura Ingalls Wilder did. Her story of the spring 1880 rush of settlers into Kingsbury County in *Pioneer Girl* and *By the Shores of Silver Lake* followed well-worn narrative patterns of relating the various aspects of the universal homestead saga. Some people arrived in wagons or buggies, others came on horses, still others traveled with their animals, tools, and belongings in emigrant cars on the railroad. They ventured out onto the prairie themselves or hired land locators to help them choose a vacant plot of government ground on which to file a homestead or tree claim. While many homesteaders fully intended to stay for five years and prove up on their claims, many others planned to acquire the land as quickly as possible, turn it over for a profit, and move on to new, presumably better locations. Once the weather was warm enough, they moved onto their new homesteads, where the men, like Charles Ingalls, knocked together a small claim shanty, dug a

---

Missouri Press, 2007), p. 195. The importance of the work ethic is often a central theme in discussions of frontier women. *See,* for example, Glenda Riley, *The Female Frontier: A Comparative View of Women on the Prairie and the Plains* (Lawrence: University Press of Kansas, 1988), chaps. 5–6; Jane Adams, *The Transformation of Rural Life: Southern Illinois, 1890–1990* (Chapel Hill: University of North Carolina Press, 1994), pp. 1–4, 84–100; Julie Roy Jeffrey, *Frontier Women: The Trans-Mississippi West, 1840–1880* (New York: Hill & Wang), pp. 59–62, 68–72, 124–25.

40. Wilder, *Pioneer Girl*, pp. 69, 96, 122–23, 133, 140, 183, 234.

Willa Cather wrote several novels about the Nebraska frontier, a landscape similar to that of Wilder's Dakota Territory. *Willa Cather Archive, Nebraska State Historical Society*

well, planted some cottonwood trees, and began plowing, while the women put the shanty in order and set up housekeeping.[41]

Wilder's narrative of homesteading overlapped considerably with thousands of similar tales written by women who experienced the midwestern homestead frontier. One of the most prominent was Pulitzer Prize-winning novelist Willa Cather (1873–1947), who set several of her twelve novels on the Nebraska frontier at about the same time that the Ingalls family was settling in Dakota Territory. The almost treeless, slightly rolling prairie landscape and the vegetation and soil types prevalent around De Smet closely approximated those in the area surrounding Red Cloud, Nebraska, which was located one degree longitude farther west and approximately three hundred miles to the south of De Smet. Both locales were near where the prairie transitions into

41. Ibid., pp. 187–98; Wilder, *By the Shores of Silver Lake* (New York: Harper & Row, 1953), pp. 224–32.

the Great Plains. The perspective that Cather brought to her work, as well as her purpose in writing, differed considerably from Wilder's. Not only was she writing for adult audiences rather than for children, she also brought a much more sophisticated educational background and literary sensibility to her craft. She was more critical of small-town society than Wilder, and she focused much of her attention on immigrant cultures, something largely lacking in Wilder's work. Each writer in her own way told stories of hope, industry, determination, and tenacity. And both made the role of women central to their narratives.

Cather's two most celebrated prairie novels, and the ones that brought her closest to Laura Ingalls Wilder, were *O Pioneers!* (1913) and *My Ántonia* (1918). The latter, considered to have been Cather's most memorable and outstanding work of fiction, depicted the immigrant Nebraska pioneer farmers sympathetically, and, some would say, sentimentally. Literary critics praised it for its emotional power, its riveting depiction of the heroic labors of the pioneers, its careful rendering of detail, and its use of myth and symbol to confer universal meanings on particular facts.[42] Different as their books were in many ways—audience, age level, complexity, sophistication, and psychological insight—Wilder and Cather complemented each other in significant ways. Each endeavored to get details correct, and each brought authenticity and believability to her work because she had lived the experience that she was writing about.

Both authors were also largely positive in their depictions of the Midwest, or the Great West as people still sometimes called it during their time. The critic John H. Randall III termed *My Ántonia* "one long paean of praise to the joys of rural living."[43] The land itself, the people who inhabited it, the social institutions they established, and their basic habits and values were essentially praiseworthy in the thinking of both Wilder and Cather. Not only praiseworthy, but heroic. The stories both novelists told took place not only in reality but also in the realm of myth, and heroic individuals inhabited both. The struggle of people against nature was epic, but, more than that, the

42. The critical literature on Cather is immense, dwarfing the work done on Wilder. For a sample, *see* James Schroeter, ed., *Willa Cather and Her Critics* (Ithaca, N.Y.: Cornell University Press, 1967). Among those critical of Cather's *My Ántonia* is James E. Miller, Jr., who contended that it "is episodic, lacks focus and abounds in irrelevancies" (Miller, "My Ántonia: A Frontier Drama of Time," *American Quarterly* 10 [Winter 1958]: 477). Deborah G. Lambert considered it "marred by many strange flaws and omissions" (Lambert, "The Defeat of a Hero: Autonomy and Sexuality in *My Ántonia*," *American Literature* 53 [Jan. 1982]: 676).

43. Randall, "Interpretation of *My Ántonia*," in *Willa Cather and Her Critics*, p. 272.

strength of will necessary to meet the challenges and threats abounding on the prairie was immense. Both Cather and Wilder, with their emphasis on the bravery, self-reliant individualism, energy, grit, and fortitude of the pioneers, fitted comfortably within the confines of the "Adamic myth" proposed by literary scholar R. W. B. Lewis, although their sense of individualism was complicated by their concurrent attachment to community and cooperation.[44] In addition, they also took account of the malevolent intentions, misguided values, and bad behaviors of a minority of community residents. Not merely a glorious celebration of American life, *My Ántonia* was more "complex, subtle, [and] aberrant" than that.[45] Cather and Wilder both ably represented the midwestern mindset for readers of different ages during the early twentieth century.

In her later novels, Wilder concentrated on the small town in the homesteading Midwest. She had witnessed the building of De Smet from the ground up. Once railroad surveyors platted the town in 1880, individuals and families were able to purchase lots on which to build houses or set up store buildings. During the rapid emergence of the town, "The business houses were all built one story high with a square, false front a story higher," Wilder wrote in *Pioneer Girl*. "Pa was building his with the idea of selling." He had bought two lots kitty-corner across from each other on Calumet Avenue (the main business street), and after constructing a store building on the first of them, he quickly sold it and put up another one on his second lot across the street. That building served as the family's home during the following hard winter of 1880–1881.[46]

A distinguishing feature of American culture for many decades was the centrality of its small towns in economic affairs and community formation. Laura Ingalls Wilder, both as a person and as a writer, was a significant participant in that phenomenon. "The civilization of America is predominantly the civilization of the small town," author Louis Raymond Reid could write as late as 1921.[47] "During most of American history, until the turn of the twentieth century, [the small town] was the basic community form for most Amer-

---

44. Lewis, *The American Adam: Innocence, Tragedy and Tradition in the Nineteenth Century* (Chicago: University of Chicago Press, 1955).

45. Blanche E. Gelfant, "The Forgotten Reaping-Hook: Sex in *My Antonia*," *American Literature* 43 (Mar. 1971): 61.

46. Wilder, *Pioneer Girl*, pp. 189, 191.

47. Reid, quoted in Guy Reynolds, "Willa Cather's Case: Region and Reputation," in *Regionalism and the Humanities*, ed. Timothy R. Mahoney and Wendy J. Katz (Lincoln: University of Nebraska Press, 2008), p. 83.

icans," cultural critic Max Lerner wrote in 1957. "But the growing point of American life is scarcely to be found in the small town today."[48] Living when and where she did, and writing about it later, Wilder paid as much, if not more, attention to town life as she did to events taking place on the countryside. The title she gave her autobiography, *Pioneer Girl*, is misleading only if readers infer from it that the town was less important than the farmstead on the frontier.

More than any other region, the Middle West demonstrated an attachment to small towns as places where the action happens. Writing in 1954, Lewis Atherton observed that the history of the Middle West could largely be written in terms of its small towns, an assessment that other scholars echoed. On average, each midwestern county contained seven towns. In discussing these places, Robert Wuthnow underscored their rootedness and sense of being grounded, their historical leanings, their attachment to story-telling, their neighborliness and community feeling, even though they frequently had few cultural amenities and suffered from lack of jobs, low wages, and excessive gossip. Richard Lingeman, for his part, pointed to the commercialism, booster spirit, practicality, and hunger for culture that, among many other things, historically characterized small communities in the Midwest.[49]

Despite the variable appearances that midwestern railroad towns like De Smet presented to the world—variations in size, local topography, wealth, economic function, date of origin, housing types, change over time, and so forth—they also shared many overlapping characteristics, rendering them similar to each other and easy to recognize. Balloon-frame construction of wooden buildings, which is said to have originated in Chicago during the 1830s, provided builders with a flexible method for executing different architectural styles, ranging from colonial and gothic to Queen Anne and Italianate. In courthouse towns, the official county building was usually situated prominently on a square in the center of town or sat two or three blocks off to the side of the main business street (as was the case in De Smet). The railroad and the main commercial street of the town constituted the two major axes around which such towns developed. De Smet, like all of the other towns located along the Dakota Central branch of the Chicago & North Western Rail-

---

48. Lerner, *America as a Civilization: Life and Thought in the United States Today* (New York: Simon & Schuster, 1957), p. 149.

49. Atherton, *Main Street on the Middle Border* (Bloomington: Indiana University Press, 1954), p. 1; Shortridge, *Middle West*, pp. 10, 140; Wuthnow, *Remaking the Heartland: Middle America since the 1950s* (Princeton, N.J.: Princeton University Press, 2011), p. 127, and *Small-Town America: Finding Community, Shaping the Future* (Princeton, N.J.: Princeton University Press, 2013), pp. 57–75; Lingeman, *Small Town America*, chaps. 3, 6.

road, was a so-called T-town. Main street ran perpendicular to the railroad, with the thoroughfare forming the stem of the "T" and the railroad serving as the cross-bar. Street widths and lot sizes in towns along the route were standardized, with plans emanating from company headquarters in Chicago.[50]

Surveyors hired by the Western Town Lot Company, a subsidiary of the Chicago & North Western Railroad, laid out the towns along the line in cookie-cutter fashion, drawing plats that varied mainly in relative size based on estimates of potential population growth made in corporate offices. Banks generally appropriated prime corner lots. Hotels, livery stables, and lumber yards tended to congregate near the railroad tracks. Churches and schools often achieved prominent locations, and opera houses, auditoriums, lodge halls, and other public or quasi-public buildings were usually located in or near the downtown business district or in other prime spots. By dint of scores of individual and organizational decisions, a certain sameness emerged in the appearance of the towns. Thus, when Wilder wrote *Pioneer Girl* and later turned part of it into *The Little Town on the Prairie*, she constructed a setting that thousands of enthusiastic readers could recognize because they had lived in towns like that or had read about them. The hotels in De Smet, Pearson's livery barn, the train depot, Jake Hopp's newspaper office, the First Congregational church, the town school, Margaret Garland's boarding house, Henry Hinz's saloon, Charles Tinkham's furniture store—all these places would have been instantly recognizable to anyone acquainted with typical small towns in the Middle West.

In like manner, the characters that peopled Wilder's stories were also recognizable. Historians have described a number of standard types of small-town residents between the Civil War and 1950, including those Wilder recalled in *Pioneer Girl*: lawyers, doctors, bankers, ministers, school teachers, newspaper editors, storekeepers, hotel managers, saloon keepers, depot agents, farmers, laborers, and immigrants.[51] Sometimes their behavior was exemplary, sometimes not. For example, the oafish behavior of railroad

50. Joseph C. Bigott, "Balloon Frame Construction," in *The Encyclopedia of Chicago*, ed. James R. Grossman, Ann Durkin Keating, and Janice L. Reiff (Chicago: University of Chicago Press, 2004), p. 60; Miller, *Wilder's Little Town*, pp. 16–34; John C. Hudson, *Plains Country Towns* (Minneapolis: University of Minnesota Press, 1985), chap. 7, and "Towns of the Western Railroads," *Great Plains Quarterly* 2 (Winter 1982): 41–54. Wilder often criticized the Chicago & North Western Railroad, without which her family would never have settled in Walnut Grove or De Smet, but which, in her view, cheated its employees and customers. Wilder, *Pioneer Girl*, pp. 151, 153, 169, 172, 174.

51. *See*, for example, Atherton, *Main Street*, chap 5; David J. Russo, *American Towns: An Interpretive History* (Chicago: Ivan R. Dee, 2001), chaps. 4–5.

storekeeper George Masters, who with his young wife and their newborn baby stayed with the Ingalls family during the winter of 1880–1881, caused Wilder to omit them from the story when she fictionalized it in *The Long Winter*. Then there was the merchant who hired Wilder to sew shirts. His prejudices, narrow-mindedness, and quarrelsome behavior, along with those of his mother-in-law, were so disconcerting to Wilder that she quit her job. Drunken men, knife-wielding housewives, stuck-up classmates, and scatter-brained railroad officials also made their appearance in her stories. By and large, however, Wilder's depictions in *Pioneer Girl* of De Smet's residents and their activities were appreciative and laudatory.[52]

Once Wilder was old enough to participate in community affairs, she engaged in the activities that she referred to as a "whirl of gaiety" in *Little Town on the Prairie*.[53] Many writers have noted how quickly the activities and accoutrements of "civilization" appeared in these little prairie towns, as the frontier continued to move westward. Wilder's description of what went on in De Smet corroborated the process of community formation, which included church programs and suppers, religious revivals, school exhibitions, hunting expeditions, house parties, literary societies, spelling bees, debates, vaudeville sketches, minstrel shows, singing schools, dancing clubs, roller-skating rinks, musical concerts, meetings of the Woman's Christian Temperance Union, sleigh and buggy riding, Fourth of July celebrations, and other events. From Alexis de Tocqueville to current-day Harvard professor Robert Putnam, a variety of observers have noted Americans' propensity to form organizations and engage in community projects, and the Middle West has been a special breeding ground of this kind of social capital over time.[54] Although

52. Wilder, *Pioneer Girl*, pp. 209, 236–37, 246, 270; Wilder, *The Long Winter* (New York: Harper & Row, 1953), pp. 203–8. The bad behavior Wilder described in De Smet was generally less egregious than the self-destructive, malicious, and abusive antics she cataloged in Burr Oak, Iowa, and Walnut Grove, Minnesota.

53. "The Whirl of Gaiety" is the title of Chapter 19 in *Little Town on the Prairie* (New York: Harper & Row, 1953), pp. 221–39. In the novels, Wilder listed more types of activities than she discussed in *Pioneer Girl*, but she did not include the many activities held in De Smet's roller-skating rink.

54. Wilder, *Pioneer Girl*, pp. 223, 251–52, 256–57, 259, 290, 292, 303, 305, 311. South Dakota and North Dakota have ranked high among the fifty states in surveys of participation in community activities. *See* Robert Putnam, *Bowling Alone: The Collapse and Revival of American Community* (New York: Simon & Schuster, 2000), pp. 291–92, 298, 300. Other books emphasizing strong community bonds in the Midwest include Merle Curti, *The Making of an American Community: A Case Study of American Democracy in a Frontier County* (Stanford, Calif.: Stanford University Press, 1959), pp. 112–15, 139, and Wuthnow, *Remaking the Heartland*, pp. 129, 146–47, 164–66, 245–46.

Wilder has been accused of overemphasizing the self-reliance of her family in her novels, the focus in her books and her activities as an adult in Missouri tended more toward supportive community than rugged individualism.[55]

The sense of community, with its attendant qualities of togetherness, obligation, and duty, was so pronounced in De Smet that some people were willing to risk their lives in order to insure the survival and benefit of the general populace. Most memorably, Almanzo Wilder and Cap Garland drove out into the countryside in hazardous blizzard conditions during the hard winter of 1880–1881 in order to bring back sacks of wheat for town residents to eat. On the other hand, storekeeper Daniel Loftus tried to profit from the situation until the citizenry rose up in collective outrage to force him to back down and lower his price.[56] Clearly, as other examples in *Pioneer Girl* also illuminate, all was not "sweetness and light" in the town. Generally speaking, however, Wilder's autobiography and the novels that emerged out of it described small towns and their surrounding countrysides as places where people were able to live life on a human scale and interact with each other on a personal basis (a process that German scholar Ferdinand Tönnies referred to as *gemeinshaft*, or "community").[57] In such towns, families formed the basis of community even as they insisted upon their own individual autonomy; they took pride in their hometowns and boosted them over neighboring towns; and they naturally formed and nourished institutions—social, economic, religious, political, educational, and legal—that made the flourishing of families and individuals more certain.

Wilder's creative treatment of Walnut Grove, Minnesota, and De Smet, Dakota Territory, and the environments they provided for her while she was growing up placed her among the scores of American writers who have dealt

55. Anita Clair Fellman, *Little House, Long Shadow: Laura Ingalls Wilder's Impact on American Culture* (Columbia: University of Missouri Press, 2008), argued that, in writing the novels, Wilder and Lane framed incidents to enhance the isolation of the family in order "to accentuate the individualist aspect of their lives" (pp. 4–5). The self-sufficiency of the family, in turn, fed into support for an anti-statist, libertarian political ideology found in the books. Ibid., pp. 3–7 and chap. 7. While it is true that Lane ended up as an extreme libertarian and her mother as a staunch, anti-Roosevelt conservative, the evidence for conservative political overtones in the Little House books, in my opinion, is scant and ambiguous; in *Pioneer Girl*, it is almost nonexistent. *See* the last chapter in my *Laura Ingalls Wilder and Rose Wilder Lane*, pp. 180–210. To her credit, Fellman admitted that different readers will discover different things in texts and that her reading may not appeal to everyone (p. 7).

56. Wilder, *Pioneer Girl*, pp. 220–21.

57. Tönnies, *Community and Civil Society* (1887; reprint, Cambridge, UK: Cambridge University Press, 2001), pp. 17–19.

with small towns in American life and especially midwestern life. Before the 1920s, a few authors such as E. W. Howe, Edgar Lee Masters, and Sherwood Anderson had cast doubt upon the small-town way of life, but most commentators had been positive and approving. The appearance of Sinclair Lewis's *Main Street* in 1920, however, and the disparaging commentaries of other writers, such as H. L. Mencken, Carl Van Doren, and Van Wyck Brooks, added up to a "revolt from the village," and the general American attitude became less appreciative of small-town ways as time went by.[58] In the 1930s, Wilder, unlike her daughter, still harbored a generally positive view of small towns as places in which to work and live, even though she had not started out that way. In *Pioneer Girl*, she had recounted episodes of family strife and abuse, infidelity, gunplay, sexual assault, drunkenness, duplicity, financial exploitation, and religious prejudice in the small towns she grew up in, but she also portrayed the positive aspects of these communities even as she claimed to prefer the homestead over the town. The discomfort that she initially felt in De Smet changed to appreciation as she grew older and engaged in more activities. By the time she wrote *Little Town on the Prairie* (1941), the shift in her attitude was complete.[59]

A final perspective on Wilder's connections to her home region can be found in the values that she acquired and the identity that she gradually took on as a girl and adult woman. In the end, she both reflected and articulated, on the one hand, and helped influence and illuminate, on the other, the values and mindsets of her native region. *Pioneer Girl* and the Little House novels can be understood in part as commentaries on the socialization process that took four young girls as blank slates and fitted them out with the attitudes, beliefs, habits, values, and motivations that made them responsible adults. Wilder's mother and father played distinctive roles in the parenting of Laura and her sisters. Charles Ingalls's friendly banter and horseplay, as well as his

---

58. Anthony Channell Hilfer, *The Revolt from the Village, 1915–1930* (Chapel Hill: University of North Caroline Press, 1969); Ronald Weber, *The Midwestern Ascendency in American Writing* (Bloomington: Indiana University Press, 1992), chap. 7. Jon K. Lauck called the idea into question in "The Myth of the Midwestern 'Revolt from the Village,'" *MidAmerica: The Yearbook of the Society for the Study of Midwestern Literature* 40 (2013): 39–85.

59. *Compare* Wilder, *By the Shores of Silver Lake* (New York: Harper & Row, 1953), pp. 247-48, 254, with her *Little Town on the Prairie*, p. 261. As a married woman in Mansfield, Missouri, Wilder engaged in many organizations and enjoyed a large coterie of friends, but she still harbored the kinds of positive and negative attitudes toward her town that most people did. Many of her *Ruralist* columns were devoted to improving life in Missouri's small towns.

example, his knowledge, and his authority provided them with a steady role model as they navigated the perils and opportunities of childhood. The girls learned from him as he loaded his gun; they delighted in playing "mad-dog" with him; they relied on him for protection from wild bears and panthers; and they benefitted from his hard work and sacrifice. His fiddle-playing enlivened family evenings; his story-telling inspired them for a lifetime; his firm setting of limits instructed them in what was proper behavior; and his infrequent spankings reinforced his status as a ruling force in a patriarchal society.

Caroline Ingalls, for her part, overlapped with her husband on a variety of these dimensions but also played the motherly role in a social order where gender roles were strictly separated and defined. Her reading to the girls from the Bible and the big green book on nature and her instructing them in cooking, sewing, house-cleaning, and all the other standard household chores socialized the girls into their proper roles. Caroline was a well-educated school teacher, providing a model for Wilder, who also taught in country schools before getting married. Caroline Ingalls's insistence that her girls get a solid education was crucial to the family's not moving beyond De Smet and created an atmosphere that valued books, education, and learning. She facilitated the girls' play time, cutting out paper dolls and letting them cook their playhouse dinners on the family stove, anticipating modern psychological research that tells us that play is an extremely effective way for children to learn. She also taught them to share and be generous with their playmates.

Within the family, the sisters engaged in some rather innocent sibling rivalry, but it was here that Wilder also learned to take on adult responsibilities, especially after Mary's blindness required her to serve as surrogate eyes. The extended family of grandparents, aunts, uncles, and cousins further provided a sense of stability, safety, predictability, and cooperation, as well as extended love and affection, which created an atmosphere of togetherness that helped shape the emotional contours of the girls' identities and motivated them to become better persons. If this portrayal of the family begins to sound too starry-eyed and idealistic, we can be sure that Wilder and her sisters also grew up in a world of reality, full of hard knocks and negative feedback. The poverty and hardship they endured during their early years on the frontier, however, were also conducive to developing ingenuity, resourcefulness, tenacity, persistence, industry, and cooperativeness, all characteristics that can be attributed to Wilder, her family, and other inhabitants of the region.

While each individual interacted with other people, social conditions, the natural environment, and metaphysical reality in his or her own unique way, there still remains value in generalizing about the sorts of people that emerged out of the social, economic, and environmental conditions on the midwestern

Frederick Jackson Turner and his ideas played an important role in framing the concept of the American frontier. *Wisconsin Historical Society*

frontier. The godfather of midwestern regionalism, historian Frederick Jackson Turner (1861–1932), grew up on the western frontier six years earlier than Wilder and approximately one hundred fifty miles southeast of her birthplace in Wisconsin. Emerging during the early 1900s as America's most influential historian and the progenitor of the "frontier interpretation" of American history, he asserted that American characteristics such as individualism, democracy, and nationalism derived largely from the encounter between westward moving pioneers and the natural environment. Beyond that, he argued, the same forces explained a whole host of American attributes: practicality, inventiveness, energy, and exuberance. In addition, he found people living on the frontier to be industrious, ambitious, courageous, egalitarian, optimistic, and idealistic. Close readers of Turner's work have pointed out that the preponderance of his examples and evidence came from his research in his own

Midwest, so, in effect, he was describing the Middle West as much as he was describing America as a whole.[60]

In *Pioneer Girl* and in her novels, Wilder, in similar fashion, described people she had known on her family's midwestern frontier as hard-working, persistent, ambitious, creative, self-reliant (and at the same time community-minded), patriotic, friendly, generous, hopeful, pious, good-hearted, and public-spirited. These kinds of attributes added up to what sometimes gets labeled midwestern (or Minnesota, or South Dakota) "niceness." Of course, one could also observe instances of envy, pride, duplicity, sloth, gluttony, narrow-mindedness, and the like. Wilder was more likely than Turner to think in moral terms, while Turner was more inclined to seek an "objective" or "unbiased" social-science/historical analysis. Both were generally hopeful, optimistic, and approving in their description of and evaluation of the Midwest as a region, while both also discerned flaws and challenges that needed attending to. While the two authors were writing for entirely different audiences and drawing upon different sources of information—one of which was narrow and personal, the other of which was eclectic, wide-ranging, and sophisticated—they painted pictures of midwestern society that overlapped with each other in significant ways.

Always, the ultimate goal, in Wilder's opinion, was to attain balance in one's personal life as well as in one's relationships with others. Cooperation and expert knowledge were both greatly needed, Wilder wrote in one of her *Missouri Ruralist* columns, "But every good becomes evil when carried to excess by poor, faulty mortals."[61] She often wrote about the need for balance between work and play, noted the necessity of keeping things even in politics, reminded readers that there are always two sides to a thing, and, in general, urged people to maintain balance in their own lives.[62] That balance has been one of the core values, too, of the Middle West as a region. Located in the center of the nation, its residents have sometimes been accused of being bland, uninteresting, and passive, while more supportive commentators have

---

60. Frederick Jackson Turner, "The Significance of the Frontier in American History," in his *The Frontier in American History* (New York: Henry Holt, 1920), pp. 1, 30, 37, 209–14; John E. Miller, *Small-Town Dreams: Stories of Midwestern Boys Who Shaped America* (Lawrence: University Press of Kansas, 2014), pp. 43–44; Michael C. Steiner, "Frederick Jackson Turner and Western Regionalism," in *Writing Western History: Essays on Major Western Historians*, ed. Richard W. Etulain (Albuquerque: University of New Mexico Press, 1991), pp. 103–35.

61. Wilder, "The Farm Home," *Missouri Ruralist*, Feb. 5, 1920, in *Laura Ingalls Wilder, Farm Journalist*, p. 213.

62. *See* her columns, ibid., pp. 52, 86, 182, 217, 220.

praised them for their steadiness, level-headedness, and common sense. All such broad generalizations are impossible to refute or verify, but whether empirical proof is forthcoming or not, people will continue to generate such observations and categorizations.

In the end, whether the Midwest is the home of pastoralism, whether the homestead frontier neatly captured the essence of the region during the time that Laura Ingalls Wilder was growing up there, whether small towns are especially midwestern, and whether midwestern values are unqualifiedly unique to the region remain debatable propositions. But the fact remains: Wilder grew up exclusively on the midwestern frontier; she lived almost all of her life in the Midwest; she bespoke generally acknowledged midwestern values; and she wrote about and lived in small towns most of her life. If we are to understand her and fully appreciate her writings, we had best acknowledge that she was, among other things, a midwesterner and that it had a significant influence on her life and work.

# { 8 }
# Women's Place
## *Family, Home, and Farm*

PAULA M. NELSON

In 1884, the year before they married, Almanzo Wilder gave Laura Ingalls one of the popular books of the day, *Mother, Home, and Heaven*.¹ The substantial volume contained poetry and prose devoted to the three subjects in the title. Written in the romantic and sentimental style of the day, the book captured dominant cultural ideals of the nation, especially the large middle class. The introduction spelled out the themes: "The *Mother* is the fountain-head of the *Home*. The home is the fountain-head of society and of the Church of Christ. And no influences in the universe contribute so much toward guiding immortal souls *Heavenward* as the Home and the Mother." The writer provided readers with the "one principle that seems to have an almost universal application, . . . "show me the mother and I will show you the man!"² Later in her life, writing from her home at Rocky Ridge Farm in Missouri, Laura Ingalls Wilder repeated that principle in her *Missouri Ruralist* columns for farm women. She saw its application in her own childhood home, which was never in one particular place for any length of time but was comprised of the love, discipline, values, work, comfort, loyalty, sharing, and striving within her nuclear family. Her home was portable, the way all good homes and good parenting should be.

While *Mother, Home, and Heaven* reflected Wilder's upbringing and her cultural ethos, the illustration on the cover of the book forecast the life she and Almanzo would build successfully in Missouri. Engraved in black ink on bronze-colored cover stock is a small farm home with a porch and smoke coming from the chimney, both symbols of comfort. Outside the door, the

---

1. William Anderson, comp., *Laura's Album: A Remembrance Scrapbook of Laura Ingalls Wilder* (New York: HarperCollins, 1998), p. 26.

2. [E. B. Treat, comp.], *Golden Thoughts on Mother, Home, and Heaven from Poetic and Prose Literature of All Ages and All Lands*, intro. Rev. Theodore L. Cuyler (Philadelphia: Monarch Book Co., 1882), p. 7 (emphasis in the original). This book, the title of which is abbreviated as *Mother, Home, & Heaven* on the cover, first appeared in 1878. Multiple editions from various publishers appeared through the 1880s.

Almanzo Wilder gave the book *Mother, Home, and Heaven* to Wilder in 1884. *Laura Ingalls Wilder Historic Home and Museum*

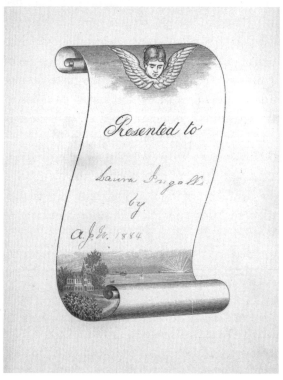

homemaker is feeding a flock of chickens, while the "man of the house" is working at the well. A small girl is spinning a hoop in the yard. The engraving provides metaphors as well: over the fence and across the road lies a tranquil sea with a small sailboat navigating life's waters. On the horizon, a large sun rises, its full rays depicting a bright day and a bright future to come. That scene must have resonated with the Wilders. While they struggled and labored, they maintained a faith in their partnership, in farm life, and in the bright, satisfying future that could be won with hard work and clear thinking.

That Laura Ingalls Wilder was not a feminist pioneer surprises and disappoints some who have studied her adult life and career. Her commitment to mostly separate spheres and the special role of women as mothers and homemakers, however, reflected the viewpoints of a majority of women at the time. Wilder's pioneering was physical and geographical, not cultural or transgressive. Her goals were more particular: (1) to be an equal partner with her husband in what she believed to be the best way of life, small-scale farming; and (2) to advocate for farm women, to teach them ways to see the world around them better, and to help them manage their work loads and family life. In many ways, Wilder was a small-scale, modern Ceres, although she was too unassuming to think of herself in those terms. Ceres, of course, was the goddess of agriculture, abundance, and motherly love.[3]

Who was Laura Ingalls Wilder? Born to Charles Ingalls, a "hunter and trapper, a musician and poet,"[4] and his quiet, serene, and unflappable wife, Caroline Quiner, Wilder and her family had become wanderers of sorts when they left their log cabin in western Wisconsin in 1869. Historian Elizabeth Jameson has tallied some of the costs: over the next twenty-six years, Wilder made eleven moves with her parents and later with her husband, Almanzo Wilder, before they found their true home in Missouri in 1894. The constants in her life were strong family ties, hard work, struggle, failure, and moving on. The young couple thought they had established a permanent home upon their marriage in 1885, a home Almanzo Wilder had built for them on his tree claim outside De Smet, Dakota Territory. On the day she married, she recalled in her autobiography, she sat on the step of their new house, thinking with satisfaction and relief of her new place, a home finally of her own. Drought, mortgages, fire, illness, and the death of their baby son changed the equation. The couple again searched for a home place, where both of them could be healthy, where they could make a living and support themselves

---

3. ceresva.org/Goddess/Ceres.htm.
4. Wilder to Rose Wilder Lane, Mar. 23, 1937, in *The Selected Letters of Laura Ingalls Wilder*, ed. William Anderson (New York: HarperCollins, 2016), p. 21.

and their daughter, Rose. Rocky Ridge Farm in Wright County, Missouri, redeemed the parents but drove their daughter to wandering to softer climes, where the work was not as repetitive and endless and where nature did not set the rules.[5]

By 1911, when Laura Ingalls Wilder began writing for the *Missouri Ruralist* farm paper, the Wilders had achieved economic stability after years of hard labor. Wilder was known for her production of eggs and chickens; the couple grew fruit, raised livestock of various kinds, enlarged their acreage from forty to one hundred acres, and had completed their plain but substantial farm house. Almanzo Wilder built much of it and much of the furniture himself, harvesting trees and rocks from their farm for materials. A paper Wilder wrote about raising chickens to contribute to an agricultural conference caught the attention of John F. Case, the editor of the *Ruralist*, who invited her to submit articles for publication. With more than half of the United States population living on farms, agricultural publications were important sources of information, advice, entertainment, and community. The *Ruralist* began in 1902 in Kansas City, Missouri. At the time Wilder began writing for the journal, the publication reached about fifteen thousand subscribers. In 1918, when editor Case wrote a lively profile of Wilder, the *Ruralist*, under new ownership, reached 88,640 subscribers. Wilder wrote for the journal until the end of 1924. She became a much-read, much-respected adviser about a host of issues of concern to farm families, especially farm women. Her optimistic outlook and her practical approaches to work in the farm home, to family life, to the roles of women on the farm, and to the values needed to live usefully had great appeal. On occasion, she told family stories that would later appear in her novels, and she celebrated the many things she had learned from her mother and her father.[6]

Wilder wrote her *Ruralist* columns in the context of rapidly changing times and sometimes controversial ideas. The decade between 1911 and 1920 brought the pinnacle of progressive politics in the United States with the

---

5. Elizabeth Jameson, "In Search of the Great Ma," *Journal of the West* 37 (Apr. 1998): 42; Wilder, *The First Four Years* (New York: Harper & Row, 1972), and *Pioneer Girl: The Annotated Autobiography*, ed. Pamela Smith Hill (Pierre: South Dakota Historical Society Press, 2014), p. 324; John E. Miller, *Becoming Laura Ingalls Wilder: The Woman behind the Legend* (Columbia: University of Missouri Press, 1998), pp. 71–113; Stephen W. Hines, ed., *Laura Ingalls Wilder, Farm Journalist: Writings from the Ozarks* (Columbia: University of Missouri Press, 2007), p. 6 (hereafter cited as *Farm Journalist*).

6. Miller, *Becoming Laura Ingalls Wilder*, pp. 99–113; Hines, Introduction to *Farm Journalist*, pp. 3–6; Pamela Hill Smith, *Laura Ingalls Wilder: A Writer's Life* (Pierre: South Dakota Historical Society Press, 2007), pp. 96–99.

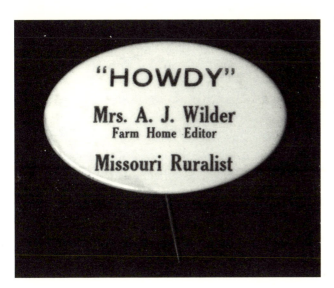

This pin is from Wilder's time at the *Missouri Ruralist*. Laura Ingalls Wilder Historic Home and Museum

election of Woodrow Wilson to the presidency. The Wilders were Democrats who supported Wilson in a Republican county. Given Wilder's libertarian leanings in the 1930s, her earlier Democratic loyalties may be surprising, but her immediate Ingalls family members were all loyal Democrats. Almanzo and Laura favored the Populist movement in the 1890s, supported William Jennings Bryan for president in 1896, and returned to the Democratic fold after the decline of Populism. Also, the Democratic Party prior to the age of Franklin Roosevelt was different from the modern version. Democrats opposed federal government power but had faith in local and state authority. They, or at least the rural wing, resisted reform elements in government and society. Democrats opposed what they saw as government policies that helped only the monied interests and advocated instead for workers and farmers, especially those who struggled. Wilson, of course, ran as a Progressive reformer, which meant that necessary reforms would be local- or state-managed without expansion of federal power. It did not work out that way. Many Progressive initiatives were institutionalized through constitutional amendments during Wilson's two terms, including the income tax and the Federal Reserve. American involvement in World War I greatly expanded federal power, as Wilson created federal bureaucracies to run the preparedness and domestic programs of wartime. Franklin Roosevelt used Wilson's system of bureaucracies to constitute the New Deal, which makes Wilder's appreciation of Wilson ironic.[7]

7. Teresa Lynn, *Little Lodges on the Prairie: Freemasonry and Laura Ingalls Wilder* (Austin, Tex.: Tranquility Press, 2014), p. 166; Miller, *Becoming Laura Ingalls Wilder*, pp.

People who live through times of great change or of emergency, such as World War I, often cannot see the long-term impact of policies and programs. Wilder wrote admiringly of Wilson's ideals as he worked to shape events on the international scene. She knew that the war had the power to remake the world, and it did. She also joined the local Red Cross during World War I, and in 1919, after the war had ended, she served as chairman of the Democratic women's group of Pleasant Township. On the other hand, while endorsing the Progressive ideal of cooperation to some extent, she argued for the traditional American emphasis on the importance of the individual.[8] Was Wilder a Progressive? Not completely. She chose among the ideals and programs, supporting those that aided agriculture or promised to bring and maintain peace. She rejected or ignored other policies that did not fit her world view, as most people do.

The decade from 1911 to 1920 also marked the return of soldiers after the war and the short, sharp depression that began in 1920. Rural-life reform had begun in 1908, when Theodore Roosevelt established a Commission on Country Life, and continued throughout the teens and beyond as public policy experts worried about mass migration from farms to the cities. They surveyed the quality of farm homes, schools, incomes, and values and found them wanting.[9] Many of Wilder's writings promote rural values and farm life and provide advice for those who wanted to improve their homes, work techniques, family relations, or create goals for the future. Finally, these years brought the success of the woman suffrage movement in the United States,

---

98–99. The literature on the parties and politics of the Gilded Age and Progressive Era is extensive. *See*, for example, Lewis L. Gould, *America in the Progressive Era, 1890–1914* (London: Routledge, 2013); Michael Kazin, *A Godly Hero: The Life of William Jennings Bryan* (New York: Anchor, 2007); John Milton Cooper, Jr., *Pivotal Decades: The United States, 1900–1920* (New York: W. W. Norton, 1990), and *Woodrow Wilson: A Biography* (New York: Vintage, 2011); R. Hal Williams, *Realigning America: McKinley, Bryan, and the Remarkable Election of 1896* (Lawrence: University Press of Kansas, 2010).

8. Wilder, "We Must Not Be Small Now," Apr. 20, 1918, "Opportunity," Nov. 5, 1918, and "The Farm Home," Feb. 5, 1920, *Missouri Ruralist*, all in *Farm Journalist*, pp. 144–45, 164–65, 213; Lynn, *Little Lodges on the Prairie*, pp. 248–49.

9. John Keegan, *The First World War* (New York: Vintage, 2000), is a good one-volume history of World War I by the late master of military history. John Milton Cooper, Jr., *The Warrior and the Priest: Woodrow Wilson and Theodore Roosevelt* (Cambridge: Belknap Press, 1985), offers a comparative biography of the two Progressive presidents and their era. For the rural-life movement, *see* Liberty Hyde Bailey, *The Country-Life Movement in the United States* (1911; reprint, Charleston: Bibliolife, 2009). Roosevelt tapped Bailey, a well-known horticulturalist from Cornell University, to head the Commission on Country Life.

with Missouri women receiving suffrage for presidential contests in 1919 and American women acquiring full voting rights in 1920 with ratification of the Nineteenth Amendment to the United States Constitution. Although the vote today is not understood as revolutionary, to Wilder and many others, it had the potential to disrupt the roles and place of women in society, impair relations within the family, and undermine family stability. On occasion, Wilder wrote about woman suffrage and the changing roles of women in American society. She was not partisan or argumentative but presented her ideas in a broader context that related to home, family, or the farm. When woman suffrage became law, Wilder urged women to do their duty, educate themselves, and go to the polls.[10]

Wilder had undoubtedly been aware of the movement since her teenage years in De Smet, Dakota Territory, a railroad town. National speakers traveled the region, bringing the message of suffrage for women to local audiences. In 1885, local representatives in the territorial legislature helped to pass a law extending suffrage to territorial women, but the governor vetoed it, fearful that it might impede the granting of statehood in Congress. In 1887, the territorial legislature granted women the right to vote in school-related elections, to serve as county superintendents, and to sit on local school boards. The statehood constitutional conventions held every two years from 1883 through 1889, when South Dakota was admitted to the Union, featured lengthy suffrage debates. Local newspaper editors, generally a highly political bunch, wrote frequently about territorial legislative sessions, bills passed, constitutional questions discussed, and anything else related to political parties and political action. In her autobiography, *Pioneer Girl*, Wilder said nothing about women's rights or suffrage and mentioned only that she did not want to promise to obey her new husband in her wedding vows.[11] Her

---

10. Margot McMillen, *The Golden Lane: How Missouri Women Gained the Vote and Changed History* (Charleston: History Press, 2011), provides a short, nicely illustrated history of suffrage in Missouri. Eleanor Flexner's *Century of Struggle: The Women's Rights Movement in the United States* (1959; New York: Atheneum, 1973) is the classic work on the subject. Marjorie Spruill Wheeler, ed., *One Woman, One Vote: Rediscovering the Woman Suffrage Movement* (Troutdale, Oreg.: New Sage Press, 1995), provides a collection of useful essays. For Wilder's advocacy, *see* her column "Women's Duty at the Polls," *Missouri Ruralist*, Apr. 20, 1919, in *Farm Journalist*, pp. 181–82.

11. Dorinda Riessen Reed, *The Woman Suffrage Movement in South Dakota*, 2d ed. (Pierre: South Dakota Commission on the Status of Women, [1975]), pp. 12–13; Doane Robinson, "History of Woman Suffrage in South Dakota," in *History of South Dakota*, 2 vols. (n.p.: B. F. Bowen & Co., 1904), 1:597–604; "Woman Suffrage," Feb. 14, 1885, and "Town and Country," Mar. 14, 1885, *De Smet Leader*; Wilder, *Pioneer Girl*, p. 322.

novel about the period, *These Happy Golden Years*, provides more detail. She asks Almanzo to talk to Reverend Brown about removing "obey" from her vows. Almanzo is surprised and asks if she favors women's rights like his sister Eliza. "'No,' Laura replied, 'I do not want to vote. But I can not make a promise that I will not keep, and, Almanzo, even if I tried, I do not think I could obey anybody against my better judgment.'"[12]

In her columns on the subject in the *Missouri Ruralist*, Wilder explained the ideals she held, the importance of women's work in the home and in voluntary associations, and her belief that the home is the foundation of society, the sanctuary where women, especially, focus on child rearing. Stephen W. Hines, who brought Wilder's *Missouri Ruralist* columns to readers' attention, has called her "something of a feminist, but a conservative one"[13] and stated elsewhere that she supported woman suffrage. Even so, her published columns do not express explicit support for suffrage, but they do tell women that they have the duty to vote, whether they want to assume the obligation or not. Hines may have mistaken her make-the-best-of-it approach for support. The Wilders were active Democrats, however, and when President Wilson publicly supported suffrage in 1918, Wilder may have become more positive about it and made statements to that effect to local people.[14]

Laura Ingalls Wilder's life philosophy shines through her columns, no matter the specific topic, and her ideals sprang from her deep Christian faith, learned at her mother's knee and practiced as a Congregationalist in her earlier life. She and Almanzo became Methodists in Mansfield, where there was no Congregational church, but she recalled a religious experience from her youth in her autobiography. The Ingalls family was in dire straits during their second stay in Minnesota, and the young Wilder was intensely worried. Her bedtime prayers were more fervent than usual, she said, when "gradually I had a feeling of a hovering, encompassing Presence of a Power, comforting and sustaining and thought in surprise 'That is what men call God!'"[15] Congregationalists required a testimony of religious awakening for full membership in the church in the nineteenth century, and this experience may have been hers.

Wilder's life philosophy rested also on the common belief that fundamental values and human nature remained unchanged over time. In her *Ruralist* column of July 20, 1917, she wrote: "'There is nothing new under the sun,' says the proverb. I think the meaning is that there are just so many truths or

---

12. Wilder, *These Happy Golden Years* (New York: Harper Trophy, 1971), pp. 269–70.
13. Hines, Introduction to *Farm Journalist*, p. 6.
14. Hines, *"I Remember Laura": Laura Ingalls Wilder* (Nashville: Thomas Nelson Publishers, 1994), p. 184; Wilder, "Women's Duty at the Polls," pp. 181–82.
15. Wilder, *Pioneer Girl*, p. 137.

laws of life and no matter how far we may think we have advanced we cannot get beyond those laws. However complex a structure we build of living we must come back to those truths."[16] Parents, especially mothers, taught fundamental precepts to their children. Each generation had to test their mothers' truths, Wilder believed, and each "must be burned by fire before we will admit the truth that it will burn." Mothers' teachings became more meaningful as children reached maturity "because our knowledge of the world and our experience of life have proved their worth," Wilder concluded.[17] She was not adverse to change or to the varieties of personal choice in her changing world, but she reminded readers that the price of it always had to be paid: "Is there something in life that you want very much? Then pay the price and take it, but never expect to have a charge account and avoid paying the bills. Life is a good collector and sooner or later the account must be paid in full." Her examples included a woman she knew who wanted to study music and become a musician. To do so, "she turned her children into the streets and neglected her husband that she might have more time for practice." The price was high, Wilder concluded, and "she will keep on paying the installments for the rest of her life."[18]

Wilder's reluctance to embrace woman suffrage resulted from her belief in the importance of women's roles as homemaker and mother and in her commitment to separate spheres broadly defined. Her ideas were similar to those expressed by organized anti-suffrage groups across the country, some of whose members' wealth and position allowed them time to write and speak against the vote for women. Their literature circulated through newspapers and booklets, providing well-argued ammunition for women who opposed the vote.[19] Wilder did not quote from their work and did not express her ideas as directly, preferring instead to use stories, humor, and moral wisdom to convey her ideals. Her convictions, however, drew from the same well.

The role of women as moral influences within the home was a relatively new idea in the nineteenth century. Historian Linda K. Kerber explained its origins in the concept of "republican motherhood," invented during the

16. Wilder, "A Bouquet of Wildflowers," *Missouri Ruralist*, July 20, 1917, in *Farm Journalist*, p. 119.

17. Wilder, "Mother, a Magic Word," ibid., Sept. 21, 1921, p. 259.

18. Wilder, "Buy Goods Worth the Price," ibid., Apr. 5, 1917, p. 105.

19. In Brookings, South Dakota, for example, prominent women of the town organized an anti-suffrage club, and one of them published excerpts from the speech given by Mrs. William Winslow Crannell at the 1896 Democratic Party convention, where she asked delegates to reject woman suffrage. Mrs. E. J. M., "Two Suffrage Arguments Scanned," *Brookings County Press*, Sept. 9, 1898.

American Revolution to provide a place for women in the new order. Republican motherhood defined the role of women as anti-suffragists understood it. The earlier organization of marriage, in the colonial period, came from British common law through the concept of coverture. Husband and wife became one person at marriage, and that person was the husband. He controlled property and assets, even the children. Dependents, including women, children, servants, and slaves, did not have a voice in politics. Women had no property and therefore no free will or independence; only the control of property provided status and entry into the body politic. Women lived within a female domain of work and home life, a sphere Kerber compares to "a tradition-bound, underdeveloped nation within a larger, more politically sophisticated one." At the time of the Revolution, American women lived in a society marked by "local isolation, political apathy, and rudimentary literacy."[20]

Following the Revolution, the new nation required active participation and a commitment to the broader national good and civic virtue. Male citizens would apply those values, but how would they learn civic virtue, broad-mindedness, and commitment to the nation? Their mothers would teach them in the family home. Women would thus participate peripherally in the "polis," the public, political world inhabited by men, through their roles as mothers instructing their children. To instruct their sons properly to be good citizens and their daughters to become good mothers of patriotic sons, women had to be educated and become committed to civic virtue. The primary role of women remained domestic, but their need to provide moral influence in the home and teach their sons to be better citizens led to greater education for women. In turn, education and the responsibility for moral influence led women to a broader awareness of the world around them. Republican motherhood, as Kerber termed it, was an enhancement of women's place in the nation.[21]

In the nineteenth century, the rapid rise of industrialization, which moved production of many goods out of the home and built the middle class, reinforced the concept of separate spheres of influence for men and women, but it also emphasized dramatic differences in male and female inclinations, virtues, and behavior. Motherhood became increasingly romanticized and sentimentalized, and the home became a refuge from the marketplace and the state. Women's moral authority within the home grew. The role of mothers as teachers of their children remained fundamental to the stability of soci-

20. Kerber, *Women of the Republic: Intellect and Ideology in Revolutionary America* (Chapel Hill: University of North Carolina Press, 1980), p. 7. *See also* pp. 120, 139–55, 189–221, 269–88.

21. Ibid., pp. 7–12, 189–231.

ety, but women's roles developed in another way that drew them out of the home. Women's voluntary associations, focused at first in churches, aimed to spread the good news of the Gospel, to reach out to the lost, aid the poor, assist widows and orphans, and perform countless other benevolent activities. The religious movement known as the Second Great Awakening prompted a revival of religious commitment across the country between 1790 and the 1840s. Women's moral influence and teaching within the home made them logical vessels of reform and uplift outside the home in certain circumstances. Wealthier women were able to fund charitable works or raise funds among men of their class. Sometimes the work of organized women moved beyond informal associations into well-organized, fully developed institutions with boards of directors, employees, and substantial fund-raising obligations. The broad-ranging catalogue of female benevolence, however, did not challenge their domesticity. Instead, their work emphasized the special roles of women within the separate-spheres ideal.[22]

By the late nineteenth century, women's activism aimed to reform society through efforts to change local, state, and federal laws, with temperance the primary issue. This kind of activism required a more public commitment from women, with organized campaigns to shutter saloons, to convince male voters to vote "dry," and sometimes to march down Main Street to declare their intentions. The Woman's Christian Temperance Union (WCTU) was the best known of the women's temperance groups, but mixed groups of men and women, like the Good Templars, flourished as well. The WCTU attracted middle-class women who were often quite traditional in their view of women's place. Frances Willard, the national president of the group, supported woman suffrage and presented it to members as a method to secure "the protection of women and the improvement of society."[23] Framing suffrage in that way prompted many women to support it who otherwise had not. The WCTU was set up so that local groups could choose their focus for work and study from a long list of social reforms. Some might incorporate suffrage advocacy with anti-liquor work; others might commit to soup-kitchen work, early childhood education, or a host of other options. Willard chose the motto "Do Everything," and WCTU women did.[24]

Caroline Ingalls, Laura Ingalls Wilder's mother, hosted a meeting of the

22. Nancy Woloch, *Women and the American Experience* (New York: Alfred A. Knopf, 1984), pp. 116–25, 167–293; Susan Goodier, *No Votes for Women: The New York State Anti-Suffrage Movement* (Urbana: University of Illinois Press, 2013), p. 2.

23. Woloch, *Women and the American Experience*, pp. 288–93.

24. Paula M. Nelson, "'Do Everything:' Women in Small Prairie Towns, 1870–1920" *Journal of the West* 36 (Oct. 1997): 58–60.

local WCTU in De Smet in 1883. In her autobiography, Wilder admitted to a "distaste" for everyone in attendance except her mother, a reflection, perhaps, of her dislike or even fear of strangers rather than any dislike for prohibition.[25] Laura Ingalls seems to have been an introvert, more at home with family and close friends and not eager to meet new people, especially if, as so often happened, she had to live with them. Perhaps their presence seemed like an invasion of her home, or at that point in her life, Wilder may not have cared for women of a reformist bent. Caroline Ingalls's membership in the organization is mentioned in other sources, but there is no information about her suffrage beliefs. Her daughter Carrie Ingalls, however, was the secretary of the De Smet chapter of the Good Templars in 1889, and Grace Ingalls's diary of the period recorded the family's interest in prohibition campaigns, which brought lecturers and rallies to town. Teresa Lynn, author of a book about the Ingalls family and Freemasonry, stated that the "entire family were prohibitionists" based on her reading of Grace's diary.[26]

When Laura and Almanzo relocated to Mansfield, Wilder found that the community had a WCTU chapter, but she did not become a regular member. Biographer John E. Miller described Wilder as sympathetic to the temperance cause but too busy with her many other obligations to join when the group reorganized in 1925. According to Rose Wilder Lane, the WCTU and the churches were active opponents of Wilder's when she ran for the office of township tax collector that same year. Their opposition may have been to Wilder's active affiliation with the Democratic Party, which most Republicans saw as the "Rumocracy" party. The Democratic Party, however, was divided into two groups, the staunch pro-alcohol urban members and the equally staunch rural anti-alcohol members, of whom the Wilders were an example. Those complexities within the party were not visible to avid prohibition partisans. In spite of her landslide loss, Wilder was active and respected in the community. She belonged to the Order of Eastern Star, serving as an officer on occasion, to the Methodist church, farmer's clubs, and several women's clubs. Over the years, she campaigned actively for restrooms for women in county towns, where they could nurse or change babies, wait for husbands, or freshen up. Another key campaign she instigated was creation of a county library system.[27]

25. Wilder, *Pioneer Girl*, p. 256.
26. Lynn, *Little Lodges on the Prairie*, p. 117.
27. Miller, *Becoming Laura Ingalls Wilder*, pp. 160, 164; Jack S. Blocker, Jr., David M. Fahey, and Ian R. Tyrell, eds., *Alcohol and Temperance in Modern History: An International Encyclopedia* (Santa Barbara, Calif.: ABC Clio, 2003), p. 191; Lynn, *Little Lodges on the Prairie*, pp. 245, 248–51; Hill, *Laura Ingalls Wilder*, p. 99.

Wilder and Almanzo (left) posed with neighbors
near Mansfield, Missouri, circa 1920.
*Herbert Hoover Presidential Library and Museum*

The vote for women had first been suggested publicly at a Seneca Falls, New York, women's rights convention in 1848. A number of female abolitionists had been struck by the many restrictions they faced as reformers because of their sex. They arranged to meet in Seneca Falls to discuss the place of women in society and what might be needed to make women's rights equal to men's rights. The "Declaration of Sentiments" that the convention produced included resolutions to allow women access to education and occupations presently closed to them, to change laws concerning rights to property they brought into marriage and income they earned during marriage, and other reforms. The final resolution, the only one not to pass unanimously, was to allow women the vote, a controversial concept. It individualized women, especially married women, and removed them from the umbrella of family relations and allowed them into political matters. The rationale for women's rights in general, and the vote in particular, in the nineteenth century was the concept of natural rights:

"All men are created equal" and "are endowed by their Creator" with rights to "life, liberty, and the pursuit of happiness" became the American creed. Even poor men might rise; many women believed themselves to be the equals of any man, no matter how rich or well-positioned. Just as the Declaration of Independence defined natural rights granted by "Nature or Nature's God" to colonial men resisting the King of England, the Declaration of Sentiments, using the same language, format, and ideals, expanded those rights to women.[28] For the next fifty years, the foundation of the women's rights movement was a female claim to natural rights, although the claim of women's moral superiority crept in by the 1860s. Elizabeth Cady Stanton, consummate natural-rights advocate, gave a speech in 1869, in which she described men as "a destructive force, . . . stern, selfish, aggrandizing, loving war, conquest, acquisition." Women had to become evangelists for "purity, virtue, morality, true religion, to lift men into the higher realm of thought and action."[29]

By the end of the nineteenth century, the arguments for woman suffrage changed to ones of expediency or usefulness. Instead of the vote liberating women from secondary status and demonstrating that all persons were equal, the vote became a tool for middle-class white women, who considered themselves different from men, possessing different virtues and ideals with which to reform society. How did this major change in thought occur? According to historian Eric Foner, the Panic of 1873 began a process of ideological change in the United States. It created economic chaos, huge financial losses for businessmen and investors, and massive unemployment, resulting in hostility towards immigrants, who took scarce jobs or worked for much less money. Reconstruction in the South failed in the 1870s, and white supremacy reasserted itself there. Many northerners turned a blind eye to the violence and increasing restrictions on African Americans. Many who had stoutly defended the rights of the former slaves began to doubt whether equality was possible; the faith that all men could rise faded. The Spanish-American War in 1898 and events leading up to it led to the creation of colonies in Cuba and the Philippines. Poet Rudyard Kipling celebrated America's colonial operations in his poem "The White Man's Burden" in 1899. Americans no longer saw their society as one made up of men like Abraham Lincoln, who rose from log-cabin poverty to the presidency. Instead, immigrants, illiterates, people of color, and many others who were not of the white, middle class seemed to be overwhelming the cities and the countryside, challenging the

28. Aileen S. Kraditor, *The Ideas of the Woman Suffrage Movement, 1890–1920* (New York: Columbia University Press, 1965), pp. 1–12, 43–52, 77; "The Declaration of Sentiments and Resolutions," *The Elizabeth Cady Stanton and Susan B. Anthony Project Papers*, ecssba.rutgers.edu/docs/seneca.html.

29. Quoted in Woloch, *Women and the American Experience*, p. 340.

old faith in universal upward mobility. When the old-line egalitarian suffragists conceded in the 1890s that the votes of white, middle-class women could counterbalance those of "undesirables," old ideas about the natural rights of all virtually disappeared from the woman suffrage movement. For women seeking the vote in this new climate, the task was to demonstrate that they had the intellectual and cultural capacity to vote and that their votes would aid society. The concurrent rise of organized women, with millions involved in Federated Women's Clubs or the WCTU, aided the suffrage movement immeasurably. Suffrage was no longer seen as quite so outlandish or bizarre.[30]

Coinciding with this shift in attitude about the vote was the rise of the Progressive movement. Born of the societal challenges that accompanied the new industrial order, the rise of massive cities, and the fear of corporate domination, Progressivism was all about government, city, and social reforms, as well as the encouragement of cooperation among affiliated groups to defend their interests in the new order. Their goals were ambitious, and as one historian wrote, "Progressives thought they could create a society run by educated citizens, without poverty, injustice, or corruption." Woman suffrage advocates, with their sense of female moral superiority and their sex-based world view, blended nicely into the Progressive order.[31]

The reforms women worked to achieve tended to be those accomplished through government legislation, which required votes to pass. Child labor laws, initiative and referendum, wage and hours laws, sanitation policy, the prohibition of alcohol, family courts, the eradication of the white-slave traffic, food and drug laws, and many other issues attracted suffragists' attention. Historian Aileen Kraditor noted that a common metaphor for pro-suffrage versus anti-suffrage approaches to social problems compared their work to that of doctors and nurses. Doctors tried to identify the cause of disease and cure it or root it out. Nurses, called in to provide care when illness or accident struck, had to "patch and bandage" to the best of their abilities to help the patient recover. Doctors were the voters, of course, solving problems through

---

30. Foner, *Reconstruction: America's Unfinished Revolution, 1863–1877* (New York: Harper & Row, 1988), pp. 512–601; Rudyard Kipling, "The White Man's Burden," *Modern History Sourcebook,* legacy.fordam.edu; Kraditor, *Ideas of the Woman Suffrage Movement,* pp. 43–47; Woloch, *Women and the American Experience,* pp. 334–37. Stuart Creighton Miller, *"Benevolent Assimilation": The American Conquest of the Philippines, 1899–1903* (New Haven, Conn.: Yale University Press, 1982), offers a classic, balanced account of the affair, while Joseph A. Fry, "Phases of Empire: Late Nineteenth Century U.S. Foreign Relations," in *The Gilded Age: Essays on the Origins of Modern America* (Wilmington, Del.: SR Books, 1996), pp. 261–88, sees all United States history as imperialism.

31. Woloch, *Women and the American Experience,* p. 336.

the ballot box. Nurses were the anti-suffrage women with their charities and benevolent organizations, trying to repair the damage that had already been done.[32]

Organized anti-suffrage activities in the United States began in the 1880s and peaked between 1895 and 1907. They continued, though more weakly, during the years of victory for suffrage advocates. Often local leaders, ministers, or editors spoke or wrote against votes for women, circulating the common anti-suffrage arguments. As the suffrage movement became more successful and began attracting middle-class women ready to use the vote to engage in social reform, anti-suffrage societies began to organize to rebut them. Such societies organized in twenty-five states, and a national anti-suffrage association appeared in 1911. A male anti-woman suffrage organization, the Man-Suffrage Association, also organized in 1912 to support the antis.[33] No evidence exists that Laura Ingalls Wilder belonged to any organized campaign to defeat suffrage. Her efforts in that direction consisted of occasional commentary in her *Missouri Ruralist* columns, where she shared many concerns expressed by anti groups.

The anti-suffrage groups based their opposition on four main arguments: (1) women's special role in society within the family, (2) women's disinterested and nonpartisan power to influence society, (3) women's biological differences from men, and (4) the rejection of the concept of equality as sameness. Women's special role and their biological differences were the most obvious, visible, and understandable concepts to their contemporaries. For anti-suffragists, the family, not the individual, was the foundation of American society. Families had one head, the husband and father, who voted in the interest of his family group. Wives and mothers reigned within the home, shaping the character of each of their children and influencing their husbands to follow the moral path. The role of mother as moral teacher and builder of character was vital to the success of the family, the community, and the nation. Anti-suffragists believed that social evils arose from the individual human heart. A better world would occur when individuals learned self-control, restraining passions and instincts. Mothers, who taught these vital precepts, held the social order in their hands. Private morality led to public morality; people who knew restraint and self-control did not need to be controlled by law. Antis did not share the suffragists' confidence that women could purify society through "municipal housekeeping," the term used to describe the use of the woman's

---

32. Kraditor, *Ideas of the Woman Suffrage Movement*, p. 63.

33. Jane Jerome Camhi, *Women against Women: American Anti-Suffragism, 1880–1920* (Brooklyn, N.Y.: Carlson Publishing, 1994), pp. 2–3, 88.

vote for social reform through groups like the WCTU. Instead, they believed that mothers in their own homes built public morality one family at a time.[34]

Women's biological differences from men also limited political participation, the antis argued. Women were physically weaker, with biological processes that required periodic rest and retreat. How would it be received if women joined the political world but had to miss important obligations due to the disabilities of their sex? Nineteenth-century understandings of health and sickness influenced these arguments. In this context, both women and men could exhaust their physical resources through excesses, exposure to extreme temperatures, eating the wrong foods, too much sexual activity, or many other things. Higher education for women came under fire for using too much brain power, for example, which would starve female reproductive organs of energy. Men could also overdo mental work and become ill or end up insane through masturbation. Balance was required to maintain health, and stepping out of one's role could cause disaster. Given the cultural and scientific understanding of the body and health at the time, the antis' focus on physical differences made sense to them. In this context, women's temperament was also considered less suited to political give-and-take because they reacted to differences of opinion too personally. People engaged in politics had to rise above the personal, antis believed, and to act in disinterested and objective fashion. Women were subjective by nature. Men and women were made differently and could not be the same nor do the same things. The division of labor had evolved over time to put each sex into its appropriate role, and society functioned best when these laws of nature were observed. When women stepped outside their roles, the consequences disrupted family and society.[35]

Laura Ingalls Wilder expressed this view when she remembered her experiences with the Brown family of De Smet in her autobiography. Anti-suffrage leaders, through widely circulated propaganda, argued that women who became politically active would neglect their homes and families. The Brown family provided Laura Ingalls with an object lesson. In *Pioneer Girl*, she told of the difficulties that her friend Ida Brown, the adopted daughter of Reverend Edward Brown and his wife Laura, faced at home. Though "always cheerful," Ida had to do the work of the household because Laura Brown was "literary," a writer, who in this case advocated for prohibition. Mrs. Brown held a time-consuming job as corresponding secretary for the Kingsbury County WCTU

---

34. Ibid., pp. 5–32.

35. Ibid., pp. 17–32; Paula M. Nelson, "'In the Midst of Life We Are in Death': Medical Care and Mortality in Early Canton," *South Dakota History* 33 (Fall 2003): 196–211.

and wrote for Congregational church publications. As a result, her home was "in a dirty disorder," as Wilder described it.[36] In the Ingalls family, of course, the women shared their household work and farm chores, and cleanliness and order were important standards.

The other two anti-suffrage arguments were more philosophical and tied to fine-tuned definitions of public and private activities. Anti-suffragists believed that women's nonpartisan power in society came through their club work, benevolent societies, and charitable social-welfare commitments. These groups met outside the home and held public events or worked with the poor or disadvantaged but fit solidly within women's domestic space. Because they did not vote or hold political party allegiances, benevolent, organized women stood above the fray. Because they applied influence through groups, they had far more impact than one woman might have with her lone vote. Through indirect action, women achieved much. If they engaged in partisan politics, however, as voting women would do, groups and individuals would associate with one party or another, influencing only members of that party and limiting their impact. Political women, the argument went, would dominate women's groups that had previously been nonpartisan. Questions of program and direction would become partisan arguments and cause division. Organized, formerly nonpolitical groups would lose their prestige and ability to influence. Related to this argument was the issue of special privileges that women enjoyed in society. Chivalry, manners, and behaviors that honored their status as women might disappear if women became political sparring partners. The special privileges that women held (not to serve on juries, not to be responsible for personal protection or for police or military duties) would change. At home, men would no longer be responsible for financial support of their wives and children, antis surmised.[37]

Finally, the anti-suffrage movement rejected the concept of equality between men and women. They believed that suffragists wanted women to have what men had. The only means to reaching this end, the antis believed, was to make women like men. Should women become equals, using the male model of rights, obligations, and behavior, society would fall apart. Men were born to protect and provide. Without those obligations, their less-evolved and more

---

36. Wilder, *Pioneer Girl*, pp. 295, 295n47. Wilder also used the Brown household in a 1917 *Ruralist* column, in which Mrs. Brown was the object of unkind gossip among people who failed to understand that she was writing for pay in order to buy her daughter a new wardrobe—a totally different interpretation of the situation. Wilder, "If We Only Understood," Dec. 5, 1917, in *Farm Journalist*, pp. 129–30.

37. Camhi, *Women against Women*, pp. 11–17.

savage elements would reassert themselves. Women's roles in society as presently constituted, included the civilization of men, as well as the training of children. Anti-suffrage women believed that men and women needed equal opportunity "for expression along their *different* lines."[38] The sexes were not the same. Women's lines included home, family, church, voluntary associations, charity, and assistance in the community in nursing the sick, caring for the elderly or infirm, monitoring the schools, and myriad other unpaid social duties. Men's primary lines were government and business, family protection and support, and war when necessary. Antis recognized that some women chose to work outside the home, at least before marriage, and some had no choice but to work for their own or their family's support. The vote, however, especially when enacted by federal amendment, would force women into politics and the political process. Voting was not a right, in this view, but an obligation that required preparation and would upset society as constituted. Anti-suffrage women considered the suffragists naive. Government is force, and political life is a form of war, they argued. Suffragists, who planned to use women's persuasive skills to achieve change and seemed to think only social advances would result, failed to see those fundamental facts.[39]

Wilder mentioned suffrage in her *Missouri Ruralist* columns for the first time in April 1916. Her words and tone conveyed some resentment about the suffrage movement and its attitude about those who opposed or were not interested in it. "I see by the papers," Wilder wrote, "that one of the suffrage leaders of the state will tour the Ozarks this spring in the interest of woman suffrage, bringing light into the dark places, as it were."[40] Suffrage leaders and speakers sometimes used the term "unenlightened" for those who did not endorse votes for women, which smacked of condescension, even ridicule.[41] Wilder's remarks reflected her sense that suffrage reformers thought highly of themselves and less of those who disagreed with their chosen remedies for social ills. This column was the only time she betrayed impatience with the pro-vote people. Other columns reflected her concerns about social changes sweeping through society, but her opposition appeared in print as thoughtful questions, not harsh critiques. What had the women now going into the paid workplace done before taking these jobs? she might ask. Who would

---

38. Ibid., p. 31 (emphasis in the original).

39. Ibid., pp. 27-32, 35-48.

40. Wilder, "Look for Faeries Now," *Missouri Ruralist*, Apr. 5, 1916, in *Farm Journalist*, p. 64.

41. Ernest Bernbaum, Introduction to *Anti-Suffrage Essays*, by Massachusetts Women (Boston: Forum Publications, 1916), p. xi.

do that work? Will that work be done? Will something vital be missing if it is not done?[42] In her first brief comment on suffrage leaders, Wilder went on to challenge the suffragist idea "of the ballot as the supreme attainment," with "everything good" to follow automatically. To her mind, Wilder said, the ballot was "incidental" to the important work of women. Corrupt politics, dishonest politicians, graft, and injustice stemmed from men who followed the wrong path. Those men were what their mothers had made them, and "their wives usually have finished the job." Wilder suggested that readers who thought she gave too much power to women's influence should study the cases of corrupt men to see the truth of her statements.[43]

In 1919, after the Missouri legislature voted to grant presidential suffrage to the state's women, Wilder again cautioned her readers to avoid utopian thinking where suffrage was concerned. Women were not all alike, she argued, and would not vote in a mass. Women's vote would "no more bring purity into politics" than men's would. Voters in California and the city of Chicago had rejected prohibition, for example, even though women there had suffrage. On the other hand, "home-loving, home-keeping women" now had an obligation to go to the polls to vote, even if it was "distasteful" to them. Here, Wilder employed arguments similar to those of suffrage supporters, that good women must do their duty to balance out the votes that would come from "the rougher class," who would certainly go to the polls. It was not that all good women would vote the same, in her view, but that the equilibrium would better be maintained if all types of women voted. Wilder also argued that women voters must prepare and not just vote as their husbands did. "We women know in our hearts, tho we would not admit it, that our men are not infallible." Men made mistakes, headed in the wrong direction, or held mistaken ideas. Women had to think for themselves. It was also important for women to vote in honor of the men who had fought in World War I to uphold American ideals.[44]

Events after World War I made the vote even more important for farm women and farm families, Wilder believed. Labor conflicts and the rise of more radical labor organizations, fear of Bolsheviks, rising food prices, the abolition of the war boards that Wilson had instituted, all led to growing national turmoil. There was hope in some quarters that women would step into politics, create their own party, and "clean house" with their votes. Wilder disagreed. "I think the idea of a woman's party, a political division on sex

42. *See*, for example, Wilder, "Who'll Do the Women's Work?," Apr. 5, 1919, and "The Farm Home," Feb. 5, 1920, in *Farm Journalist*, pp. 179–181, 213.
43. Wilder, "Look for Faeries Now," p. 64.
44. Wilder, "Women's Duty at the Polls," pp. 181–82.

lines, is distasteful to women, especially farm women." People must work together, Wilder believed, not add more division. Farm women should read about national politics, study the role of Congress in instigating or extending internal conflicts, ponder their own interests, discuss it at home with their "men folks," and choose candidates that way. If farm families were worried about political figures selling them out, they needed to study and to vote their mutual interests. Wilder believed that women might be able to overcome the anger, "'hot air' and insults," and help bring "sane, sensible discussion" back to politics, a hope she shared with suffragists.[45]

In a 1918 column titled "New Day for Women," Wilder asked her readers if they remembered the term "old maid," which had been the label for unmarried women in her youth. There had been just two life choices for females in that era: to marry or to be an old maid. Some of the older girls, she remembered, rejected the term and wanted to be known as "bachelor girls" instead, which was controversial at the time. Now, Wilder wrote, people just referred to women, with such "descriptive adjective[s]" as young, married, older, divorced or widowed "in the background." Women worked successfully at a host of occupations. Marriage was no longer a woman's sole aim. Of course, Wilder stated, "everyone knows that a woman's most important work is still her children," but the "activities and absorbing interests" now available filled much of her time. Across the western world, women were voting, participating in government, and adding their voices to their nations' directions. Wilder recognized that American women would win the vote soon. Her concern was their preparation. Would women use their new power for good? Women had criticized men for the direction of events in the past. When the war ended, society could be remade. Would inexperienced women make the right choices? "I wish I might be sure," Wilder wrote, "that we would be equal to our opportunity." She described her discussion with a "liberal-minded man," one who fully endorsed woman suffrage. When she asked him about "the coming power of women" and the preparation, or lack thereof, of women voters, he compared them to citizens in Russia whom he considered totally unprepared to vote. Women, he said, "'are ignorant along the lines of government and too uncontrolled in their emotions.' I wonder if he is right!" Wilder worried.[46]

---

45. Wilder, "The Farm Home," *Missouri Ruralist*, Dec. 5, 1919, in *Farm Journalist*, pp. 206-7. The *Ruralist* began publishing Wilder's work under the set title "The Farm Home" on May 5, 1919, and continued the title through Dec. 5, 1920, with occasional individually titled pieces in between.

46. Wilder, "New Day for Women," *Missouri Ruralist*, June 5, 1918, in *Farm Journalist*, pp. 149-51.

Daughter Rose Wilder Lane's world travels occasionally provided Wilder with material for her *Ruralist* column. Lane's letter about postwar Poland allowed Wilder to comment again on suffrage. "Women who feel that they had quite enough to do without taking part in politics and who are inclined to shirk the duties of full citizenship should be thankful they have escaped so easily and consider the situation of Polish women," Wilder wrote. In Poland, women were advocating for "a universal military service law for women," which included a year of military training at age nineteen but could include health-care work or other public service instead. Young women would be unable to marry until their service was completed. The Polish women advocating for this law believed that "all privileges carry duties."[47] Although Wilder did not include this information in her column, American anti-suffrage women had used the possibility of such service as an argument against woman suffrage. Those who participated in the affairs of state had the duty to defend the state when called upon, antis argued, which might mean military service for women if they won the franchise.[48]

Another postwar issue that interested Wilder involved the new place of women. When the men marched off to war, their jobs and many of the new ones created to support the war effort were filled by women. When these women refused to leave their posts in the postwar economy so that returning soldiers could go back to work, Wilder wondered: Where were these women before the war? Were they employed? Where did they work? Who had their old jobs now? Was their work being done? Who was doing the work they left behind to take the new jobs the war created? How would the conflict over these jobs resolve? "Where are [these women] going," Wilder wondered, "and with them all of us?" While she was proud of women's many accomplishments, and sure that no one could now contest women's place in world affairs, she worried about the future. Who would do the work women had always done? "If in their haste to do other, perhaps more showy things, their old and special work is neglected and only half done, there will be something seriously wrong with the world, for the commonplace, home work of women is the very foundation upon which everything else rests."[49]

Wilder's columns over the years discussed many issues beyond women's changing world. She wrote frequently about the impact of World War I on her and her neighbors' attitudes about cutting back on food, on purchasing luxury items, on the high cost of living, and on Wilson's plans for war and

47. Wilder, "Women and Real Politics," ibid., Apr. 15, 1921, pp. 246–47.
48. Kraditor, *Ideas of the Woman Suffrage Movement*, pp. 28–29.
49. Wilder, "Who'll Do the Women's Work?," p. 180.

peace. American involvement in the war, however, occupied only two years of her thirteen-year career with the *Ruralist*. The tumultuous years in the immediate aftermath of war provided more columns on farmers, labor, and the problems of big business intervening between producers and consumers to earn big profits at the peoples' expense. Much of her language comes from the Progressive understanding of economic relations so much under discussion in this era and shows Wilder's eagerness to win farmers better prices and more respect. Underlying those inclinations, however, was always her understanding of the role of individuals, of the power of each human heart. In "The Farm Home" column for February 5, 1920, she explained: "Co-operation is the keynote of affairs today and our lives seem to be governed mostly by the advice of experts. These both are greatly needed, and I heartily say, more power to them." On the other hand, cooperation and the authority of experts could be harmful if "individual thinking and initiative" were pushed aside and replaced with the new ideology. Reliance on government experts cost money, "which is really our money," she reminded her readers, when people would do better to solve problems on their own. Her example came from her childhood, when it had been common knowledge, passed on by parents and grandparents, that to clean and then oil shoes made them last longer. Now government experts were saying the same thing at taxpayers' expense. Parents and grandparents had instructed family members for free! "So you see that expert advice was given in our homes years ago. And after all that is the best place for teaching many things, first and most important of which is how to think for one's self," she concluded.[50]

Wilder's forays into politics, government policy, and the war and its impact indicated her interest in current events and her ability to write about them in ways that interested and edified her readers. Most of her writings, however, combined her avid interest in farm life, stories of her own farm partnership with her husband, and the circumstances confronting farm women and families. She was an "expert" herself, offering advice and inspiration, but in the tone of a helpful neighbor who had been in their shoes. She wanted her readers to think about the problems of their farms, of production, of modernization of their homes to reduce the work, and of many other farm issues and to find solutions that would work for them. She loved farm life, was an equal partner in the affairs and direction of their place, and wanted others to share in her enthusiasm. Wilder understood that many farm women were overworked and underappreciated and were often eager to leave the farm for good. She was convinced that farms were the best places for wives to forge

---

50. Wilder, "The Farm Home," *Missouri Ruralist*, Feb. 5, 1920, p. 213.

equal partnerships with husbands and then to build something for the future. Her advice and inspirational essays were designed to encourage just that.

Wilder's longest article on the roles of women on the farm did not appear in the *Ruralist* but in *McCall's*, the national women's magazine. A product of her ideas and Lane's insistence that she start writing for larger publications, the article "Whom Will You Marry?" appeared in the June 1919 issue. Wilder or Lane, who edited the piece, set up a scenario that allowed Wilder to explain her ideas. A young friend, "Elizabeth," dropped in at Wilder's house to ask her if she would still be a farmer's wife if she could start her life over. The young woman's fiancé was coming home and had decided to be a farmer rather than work at the bank as he had before the war. Elizabeth had to decide if she wanted to be a farmer's wife. The scene takes place in Wilder's kitchen, where so much of the work of the farm took place. The author ponders how embarrassed she would have been at Elizabeth's age to be entertaining while kneading bread at the work table and boiling potato peelings to feed the hogs. She recognizes, too, that the snappily dressed young visitor looks out of place in her kitchen. The question of fashionable Elizabeth's adaptability is crucial; the burden of mentoring her is a heavy one. For the reader and the young woman, seeing the farm kitchen as it is, a workshop always busy, is important to the decision at hand.[51]

In the *McCall's* article, Wilder contemplates her generation and Elizabeth's and her own ideas about the importance of farms and the economic partnerships that women can enjoy on them. Wilder rejected much of the overstated, oppressed, and tragic view of women's lives as farm wives. She believed that women on farms were economic producers and homemakers who could make their lives satisfying. The farm wife was vital to the success of the operation. Her and her husband's economic interests were entwined, and unlike in the cities where women worked away from home and husbands, farm couples built their futures together. The work could be hard, of course, but Wilder believed that it was wrong to be idle. Farm life strengthened the physical body, and newspapers, books, and magazines arrived to enrich the mind through rural mail delivery. Her discussion of city women included the term "parasite life." Conditions in the city "inevitably pull married women into economic dependence and partial idleness." In contrast, farm women had "independence and security," and through "the labor of her hands, she is producing food for humanity and is, in the old and delightful sense, a lady,

---

51. Wilder, "Whom Will You Marry?," *McCall's*, June 1919, reprinted in *Little House in the Ozarks: The Rediscovered Writings*, ed. Stephen W. Hines (New York: Galahad Books, 1991), pp. 183–90.

WOMEN'S PLACE {201

8 McCall's Magazine for June, 1919

# Whom Will You Marry?

"Rich man, poor man, beggar man, thief,
Doctor, lawyer, merchant, chief."

## THE FARMER'S WIFE SAYS:

"Whether or not you are fitted for my life depends on what you want from marriage."

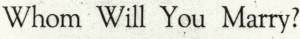

WHEN a man marries, his business life goes on as usual. He doesn't suddenly stop being a doctor and become a tailor, just because he has ceased to be a bachelor.

When a woman marries, what happens?

Her work, interests, environment, friends are determined by her husband's occupation.

Is this as it should be? Or need be?

We are going to give you the intimate stories of wives. The minister's wife, the doctor's, the artist's, the artisan's and many others. They will tell you where they failed and how they succeeded.

Perhaps, in them you will find the answer to some vital, perplexing question of your own.

R· I·

By Laura Ingalls Wilder

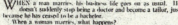

ELIZABETH came out from town this morning to talk over a problem with me. I was kneading bread, and, because twenty-five years of it have not taught me to like this part of the work of a farmer's wife, I had put the bread pan near the kitchen window, where I could look up now and then at the clean, cool beauty of the budding oak trees. So I saw Elizabeth as she came up the south slope between the gray tree trunks and I thought she looked like a redbird, in her bright sweater and cap.

I felt a twinge of envy. I thought how glad I would be if I could forget housework and get out into the spring woods. We always forget our own compensations in looking at others who have joys that we have not. But by the time I had opened the door to Elizabeth and had her in by the stove, taking off her muddy rubbers, the envy was gone. It is a poor life that does not teach us to shed envy as a duck sheds raindrops, and besides, I saw that Elizabeth was troubled.

There was a time when I would have been ashamed to receive Elizabeth, a banker's granddaughter, in the farm kitchen. Farm kitchens are not like city kitchenettes, nor even like the white-painted, muslin-curtained kitchens that some of the town people have. All the work of a farm centers in the farmer's wife's kitchen. I skim milk, make butter, and cook bran mashes for the chickens and potato parings for the hogs, in mine. A big iron pot of parings was steaming on the stove when Elizabeth came in.

I may as well admit that Elizabeth, in her dainty, gay clothes, was out of place in my kitchen. Twenty-five years ago, when I was her age, I would have bustled her into the front room and entertained her there, feeling embarrassed because my rag carpet was not Wilton and my furniture was not mahogany. The bread would have waited until she was gone, and if the family ate sourish bread for a week I would have felt it was not my fault.

But this morning I gave her a kitchen chair and went on kneading, thumping the dough and sprinkling flour over the bread-board while she talked. Good bread is my pride now, rather than Wilton rugs, and I have found that friendliness not genuine in a kitchen is not improved by a parlor.

"Jim's coming home next week," Elizabeth said.

"That's good!" I answered, heartily, for I had watched that romance from the time Elizabeth was in pigtails till the day Jim went away in khaki. But Elizabeth's tone made it clear enough that Jim's coming back brought a little doubt into her mind.

WOULD—would you be a farmer's wife if you had the chance to live your life over again?" she asked, in that breathless rush in which girls blurt out things they have been thinking about for a long time. "I wanted to talk to you about it. Jim says he wants to buy a farm when he comes back. He says he doesn't want to go into the bank again. I don't know what to do about it. I don't know whether I want to be a farmer's wife or not. Would you, if you were me? I guess I could talk him out of it, but—"

I had no doubt she could talk him out of it. Giving advice to Elizabeth seemed to me a heavy responsibility, though the advice we older women give girls now has not the weight it had when I was a girl. It seems to me that girls nowadays handle their lives and the lives of their husbands with much more assurance than we used to have. Elizabeth is really the one who is deciding Jim's future, as well as her own.

In my girlhood we had, one might say, the right of veto on some things in our own lives; we married the man who asked us, or we did not marry him. But now girls make their own laws, and to an astonishing extent, their own husbands—after they have married them.

While I talked to Elizabeth and kneaded the bread I thought of many things I did not say. Many persons think that a farmer, and of course, his wife, are isolated from the current of affairs in the nation, but sometimes I think we have a better viewpoint on them because we are farther away. The mail carrier brings out our papers and magazines in the morning, and after the chores are done I usually have a few minutes to run down to the mail-box and bring them up. During the day I snatch a glance at them now and then, and after the chores are done at night we sit by the fire and read and talk. We have a great deal of time for thinking at our work, and for making our own opinions about the happenings in the world.

SO Elizabeth's question seemed to me to mean more than the problem of one girl. I thought of Secretary Lane's plan for placing returning soldiers on farms, and I thought how badly our country needs good farmers and good farm conditions. I thought of the million dollars asked by the Senate Committee on Public Lands for making surveys of farms for our soldiers, and I thought of all the girls and women whose opinions mean far more in the matter than any decision of any Senate committee.

There must be a great many of them who, like Elizabeth, are undecided because of their ignorance of the real conditions of life on a farm, and nothing I have ever read seems to tell the truth about these conditions.

There has been a great deal of pity spent on the farmer's wife, and a great deal of condescending effort has been spent to educate her, while, on the other hand, some very pleasant and poetic things have been written about country life. But I have never seen it pointed out that the farm woman's life combines the desires of the "modern woman" with all the advantages and traditions of home-keeping.

On the farm a woman may have both economic independence and a home life as perfect as she cares to make it. Farm women have always been wage-earners and partners in their husband's business. Such a creature as the woman parasite has never been known among us. Perhaps this is one reason why "feminism" has never greatly aroused us.

IT has been rather amusing to farm women to read flaring headlines announcing the fact that women are at last coming into their own, that the younger ones at least can now become self-supporting. About the woman past forty there seems to be a little doubt, in the papers. But the woman past forty, on the farm, is still sure of her position, even the woman past fifty or sixty.

There is always plenty of self-supporting, self-respecting work for women on the farm, even though their youth is gone, and the work is within the shelter and quiet security of their own homes. While the discussion for and against women in business has been raging over the country, farm women have always been business women and no one has protested against it. No one has even noticed it.

Yet I remember well my husband's mother, undisputed head of her household, and fully a partner in all the business of the northern Minnesota farm, where I lived for a few months many years ago. She was not a "feminist." I never heard the words "economic independence" on her lips, and when her daughter, who went to the city and worked in an office, came back to talk of these things, she listened with an indulgent smile. She was too busy to bother her head with such notions, she said. But her husband was never so rash as to sell a herd of hogs or turn meadow land into corn fields without consulting her, and the butter-money went into her own purse without a question.

Perhaps the reason this economic value of farm women has gone unnoticed is because they have taken the advice the small boy gave the hen. When he heard her wildly cackling to announce that she had laid an egg he exclaimed, "Aw, shut up! What's the use of making such a fuss? You couldn't help it!"

It is true that a farmer's wife can never stop contributing her share to the success of the farm without ruining her husband's business as well. Many times when the churning had to be done and the hens fed I have felt like running away into the woods, "just to walk and to walk and to stun my soul and amaze it—a day with the stone and the sparrow and every marvelous thing." And I have felt that the life of a parasite woman has its attractions. But it lacks certain sturdy virtues that are good for a woman to have.

Women in the cities have tried the parasite life, and it appears that they do not like it. Yet, in the city, conditions inevitably pull married women into economic dependence and partial idleness.

It is not good for any living creature to be idle. A horse that does not work becomes unmanageable and fractious in his stall; he begins eating the wood of the manger, which is not a good thing for a horse to do. Hens, if they are to be kept healthy, must be kept busy, and every good poultry raiser gives them straw to scratch, so that they may earn part of their food by good, honest toil. I think it is not unreasonable to suppose that women, too, must use their energies to some purpose, good or bad, and no woman can make a success of her marriage if she uses her energies in eating the wood of the manger.

Yet, if, in order to avoid the restlessness and uneasiness that go with idleness, the city woman works outside her home, her business interests and occupations pull away from the home life and from marriage.

A SPECIES of business rivalry enters into the relations of herself and her husband, and, if she is successful, she has a pride in her pay envelope which is only equaled by her husband's jealousy of it. A man is perhaps slower to adapt himself to new things than a woman, or it may be that there is some deep, possessive instinct in him that resents any rival in the attention of the woman he loves. Combating this feeling in her husband gives a woman a sense of power, and nothing tears the delicate fabric of intimacy between two persons so surely as this sense of power in one and of futile protest in the other.

With separated interests, differing ambitions, a different set of business friends and a jealous rivalry between them, it is no wonder that so many fine men and women in the cities are finding marriage impossible. The divorce court makes legal a separation which already exists, and their marriage is a failure, whatever their business successes may be.

It is in the cities that the divorce statistics pile higher with every year. Divorce is rare in the country.

The farm woman's economic independence pulls in the direction of making her marriage a success. Her interests and those of her husband are the same; their success is a mutual success, of which each may be equally proud. In the event of a threatened failure, their interests still hold them together, instead of pulling them apart, and failure may often be averted because of the simple fact that two heads are better than one.

A farmer's wife may and should be—I may almost say must be—her husband's partner in the business, and she may be this without detracting from the home life.

Meals on time; the surplus of

[Con. on page [illegible]]

a 'bread-giver.'" Wilder believed that farm life offered the truest values in a changing world: "simplicity, money honestly earned, difficulties overcome, service lovingly given, respect deserved." What did Wilder tell Elizabeth? "If you want ease, unearned luxuries, selfish indulgence, a silken-cushioned, strawberries-and-cream life, do not marry a man who will be a farmer." On the other hand, "If you want to give, as well as to take; if you want to be your husband's full partner in business and in homemaking; if you can stand on your own feet and face life as a whole; . . . if you want an opportunity to be a fine, strong, free woman, then you are fitted for the life of a farmer's wife."[52] Wilder does not tell the reader which path Elizabeth chose.

Along with the joys of work, partnership with husbands, and the importance of the farm, Wilder wrote frequently about the vital role of parents, especially mothers. In her 1921 essay "A Homey Chat for Mothers," she told of receiving a letter from her elderly mother, a letter that made her "a child again" longing for her mother's wisdom and advice.[53] Charles Ingalls appeared in her essays, too, but not as often. Wilder's "Let Us Be Just," published September 5, 1917, is a story about her father, although it does not specify which parent was involved. The essay recounted in great detail the fight between Mary and Laura over Aunt Lottie's praise of Mary's golden hair and Mary's taunting of Laura for having plain brown hair, an incident that occurred in Wisconsin. Wilder described "two little girls who had disagreed" because "they were so temperamentally different." Mary, called here "the elder of the two," was sharp tongued and used her words as weapons. The younger girl, deeply hurt when her sister told her of Aunt Lottie's remarks about her plain hair and snub nose, grew angry when Mary continued to talk, telling Laura to obey her because she was older. In response, Laura, not as good with words but eager for action, slapped her smug older sister as hard as she could. Mary ran to tell their parents, conveniently leaving out her own taunting words. "I hate to write the end of the story," Wilder told *Ruralist* readers. "No, not the end! No story is ever ended! It goes on and on and the effects of this one followed this little girl all her life, showing in her hatred of injustice."[54] In *Little House in the Big Woods*, Pa spanks Laura with a strap, but he comforts her later when he holds her on his lap and reminds her that he has brown hair.[55] *Pioneer Girl* contains a similar story, but in that

---

52. Ibid., pp. 186–90.
53. Wilder, "A Homey Chat for Mothers," *Missouri Ruralist*, Sept. 15, 1921, in *Farm Journalist*, p. 260.
54. Wilder, "Let Us Be Just," ibid., Sept. 5, 1917, p. 121.
55. Wilder, *Little House in the Big Woods* (New York: Harper Trophy, 1971), pp. 184–85.

one, Laura cries in the corner. Later, Pa tells a story of his own disobedience and his father's response, saying, "And then he tanned my jacket because I hadn't minded."[56] In the *Ruralist* essay, Wilder described herself sitting in the corner, refusing to cry, and "glowering at the parent who punished her." She planned a return spanking when she was big enough to deliver it.[57]

Wilder used this story to teach about children's sense of justice and the need for parents to appeal to it, to explain any punishments they give. "When children are ruled thru their sense of justice," she wrote, "there are no angry thoughts left to rankle in their minds. . . . The punishment [becomes] the inevitable consequences of their own acts." This approach to childrearing would help children learn "self control and self government" that would last a lifetime.[58] Her frank recounting of her childhood anger and desire for revenge was designed to reach her readers, mostly mothers, with effective advice on a thorny topic. Her treatment of the incident in *Little House in the Big Woods* is part of a children's story. Children would not be properly edified by the tale of a brooding little girl with grim thoughts of revenge spankings burning in her heart. Wilder's *Pioneer Girl*, her autobiography, is a not a deeply reflective book. It tells an important story of pioneering, of daily life, of work, and of human relationships of all kinds, but Wilder did not ponder the human condition in its pages. That, in fact, may be why publishers rejected it when Rose Wilder Lane first presented it to them. *Pioneer Girl* provides much in the way of motion, day-to-day activity, and detail but not much from the heart.

On other occasions, Wilder wrote about selfishness, which she saw as the cause of "unrest and strife" everywhere in the world. "It seems rather impossible that such a small thing as individual selfishness could cause so much trouble," she wrote in 1919, but selfishness compounds when it is in each human heart. Neighborhoods, local regions, states, and the nation, all full of selfish people, create troubled relations in each.[59] Wilder's discussion of selfishness as a core problem of human nature channels her mother's voice into her adult world. As children, Mary and Laura Ingalls had shared their cookies or other treats with their sister Carrie. Each older girl gave Carrie half, leaving only half for themselves and a whole treat for the youngest. During their Minnesota years, Caroline Ingalls told Laura to give her cherished doll to a crying two-year-old neighbor. Laura was too old for dolls, Caroline

---

56. Wilder, *Pioneer Girl*, pp. 47–49.
57. Wilder, "Let Us Be Just," p. 122.
58. Ibid.
59. Wilder, "The Farm Home," *Missouri Ruralist*, Dec. 20, 1919, in *Farm Journalist*, p. 207.

said; little Anna Nelson should have it. Then there was the time that Charles Ingalls gave his boot money to the church for the purchase of the bell. The theme in the Ingalls home was always unselfishness and sacrifice.[60]

Many things in Wilder's life at Rocky Ridge Farm brought memories of her parents and her childhood home. Inevitably, those memories brought her back to a favorite theme: the importance of home influence on the young. "Across the years, the old home and its love called to me and memories of sweet words of counsel came flooding back. I realized that all my life the teachings of those early days have influenced me and the example set by father and mother has been something I have tried to follow . . . always coming back to it as the compass needle to the star." Wilder reminded her readers of recent newspaper accounts of child suicides, something they knew nothing of in her youth. "So much depends on the homemakers," she reflected. "I sometimes wonder if they are so busy now, with other things, that they are forgetting the importance of this special work." With society changing so rapidly, she noted, the home influence must not be neglected, "For when tests of character come in later years, strength to the good" will not come from the latest entertainment or gadget but from "the 'still, small voices' of the old home." Good upbringing of children did not depend on wealth or luxuries, she argued. Both rich and poor could provide; it was "a heritage from all fathers and mothers to their children."[61]

Avid fans of Laura Ingalls Wilder and her loving, intrepid family are sometimes disappointed when they discover that the real Laura was not a feminist pathbreaker, that her pioneering was physical, geographical, and confined to the nineteenth century. Wilder's professed values stand in sharp opposition to much of the modern trend: the liberation of people from institutions, such as the family and the church that Wilder revered, and the attendant virtues those institutions taught, such as restraint, self-control, modesty, courtesy, self-sacrifice, respect for authority, and a conformity of manner designed to smooth social relations and keep the peace. That she celebrated home and child-rearing as the special role of women, reminded readers that human nature does not change, and suggested that there is a price to pay for human actions that challenge virtue or tradition seems out of step with her assertive personality as described in her autobiography and her novels. That she recognized and appreciated some changes is clear. The technologies that made women's work easier and allowed swifter travel or brought books and maga-

---

60. Wilder, *Pioneer Girl*, pp. 52, 74, 76.

61. Wilder, "As a Farm Woman Thinks," *Missouri Ruralist*, Aug. 1, 1923, in *Farm Journalist*, pp. 290–91.

zines to her mailbox regularly were worthy of celebration, as long as using them did not become part of social display, "keeping up with the Joneses," as it were.

For Wilder, the fact that modern young women could now work and earn enough to make a living was good but not unequivocally so. Would such work keep them from marriage and motherhood? What about older women? Would they get or keep better-paid work as they aged? On the farm, older women would still have their "workshop" and home; might that not be better? When she spoke about farm life to the imaginary Elizabeth in the *McCall's* article, Wilder recognized that young women had more power than she had had in shaping her marriage back in 1885. "In my girlhood we had, one might say, the right of veto in some things in our own lives; we married the man who asked us, or we did not marry him." She might have referenced her own mother's veto of her father's hope to move on from De Smet into the disappearing frontier, but Wilder saw the modern woman as the one with the power. "Girls nowadays," she wrote, "handle their lives and the lives of their husbands with much more assurance than we used to. . . . But now girls make their own laws, and, to an astonishing extent, their own husbands' after they have married them."[62] Wilder recognized as well that modern young women did not take older women's advice as seriously as Wilder's generation had taken the advice of their mothers and grandmothers. She does not speculate about why that might be, but the advent of film, mass-circulation magazines, advertising, and the beginnings of a youth culture offered the 1920s generation many more sources of information and counsel. Wilder lived in a time of tumultuous social, technological, and economic change. She also had insight and a sense of the past and its values that helped her weigh and measure the new ideas in comparison to the old. That her daughter was so different from her parents, so accomplished and well-traveled, yet so often miserable, may have added into the equation as well.

Laura Ingalls Wilder was not a feminist or suffrage advocate, and she stressed the old and tried in many aspects of human relations. For any modern readers who may be disappointed in her ideals, it is important to note that she was part of the disinterested majority of women who had other things to do or who were satisfied with their lives. Once women got the vote, decades passed before they voted in the same numbers as men did. Women were more enthused about economic changes that provided opportunities for work and about cultural changes that added interest, excitement, and mobility to everyday life. Women did eventually become politically interested in large num-

62. Wilder, "Whom Will You Marry?," pp. 184–85.

bers, but it was long after Wilder was gone. The past always fails us when we turn to it for endorsements of our own passions or visions. Wilder and other residents of worlds long gone had their own questions, problems, and ways of thinking; they lived their lives for their own purposes. In Wilder's case, her purposes were to be a partner and "bread-giver" on her own place, an advocate for farm women and farm life, and, ultimately, a writer and storyteller. In each of these aspirations, she achieved success, but especially in the last. Her books are a gift to the ages.

# Enduring Fairy Tales and Childhood Myths

# { 9 }
# Fairy Tale, Folklore, and the Little House in the Deep Dark Woods

## SALLIE KETCHAM

*You have a sketch map and a rough guide;*
*the lights are lit in the windows of that house in the deep dark forest*
*ahead of us. We can begin to move in, listening out, eyes open,*
*trying to find our bearings.*
MARINA WARNER, *Once Upon a Time*[1]

During the bleakest days of the Great Depression, Laura Ingalls Wilder made a remarkable, highly original, and now largely overlooked artistic decision, one that would distinguish her life, her legacy, and the cultural significance of her work. This key decision proved central to Wilder's broad, enduring appeal and has contributed to the continual reinvention and adaptation of her writing. From the outset, Wilder chose to frame her wandering, hardscrabble childhood on the western plains as the nation's frontier fairy tale. "Once upon a time," she wrote, "sixty years ago, a little girl lived in the Big Woods of Wisconsin, in a little gray house made of logs."[2] This introductory sentence was no conventional cliché, no throw-away line for the juvenile market. Wilder's lavish use of fairy-tale elements in her work—most notably in her first novel, *Little House in the Big Woods*, but to varying degrees in all of the Little House books—resulted in something unprecedented in American children's literature. Wilder's irresistible story, reworked and reimagined as historical fiction but shot through with golden threads of ancient and timeless fairy

---

1. Warner, *Once Upon a Time: A Short History of Fairy Tale* (Oxford, UK: Oxford University Press, 2014), p. xxiv.

2. Wilder, *Little House in the Big Woods*, illus. Garth Williams (New York: Harper & Bros., 1953), p. 1 (page numbers hereafter appear in the text). Wilder first used this framing concept in 1929 or 1930 when she began writing her life story: "Once upon a time years and years ago, Pa stopped the horses and the wagon they were hauling away out on the prairie in Indian Territory" (Wilder, *Pioneer Girl: The Annotated Autobiography*, ed. Pamela Smith Hill [Pierre: South Dakota Historical Society Press, 2014], p. 1).

tale, dramatized America's western experience for generations of young readers. In effect, Wilder reinterpreted Manifest Destiny and the Mythic West for young children, subtly shaping their understanding of frontier life through her compelling personal narrative based on childhood memory, family history, historic fact, and last, but by no means least, Wilder's own shrewd grasp of fairy tale and its power to capture the hearts, minds, and imaginations of young readers. By deploying the classic concepts and framing features of fairy tale, Wilder completely transformed her monotone and comparatively plodding autobiographical memoir, *Pioneer Girl*, into a prize-winning series of best-loved children's books.

"I had no idea that I was writing history," Wilder stated, somewhat disingenuously, in 1953.[3] The degree to which she did or did not know exactly *what* she was writing is debatable and remains a contentious subject among historians, critics, biographers, and Wilder's voracious fans. The issue was complicated early on by the insistence of Wilder's daughter, fellow writer Rose Wilder Lane, that every word her mother wrote was indisputable fact (although it is clear from their correspondence that both mother and daughter acknowledged that the Little House books were works of historical fiction, subject to artistic license).[4] The recently released *Pioneer Girl: The Annotated Autobiography*, edited by Pamela Smith Hill, and *The Selected Letters of Laura Ingalls Wilder*, edited by William Anderson, have sparked yet another reappraisal of Wilder's long eventful life, her collaborative writing process with daughter Rose Wilder Lane, and the continuing relevance of her work. Wilder's narrative treatment of the removal of the Osage Indians from Kansas in *Little House on the Prairie* and her depiction of American Indians in general have come under scrutiny by other scholars, most notably John E. Miller and Frances W. Kaye, who drew different conclusions from Wilder's work. Kaye, who deemed *Little House on the Prairie* (1935) nothing "other than an apology for the 'ethnic cleansing' of the Great Plains," argued that the books should no longer be read, taught, or considered in the class-

---

3. Wilder to Everett Lantz, Editor, *Walnut Grove Tribune*, Oct. 21, 1953, Laura Ingalls Wilder Museum, Walnut Grove, Minn.

4. For Lane's insistence, *see*, for example, Lane to Mortenson, reprinted in Louise Hovde Mortenson, "Idea Inventory," *Elementary English* 41 (Apr. 1964): 428–29. For the correspondence between the two women, *see* Box 13, files 193–95, Laura Ingalls Wilder Series, Rose Wilder Lane Papers, Herbert Hoover Presidential Library, West Branch, Iowa, and Folder 19, Laura Ingalls Wilder Papers, Laura Ingalls Wilder Home Association, Mansfield, Mo., Microfilm ed., University of Missouri Western Historical Manuscript Collection & State Historical Society of Missouri, Columbia.

room.⁵ Given their "considerable strengths and appeal to young readers," Miller countered, the books provide "a useful teaching opportunity" if given context and should not be suppressed too quickly.⁶ Feminist critics such as Ann Romines and Dolores Rosenblum have argued for a more nuanced reading of all the novels and have focused attention on gendered and mythic spaces in the books. Wilder's legacy has also become increasingly politicized in recent years, resulting in the occasional call for book banning and immediate pushback on the part of her outraged, lifelong readers. Wilder's libertarian political leanings and anti-government messages throughout the Little House series were the subject of Anita Clair Fellman's book *Little House, Long Shadow*. In *Ghost in the Little House*, William Holtz flatly rejected the idea of Wilder as the actual author of the series, crediting Rose Wilder Lane instead.⁷

But in the ongoing hunt for any new biographical detail regarding her life and the evaluation of historical accuracy in Wilder's work, another fundamental feature of Wilder's writing has gone relatively unnoticed, despite the many ways in which she drew attention to it. A significant part of Wilder's art is in the telling. Her classic American stories of the western frontier have old-vine roots, deeply entangled in European fairy tale, which Wilder used to strange and surprising effect. Fairy tale resonates throughout her work like an old bell and ultimately enriches it, not because it is trivial, childish, and superficial, but because it is dark and cautionary, profound and true. Fairy tale is particularly relevant to Wilder's work because fairy tale, in its traditional form, preserves and passes down complicated stories of faith, hope, identity, betrayal, struggle, and redemption. Fairy tale is philosophical and universal, but it is not necessarily inclusive, unbiased, or impartial. It does not claim to be. It is subjective and contradictory, intimate and archetypal. In Wilder's work, fairy tale requires the reader to stand in the Literary East and

---

5. Kaye, "Little Squatter on the Osage Diminished Reserve: Reading Laura Ingalls Wilder's Kansas Indians," *Great Plains Quarterly* 20 (Spring 2000): 123.

6. Miller, *Laura Ingalls Wilder and Rose Wilder Lane: Authorship, Place, Time, and Culture* (Columbia: University of Missouri Press, 2008), p. 173.

7. Romines, *Constructing the Little House: Gender, Culture, and Laura Ingalls Wilder* (Amherst: University Press of Massachusetts, 1997); Rosenblum, "'Intimate Immensity': Mythic Space in the Works of Laura Ingalls Wilder," in *Where the West Begins: Essays on Middle Border and Siouxland Writing, in Honor of Herbert Krause*, ed. Arthur R. Huseboe and William Geyer (Sioux Falls, S.Dak.: Center for Western Studies Press, 1978), pp. 72–79; Fellman, *Little House, Long Shadow: Laura Ingalls Wilder's Impact on American Culture* (Columbia: University of Missouri Press, 2008); Holtz, *The Ghost in the Little House: A Life of Rose Wilder Lane* (Columbia: University of Missouri Press, 1993).

look to the Untamed West, even as it articulates prescient, distinctly modern, and rebellious ideas about the destruction of wilderness, the encroachment of "civilizing" forces, the clash of cultures, the loss of innocence, and the role of women in society. Fairy tale is the native language of childhood; children recognize its symbols, adages, and images. It is the charming red apple in Wilder's work, pulling the young (and not so young) reader into the heroine's journey for self-realization, existential meaning, and the elusive place called home.

*Little House in the Big Woods*, released in 1932, could hardly have appeared at a more fortuitous time. The first installment in Wilder's highly personal narrative of Manifest Destiny, it contained a nostalgic and reassuring story as seen through the eyes of a determined, compelling, and occasionally conflicted child. It appealed to an American audience fearing for its future, looking to its past for hope and glory, and yearning for what it perceived as its long-lost Golden Frontier, the place where hard work met opportunity and reaped success. It was, as Wilder's editor Virginia Kirkus noted, "the book no depression could stop."[8] By 1943, when Wilder quietly set down her Big Chief notebook and her pencil, her carefully executed tale had come full circle, culminating in the happily-ever-after marriage of Laura Ingalls and Almanzo Wilder, the beloved storybook couple of *These Happy Golden Years*.

In all likelihood, Wilder was still filling notebooks with her painstaking longhand when Albert Einstein gave his now famous answer to a mother's persistent question about the best possible education for her son: "If you want your children to be intelligent," he told her, "read them fairy tales. If you want them to be very intelligent, read them more fairy tales."[9] Even today, Einstein's comment tends to elicit as much bafflement as shock, but during the first half of the twentieth century, the academic field of fairy tale was almost nonexistent. The grisly old tales of adolescent girls devoured by beasts or raped, chopped up, and salted by men, of unwanted children abandoned to the woods, or of beautiful daughters forced to flee their homes disguised in ashes or animal pelts (like the princess in the tale of *Peau d'Ane*, or Donkeyskin, who bolts the castle when she learns of her father's plan to marry her after the death of his queen) had been purged, stripped of their complexity, and sanitized for children. The 1937 premiere of Walt Disney's landmark

---

8. Kirkus, "The Discovery of Laura Ingalls Wilder," *The Horn Book Magazine* 29 (Dec. 1953): 429.

9. Einstein, quoted in Maria Popova, "Einstein on Fairy Tales and Education," *Brain Pickings*, brainpickings.org. Jack Zipes, *Breaking the Magic Spell: Radical Theories of Folk and Fairy Tales*, rev. ed. (Lexington: University Press of Kentucky, 2002), p. 1, turned this quotation into a fairy tale.

animated film *Snow White* also influenced the re-introduction, revision, and commercialization of the old tales. But historically, scholars of myth and fairy tale from G. K. Chesterton to Bruno Bettelheim and Joseph Campbell insisted that while the original tales may be *unreal*, they are not *untrue*.[10] Like Einstein, they argued that fairy tales are universal stories of personal discovery, stories that expand the developing mind, unleash the imagination in unpredictable ways, and illustrate the Hero's Journey for children. Although writers as diverse as J. R. R. Tolkien, C. S. Lewis, and J. K. Rowling have reworked the Hero's Journey countless times, at its core, it is the story of Every Child. As Chesterton noted in 1909: "The old tales endure forever. The old fairy tale makes the hero a normal human boy [or pioneer girl]; it is his adventures that are startling; they startle him because he is normal."[11]

Today, the field of fairy tale is rich, crowded, and teeming with new research. Fairy tale and folklore are the essential seeds of story, our enduring link to the minds and imaginations of ordinary men and women who lived millennia ago. Recent phylogenetic analyses of fairy tales suggested that they are far older than previously thought, older than the Bible and Greek myth, with origins dating back to the Bronze Age.[12] Interestingly, Wilhelm Grimm of the famous Brothers Grimm suspected this fact in 1812, when he and his brother Jacob published their first collection of folk tales, *Kinder und Hausmarchen (Children's and Household Tales)*. Although traditional fairy tales cross all settings and cultures—from Hans Christian Andersen's cold Danish ocean to the sacred forests of Japan—American fairy tales are comparatively rare, and American authors have often struggled to adapt the language, heritage, and imagery of European fairy tale to American children's literature. In fact, Cornell professor of American literature Alison Lurie has pointed out that the best American fairy tales have "a different underlying message than the ones from across the Atlantic." In the standard European fairy tale, which occurs within a fixed social order, a poor boy or girl "becomes rich or marries into royalty," or a prince or princess falls under "an evil enchantment" or is "cast out by a cruel relative" and has to regain position. "In both types of story the social system is unquestioned and remains unchanged." In contrast, Lurie continued, in the most unique American fairy tales:

---

10. Bruno Bettelheim, *The Uses of Enchantment: The Meaning and Importance of Fairy Tales* (New York: Alfred A. Knopf, 1976), p. 73 (emphasis in the original).

11. Chesterton, *Orthodoxy* (New York: Lohn Lane Co., 1909), p. 26.

12. Sara Graça and Jamshid J. Tehrani, "Comparative Phylogenetic Analyses Uncover the Ancient Roots of Indo-European Folktales," *Royal Society Open Science*, Jan. 14, 2016, rsos.royalsocietypublishing.org.

the world within the story alters or is abandoned. Rip Van Winkle falls into a twenty-year sleep and wakes to find that a British colony has become a new nation in which "the very character of the people seemed changed." A hundred years later, the family in Carl Sandburg's story repeats the experience of many nineteenth-century immigrants and Western settlers. They sell all their possessions and ride "to where the railroad tracks run off into the sky"—to Rootabaga Country, which is not a fairy kingdom but rich farming country named after a large turnip.[13]

Laura Ingalls Wilder borrowed heavily from this uncommon American storytelling tradition in the creation of her semi-autobiographical, historical novels of the western frontier. What makes her work uniquely her own is the organic way in which she grafted elements of European fairy tale directly onto a real place and time—the western woods and prairie homesteads of nineteenth-century America. Just as Dorothy Gale of Kansas journeys to the utopian Land of Oz, little Laura Ingalls roams the Great Plains of the western frontier, a place Wilder would later refer to as "The Land of Used-to-Be."[14] To Wilder, nothing had altered more irreparably (or regrettably) than the dense green forests, the wetlands, and the wild living prairie of her childhood, despite the fact that much of her work chronicled and seemingly sanctioned the arrival of the homesteaders, the growth of their towns, and the checkboard expansion of their dusty wheat fields. In all of her books, Wilder deployed elements of fairy tale and folklore to engage her reader, memorialize her peripatetic childhood, and illustrate her version of America's westward expansion, a historical "process" much in accordance with Frederick Jackson Turner's thesis of successive frontiers. But it is in her first, most episodic novel, *Little House in the Big Woods*, that Wilder's suggestive use of European fairy tale is most transparent to her readers. In the book, Wilder transformed the already heavily-logged woods of nineteenth-century Wisconsin into America's own enchanted forest.

In traditional fairy tales, the woods represent power and mystery; they are immense and life-altering. They demand a path, often the first step in a long journey. The woods also represent a choice, as writer Joseph Campbell noted: "You enter the forest at the darkest point, where there is no path. Where there is a way or path, it is someone else's path. You are not on your

13. Lurie, Preface to *American Fairy Tales: From Rip Van Winkle to the Rootabaga Stories*, comp. Neil Philip (New York: Hyperion, 1996), p. 7.

14. Wilder, "The Land of Used-to-Be" (1940), reprinted in Wilder and Lane, *A Little House Sampler*, ed. William Anderson (Lincoln: University of Nebraska Press, 1988), pp. 226–31.

own path. If you follow someone else's way, you are not going to realize your potential."[15] Wilder understood this path; she literally created it for her heroine at the beginning of the book. "A wagon track ran before the house, turning and twisting out of sight in the woods where the wild animals lived, but the little girl did not know where it went, nor what might be at the end of it" (p. 2). But the little girl, Laura, will ultimately follow that winding road out of the Big Woods, all the way to edge of the tall grass prairie, where she will have to learn to make her way and carve her own path.

Wilder's Big Woods exude compelling power, compounded by wistfulness. The reader's awareness that these woods once occupied a real space (and to a lesser extent still do) in the American heartland, a place where the Ingalls family toiled on their small subsistence farm, enhances their appeal. Although Wilder was memorializing a lost way of life, the lifestyle was one that many of her rural readers could still remember, visualize, and relate to in the 1930s. British writer Sarah Maitland made a similar observation about the impact of the forest in European fairy tales: "It is obvious that playing in a [modern] forest for which you have no responsibility, in which you never have to labour, in which you have no investment, and to which you have been mechanically conveyed by an adult is not the same thing as playing in the forest which is both your home and your workplace and whose well-being is your well-being." The "robust and lovely" European fairy stories, she continued, "come out of that older forest, they reunite us with our cultural roots there, and children should have access to them particularly as it gets harder to access the real thing; these stories teach them both that the forest is magical and generous and also that it is dark and terrible."[16]

In *Little House in the Big Woods*, the lost world of Wilder's childhood fairly quivers with magic and mystery, "sunshine and shadow" (in Wilder's words),[17] and even the occasional talking animal. Like Little Red Riding Hood, Laura lives in a lonely house in the darkening wood, where wolves that "eat little girls" prowl just outside the walls (p. 3). Like Snow White and Rose Red, Laura (the dark and stormy) has a beautiful sister she loves, Mary (the good and fair). Their little house is staunchly defended by Pa, the Huntsman, with his mighty gun. Pa is also the Woodcarver, who whittles wonderful gifts at Christmastime. Ma is good and gentle and kind. Susan

15. Campbell, quoted in *A Joseph Campbell Companion: Reflections on the Art of Living*, ed. Diane K. Osbon (New York: HarperCollins, 1991), p. 22.

16. Maitland, *From the Forest: A Search for the Hidden Roots of Our Fairy Tales* (Berkeley, Calif.: Counterpoint, 2012), p. 107.

17. Wilder, "Dear Children" (1947), reprinted in *Dear Laura: Letters from Children to Laura Ingalls Wilder* (New York: HarperCollins, 1996), p. 149.

the Black Cat sleeps curled upon the hearth; loyal dog Jack guards their door. Wild bears and stalking panthers and talking owls haunt the woods at night, but Pa's magic fiddle dispels the fear and the darkness. The wolves in particular fascinate little Laura and prey upon her mind. Wilder returned to the wolves numerous times in all the subsequent Little House books; eventually, they will come to represent Laura's yearning for solitude, wilderness, freedom, and flight.[18] In American Indian mythology, the wolf often signifies power and pathfinding.

Wilder intentionally isolated this little house, which, although historically inaccurate—the Ingalls had many neighbors in Pepin County, Wisconsin, both native and white, including a large contingent of Swedes—is a recurring motif in fairy tale, where the heroine must proceed for a time in relative isolation before launching on her journey of discovery and fulfilling her destiny. "The great, dark trees of the Big Woods stood all around the house," Wilder wrote in her taut and lyrical opening lines. "As far as a man could go to the north in a day, or a week, or a whole month, there was nothing but woods. There were no houses. There were no roads. There were no people. There were only trees and the wild animals who had their homes among them" (pp. 1–2). This haunting passage is the language of fairy tale, not history, and it underscores the artistic tension between fact and fable in Wilder's work. She segued between the two throughout the book, but here, as she set her scene, Wilder was clearly working within the conventions of fairy tale. Many historians and critics, in particular the late anthropologist Michael Dorris, himself part Modoc, justifiably objected to Wilder's assertion "there were no people," noting the omission of "the thousands of resident Menominees, Potowatomis, Sauks, Foxes, Winnebagos, Ottawas who inhabited mid-nineteenth-century Wisconsin, as they had for many hundreds of years." Dorris continued, "This cozy, fun-filled world of extended Ingallses was curiously empty, a pristine wilderness in which only white folks toiled and cavorted, ate and harvested, celebrated and were kind to each other."[19]

Others noted the omission, as well, and the issue became increasingly problematic, particularly in midwestern classrooms where Wilder's books were often read with the gravitas accorded to supplemental history texts. In 1953, before the newly-illustrated Garth Williams edition of the Little House series was released, Wilder and her editor readily changed a similarly offensive line in *Little House on the Prairie* from "no people" to "no settlers."

18. Caroline Fraser, "Laura Ingalls Wilder and the Wolves," *Los Angeles Review of Books*, Oct. 10, 2012, lareviewofbooks.org.

19. Dorris, "Trusting the Words," *Booklist* 89 (June 15, 1993): 1820.

Wilder termed the omission, "a stupid blunder of mine."[20] Although it is a glaring historical error, Wilder's concept of a curiously empty and pristine wilderness, as essayist Caroline Fraser explained, is central to Wilder's artistic vision:

> The Little House books have always been stranger, deeper and darker than any ideology. While celebrating family life and domesticity, they undercut those cozy values at every turn, contrasting the pleasures of home (firelight, companionship, song) with the immensity of the wilderness, its nobility and its power to resist cultivation and civilization. In her hymn to the American west, Wilder treasures forest, grasslands, wetlands, and wildlife in terms that verge on the transcendental. Alive in Laura Ingalls Wilder's memory of it, the wilderness she knew—now lost—continues to reflect her longing for a vanishing world, a rough paradise from which we are excluded by a helpless devotion to our own survival.[21]

In the Little House, survival is paramount, and as Fraser also pointed out, not everything is entirely cozy. Just thirteen pages into the story, the big butcher knives appear, and it is hog-killing time. Wilder did not spare her youngest readers the unpleasant details:

> Near the pigpen, Pa and Uncle Henry built a bonfire.... When the water was boiling they went to kill the hog. Then Laura ran and hid her head on the bed and stopped her ears with her fingers so she could not hear the hog squeal.
> "It doesn't hurt him, Laura," Pa said. "We do it so quickly." But she did not want to hear him squeal.
> In a minute she took one finger cautiously out of an ear, and listened. The hog had stopped squealing. After that, Butchering Time was great fun. (p. 13)

The Ingallses boil the family pig in a great cauldron, scrape off its bristles, then roast and eat its curly tail. Laura and Mary are given a balloon made of the pig's inflated bladder to bat about.

Writers for children know that the death of animals is deeply disturbing to the majority of young readers; yet, many fairy tales and other classic children's stories from *Bambi* to *Charlotte's Web* prominently feature it. Like the

---

20. Wilder to Ursula Nordstrom, quoted in Pamela Smith Hill, *Laura Ingalls Wilder: A Writer's Life* (Pierre: South Dakota Historical Society Press, 2007), p. 191.
21. Fraser, "Laura Ingalls Wilder and the Wolves."

old tales, Wilder's story took on life and death in the woods, and her language deftly juxtaposed the beautiful, the visceral, and the grim:

> When the grass was tall . . . and the cows were giving plenty of milk, that was the time to make cheese.
> Somebody must kill a calf, for cheese could not be made without rennet, . . . the lining of a young calf's stomach. The calf must . . . never [have] eaten anything but milk.
> Laura was afraid that Pa must kill one of the little calves in the barn. They were so sweet. . . . their large eyes so wondering. Laura's heart beat fast when Ma talked to Pa about making cheese. (p. 186)

In nearly every fairy tale, Grim Death or the threat of death stalks animals and humans alike. In the old stories, friends, family, and beloved creatures may fall cruelly, but death itself (if not the resulting fear, shock, or grief of death) must pass over the heroine as she learns to recognize death's finality and life's brutal truths. The heroine must come to terms with death, then stoically soldier on to her eventual reward: Snow White and Sleeping Beauty ultimately awaken; Goldilocks, Gretel, and Little Red Riding Hood escape (in most versions); the beautiful miller's daughter watches in triumph as Rumpelstiltskin tears himself to bloody shreds. In other tales, gentle animals are sacrificed in lieu of, or sacrifice themselves for, innocent children; in some of the oldest, unsanitized stories, the tales in which little children are eaten by wild animals or consumed by witches, we can assume the point of death was equally well taken, the lesson learned.

The last chapter of *Little House in the Big Woods*, "The Deer in the Wood" (pp. 229–38), sets up the first happy ending of the series, and the lesson is one of compassion, grace, and wonder. The scene is also strongly reminiscent of scenes in *Bambi*, written by Felix Salten and first published in translation by Simon and Schuster in 1928. Either Wilder or Lane could have been familiar with the bestselling book. In Wilder's final chapter, Pa has set a salt lick—a lure—for deer in the winter woods, while he waits in a tree with his gun. His family is hungry, and he has three opportunities to shoot animals drawn to the salt lick. (Three is fairy tale's magic number; often, the protagonist will be presented with three chances or choices, three wishes, three bears, or three witches.) First comes a big buck. "It was a perfect shot," Pa says. "But he was so beautiful, he looked so strong and free and wild, that I couldn't kill him. I sat there and looked at him, until he bounded away into the dark woods" (p. 233). Then along comes a great, lumbering bear. "He was a perfect mark to shoot at, but I was so much interested in watching him, and the woods were so peaceful in the moonlight. . . . I did not even think of shooting him, until he was waddling away into the woods" (pp. 234–35). Finally, a doe and her fawn arrive. "They were not afraid at all. They walked over to the place where I had sprinkled the salt.... They stood there together, looking at the woods and the moonlight. Their large eyes were shining and soft. I just sat there looking at them, until they walked away among the shadows. Then I climbed down out of the tree and came home" (pp. 235–36).

As Jack Zipes argued in *When Dreams Came True*, "Ultimately, the definition of both the wonder tale and the fairy tale, which derives from it, depends on the manner in which a narrator/author arranges *known* functions of a tale aesthetically and ideologically to induce wonder and then transmits the tale as a whole according to customary usage of a society in a given historical period."[22] As she did with Pa the Huntsman sparing the innocent creatures of the forest, Wilder skillfully inserted other elements of classic fairy tale and fable into the pioneer time frame of *Little House in the Big Woods*, transferring their charm and wonder to real-life activities and events. The chapter "Dance at Grandpa's" (pp. 131–55) describes a great ball in celebration of the maple-sugar harvest. Although Cinderella does not actually make an appearance, Wilder provided the reader with a wealth of familiar details from the vantage point of little Laura. Sleigh bells ring out in the frosty air as beautiful young women pile into cutters and race over the snow-covered hills to the ball. Pa points out animal tracks along the way, "the small, leaping tracks of cottontail rabbits, the tiny tracks of field mice, and the feather-stitching tracks of snowbirds" (pp. 132–33). A heated debate breaks out at Grandma's regarding which of the many babies piled on Grandma's bed is the fairest of them all. Pa's entertaining sisters, Ruby and Docia, preen before the mirror as they fuss with their hair and struggle into their corsets. When Ma finally appears in her flounced and ruffled gown—the beautiful delaine—she "looked so rich and fine that Laura was afraid to touch her" (p. 142). Later, in the chapter entitled "Harvest" (pp. 199–209), Wilder reached even further back in literary time—all the way back to Aesop—in order to retell the story of lazy cousin Charley, the Boy Who Cried Wolf once too often, and who receives his just deserts when a swarm of angry yellow jackets attacks him.

In fairy tales, the nature of magic is the magic of nature. Deep in the woods, where the birds and the animals can talk, the forest creatures may be rescuers, or they may be shapeshifting tricksters. Even rocks and trees have the ability to morph from inanimate objects into friends or foes. Laura and Ma mistake a threatening black bear for Sukey the cow. Pa attacks and beats a gnarled

---

22. Zipes, *When Dreams Came True: Classical Fairy Tales and Their Tradition* (New York: Routledge, 1999), p. 7 (emphasis in the original).

tree stump with nothing but a club, convinced that the shadowy stump is yet another dreaded bear. Wilder borrowed directly from this old tradition and set other vignettes even further into the legendary past by casting them as the childhood adventures of her father or grandfather, Lansford Ingalls. In one chapter, Wilder recounted the tale of Pa's boyhood encounter with a talking owl that pursues him through the forest; in another, Pa's father goes sledding with a hitchhiking pig. Similarly, Laura and Mary have their own "real" fairy encounter. Jack Frost arrives in the night, allowing the girls to admire his handiwork on a dark, wintry morning.

Before fairy tales were collected and recorded, they formed the core of storytelling's oral tradition. Listeners were required to pay close attention to the language of fairy tales, to what was said and repeated, in order to comprehend fully, reproduce, and disseminate the stories. And so the tales were usually loaded with mnemonic prompts: riddles, folk rhymes, lyrics, couplets, charms, and verses. ("Mirror, mirror on the wall" and "Fee, fie, foe, fum, I smell the blood of an Englishman" are just two of many examples.) In *Little House in the Big Woods*, Pa's marvelous singing fiddle functions in much the same way as these age-old prompts and harkens back to the classic tales in which magical instruments (particularly fiddles and flutes) figure so prominently. The recurring songs, lyrics, and aphorisms of the *Little House* books foster more than a sense of nostalgia for the reader; they serve as a recurring literary device, linking Laura over many years and many books to the most significant and memorable moments of her life. Wilder herself attached great significance to her father's musicianship. "Whatever religion, romance and patriotism I have," she wrote, "I owe largely to the violin and my Father playing in the twilight."[23]

Because *Little House in the Big Woods* was written as a chapter book for beginning readers, Wilder tended to preserve simple tunes and nursery rhymes, including "Pop Goes the Weasel" and "Old Grimes," as well as such buoyant folksongs from the American repertoire as "Yankee Doodle," "Oh, Susanna," and "Captain Jinks of the Horse Marines." But Wilder also included the racist minstrel show standard "Old Uncle Ned," which she inserted at the end of the chapter called "Sundays." It is a jarring selection, a song of slavery, privation, and death, played for Laura and her sisters as they drift off to sleep (p. 100). As in most traditional fairy tales, it casts a pall over the proceedings, undercuts the jollity, and raises troubling questions for children.

23. Wilder, "First Memories of Father," in *A Little House Reader: A Collection of Writings by Laura Ingalls Wilder*, ed. William Anderson (New York: HarperCollins, 1998), p. 161.

In *Little House, Long Shadow*, Anita Clair Fellman argued that the *Little House* books encourage negative attitudes toward government, regulation, and social welfare programs, serve up "covert" conservative messages to young readers, and ultimately paved the way for the resurgence of cultural conservatism in American society.[24] However, many Wilder readers—fans and critics alike—would be hard pressed to find anything covert about Wilder's message of individualism, resourcefulness, and self-reliance or anything particularly oblique in her approach to storytelling. Many readers who begin the series never finish. If anything, they find Wilder's style and message too overt, too didactic, or too moralizing, her wisdom too homespun, her humor too corn-fed. The Little House books often echo the tone Wilder honed in her years as a column writer for the *Missouri Ruralist*, which in turn owed much to Wilder's Calvinistic childhood and to her family's Victorian sense of decorum. As Caroline Fraser noted, there are times when Wilder undercut her own message, a message more complicated than it initially appears, but within the conventions of fairy tale, Wilder's self-consciously uplifting, straightforward, and unambiguous storytelling style is strictly orthodox.

In the 1970s, Bruno Bettelheim's provocative new theories sparked an ongoing debate over the ways in which folk and fairy tales, acting as agents of socialization, exert their profound influence on the moral, intellectual, and personal development of young children. Jack Zipes, whose work focuses on the political, revolutionary, and materialist aspects of literary fairy tale, has written extensively on their history, dissemination, and socializing functions. He identified six key framing features that illustrate how the traditional fairy tale was institutionalized for children:

> (1) the social function of the fairy tale must be didactic and teach a lesson that corroborates the code of civility; . . . (2) it must be short so that children can remember and memorize it and . . . both adults and children can repeat it orally; this was the way that many written tales worked their way back into the oral tradition; (3) it must pass the censorship of adults so that it can be easily circulated; (4) it must address social issues such as obligation, sex roles, class differences, power, and decorum so that it will appeal to adults, especially those who . . . publicize the tales; (5) it must be suitable to be used with children in a schooling situation; and (6) it must reinforce a notion of power within the children of the upper classes and suggest ways for them to maintain power.[25]

24. See Fellman, *Little House, Long Shadow*, esp. p. 5.
25. Zipes, *Fairy Tale as Myth, Myth as Fairy Tale* (Lexington: University Press of Kentucky, 1994), p. 33.

By the time Wilder finished spinning the events of her frontier childhood into gold, her highly-burnished version of personal, family, and national history displayed all six of these traditional and institutional framing features. Although at thirteen chapters, *Little House in the Big Woods* is not particularly "brief," it is highly episodic. Each chapter stands alone, a detailed and memorable portrait of a specific moment in time. Short, moralizing vignettes are often embedded within these chapters, usually emphasizing duty, responsibility, proper behavior, and the consequences of personal negligence or disobedience. Since its publication in 1932, parents, reviewers, and educators alike have lauded the "wholesomeness" of the novel (much like the *Little House on the Prairie* television series), which remains a major selling point. Wilder's writing even exhibits Zipes's sixth framing point. Despite the fact that Wilder's family did not belong, strictly speaking, to the "upper classes," they most certainly represented members of a conquering class: the white homesteaders, settlers, and newcomers who displaced the native populations of the American Plains, a subject Wilder addressed with a decided uneasiness in the Little House books. In fact, one of the unifying themes of the series is the idea that the acquisition of "free" land, and the work required to transform it, is the means to status, respectability, and a useful, worthy life. Yet, in Wilder's wolf-haunted world, that transformation also comes at great cost, often with unsettling financial, physical, emotional, and environmental consequences.

*Little House in the Big Woods* is a rare example of an American classic that has managed to work its way in and out of the oral tradition. It has been a standard "read aloud" story book at home and in the classroom for over eighty years. Multiple generations of Wilder fans have had the story read to them or have themselves read the story to students, children, or grandchildren. Many Wilder readers pride themselves on having read the entire Little House series dozens of times. Thousands more can recall and relate the events described in *Little House in the Big Woods* even though they have never cracked the book's cover; they simply heard the story read aloud in elementary school. At least as many can recount the "true stories" contained in Wilder's novels, although they may only be familiar with the stage version of Wilder's work, as popularized by the long-running television series.

Orality, that key component of fairy tale, helps explain another root cause of Wilder's unusually strong and continuing appeal. For many readers, an intense familiarity and identification with Wilder's characters is the result of what art critic and novelist John Berger termed fairy-tale *fusion*. "If you remember listening to stories as a child, you will remember the pleasure of hearing a story repeated many times, and you will remember that while you were listening you became three people. There is an incredible fusion: you became the story-teller, the protagonist and you remember yourself listening to the story."[26] Wilder's most devoted fans do not simply identify with Laura or want to read about her, they want to be Laura. They attend conferences based on Wilder's work. They research the lives of her friends, family, and acquaintances. They buy tickets to Wilder museums, pageants, and plays. They go on literary pilgrimages to the prairie towns and home sites associated with the books. They knock back their sunbonnets, kick off their shoes, and go wading on the banks of Plum Creek.

Wilder's interest in fairy tale and folklore predated the publication of the *Little House* books. Years before she began work on the series, several of her writings made mention of fairies, magic, or the folk customs of the past. In 1915, when visiting Rose Wilder Lane in San Francisco, Wilder broke into children's writing with a series of short ethereal fairy poems for the "Tuck 'Em In Corner," a children's feature in the *San Francisco Bulletin*.[27] Up to this point in her fledgling writing career, Wilder had been working as a farm journalist. Her expert articles on poultry production and her columns ran regularly in the *Missouri Ruralist*. In 1916, she mused, "I have a feeling that childhood has been robbed of a great deal of its joys by taking away its belief in wonderful, mystic things, in fairies and all their kin. It is not surprising that when children are grown they have so little idealism or imagination."[28]

In one of her 1922 columns, in which she combined two of her favorite subjects—fairies and horses—the fairies were still on her mind. She recalled an Irish story in which a mortal was invited to go hunting with the fairies. He was given the choice to become "small enough to ride the horse as it was" or ride "a man-sized" horse. He chose to become small and rode gaily in the fairy king's company "until he came to a wall so high he feared his tiny horse could not carry him over." The fairy king told him: "'Throw your heart over the wall, then follow it!' So he rode fearlessly at the wall, with his heart already bravely passed it, and went safely over." Wilder told her readers that she often thought "of the fairy's advice" because "anyone who has ridden horses much, understands how the heart of the rider going over, fairly lifts the horse up and across an obstacle." She continued: "the uplift of a fearless

26. Berger, quoted in Marina Warner, *From the Beast to the Blonde: On Fairy Tales and Their Tellers* (New York: Farrar, Straus & Giroux, 1995), p. 215.

27. These poems were published as *Laura Ingalls Wilder's Fairy Poems*, ed. Stephen W. Hines (New York: Doubleday, 1998).

28. Wilder, "Look for Fairies Now," *Missouri Ruralist*, Apr. 5, 1916, reprinted in *Laura Ingalls Wilder, Farm Journalist: Writings from the Ozarks*, ed. Stephen W. Hines (Columbia: University of Missouri Press, 2007), p. 63.

heart will help us over other sorts of barriers. In any undertaking, to falter at a crisis means defeat." She concluded that if we are to succeed in anything, "when we come to a wall that bars our way we must throw our hearts over and then follow confidently. It is fairy advice, you know, and savors of magic, so following it we will ride with the fairies of good fortune and go safely over."[29]

It is fairy advice; it was Wilder's credo; and it sums up yet another defining characteristic of classic fairy tales: *heroic optimism*. According to Marina Warner, citing feminist writer Angela Carter, fairy tales accept and address the existence of hardship, suffering, loss, and sorrow, but they do not allow for universal defeat.[30] Fairy tales may flash their bloody teeth and claws, but it is the protagonist's heroic optimism that drives the inevitable happy ending. As Warner noted, "The more one knows of fairy tales the less fantastical they appear; they are vehicles of the grimmest realism, expressing hope against all the odds with gritted teeth."[31] Wilder regularly used this concept of heroic optimism to propel her characters and her plots, particularly in her most harrowing and accomplished novel, *The Long Winter*. Conversely, as Wilder transformed the raw material of *Pioneer Girl* into the Little House series, she deliberately scrubbed several real-life childhood events that had proved tragic beyond any hope of success or redemption. Wilder chose to erase an entire year of her childhood for the series. She silently passed over the irredeemably pessimistic year of 1876, the year her family lived in Burr Oak, Iowa, including the devastating death of Wilder's baby brother, Freddy, on the way there. "It is a story in itself," she wrote to Lane, "but does not belong in the picture I am making of the family."[32]

"My mother loves courage and beauty and books," Lane wrote in 1918.[33] Like her mother Caroline Quiner Ingalls, Wilder was an avid reader who carefully selected and maintained a small library of her own. Even in times of serious financial hardship, all three women prioritized books and continued to acquire them. Lane also recorded the fact that her mother frequently read aloud in the evenings, often from the collected poems of Tennyson or Walter Scott who, along with Shakespeare and Robert Burns, were among Wilder's favorite authors, and all of whom are noted for fairy verse or tales of enchant-

29. Wilder, "As a Farm Woman Thinks," ibid., Nov. 1, 1922, p. 278.
30. Warner, *Once Upon a Time*, pp. xxiii–xxiv.
31. Warner, *The Absent Mother, or Women against Women in the 'Old Wives' Tale* (Hilversum, Neth.: Verloren, 1991), p. 47.
32. Wilder to Lane, n.d. [ca. Dec. 1937–Jan. 1938], Box 13, file 193, Lane Papers. Wilder told this story in *Pioneer Girl*, pp. 99–113.
33. Lane, "Rose Wilder Lane, by Herself," in Wilder and Lane, *Little House Sampler*, p. 12.

Wilder filled her library, nestled to one side of the
living room at Rocky Ridge Farm, with her favorite books.
*South Dakota Historical Society Press*

ment.[34] *Little House in the Big Woods* reflects Wilder's personal tastes and literary influences, but paradoxically, of all the volumes in the Little House series, it is also the book most indebted to the heavy editorial pen of Rose Wilder Lane.

By 1910, two decades before the release of *Little House in the Big Woods*, Wilder had already written several children's stories for Lane's review. Unfortunately, these early stories did not survive. At the time, Lane expressed limited enthusiasm for the children's market.[35] But when Wilder's autobiographical memoir *Pioneer Girl* failed to sell, Lane took matters into her own

34. Lane, "Setting" for Wilder, *On the Way Home: The Diary of a Trip from South Dakota to Mansfield, Missouri, in 1894* (New York: Harper & Row, 1962), p. 95. Wilder's appreciation for Shakespeare is apparent in her column, "The Farm Home," Nov. 5, 1920, reprinted in *Laura Ingalls Wilder, Farm Journalist*, pp. 237–39. She quoted Burns in "Thanksgiving Time," Nov. 20, 1916, ibid., p. 91.

35. John E. Miller, *Becoming Laura Ingalls Wilder: The Woman behind the Legend* (Columbia: University of Missouri Press, 1998), p. 139.

hands. She surgically extracted—apparently without Wilder's knowledge or consent—key scenes from the manuscript and (as she informed her mother by letter) "strung [them] together as you will see" to create a picture or chapter book for children.[36] Lane often acted unilaterally on her mother's behalf as ersatz editor and agent. On more than one occasion, Lane also helped herself to her mother's material. But in this case, Lane's intervention resulted in the first draft of a new manuscript that would become *Little House in the Big Woods*. Lane apparently dramatized the static reminiscences of *Pioneer Girl*, defined the manuscript's episodic form, and then worked her connections to secure a sale. Lane was a writer in search of a subject; Wilder was a writer in search of form and structure. However, as the manuscript passed through two editors at two separate publishing houses, Wilder took back creative control at the time she began revisions.[37]

Originally, Wilder may have been inspired to write a story based upon the childhood adventures of Caroline Quiner Ingalls, not her own. About a year after her mother's death in 1924, Wilder wrote to her aunt Martha Quiner Carpenter, Caroline's sister, asking for specific details regarding Carpenter's childhood, family history, daily activities, pioneer pastimes, old recipes, and more. "I want lots of it," Wilder wrote, "pages and pages of things you remember. . . . the little everyday happenings and what you and Mother and Aunt Eliza and Uncle Tom and Uncle Henry did as children and young folks, going to parties and sleigh rides and spelling schools. . . . work and school too."[38] In the end, Wilder modified and adapted some of the detail Martha Carpenter obligingly provided for the experiences of Laura in *Little House in the Big Woods*.

"I went to a hot maple sugar party at Mr. Petres' at Kellogg," Martha Quiner Carpenter replied to Wilder, "we ate hot sugar till all were satisfied and then they did dance till early morning [and] then went home happy." Carpenter also recalled, "The wolves would howl first at the North then the East the South and at last to the west [and] we would think they [might] catch father before he got home and the Panthers they was around with their noise to frighten us but I never saw one."[39] Wilder incorporated these and other incidents into the Little House books. When editor Marion Fiery requested more specific detail regarding nineteenth-century cabin life, Wilder bolstered her Aunt Martha's recollections with her own and responded with a treasure

36. Wilder, quoted in Hill, *Laura Ingalls Wilder*, p. 134.
37. Hill, *Laura Ingalls Wilder*, p. 139.
38. Wilder to Carpenter, June 22, 1925, reprinted in *The Selected Letters of Laura Ingalls Wilder*, ed. William Anderson (New York: HarperCollins, 2016), p. 34.
39. Carpenter to Wilder, Sept. 2, 1925, Box 14, file 204, Lane Papers.

"WHO?"

Helen Sewell's illustrations from *Little House in the Big Woods* evoke a classic fairy-tale setting. *Helen Sewell,* Little House in the Big Woods, *1932*

trove of frontier folklore: how to make cheese, braid straw hats (another Martha Carpenter contribution), mold bullets, build a log smoker to cure ham, tap maple trees, dangle dead deer from trees to protect the meat, roast pig's tail on a stick, and make candy in the snow. Wilder included such "how-to" scenes throughout the series; they proved a kind of "folklure," particularly appealing and satisfying to young children intensely curious about the way things work.

Once they had accepted the revised manuscript, Harper & Brothers selected artist Helen Sewell to illustrate the book. Although some children's books are author illustrated, it is unusual for the author and the illustrator to collaborate actively on a project. Publishers prefer to hand-select the illustrator in order to maintain artistic control over the layout, drawings, and overall design. In 1929, Helen Sewell had illustrated *Sally Gabble and the Fairies* by Miriam Clark Potter for Macmillian Company. Harper & Brothers clearly knew the look they wanted for Wilder's book, and they found it in Sewell.

In an earlier work, *Sally Gable and the Fairies*, illustrator Helen Sewell showcased her ability to recreate the fairy-tale forest. *Helen Sewell,* Sally Gable and the Fairies, *1929*

*Little House in the Big Woods* and *Sally Gabble and the Fairies* share an unmistakable visual aesthetic. Sewell would go on to illustrate an edition of *Cinderella* (1934) and other whimsical stories while she continued to draw the Little House series. Her clean, understated line drawings mimic Old World wood-block prints and focus direct attention on the fairy-tale aspects of *Little House in the Big Woods*. Her drawings also emphasize the eeriness of the forest, the contrast between light and dark, and the wild creatures that haunt the woods. In one illustration, she clearly depicted Laura Ingalls as Little Red Riding Hood.[40] Not all readers are familiar with Sewell's artwork for the first edition because, in 1953, the publisher reissued the Little House books in a uniform set. This new, postwar edition featured the charming and dynamic—but decidedly different—artwork of Garth Williams. Williams's illustrations de-emphasized the forest and surroundings in favor of the now better-known

40. Wilder, *Little House in the Big Woods*, illus. Helen Sewell (New York: Harper & Bros., 1932), frontispiece.

drawings of the buoyant, nuclear Ingalls family at work and at play, learning new skills or tending to daily tasks and chores.

Like the West of James Fenimore Cooper, George Catlin, Frederic Remington, Samuel Clemens, Albert Bierstadt, Mari Sandoz, Willa Cather, Zane Grey, Wallace Stegner, Louise Erdrich, Cormac McCarthy, and a host of others, the American West of Laura Ingalls Wilder is an artistic creation. In art, the frontier experience belongs to the territory of the imagination (even when grounded in personal experience), but that does not invalidate its powerful appeal, its historical significance, or its ability to inform, however imperfectly. Many readers who begin their introduction to western history with Laura Ingalls Wilder ultimately find themselves moving on to other voices, other sources, and the nonfiction of historians such as Vine Deloria, Jr., Patricia Nelson Limerick, Howard Zinn, or Robert Berghofer. And although Wilder's conception of the frontier was built on a foundation of fairy tale, generations of readers have refused to relegate it to the nursery. Wilder's frontier remains a place of personal and social conflict, a tenuous new world balanced precariously on the ridgeline between great romance and high anxiety. In her essay "Intimate Immensity," Dolores Rosenblum described the dominant theme of Wilder's frontier narratives:

> The basic "human" plot of all the narratives . . . is "to survive," that is, to learn the rules—and internalize them as self-regulation—so that you can enjoy life as a civilized human. Learning the rules means learning how to "read" the world, or rather how to make the world signify. . . . Wilder's central metaphor for the process of human survival and development always involves the problem of inhabiting space: how do you fill with your presence an emptiness that threatens to efface you? The narratives are thus organized around a variety of habitations constructed against and in compliance with the vast outer space surrounding the human figures. That space is both threatening and inviting—the true American sublime.[41]

And it is the forest primeval of fairy tale.

In his groundbreaking Freudian analysis, *The Uses of Enchantment: The Meaning and Importance of Fairy Tales*, Bruno Bettelheim made a similar argument about the profound way in which fairy tales help children to understand, process, and internalize difficult or frightening realities:

> The fairy-tale hero proceeds for a time in isolation, as the modern child often feels isolated. The hero is helped by being in touch with

---

41. Rosenblum, "Intimate Immensity," p. 74.

primitive things—a tree, an animal, nature—as the child feels more in touch with those things than most adults do. The fate of these heroes convinces the child that, like them, he may feel outcast and abandoned in the world, groping in the dark, but, like them, in the course of his life he will be guided step by step, and given help when it is needed. Today even more than in past times, the child needs the reassurance offered by the image of the isolated man [or pioneer girl] who nevertheless is capable of achieving meaningful and rewarding relations with the world around him.[42]

In *Little House in the Big Woods,* Wilder may have chosen to lead with Once Upon a Time in the West, but it is the enigmatic Zen of the ending that stays with the reader. Wilder decided to close her narrative with an unexpected and evocative image of her feisty, perceptive heroine. The image brings the story full circle, conflates past, present, and future time, and merges Laura of the story with Laura Ingalls Wilder, the teller of the tale. Zipes described this archetypal feature of fairy tale as an "uplifting of time," a dissolution of normal sequential patterns that fuse the boundaries between fantasy and the real world.[43] The final scene begins with Pa playing the fiddle. Laura asks:

> "What are the days of auld lang syne, Pa?"
> "They are the days of a long time ago, Laura," Pa said. "Go to sleep, now."
> But Laura lay awake a little while, listening to Pa's fiddle softly playing and to the lonely sound of the wind in the Big Woods. She looked at Pa sitting on the bench by the hearth. . . . She looked at Ma, gently rocking and knitting.
> She thought to herself, "This is now."
> She was glad that the cozy house, and Pa and Ma and the firelight and the music, were now. They could not be forgotten, she thought, because now is now. It can never be a long time ago. (pp. 237–38)

Of course, even the youngest reader knows otherwise. It actually *can* be a long time ago; in fact, it is and it was and it always will be. And yet also, it is not. Because, as Wilder understood, in fairy tales—the first stories, the bedtime stories, the enduring stories that have always mattered most—time is timeless.

---

42. Bettelheim, *Uses of Enchantment*, p. 11.
43. Zipes, *Breaking the Magic Spell*, p. 101.

# { 10 }
# The Myth of Happy Childhood (and Other Myths about Frontiers, Families, and Growing Up)

ELIZABETH JAMESON

*"I was not a happy child. Few children are happy. The myth of happy childhood is created by adults."*

ROSE WILDER LANE, *Cosmopolitan* (1926)

As Laura Ingalls Wilder's daughter broadcast her unhappy childhood to the readers of *Cosmopolitan*, Wilder was on the brink of writing *Pioneer Girl*, the autobiography of her childhood and adolescence on American frontiers. Though millions of fans have believed that the fictional Little House books were Wilder's unfiltered personal story, *Pioneer Girl* offered a more complex portrait of an often insecure and impoverished reality. Submitted in 1930 to literary agent Carl Brandt and in the following year to George T. Bye, the manuscript failed to attract a buyer and would likely have reached few readers but for Wilder's subsequent success as a children's author. Valuable in its own right as a historical source, *Pioneer Girl* remained unpublished, accessible only in archives until the South Dakota Historical Society Press undertook the carefully edited and annotated 2014 volume.[1] Its publication allows a wider public audience to explore how Wilder transformed lived experi-

---

1. Laura Ingalls Wilder, *Pioneer Girl: The Annotated Autobiography*, ed. Pamela Smith Hill (Pierre: South Dakota Historical Society Press, 2014). Wilder wrote "Pioneer Girl" between 1926 and May 1930; Rose Wilder Lane typed several drafts and submitted them to agents Carl Brandt and George T. Bye. Copies of the manuscripts sent to Brandt and Bye are in the Laura Ingalls Wilder Series, Rose Wilder Lane Papers, Herbert Hoover Presidential Library, West Branch, Iowa (Lane Papers), identified as "*Pioneer Girl*–Copy sent Brandt" and "*Pioneer Girl*–Copy sent Bye." In this article, the citation *Pioneer Girl* refers to the 2014 publication based on Wilder's original handwritten draft housed at the Laura Ingalls Wilder Historic Home and Museum, Mansfield, Missouri, as distinct from the two subsequent manuscripts, referenced hereafter as Brandt and Bye, respectively.

Lane posed for this portrait between 1928 and 1930, around the time *Pioneer Girl* was being written. *Herbert Hoover Presidential Library and Museum*

ence into the mythic childhood of her spectacularly successful Little House books. In the journey from *Pioneer Girl* to children's bookshelves, memory, history, ideology, and imagination converged to reinforce popular narratives of American frontier settlement, childhood and maturation, and particular templates of family and gender.

That literary transformation owed much to Wilder and Lane's evolving collaboration during the 1930s, when their hostility to the New Deal led them to emphasize independence and to denigrate government in the Little House books.[2] Lane's negative view of childhood became one element of her liber-

---

2. On the women's literary collaboration, *see* Rosa Ann Moore, "Laura Ingalls Wilder and Rose Wilder Lane: The Chemistry of Collaboration," *Children's Literature in Education* 11 (Sept. 1980): 101–9, and "The Little House Books: Rose-Colored Classics," *Children's Literature* 7 (1978): 7–16; Anita Clair Fellman, "Laura Ingalls Wilder and Rose Wilder Lane: The Politics of a Mother-Daughter Relationship," *Signs: Journal of Women in Culture and Society* 15 (Spring 1990): 535–61; William Holtz, *The Ghost in the Little House: A Life of Rose Wilder Lane* (Columbia: University of Missouri Press, 1993); John E. Miller, *Becoming Laura Ingalls Wilder: The Woman behind the Legend* (Columbia: University of Missouri Press, 1998), pp. 155–240, and *Laura Ingalls Wilder and Rose Wilder Lane: Authorship, Place, Time, and Culture* (Columbia: University of Missouri Press, 2008), pp. 1–23; Pamela Smith Hill, *Laura Ingalls Wilder: A Writer's Life* (Pierre:

tarian philosophy, expressed in her *Saturday Evening Post* article "Credo" in 1936 and the expanded book version, *Give Me Liberty*, and in her *The Discovery of Freedom* in 1943.³ Historian Jennifer Burns has argued that, for Lane, as for fellow libertarians Ayn Rand and Isabel Paterson, childhood represented a period of dependence and powerlessness. In Lane's case, the political was also personal. "This identification of childlike dependence as the root of political authority," Burns observed, "can be seen as a vestige of Lane's ongoing struggle for independence from her mother."⁴ However we characterize Wilder and Lane's admittedly complex relationship, Lane's words in 1926 remained ironically prophetic: "The myth of happy childhood is created by adults."⁵ She and her mother collaboratively crafted one of the more mythically secure and happy childhoods in American juvenile fiction. In the process, they helped mythologize the American frontier and the American family as well.

The Little House books have captured the imaginations of countless children and imprinted a popular portrait of pioneer childhood since the first volume appeared in 1932. I treasured the copies my grandmother sent me, beginning in 1953 with the publication of the uniform edition illustrated by Garth Williams.⁶ I was captivated with the daily details of female experience:

South Dakota Historical Society Press, 2007), pp. 134–80. On both women's antipathy to the New Deal, *see* Anita Clair Fellman, "Everybody's 'Little Houses': Reviewers and Critics Read Laura Ingalls Wilder," *Publishing Research Quarterly* 12 (Spring 1996): 3–19, "'Don't Expect to Depend on Anybody Else': The Frontier as Portrayed in the Little House Books," *Children's Literature* 24 (1996): 101–16, and *Little House, Long Shadow: Laura Ingalls Wilder's Impact on American Culture* (Columbia: University of Missouri Press, 2008), pp. 55–68.

3. Lane, "Credo," *Saturday Evening Post* 208 (Mar. 7, 1936): 5–7, 30–31, 34–35, *Give Me Liberty* (New York: Longmans, Green & Co., 1936), and *The Discovery of Freedom: Man's Struggle against Authority* (New York: John Day Co., 1943). See also Holtz, *Ghost in the Little House*, pp. 247, 262–63, 267, 309, 315, 318, 325, 347, 361, 373. Wilder expressed her views in letters to her daughter. *See* Wilder to Lane, Feb. 20, Mar. 17, Apr. 2, May 24, 1939, Box 13, file 195, Lane Papers.

4. Burns, "The Three 'Furies' of Libertarianism: Rose Wilder Lane, Isabel Paterson, and Ayn Rand," *Journal of American History* 102 (Dec. 2015): 762. On Lane's relationship with her mother, *see* Holtz, *Ghost in the Little House;* Fellman, "Laura Ingalls Wilder and Rose Wilder Lane"; and Miller, *Laura Ingalls Wilder and Rose Wilder Lane*.

5. Lane, "I, Rose Wilder Lane, Am the Only Truly Happy Person I Know, and I Discovered the Secret of Happiness on the Day I Tried to Kill Myself," *Cosmopolitan* 80 (June 1926): 42.

6. Wilder considered the eight volumes, all published by Harper & Brothers, a composite children's novel: *Little House in the Big Woods* (1932), *Farmer Boy* (1933), *Little*

*Helen Sewell,* Little House in the Big *Woods, 1932*

Mary and Laura playing with homemade paper dolls, tossing a balloon made from a pig's bladder, making molasses candy; Ma's deft skill manufacturing straw hats, making cheese, churning butter and coloring it with grated carrots, producing headcheese and hominy, trying out lard. I was equally intrigued when Pa's masculine labors occasionally crossed the domestic threshold, absorbing each intricate step as he cleaned his traps or made bullets to hunt game for his girls.[7]

I became more conflicted later, as I analyzed the narrative that chronicled the Ingalls family's trek from the Little House in the Big Woods to Indian Territory, to Plum Creek near Walnut Grove in western Minnesota, and finally to their homestead outside De Smet, Dakota Territory (now South Dakota). I became troubled by tensions between the pioneer family's pursuit of opportunity along the nation's westward trek and what could, on closer examination, be read as a narrative of decline from the security of *Little House in the Big Woods* to increasing poverty and insecurity on a homesteading frontier.

---

*House on the Prairie* (1935), *On the Banks of Plum Creek* (1937), *By the Shores of Silver Lake* (1939), *The Long Winter* (1940), *Little Town on the Prairie* (1941), *These Happy Golden Years* (1943). All citations in this article are from the 1953 uniform edition of the series, with new illustrations by Garth Williams. In most cases, page numbers are given in the text.

7. Wilder, *Little House in the Big Woods,* pp. 14-15, 17-18, 20-22, 29-33, 45-46, 63-64, 186-90, 212-14, 218-21.

Despite idealized appeals to American pioneer progress personified in Pa's and Laura's desires to keep moving west, the promise of frontier opportunity and independence fades as the family moves from Wisconsin to Kansas to Minnesota to South Dakota. The cozy self-sufficiency in the Big Woods leads to government eviction from the *Little House on the Prairie,* to precarious years battling grasshoppers, fire, and drought *On the Banks of Plum Creek*, to near starvation during *The Long Winter* in De Smet. The abundant larder of wild game, home-raised meat, garden vegetables, and dairy products from their own cow that stuffed the family's Wisconsin larder contracts on the South Dakota homestead to a diet increasingly dependent on flour and salt pork bought in town.[8]

Those changes accurately reflect a period in American agriculture when production for household consumption gave way to more specialized crops for urban markets. That changing reality, however, does not fit the Little House narrative of girlhood in a self-sufficient pioneer family. Larger nineteenth-century economic and technological changes appear in the novels occasionally, when they directly impact the Ingalls family. Pa hires a "wonderful machine" to thresh his wheat in *Little House in the Big Woods*, announcing, "As long as I raise wheat, I'm going to have a machine come and thresh it" (p. 228). Railroad construction draws the Ingallses west from Walnut Grove to De Smet when Aunt Docia's husband, a railroad contractor, hires Pa as his storekeeper and timekeeper at the beginning of *By the Shores of Silver Lake*. New industrial technologies and the transcontinental railroads that transformed American agriculture, however, hold little explanatory power in the Little House narrative, which relies for context on a nostalgic frontier past. Farmers' increasing dependence on distant markets lurks implicitly in *The Long Winter*, when interminable blizzards halt the trains carrying processed flour, salt pork, and other staples to De Smet. But the emphasis is not on adaptation to a new industrial reality, much less the populist challenge to railroads' freight rates, but rather on nuclear family survival.

The 2014 publication of *Pioneer Girl* clarifies some of these narrative tensions, painting a grittier, less-secure childhood than the eight-volume fiction. For many years, scholars consulted the unpublished *Pioneer Girl* manuscripts to probe differences between the historical Ingalls family and

---

8. Elizabeth Jameson, "Unconscious Inheritance and Conscious Striving: Laura Ingalls Wilder and the Frontier Narrative," in *Laura Ingalls Wilder and the American Frontier: Five Perspectives*, ed. Dwight M. Miller (Lanham, Md.: University Press of America, 2002), pp. 69–94.

the fictional characters who bear their names.⁹ The 2014 published version, which relies on Wilder's original handwritten text, adds new layers of edits, annotations, and fact checking. The annotations catch some factual errors within the manuscripts, cautioning against simple assumptions that *Pioneer Girl* represents "real history" in contrast to the fictional Little House books. *Pioneer Girl*, like most historical sources, was created in particular contexts for an imagined audience. Specific details and the narrative itself were filtered through Wilder's memories of her childhood, reinforced by her subsequent experience. Wilder sometimes confused dates and chronologies.¹⁰ Many memoirs do. Few have been annotated and corrected as *Pioneer Girl* has been. Nor do such lapses of memory necessarily negate authors' essential truths. Even with confused dates and chronologies, autobiographies can reveal a great deal about events and values that were, in retrospect, important to an author, that influenced how he or she interpreted the world and acted in it. Memory, in other words, affects behavior and has historical impact.

In Wilder's case, authorial intent, imagination, and personal values helped shape a memoir of childhood into the fiction she considered appropriate and marketable for young readers. The narrative she crafted combined elements of Frederick Jackson Turner's frontier thesis and conventional romance—of Manifest Destiny and Cinderella. The Little House books follow America's westward movement and Laura's gradual maturation from a secure childhood into increasing adolescent responsibility and independence. A long foreground of pioneer childhood ends according to roman-

---

9. *See*, for example, Elizabeth Jameson, "In Search of the Great Ma," *Journal of the West* 37 (Apr. 1998): 42-52, which can also be found in *Myths and the American West*, ed. Richard W. Etulain (Manhattan, Kans: Sunflower University Press, 1998). In distinguishing the fictional Laura from Laura Ingalls Wilder and the fictional Ma from the actual Caroline Quiner Ingalls, I used the Brandt and Bye manuscripts. *See also* William T. Anderson, "The Literary Apprenticeship of Laura Ingalls Wilder," *South Dakota History* 13 (Winter 1983): 287-90, which describes some of the early questioning of differences between the actual lives and the fictional accounts. Other scholarship on the topic includes Donald Zochert, *Laura: The Life of Laura Ingalls Wilder* (Chicago: Contemporary Books, 1976); Holtz, *Ghost in the Little House*; Louise Hovde Mortensen, "Idea Inventory," *Elementary English* 41 (Apr. 1964): 428-29; Rosa Ann Moore, "Laura Ingalls Wilder's Orange Notebooks and the Art of the Little House Books," *Children's Literature* 4 (1975): 105-19; Ann Romines, "*The Long Winter*: An Introduction to Western Womanhood," *Great Plains Quarterly* 10 (Winter 1990): 36-47, among others.

10. For errors in dates and/or chronologies, *see* Wilder, *Pioneer Girl*, pp. 69, 86n72, 145n93, 176, 260-61, 281, 295. For other factual errors, *see* pp. 117n10, 131, 140n73, 203n6, 227n3.

tic formula when Laura marries her pioneer Prince Charming at the end of *These Happy Golden Years*.[11]

*Pioneer Girl* had its own happy ending when Laura Ingalls married Almanzo Wilder. "I was a little awed by my new estate," Wilder wrote, "but I felt very much at home and very happy and among the other causes for happiness was the thought that I would not again have to go and live with strangers in their houses. I had a house and a home of my own."[12] The path to that happy ending was much rockier in *Pioneer Girl* than in the Little House narrative. The ending of *These Happy Golden Years* is similar, but the fictional conclusion promises increasing prosperity as Laura and Almanzo, backed by a secure homestead, begin their own family saga amid the sprouting saplings on Almanzo's tree claim:

> Laura's heart was full of happiness. She knew she need never be homesick for the old home. It was so near that she could go to it whenever she wished, while she and Almanzo made the new home in their own little house.
> 
> All this was theirs; their own horses, their own cow, their own claim. The many leaves of their little trees rustled softly in the gentle breeze [p. 289].

Two years after that happy ending, though, in late 1887, Charles and Caroline Ingalls left the "old home" on their hard-won homestead and moved their family to town. Within four years, Laura and Almanzo Wilder lost everything—homestead, tree claim, and their newborn son, leaving them homeless and Rose an only child. They traveled east briefly in 1890 to his family in Minnesota and Florida and then labored and scrimped in De Smet from 1892 to 1894 to finance one last move. That final journey led southeast, to their Rocky Ridge Farm near Mansfield, Missouri. Decades of labor followed before they could build a home on their land. They did not move into their farmhouse until they were both well into middle age, long after Rose had left home.[13]

---

11. These concepts are explored in Jameson, "Unconscious Inheritance and Conscious Striving" and "In Search of the Great Ma."

12. Wilder, *Pioneer Girl*, p. 324.

13. On the difficult years in Missouri, *see* William Anderson, *The Story of the Ingalls Family,* new ed. (n.p., 2006), *The Story of the Wilders* (Davison, Mich.: Anderson Publications, 1983), pp. 22-28, *Laura's Rose: The Story of Rose Wilder Lane,* Centennial ed. (De Smet, S.Dak.: Laura Ingalls Wilder Memorial Society, 1986), pp. 7-13, *Laura Wilder of Mansfield* (De Smet, S.Dak.: Laura Ingalls Wilder Memorial Society, 1982), and *Laura Ingalls Wilder: A Biography* (New York: HarperCollins, 1992), pp. 143-81; Holtz, *Ghost in the Little House*, pp. 29-46.

Though they differ in tone, the happy endings of both *Pioneer Girl* and *These Happy Golden Years* proved elusive in real life. Both stories had to end before the difficult years when the Wilders' hardships, poverty, and backtracking east repeated less-happy chapters of Ingalls family history. *Pioneer Girl* makes it easy to understand the relief Wilder felt at having a home of her own. The little houses in which she was raised rarely promised prosperity or stability, but rather a childhood that took her all-too-often into strangers' homes.

Wilder navigated the distance between myth and history as she tailored her family's lived experience to fit Frederick Jackson Turner's frontier thesis. In the process, though, she also modified the categories and boundaries of Turnerian frontiers, charting a sometimes conflicted course between a mythic frontier and her mythic family. Born in Portage in 1862, Turner, like Wilder, began childhood on a Wisconsin frontier. Laura Elizabeth Ingalls entered the world a bit farther west in Pepin on 7 February 1867. Their interpretations of their respective frontiers were compatible, but they differed in focus.

Turner's "Significance of the Frontier in American History," arguably the most stubbornly influential essay in United States history, identified national progress with constant westward movement. Turner argued in 1893 that Americans' engagements with a succession of westward-moving frontiers created American values and institutions. American democracy, individualism, and a uniquely American "composite nationality" and character were forged on frontiers that separated "savagery from civilization" as progressive waves of traders, ranchers or miners, and farmers claimed ever-receding free land. The process continued until the frontier had passed, the elbow room was gone, and it was time for a new wave of pioneers to move farther west.[14]

Turner's frontier followed a male occupational hierarchy, from trapping

---

14. Turner, "The Significance of the Frontier in American History," reprinted in *History, Frontier, and Section: Three Essays by Frederick Jackson Turner*, ed. Martin Ridge (Albuquerque: University of New Mexico Press, 1993), pp. 59, 62–65, 67–70, 75–76, 82–84, 87–88. Turner's "Significance of the Frontier" was first presented at the Historical Congress in Chicago at the World's Columbian Exhibition of 1893 and printed in *Annual Report of the American Historical Association for the Year 1893* (Washington, D.C.: Government Printing Office, 1894), pp. 199–227. Turner wrote his thesis the year after the superintendent of the United States census declared that the frontier had closed, and Turner believed he was describing a first period of American history that had come to an end. The superintendent said that there was no longer a frontier line, defined as an unbroken line with two or fewer settlers per square mile. U.S., Department of the Interior, Census Office, *Distribution of Population According to Density,* Extra Census Bulletin, no. 2 (Apr. 20, 1892).

and hunting at the bottom on the fur trader's frontier, to herding (ranching), to farming (the most "civilized" stage). Those frontiers of masculine work erased Ma Ingalls. There was no cheese- or butter-maker's frontier, no teacher's frontier, no child-bearer's frontier. Turner might have included Ma by inference in one isolated sentence: "Complex society is precipitated by the wilderness into a kind of primitive organization based on the family." For Turner, society progressed from the isolated family to the state. The Little House books inverted Turner, who considered the primitive stage of the family "anti-social" and who lamented an ethic that too easily confused "individual liberty . . . with absence of all effective government."[15]

In contrast, Wilder and Lane focused on Turner's "primitive organization" —on the family itself. They marginalized the state, which they generally erased or characterized as meddling, stupid, and/or intrusive. Government troops evict the family from their little house on the prairie in Indian Territory. The foolish government requires Almanzo to be twenty-one before he can claim land. The Homestead Act unreasonably requires Mrs. McKee and other women to sit idle on homestead claims while their husbands labor for wages to develop their land.[16] The role that the United States government actually played in securing the western territories and offering homestead land to settlers goes unheralded. The inconvenient fact that Mary Ingalls attended the Iowa College for the Blind through an agreement between Dakota Territory and the state of Iowa disappears in translation from reality to fiction.[17]

Turner, on the other hand, erased women, along with the indigenous inhabitants of the "free" western land. Casually dismissing the "primitive or-

15. Turner, "Significance of the Frontier," p. 82. For more on the absence of women in Turner's frontier theses, *see* William Cronon et al., "Women and the West: Rethinking the Western History Survey Course," *Western Historical Quarterly* 17 (July 1986): 269–90, and Elizabeth Jameson, "Halfway across That Line: Gender at the Threshold of History in the North American West," *Western Historical Quarterly* 47 (Spring 2016): 16–19.

16. Wilder, *Little House on the Prairie*, pp. 316–18, and *The Long Winter*, pp. 99–100.

17. While both Wilder and her fictional character worked to enable Mary to attend the Iowa College for the Blind in Vinton, Iowa, where Charles and Caroline Ingalls enrolled her in November 1881, neither *Pioneer Girl* (pp. 239–41) nor *Little House on the Prairie* make reference to the subsidy from Dakota Territory. Interestingly, Wilder had included it in her original draft of *Little Town on the Prairie:* "Dakota Territory still had no school where the blind could be educated, but the territory would pay tuition, to the state of Iowa, for all Dakota blind children. And Mary could go to the Iowa College for the blind at Vinton. Tuition included board and room and books" (quoted in Holtz, *Ghost in the Little House*, p. 384). In reality, the family worked to provide Mary's clothes, railroad fare, and spending money. For more, *see* Nancy Tystad Koupal, "Mary Ingalls Goes to College," Oct. 2014, *Pioneer Girl Project*, pioneergirlproject.org.

Caroline Ingalls differed from her fictional counterpart in significant ways. *South Dakota State Historical Society*

ganization based on the family," he buried women in a history of the nation in which they had no visible role. Part of what drew me to the Little House books was precisely their focus on the family, which restored Ma and Laura to the historical landscape, giving me women and girls with whom I could identify. The books also created nascent tensions with the American history I learned in school, which focused on the nation and valorized the independent frontiersman. In contrast, Ma's "effeminate" urge to civilize, her desire to settle amidst neighbors, schools, and churches, seemed to me, as to Laura, less adventurous and less fun than Pa's restless desire to keep moving west whenever neighbors crowded in and the game fled.

Ma was up against an avalanche of early childhood messaging. American history texts, TV shows like *The Lone Ranger* and *Gunsmoke*, and movies like *Davy Crockett* and *Westward Ho the Wagons*, all conditioned me to side with Pa in the choice between the interdependence of town and the presumed freedom of the frontier. I wanted the westward saga to continue, obliviously ignoring the fact that the libraries and schools that Ma valued enabled me to read the treasured stories.

Even so, the tensions between Ma's yearnings for civilization and Pa's frontier ethos were not absolute. Pa went to church; he stayed put in De Smet when Ma refused to move on; the family itself was an interdependent unit. But the tensions between the frontiers of western expansion and those of an interdependent nuclear family can be reconciled only if we abandon both the frontier myth and the mythic security of frontier childhood.

As she crafted her story for young readers, Wilder omitted troubling chapters in her own childhood and tailored the Ingalls family journey to move always farther west. To reflect that westward-moving frontier line of progress, Wilder's fictional narrative eliminated periods when the Ingalls family backtracked from the Osage Diminished Indian Reserve to return to Wisconsin ("the place we had left when we went west"), not because government troops "were taking all the white people off the Indian's land," but because the man who bought the land from Charles Ingalls "had not paid for it."[18] She erased the period from 1875 to 1879, a time that included the birth and death of the only Ingalls son, years when successive crop failures forced Charles Ingalls to sell the farm on Plum Creek and move to Burr Oak, Iowa, where the whole family labored in a hotel.[19] Deleting the moves east to Pepin and Burr Oak propelled the family along the trajectory of Manifest Destiny.

Wilder made her pioneer family self-sufficient as she excised extended family and friends who lived nearby in the Great Woods of Wisconsin and those who shared the hardships of the long winter of 1880–1881 in De Smet. By erasing their support, and by eliminating all vestiges of government assistance, she recast the family story from a typical experience of extended family settlement and rural interdependence to a more isolated and self-sufficient nuclear family that ultimately triumphed to win a western homestead.

*Pioneer Girl*, in contrast, chronicled a childhood of periodic poverty, hunger, and early exposure to sexuality and violence. Though Charles and Caroline Ingalls clearly tried to support and protect their children, their circumstances often placed safety, security, and childhood innocence beyond parental control. *Pioneer Girl* offers a version of childhood that was far from idyllic and of adult gender roles that were more interdependent and less securely anchored within domestic boundaries than their fictional counterparts.

Wilder thus etched her longing for a secure home of her own in *Pioneer Girl*'s extended foreground of constant moving, poverty, and childhood labor. The fictional Mary and Laura perform household chores in all the little

---

18. Wilder, *Pioneer Girl*, pp. 18, 22.

19. Ibid., pp. 99–113. *See also* William Anderson, *Laura Ingalls Wilder: The Iowa Story* (Burr Oak, Iowa: Laura Ingalls Wilder Park & Museum, 1990).

houses and help Ma with her domestic labors. But perhaps understandably in books intended for children, Wilder deleted periods of child labor during the precarious years from 1875 to 1879, when the wages of an eight- to twelve-year-old child aided family survival. In the Little House books, Laura's entry into the work world comes later and is a gradual part of growing up. In the more realistic *Pioneer Girl*, working for strangers was a constant and often frightening element of an impoverished childhood. Wilder's *Pioneer Girl* work record began to resemble the Little House story only at Silver Lake, when thirteen-year-old Laura cooked and washed for hordes of settlers during the spring land rush in a house that "was always full of strange men."[20] In *The Long Winter*, Laura labors endlessly, twisting hay for fuel and grinding wheat for bread. *Little Town on the Prairie* and *These Happy Golden Years* include her three terms as a school teacher, two of which took her away from home, her job claim-sitting with Mrs. McKee, her paid work in town as a seamstress and then as a milliner's assistant. "Of course," she shared in her autobiography, "the money I earned [for her work with milliner Florence Bell] had gone into the home fund."[21] She had by then contributed to the home fund for many years.

After they left Plum Creek the first time in 1876, Charles and Caroline Ingalls ran a hotel in Burr Oak with the Steadmans, a couple they knew from Walnut Grove. Laura and Mary worked there as well, washing dishes, waiting on tables, and caring for the Steadman's baby "all day saturdays [*sic*] and Sundays." The domestic chores of the fictional Laura and Mary teach them adult skills and contribute to family well-being. The real world of child labor, however, guaranteed neither security nor just reward for their efforts. In return for their caring for Tommy, Mrs. Steadman promised the girls "something nice for Christmas." But in contrast to the cozy Christmas in the Big Woods with Aunt Eliza, Uncle Peter, and the cousins, in Burr Oak "Christmas was disappointing. Ma was always tired; Pa was always busy and Mrs[.] Steadman did not give us anything at all for taking care of her disagreeable baby, Tommy!"[22]

20. Wilder, *Pioneer Girl*, p. 187. In the Brandt manuscript, this passage was edited slightly to "the house was always full of strangers" (p. 87), a change that removed a degree of the sexual threat that may have troubled an adolescent girl, but the original wording appears in Bye (p. 107). *By the Shores of Silver Lake* also references "strange men" (p. 22).

21. Wilder, *Pioneer Girl*, p. 287.

22. Ibid., p. 103. For the Wisconsin Christmas, *see Little House in the Big Woods*, pp. 59–82, and *Pioneer Girl*, pp. 32–35. The Ingallses and Steadmans were apparently partners in the Burr Oak hotel, but Steadman cheated Charles Ingalls of what little money, if any, the venture produced. *See Pioneer Girl*, p. 104n15.

The Ingalls family left Burr Oak and returned to Walnut Grove in 1877, living in town for two years until 1879. They arrived in Minnesota in wretched financial straits. During their stay in Burr Oak, Wilder wrote:

> Pa worked catchely [sic] here and there but never enough to pay expenses. When we left there was not money enough to pay the last months [sic] rent and feed us on the way back to Walnut Grove. There Pa bought a lot and built a house on just his credit. "Old Man Masters," who used to own the hotel in Burr Oak owned the land and lumber yard. Pa bought from him. It was not all paid for when Pa went to work on the R.R. west from Tracy.

Charles Ingalls apparently was never able to pay more than the interest on the loan and turned the property back to Masters when the family left Walnut Grove.[23]

Mary and Laura Ingalls had both worked in the family hotel in Burr Oak. Beginning in Walnut Grove in 1878, the burden of work fell most often on Laura after Mary became ill and then blind. Charles Ingalls struggled to eke out a living, working in a store, briefly operating a butcher shop, serving as justice of the peace, and doing carpentry. Laura Ingalls worked away from home, earning fifty cents a week at the hotel of William and Emmeline Masters, "washing dishes, waiting on table," sweeping and dusting, and helping to care for baby Nan, daughter of the Masterses' son Will and his wife Nannie. Later, Wilder worked "away from home a good many days . . . helping Mrs. Goff on Saturdays and holidays." She then stayed for two weeks with Sadie Hurley in "a little two roomed house in the country" because Sadie was "not . . . very well" (perhaps a euphemism for pregnant) and her husband John was absent much of the time turning "his crop of broom straw into brooms to sell in town." Wilder reported feeling "lonely" and "homesick." She was worried as well. "I knew things were not going well at home, because Pa could not get much work and we needed more money to live on."[24]

What work Charles Ingalls scraped up often involved working for William Masters ("Old Man Masters"), doing carpentry, repairing a pasture fence, and other jobs. After Masters built a store next to the hotel, his son Will moved into rooms above it with Nannie and their baby. "[Emmeline] Masters persuaded Ma to let me stay with Nannie," Wilder wrote, "because she had fainting spells and it was not safe for her to stay alone with Little Nan." Though Wilder was not required to do much housework, the job "was not

---

23. Wilder to Lane, Mar. 23, 1937, Box 13, file 193, Lane Papers.
24. Wilder, *Pioneer Girl*, pp. 122–23, 137.

pleasant, for I never knew at what moment Nannie would fall without a word or a sign and lie as if dead."[25]

Poverty and living conditions also exposed the Ingalls children to drinking, violence, and sexual abuse in both Burr Oak and Walnut Grove. Will Masters came to personify these threats in both communities. William and Emmeline Masters had owned the Burr Oak hotel before they sold it to the Steadmans and Ingallses and left Iowa to operate their hotel in Walnut Grove. Wilder wrote in *Pioneer Girl* that a door in the Burr Oak hotel was scarred by "several bullet holes made by the son of the man who had sold us the hotel, when he shot at his wife as she ran from him.... He had been drunk!" His drinking had caused his father to take him "west away from the saloon next door. Pa and Ma didn't like the saloon next door either and we were a little afraid of the men who were always hanging around its door."[26]

Even when Charles and Caroline Ingalls moved their family out of the Burr Oak hotel to rooms over a grocery store, they could not shield their children from domestic violence. Nor could they seem to escape saloons—another one operated on the other side of the wall from their rented rooms. The store owner, Mr. Cameron, spent considerable time at the saloon, and Charles Ingalls had to intervene one night when Mrs. Cameron screamed and he found her husband "dragging her around the room, by her long hair." Doubly alarming, Cameron was carrying a kerosene lamp upside down, and the kerosene was "catching fire and flaming up around his hand." The incident occurred not long after the saloon caught fire one night and threatened to burn the whole building down.[27]

The hazards of alcohol climaxed when a man called Hairpin ended a several-day drinking binge at the saloon by lighting a cigar before swallowing yet another mouthful of whiskey. The whiskey ignited in his mouth. Hairpin breathed the flames into his lungs and died virtually immediately. The Ingalls girls knew Hairpin because he had courted Amy, a servant at the Burr Oak hotel. After Hairpin's gruesome death, Charles Ingalls moved the family away from the saloon to a rental house on the edge of town.[28]

Charles and Caroline Ingalls took action to combat the dangers of alcohol, joining the Good Templars Lodge to support sobriety in Walnut Grove. They did not, however, keep their daughter away from Will Masters, whom they knew to be a violent and abusive drunk. Perhaps they had no choice.

25. Ibid., p. 140.
26. Ibid., pp. 99, 101.
27. Ibid., p. 105.
28. Ibid., pp. 106, 108.

Maybe they were simply so poor that they had to let Laura work in the Masters Hotel in Walnut Grove and then live with Will and Nannie Masters. At least Laura got fed where she worked; at least she earned meager wages. Perhaps they could not afford to antagonize William and Emmeline Masters, to whom Charles Ingalls was in debt and who provided much-needed wage work.[29] Whatever their motives or reservations, Wilder's parents allowed her to work in environments about which they had considerable grounds for concern, including her job as companion to Nannie Masters that produced one of the most disturbing scenes in *Pioneer Girl*:

> I hadn't stayed with Nannie very long when one night I waked from a sound sleep to find Will leaning over me. I could smell the whiskey on his breath. I sat up quickly.
> 'Is Nannie sick,' I asked.
> "No," he answered, ["]lie down and be still!"
> 'Go away quick,' I said, 'or I will scream for Nannie.'
> He went and the next day Ma said I could come home.[30]

Laura Ingalls had already witnessed the manipulative powers and potential dangers of sexuality while working for Emmeline Masters at the Walnut Grove hotel. The Masterses' daughter Mattie (Mary Masters, called "Matie" in *Pioneer Girl*) impressed Wilder as lazy and spoiled. She complained that Mattie "never helped with the work, not even making her own bed," that she slept late and was used to getting her own way. Mattie Masters's self-absorbed sense of entitlement manifested in her campaign to woo Dr. Robert Hoyt, who boarded at the hotel. When Hoyt's former girlfriend, Fanny Starr, came to visit, Mattie apparently seduced the doctor to secure her conquest. Soon thereafter, Fanny Starr left town, and Caroline Ingalls helped with the sewing as "right away Mrs[.] Masters began to get Matie ready for her wedding."[31]

But within five short months of her marriage, Mattie died on March 5, 1879, not long after Wilder returned from working at the Hurleys. "No one ever said what the sickness was," Wilder recalled, "but I heard Ma tell Pa that Dr. Hoyt had been trying some experiment and she said, 'Matie would

---

29. Ibid., pp. 133, 140. The editors of *Pioneer Girl* speculate that John Hurley may have been Emmeline Masters's brother, and it was Mrs. Masters who requested that Laura stay with Sadie Hurley while John made his brooms, adding yet another potential link between the Masters family and the wage work that took young Laura Ingalls away from home. *See* pp. 137, 137n67.

30. Ibid., pp. 140–41.

31. *Pioneer Girl*, pp. 122–25.

better have let Fanny Star have him than to have gotten him that way.'"[32] In the Bye manuscript, Wilder changed it slightly: "No one ever said what the sickness was, but I heard Ma tell Pa that the disgrace wouldn't have been any worse than what Dr. Hoyt did, and he shouldn't have done it. She said, 'Matie would better have let Fanny Starr have him, than to get him that way.'"[33]

More members of the extended Masters family followed the Ingallses to De Smet and contributed further to Wilder's knowledge of pre-marital sexuality. George Masters, "the eldest son of Uncle Sam Masters of Walnut Grove," came through De Smet in the fall of 1880 on his way to work farther west and "begged Ma to let his wife Maggie stay with us to be nearer to him."[34] George and Maggie Masters ultimately shared the Ingallses' house during the hard winter of 1880–1881. Wilder excised them from *The Long Winter* to portray her family as more isolated and self-reliant during that ordeal. She wrote her daughter about how the couple came to be in the Ingalls household in the first place:

> When Maggie came, Ma saw she would soon have a baby, much too soon after the time she was married.
>
> Maggie didn't want the baby to be born at her folks' and disgrace them. George's folks were mad because he married her and wouldn't have her there.
>
> Maggie had always been a nice girl and Ma was sorry for her and let her stay, the baby was born before winter came.

After George's work ran out, he returned to De Smet for the winter because "Pa couldn't put them out in the street."[35]

Although the family liked Maggie, they became increasingly weary of George, who avoided the endless labor of grinding wheat in the coffee mill or twisting hay to burn but instead hogged the meager warmth near the stove while Charles Ingalls did all the chores. George and Maggie Masters finally left in May 1881. "We parted friendly enough," Wilder wrote, "but I at least was glad to say good by."

The Ingallses' relationships with the Masters family, however fraught, also epitomized the cooperative aid and interdependence of frontier communities.[36] Ideally, such assistance was rooted in the mutuality of egalitarian re-

32. Ibid., pp. 125, 137–38.
33. Bye, p. 59.
34. Wilder, *Pioneer Girl*, p. 203.
35. Wilder to Lane, Mar. 7, 1938, quoted in *Pioneer Girl*, p. 205n10.
36. Wilder, *Pioneer Girl*, pp. 229, 229n8. *See also* pp. 205n10, 213, 215, 220.

lationships, exemplified in community barn raisings. At other times, dependency could lead to less-balanced relationships of obligation and assistance, like those that sent eleven-year-old Laura Ingalls to labor for other Masters in Walnut Grove. George's refusal to shoulder his share of labor contributed to Wilder's decision to eliminate him from *The Long Winter*. Perhaps he had to disappear to reinforce the independent self-sufficiency that she clearly preferred to his selfish dependence or to her family's compromises with necessity.

Sexuality was but one of the potential threats to children's lives and security that Wilder recorded in *Pioneer Girl*. In addition to poverty, fire, and alcohol, Wilder knew of children who perished in tornadoes and blizzards. During their sojourn in Walnut Grove, Charles Ingalls joined the searchers who discovered five children buried in a snowdrift after a blizzard struck while their parents were gone. The children had fled their house when the stovepipe fell down, sending sparks flying and convincing them that the house was on fire. Three of the children froze to death. The oldest daughter, age twelve, saved the baby under her coat but was herself badly frozen and lost a leg.[37]

Wilder also recorded events that were less dangerous but made her uncomfortable nonetheless. When Charles and Caroline Ingalls left their homestead for a week to enroll Mary in the Iowa College for the Blind in Vinton, Iowa, they hired Gaylord Ross to do the chores and Jennie Ross to look after the younger girls. This arrangement might seem to be more protective than leaving Grace and Carrie in Laura's care, as Ma and Pa do in *Little Town on the Prairie*. However, Wilder wrote, Gaylord was "unpleasant in a way I couldn't explain" and Jennie "told dirty stories that I only half understood, tormented our pet cat and was lazy and quarrelsome besides."[38] Jennie Ross was a twenty-one-year-old schoolteacher at the time. Wilder erased the disagreeable Rosses from the Bye manuscript and from *Little Town on the Prairie*. She excised other scenes of discord and discomfort as well. An argument she witnessed between a Manchester hotelkeeper and his wife when she was traveling with Mrs. McKee to claim-sit on the McKee's homestead disappeared from *These Happy Golden Years*, along with adolescent kissing games that made her uncomfortable.[39]

Wilder also laundered the actual details of her first job in De Smet, sewing shirts that the mother-in-law of a local merchant made and sold to bachelors.

---

37. Ibid., p. 139; for the boy killed by a tornado, *see* p. 310. Later, Wilder described a blizzard that claimed other lives, likely misdating the storm known as the Children's Blizzard of 1888. Ibid., pp. 315, 315n90.

38. Ibid., p. 239.

39. Ibid., pp. 240–41n36, 257, 259, 284.

In *Little Town on the Prairie,* Laura walks to work from the homestead claim every day. *Pioneer Girl,* however, revealed that she "slept with [the mother-in-law] in the [merchant's] attic and ate with them in the kitchen." Their behavior was often distressing. "Mrs[.] Clancy quarreled constantly with her son-in-law, so that at times it was unpleasant." Her daughter, who was consumed with nativist fears of Catholics, "would wring her hands and pace the floor declaring that the Catholics should never take her Bible away from her."[40] In *Little Town on the Prairie,* Mr. Clancy swears at his mother-in-law, and the family quarrels, but Laura can go home at the end of the work day. For six weeks' work she brings home nine dollars.

Wilder's awareness of sexuality, poverty, and danger were not unusual for a girl growing up in her time and place. Children who grew up in little one-room houses likely heard and witnessed adult stories, intimacies, and violence. And simple demography shaped the meaning of frontier "opportunity" for girls and women. Women were outnumbered on all frontiers by an excess of men. Skewed sex ratios (the number of men per hundred women) provided women with only limited options. They could teach, do domestic wage work like sewing, cooking, or laundry, keep boarders, or engage in sex work. Or they could marry—usually young and often men considerably older than themselves. In *Pioneer Girl,* Wilder recounted one marriage of a thirteen-year-old girl. One day after the family came to the railroad camp, Wilder and her cousin Lena went to pick up laundry from a nearby farmers' wife who had not delivered the laundry herself "because her daughter had just been married and she had been busy with the wedding. 'She is only thirteen,' she said proudly, 'but it is just as well to be married young.'" Realizing that she was the same age as the bride and that Lena was only a year older, Wilder reflected, "we were glad we were not in her place but could run around and play as we were doing. We decided we didn't mind helping with the work and the babies but . . . let some one [sic] else be responsible."[41]

Wilder retained the story in *By the Shores of Silver Lake* as she began slowly to include material from *Pioneer Girl* that she considered acceptable for older juvenile readers. In the novel, Laura concludes, "I'd like my own house and I like babies, and I wouldn't mind the work, but I don't want to be so responsible. I'd rather let Ma be responsible for a long time yet." Lena is more reluctant, announcing, "I don't want to settle down. . . . I'm not ever going to get married, or if I do, I'm going to marry a railroader and keep on moving west as long as I live" (p. 50). For Lena, the westward journey prom-

---

40. Ibid., p. 237. *See* Wilder, *Little Town on the Prairie,* pp. 35–56.
41. Wilder, *Pioneer Girl,* p. 153.

ises freedom from adult female responsibility. Settling down threatens the constraints of home and children. It is a particularly female spin on the urge to keep moving west with the frontier.

From these perspectives, Wilder's own marriage at age eighteen seems appropriately conservative. She recorded in *Pioneer Girl* her oblivious failure to respond, at age fifteen or sixteen, when a De Smet lawyer wanted to escort her to an entertainment in town. The annotator explained: "The attention he and other single men paid Wilder as a schoolgirl reflected the fact that De Smet was 'a bachelor community.' Unmarried men were 'here in force, the local newspaper reported.'"[42] Their object, the *De Smet Leader* concluded, was "the building up of happy homes when they have brought the wilds under subjection." Therefore, the paper announced, "Dakota wants more women—young women especially. Send on your girls from the overcrowded East."[43]

The *Leader* broadcast one stereotypical version of female frontier "opportunity": the belief that an excess of men created marriage options for women without marital prospects elsewhere. Barring that, the skewed sex ratios held the promise of a lucrative living satisfying the domestic and social desires of the surplus male population. Such options, however, could be more constraining than liberating. It was monotonous and taxing to sew buttonholes on shirts all day or to feed hungry boarders their daily meals. The rigors and isolation of pioneer settlement, moreover, also created conditions conducive to spousal and child abuse.[44]

Of all the domestic discord recorded in *Pioneer Girl*, the only major incident included in the Little House books appeared in *These Happy Golden Years,* when, during Laura's first job as a teacher, she boarded with the fictional Brewster family. The Brewsters were based on the Bouchie family in *Pioneer Girl*—one of the few name changes Wilder made in the Little House

---

42. Ibid., pp. 256, 256n68.

43. "A Bachelor Community," *De Smet Leader*, 23 June 1883. On gender ratios on other frontiers, *see* Albert Hurtado, *Intimate Frontiers: Sex, Gender and Culture in Old California* (Albuquerque: University of New Mexico Press, 1999), pp. 75–77; Elizabeth Jameson, *All That Glitters: Class, Conflict, and Community in Cripple Creek* (Urbana: University of Illinois Press, 1998), pp. 33–38.

44. *See* Elizabeth Hampsten, *Settlers' Children: Growing Up on the Great Plains* (Norman: University of Oklahoma Press, 1991); Melody Graulich, "Violence against Women: Power Dynamics in Literature of the Western Family," in *The Women's West,* ed. Susan Armitage and Elizabeth Jameson (Norman: University of Oklahoma Press, 1987), pp. 111–26; Jameson, "Halfway across That Line," pp. 20–21.

stories.[45] Laura's unhappy sojourn with the Brewsters punctuates the first third of *These Happy Golden Years*, the final volume of the Little House saga, when the fictional Laura leaves the security of her family home for the first time at age fifteen to teach school and board in the unhappy Brewster household. Mrs. Brewster, an angry, rude, and sullen woman, does not want to board the teacher and does not want to be on a western homestead at all. She refuses to clean the house or make the bed, and aside from cooking potatoes and salt pork twice a day, she spends most of her time brooding. Baby Johnny squalls incessantly; the Brewsters quarrel or endure hostile silences. The ordeal climaxes one night when Laura is awakened by a scream to see Mrs. Brewster standing over her husband with a butcher knife. Claiming that he kicked her, she threatens, "If I can't go home one way, I can another." "I've got you and Johnny to support," he replies, "and nothing in the world but this claim. Go put up that knife and come to bed before you freeze" (pp. 65–66).

The Bouchies appeared more briefly in *Pioneer Girl*, but their household was clearly oppressive: "Mrs[.] Bouchie was never pleasant, she was always sullen and seldom spoke." Sometimes, however, after going to bed, Wilder "could hear Mrs[.] Bouchie raging, seemingly perfectly able to talk." In the *Pioneer Girl* rendition of the butcher knife scene, the only apparent provocation was Mrs. Bouchie's claim that her husband kicked her, and she quickly "turned and took the butcher knife to the kitchen, muttering a jumble of words as she went." In the original manuscript, Wilder wrote, "I never knew what she was furious about."[46] In the George T. Bye version, she wrote simply, "I never knew why she acted so, but Mr. Bouchie seemed used to her spells."[47] In *These Happy Golden Years*, however, a new motive emerges. Mrs. Brewster becomes a stereotypical reluctant pioneer, who hates "this horrible country out here" and wants her husband to abandon his homestead claim and take her back east to her old home (p. 10).[48]

Understandably, the hostility and violence at the Bouchie house terrified

---

45. The others were the Clayson (Clancy) family and her nemesis Nellie Oleson and her family. She based the character of Nellie Oleson partially on Nellie Owens, the daughter of a Walnut Grove storekeeper, who had a brother named Willie, as did the fictional Nellie Oleson.

46. Ibid., pp. 263, 270, 272. *See also* Brandt, p. 132.

47. Bye, p. 158.

48. On stereotypes of western women as civilizers and reluctant pioneers, *see* Beverly Stoeltje, "A Helpmate for Man Indeed: The Image of the Frontier Woman," *Journal of American Folklore* 88 (Jan.-Mar. 1975): 27–41; Elizabeth Jameson, "Women as Workers, Women as Civilizers: True Womanhood in the American West," in *Women's West*, pp. 145–64.

young Laura Ingalls. Her time with the Bouchies was one more unhappy experience of working away from home that made her want never again to live among strangers. Those grim memories were either so personally significant or they occurred sufficiently late in her story that, of all the violent and disturbing scenes in *Pioneer Girl* left on the cutting-room floor, the vivid memory of Mrs. Bouchie and the butcher knife was not among them. Instead, that memory got slotted into a Turnerian narrative in *These Happy Golden Years,* where Wilder cast Mrs. Brewster as a woman reprehensible not only for her behavior but for her rejection of the frontier as well.

Feminist scholars have questioned the judgmental stereotypes that demonized women who rejected difficult lives in sod houses or flimsy frame shacks, who feared isolation on homesteads far from friends, family, and communal support.[49] Without the rosy glow of frontier nostalgia, we might even sympathize with Mrs. Brewster, cooped up with a cranky baby in a drafty claim shanty, cooking the same monotonous salt pork and potatoes twice a day every day. The irony, though, is that the real Mrs. Bouchie was not a reluctant pioneer at all. Nor did she reject homesteading. Oliv Delilah Isenberger Morrison filed on her own homestead adjoining Louis Bouchie's on the same day in November 1882, shortly before their marriage on Christmas day that year.[50]

Oliv Morrison could claim land in her own name under the provisions of the 1862 United States Homestead Act, which specified in unusually gender-inclusive language: "That the *person* applying for the benefit of this act shall, upon application to the register of the land office in which *he or she* is about to make such entry, make affidavit before the said register or receiver that *he or she* is the head of a family, or is twenty-one years or more of age," and "that such application is made for *his or her* exclusive use and benefit." Beyond this, a woman had only to swear that she was unmarried when she filed her claim or, if married, that she was the sole support of her family, and that she was or had declared her "intention to become" a United States citizen. All homesteaders had to reside on their land part of the year and put it to productive use.[51] If couples married before satisfying the five-year residency re-

49. *See* Susan Armitage, "Through Women's Eyes: A New View of the West," in *The Women's West,* pp. 9–18.

50. Final Certificate #5537, issued to Oliv D. Morrison, Land Entry Files, General Land Office, Department of the Interior, Record Group 49, National Archives and Records Administration, Washington, D.C.

51. Homestead Act, 1862, National Archives and Records Administration, www.ourdocuments.gov (emphasis added). For proportions of women homesteaders in various times and places, *see* Sheryll Patterson-Black, "Women Homesteaders on the Great

Charles Ingalls frequently subsidized the family income with carpentry work in addition to hunting and farming. *South Dakota State Historical Society*

quirement, they both had to reside on their respective homesteads, a requirement the Bouchies met by building their house on the boundary line between their claims. "My house and my husband's are the same," Oliv Bouchie wrote on her 1889 final claim statement, "and is built on both claims and across the line, and my part of the house is on my claim, and his on his claim."[52]

Oliv Isenberger Morrison, who was either widowed or divorced, had moved from Iowa to Kingsbury County, Dakota Territory, with her two-year-old son a few months after Louis Bouchie got there. The couple deliberately filed for adjoining homesteads shortly before they married, when she could still claim land in her own name, a not-uncommon strategy for engaged cou-

---

Plains Frontier," *Frontiers: A Journal of Women Studies* 1 (Spring 1976): 67–88; Paula Nelson, "No Place for Clinging Vines: Women Homesteaders on the South Dakota Frontier, 1900–1915" (M.A. thesis, University of South Dakota, 1978), pp. 1–5; H. Elaine Lindgren, *Land in Her Own Name: Women as Homesteaders in North Dakota* (Fargo: North Dakota Institute for Regional Studies, 1991), pp. 51–54; and Jameson, "Halfway across That Line," pp. 6–14.

52. Final Certificate #5537.

ples seeking to double family landholdings, though it was by no means the norm for unmarried women homesteaders.[53] Given these facts, the fictional motivation Wilder ascribed to Mrs. Brewster is particularly interesting. Laura Ingalls was young, working away from home again, staying in yet another frightening house, once again with unpleasant strangers. Mrs. Bouchie's frightening behavior mystified Wilder, who made no explanation for it in *Pioneer Girl*. The fictional Mrs. Brewster's behavior could be explained because she rejected the frontier. This difference in explanation matters. So does the range of female opportunity presented in the Little House books, which eliminate the fact that Carrie Ingalls and Eliza Wilder also homesteaded as single women. The opportunity for unmarried women to claim land in their own names was effectively deleted from American history texts and American fiction until feminist scholars began researching women homesteaders in the 1970s.[54]

It is not my primary intention to prove that Laura Ingalls Wilder did not have an idyllically secure and happy childhood, however much we might empathize with a lonely and frightened little girl working away from home. Lots of pioneer children had scary, dangerous, and difficult childhoods. And that is the larger point. In crafting her own sometimes-hard and often-prosaic childhood into the much-beloved children's classics, Wilder implanted a ver-

---

53. See *Pioneer Girl*, p. 262n87.

54. For Eliza Jane Wilder's homesteading experience, *see* William Anderson, ed., *A Wilder in the West: The Story of Eliza Jane Wilder* (De Smet, S.Dak.: Laura Ingalls Wilder Memorial Society, 1971). Eliza Jane Wilder and her brothers Royal and Almanzo Wilder filed their adjoining homestead claims in 1879; they each also filed for tree claims and achieved final title to their claims. Final Patents, nos. 200, 410, 1490, 1505, 2263, and 10979, Bureau of Land Management, General Land Office Records, U.S. Department of the Interior, Springfield, Va., glorecords.blm.gov. Carrie Ingalls proved up in 1909 to gain title to a quarter section twenty miles north of Philip, South Dakota. After proving up, she became a printer, one of the few skilled trades open to women, and worked for the Senn newspaper chain in various South Dakota communities. *See* William Anderson, *Story of the Ingalls*, pp. 23-24. On South Dakota women homesteaders, *see* Nelson, "No Place for Clinging Vines." In addition to the previously mentioned works by Patterson-Black, Nelson, and Lindgren, histories of women homesteaders include Katherine Benton-Cohen, "Common Purposes, Worlds Apart: Mexican-American, Mormon, and Midwestern Women Homesteaders in Cochise County, Arizona," *Western Historical Quarterly* 36 (Winter 2005): 429-52; Dee Garceau, "Single Women Homesteaders and the Meanings of Independence: Places on the Map, Places in the Mind," *Frontiers: A Journal of Women Studies* 15: 3 (1995): 1-26; Sherry L. Smith, "Single Women Homesteaders: The Perplexing Case of Elinore Pruitt Stewart," *Western Historical Quarterly* 22 (May 1991): 163-83; and Jameson, "Halfway across That Line," pp. 6-14.

sion of pioneer childhood and family security into the collective memory of generations of readers, crafting a nostalgic and false historical memory that has continued to influence collective understandings of American history and how it was forged.[55] Abandoning the myth of happy childhood opens new questions about the idealized self-sufficient nuclear family that Ma and Pa Ingalls created and about the mythic frontiers on which they raised their girls.

Childhood in the Little House books is not always safe. The fictional family, like the actual Ingallses, have to contend with danger and adversity. Laura and her sisters face threats and insecurity, but adult protectors mediate the dangers and gradually teach the children to care for themselves. Initially, they are simply taught to obey the adults who protect them. In *Little House in the Big Woods*, Laura watches Ma slap a bear, mistaking it for a cow. Ma instructs, "Laura, walk back to the house," and then "snatched her up, lantern and all, and ran. . . . into the house, and slammed the door." Ma praises Laura for her obedience. "You were a good girl, Laura, to do exactly as I told you, and to do it quickly, without asking why" (pp. 104–6). In *Little House on the Prairie*, Laura and Mary are frightened when they see two Indians enter the house while Pa is away. They debate untying their dog Jack, but Pa had told them not to. The Indians signal that they want Ma to make cornbread for them, and though frightened, she manages the situation. When Pa returns, Laura tells him that if they had "turned Jack loose, he would have eaten those Indians right up." Alarmed, Pa admonishes the girls. "'After this,' he said, in a terrible voice, 'you girls remember to always do as you're told. Don't you even think of disobeying me. Do you hear?'" (pp. 145–46).

Wilder was too young to remember much of her family's time in Indian Country, and she apparently based *Little House on the Prairie* and the opening chapter in *Pioneer Girl* on stories she had been told. Both are punctuated by threats of potential Indian attacks, but Ma and Pa attempt to protect the girls from adult fears. In the novel, Ma stops Mrs. Scott from describing the "Minnesota Massacre" (a reference to the Dakota Uprising of 1862) to protect the girls from her own perceptions of Indian threats.[56] Then, when Pa is late returning from a trip to Independence, Ma bars the door and sits up late into the night holding Pa's pistol as protection. Ma is capable and courageous, but

---

55. *See* Fellman, *Little House, Big Shadow*.

56. I am describing these events as they are portrayed in the Little House books, not as I would portray them in a history of the impacts of settler colonialism for indigenous peoples. The circumstances that made "free land" available for advancing American settlers is beyond the scope of this essay, but they clearly underlie the events in *Little House on the Prairie* in particular. In the other books, American Indians are simply erased, as

no one feels really safe until Pa returns with his rifle. Laura wakes up in the middle of the night to find Pa home at last, warming himself before the fire. He wraps her in Ma's shawl and hugs her. Then, "Everything was all right. The house was cozy with firelight, there was the warm brown smell of coffee, Ma was smiling, and Pa was there" (pp. 220-21).

Laura begins to exercise independent agency in the face of danger in *On the Banks of Plum Creek*, when, facing a sudden blizzard while Ma and Pa are in town, she and Mary lug the entire woodpile into the house. Her parents still try to shelter her from the full threat the blizzard posed after Pa goes to milk the cow and, blinded by the snow, nearly misses the house. "I thought I was on the path, but I couldn't see the house.... Another foot to the left and I never would have got in," he says. Ma cuts him short with her characteristic, *"Charles!"* He recoups and reassures the girls, "Nothing to be scared about now" (p. 291).

In the Little House fiction, Ma and Pa are more able to shield the girls from full knowledge of potential dangers than Charles and Caroline Ingalls could their children. Wilder wrote hardships and hazards enough into the children's books for the pioneer family to triumph over adversity, but, with the lone exception of Mary's blindness, no adversity causes enduring harm, and adults provide safety and security. If Pa is not home, a male surrogate usually aids and protects the family, as Mr. Edwards does in *Little House on the Prairie*.

It is not until Chapter 24 of *By the Shores of Silver Lake* that the threats of alcohol, strangers, and fire that filled early chapters of *Pioneer Girl* converge for the adolescent Laura. "The Spring Rush" narrates the stresses of caring for the influx of "strange men" who flood the surveyors' house. Mr. and Mrs. Boast come to stay when Pa must go away to file his homestead claim, leaving Ma and the girls to provide board for the incoming strangers. Laura is overwhelmed when a new wagonload arrives: "The house was so full of strange men, strange eyes and strange voices and bulky coats and muddy boots, that she could hardly get through the crowd." Throughout the night, Laura hears loud noises as the men drink and carouse, but when "another crash woke her out of a sound sleep[,] Ma said, 'It's all right, Laura. Mr. Boast is there'" (pp. 229-30).

they are in the opening pages of *Little House in the Big Woods*: "As far as a man could go to the north in a day, or a week, or a whole month, there was nothing but woods. There were no houses. There were no roads. There were no people" (p. 1). On this casual erasure of thousands of indigenous Ojibwe, Menominees, Potawatomis, Sauks, Foxes, Winnebagos, and Ottawas, *see* Michael Dorris, "Trusting the Words," *Booklist* (June 1 & 15, 1993): 1820-22.

Friendly characters like the Boasts, Mr. Edwards, and Almanzo Wilder provide welcome company and support in the Little House saga, but outsiders can also be unwelcome intruders who disrupt the balance of family well-being. True safety and security return only when the household contracts to the nuclear family. Domestic order is restored when Ma and Pa are both there with their girls, snug inside the walls of each little house, when Pa's rifle rests above the door, his fiddle handy to bring joy and comfort, and Ma's china shepherdess stands once more on the shelf Pa carved for her.

People outside that safe family circle evoke different responses from the fictional Ma, Pa, and Laura and from their real-life counterparts. Each reacted somewhat differently to neighbors and strangers and to the benefits and constraints of civilized society beyond the nuclear household. These differences can illuminate how American frontiers reverberated across genders and generations. Each vantage point within the interdependent nuclear family complicated the rugged individualism and independence of a Turnerian frontier.

The fictional Ma and Pa are an interdependent partnership. They appreciate one another's skills and contributions to family security. Ma, however, remains more securely ensconced within the domesticity of the little houses than Caroline Ingalls was in real life. Ma is strong, but her strength is gentle and often responsive as she protects her girls from learning too early the dangers of pioneer life. Her quiet "Charles" usually stops her husband from revealing too much for innocent ears. Caroline Ingalls of *Pioneer Girl* left her home to work in a hotel in Burr Oak to help support the family, to sew Mattie Masters's trousseau, and to provide neighborly assistance. On the way to Dakota Territory, as work concluded in the railroad camp, Wilder reported: "One Irish family, ready to leave, had a sick baby, and could not go. Ma heard of it and went to see if she could help. By great good luck she did know what to do and cured the baby." This rare account of Caroline Ingalls acting outside her own family appeared only in the original draft of *Pioneer Girl*; it was excised from all subsequent versions.[57]

Ma and Caroline Ingalls each responded somewhat differently to the lures of new frontiers. Ma is usually more reluctant. She insists on schools for her girls and ultimately refuses to move beyond De Smet. Even so, she appears less resistant to the first move west, from the Big Woods to Indian Country. *Little House on the Prairie* explains that the Ingallses left Wisconsin because "Pa said there were too many people in the Big Woods now.... Wild animals would not stay where there were so many people." As he tries to persuade Ma, he describes the promise of Indian Territory: "In the West the land was

---

57. Wilder, *Pioneer Girl*, p. 172.

level, and there were no trees. The grass grew thick and high. There the wild animals wandered and fed as though they were in a pasture, . . . and there were no settlers. Only Indians lived there." Living surrounded only by wild animals and Indians would not seem to be Ma's cup of tea, but she apparently acquiesces. Pa concludes, "Seeing you don't object, I've decided to go see the West" (pp. 1–2). In this common pattern, Pa is the active partner; Ma's power is the power to refuse.

This scene does not appear in *Pioneer Girl*, which opens as the family is already traveling west to Indian Country. The motives behind the actual move remain unclear. We do not know why the family left Wisconsin or how Caroline Ingalls felt about leaving her home, her apparently well-stocked larder, or the neighbors and extended kin who lived near the real little house. Perhaps her subsequent reluctance to leave settled country began with her experience living alone on the prairie surrounded by wild animals and the Indians she feared. Ma becomes increasingly reluctant as the fictional journeys unfold. The difference between Ma and Caroline emerges most clearly in the context of the family's move west from Walnut Grove, when Charles Ingalls's sister Docia offered him the chance to work for her husband, a contractor for the Chicago & North Western Railroad. In each iteration of *Pioneer Girl*, Caroline supported her husband's decision to take the job. "Pa was glad of the chance and Ma told him to go along, we would be all right until we could come later."[58]

When Aunt Docia arrives in the fictional version, at the beginning of *By the Shores of Silver Lake*, Laura at first thinks she is "a strange woman" (p. 2), but Docia is family. The reasons for Pa to accept her offer are abundantly clear. Mary is still recovering from the illness that left her blind. Food is scarce. For a company dinner, Ma can offer only bread, molasses, and potatoes. Even game was scarce: "Pa did not like a country so old and worn out that the hunting was poor. . . . For two years he had wanted to go west and take a homestead, but Ma did not want to leave the settled country. And there was no money. Pa had made only two poor wheat crops since the grasshoppers came; he had barely been able to keep out of debt, and now there was the doctor's bill" (pp. 2–3).

In these circumstances, the prospect of a job that paid "fifty dollars a month" offers welcome relief. "A kind of tightness smoothed out of Pa's thin cheeks and his blue eyes lighted up. He said slowly, 'Seems like I can draw good pay while I'm looking for that homestead, Caroline.'" Ma does not want to go. She agrees that the pay "does seem providential," but she protests,

---

58. Ibid., p. 142.

"we're settled here. We've got the farm." She worries that Mary is "not strong enough to travel." For Pa there is no contest. "We can get a hundred and sixty acres out west, just by living on it.... If Uncle Sam's willing to give us a farm in place of the one he drove us off of, in Indian Territory, I say let's take it. The hunting's good in the west, a man can get all the meat he wants." Laura agrees. She wants "so much to go that she could hardly keep from speaking." Pa urges, "It's fifty dollars a month, Caroline.... And a homestead." Ma characteristically capitulates, saying gently, "Well, Charles, you must do as you think best" (pp. 4-5).

The fictional decisions to move west are always Pa's; Ma must agree, but she leaves the choice to him. She remains reluctant as Pa drives the family to their temporary home at the railroad camp. Two strange men approach from the distance, but an ally, Big Jerry, protects the family. "Ma looked back to see that her girls were all right, and she held Grace snugly on her lap. She did not say anything because nothing she could say would make any difference. But Laura knew that Ma had never wanted to leave Plum Creek and did not like to be here now; she did not like traveling in that lonely country with night coming on and such men riding on the prairie" (p. 66).

If concern for her girls makes Ma wish they had not left Plum Creek, that same concern prompted Caroline Ingalls to approve the journey. Her family's situation was even more precarious than that in the fictional version. They had lost the farm; Mary had been ill and was blind; and they were in debt. They lived on whatever wage work Charles Ingalls could scrounge, augmented by whatever young Laura could earn. Caroline Ingalls may well have preferred to stay in town, where she had a home, friends, a church, school, and the Good Templars Lodge. But she was also a realist, and concern for her family trumped her understandable desires. So, just as she had left a house and farm to run a hotel in Burr Oak, she left a familiar community in Walnut Grove to venture to yet another unknown frontier on the Dakota prairie. She did it for her family.

If Caroline Ingalls appeared stronger and less domestically isolated in *Pioneer Girl* than in the Little House books, Charles Ingalls violated the simple typologies of frontier manhood. Regardless of Turner's trajectory of economic progress, for Charles Ingalls the best frontier remained the hunter's frontier. In Wisconsin, he hunted and trapped for meat and for skins to barter, thus combining "the trader's frontier" with "the farmer's frontier." The fictional Pa always wanted to move when the game got scarce. During the difficult years on Plum Creek, his family's survival required Charles Ingalls to combine periodic wage work with farming. He abandoned farming altogether from 1875 until he claimed the Dakota Territory homestead in 1880.

Carrie Ingalls, pictured here at her claim shack near Top Bar, South Dakota, circa 1907, was among many single women who took advantage of the Homestead Act.
*Laura Ingalls Wilder Memorial Society*

Even then, he worked frequently at carpentry and secured rental income from the buildings he erected in De Smet. Perhaps it is not surprising that he seemed at times even more restless than his fictional counterpart. Wilder wrote in *Pioneer Girl*:

> Pa had been working very hard all summer [1883] at Carpenter work and on the farm. He and Ma had put up the hay and now he was harvesting his little fields of wheat and of oats with the old hand cradle, because he couldn't afford a harvester and the fields were too small to pay to have one. Pa was very thin and tired from the hard work of harvesting but strong and hard as nails.
>
> I think though that he was not very happy. People had crowded in too thick for him some time before. He wanted to go to Oregon.... but Ma said she was tired of wandering around from "pillar to post" and would not go.
>
> We moved back to town when cold weather came so that we could be nearer school and Pa's work.[59]

59. Ibid., pp. 287–88.

Towns provided schools for the children and wage work for Pa and Laura. Towns and the constraints of government meant different things for Ma and Pa, Charles and Caroline, the fictional Laura, and Laura Ingalls Wilder. Although she excised from the Little House series the unhappy childhood jobs in Walnut Grove and De Smet, both the fictional Laura and her *Pioneer Girl* counterpart were often uncomfortable in town. In the novels, Laura's discomfort centers on her fear of strangers and resentment of stuck-up town children. In *On the Banks of Plum Creek*, she and Mary are poor country girls who cannot compete with Nellie Oleson. In *Little Town on the Prairie*, Pa takes Laura and Carrie to town for the Fourth of July, but the girls do not like the noise, crowds, and popping firecrackers: "They had never been in such a crowd before, . . . and to be among so many strangers made them uncomfortable" (p. 68). Pa takes the girls into his store building. After lunch, the celebration takes a more positive turn, with free lemonade, horse races, a long rendition of the Declaration of Independence, and Laura's reflections on the meaning of liberty (pp. 70–85). In *Pioneer Girl*, Wilder found the entire day "tiresome." She wrote, "I didn't like the crowd and would much rather be home where it was quiet." Later, she similarly described her discomfort facing strange new schoolmates and a "strange teacher. . . . It seemed some mornings as though I simply could not face the crowd on the school grounds and the palms of my hands would grow moist and sticky."[60]

Although she made friends at school, and did well in her studies, Wilder repeatedly identified town with the strangers who made her so uncomfortable. Perhaps Laura Ingalls was simply shy. Perhaps her childhood work experiences fostered her aversion to towns and to strangers who drank, fought, and sometimes presented sexual threats. Her alternative lay in marriage, which she realized meant domestic responsibility. She felt understandably conflicted about both growing up and the more unhappy chapters of her own childhood. No wonder that she and Lena would rather play and let someone else be responsible for a while. Childhood had already held responsibility enough.

For Ma and for Caroline Ingalls, towns promised civilized amenities: schools, churches, temperance societies, and Masonic lodges. Towns offered her and other western women the means to earn a livelihood. After the family moved into town, Caroline sometimes kept boarders in their house on Third Street. That income became particularly important after Charles Ingalls died in 1902; after that, Caroline Ingalls supported herself and Mary with income from boarders and help from Carrie and Grace.[61]

60. Ibid., pp. 236, 242.
61. Anderson, *Story of the Ingalls Family*, pp. 25–27.

As justice of the peace for Kingsbury County, Dakota Territory, Charles Ingalls issued this arrest warrant for Henry Hinz for selling liquor without a license in December of 1883. *Kingsbury County Courthouse*

Charles Ingalls was at home alone in nature, preferably hunting, armed against predators, both animal and human. He embodied the frontiersman in his desire to move whenever the human population got too large and the wild animals too scarce. He hoped that something better lay somewhere farther west. But Charles Ingalls, like Caroline, compromised for his family, to please his wife, to educate his girls, and to earn a living. Pa in the Little House books is often a gentle nurturer. Charles Ingalls frequently supported his family through wage work, at times working on a threshing crew, as railroad storekeeper, and more frequently in town as a millwright or carpenter. After he got title to his homestead in 1888, he never farmed again. And after Caroline Ingalls refused to move any more and he settled his family in De Smet, Charles worked as a carpenter and sold insurance and binding twine. He opened a general store in 1892, which did not last long in the dismal economy of the 1890s; it folded within a year, like the Burr Oak hotel and his butcher shop in Walnut Grove. Charles Ingalls does not appear to have been hostile to all government. He served in numerous appointed offices: as justice of the peace in Walnut Grove and as town clerk, deputy sheriff, street commissioner, chief of police, constable, and justice of the peace in De Smet.[62]

Both Pa and Charles Ingalls embraced some civilized amenities. Charles Ingalls was even more active than his wife in De Smet civic and community life. A devout Congregationalist who helped found churches, schools, and lodges, he may have valued male companionship as much as Caroline valued family and neighbors. During the long winter in De Smet, he found masculine company at the local stores and with the Wilder brothers.[63] He joined the other men of De Smet who united to stop storekeeper Daniel Loftus from profiting from the seed wheat that Almanzo Wilder and Cap Garland had bought for him from a homesteader, charging "nothing for making the trip at the peril of their lives . . . for the sake of the community." Community interdependence won the day. The men persuaded Loftus to charge only the cost of the wheat and to sell it on the basis of need.[64]

Confronting the realities of pioneer childhood opens more realistic windows on the meanings of frontier opportunity for nineteenth-century Americans. The "primitive organization" of the family illuminates the roles that women, girls, and ordinary men played in western economic development and community formation—but only if we do not envelop that family in nostalgia and isolate it behind domestic walls, secure from public dangers and from community and governmental support. Discarding the mythic security of pioneer childhood and of frontier opportunity helps fill in the blank years in the fast flyover from the young couple starting out on a Dakota tree claim to the perspectives from which, in the 1930s, Wilder and Lane crafted the pioneer fiction so many Americans have come to see as historical fact. Gauged against a myth of frontier independence and self-sufficiency, the only successful conclusion to a homesteader's frontier was to gain title to the land and live on it contentedly ever after. By that calculus, the years after the happy endings

62. Ibid., pp. 16–19; Wilder, *Pioneer Girl*, pp. 125, 203–4.
63. Wilder, *Pioneer Girl*, pp. 72n34, 187, 215, 220; Anderson, *Story of the Ingalls Family*, pp. 13, 18.
64. Wilder, *Pioneer Girl*, p. 221.

of both *Pioneer Girl* and *These Happy Golden Years* were years of failure. But most aspiring homesteaders did not succeed in winning title to their land. Viewed as a shared collective dilemma, there was difficulty but no shame in losing a farm to drought and economic depression. Many who did succeed used the land for goals other than farming—their hard-won acres became equity to finance a business, an education, or some other goal. Charles and Caroline Ingalls were fairly typical in leaving their homestead soon after gaining title. For some people, losing the land felt like betrayal—the failure of a government program to provide the security and independence it promised. That sense of betrayal could breed distrust of all government, as manifested in the Wilders' antipathy to the New Deal.

Myths, by definition, are not real. The Homestead Act offered 160 acres, not security. Charles and Caroline Ingalls did their best but could not guarantee perpetually happy childhoods for their daughters. To abandon the frontier myth and mythically happy pioneer childhoods is not to renounce the values of secure families, hard work, or opportunity. It is to admit that reality often fell short of the ideal and that security lay not in domestic isolation but in collective responsibility and interdependence. The Ingalls family sometimes needed the help of neighbors. And sometimes strong families and secure childhoods require government aid and authority to insure that schools are staffed, saloons regulated, and fire departments funded; that natural disasters and poverty do not propel youngsters into the workforce; and that children are protected from predators like Will Masters in their young worlds.

# { 11 }
# Frontier Families and the Little House Where Nobody Dies

## ANN ROMINES

At the center of all of Laura Ingalls Wilder's Little House books, from the first to the last, is her own Ingalls family, contained in their Little House. As the first book of the series, *Little House in the Big Woods*, begins in Wisconsin, we read these words: "So far as the little girl could see, there was only the one little house where she lived with her Father and Mother, her sister Mary and baby sister Carrie."[1] That iconic Little House took many forms and locations during Laura Ingalls's childhood. But it was always the same place, shaped by Ma's domestic rituals and treasured, instructive objects (such as the china shepherdess), by Pa's stories and music, and by both parents' insistence on the primacy of their close, tight nuclear family.

Wilder was clear about this primacy when she corresponded with her daughter, Rose Wilder Lane, about their plans for the fifth novel in the series, *On the Shores of Silver Lake*. She insisted, "The story is of family and the family life.... Our interests all centered at home." As I was surprised to learn when I first read this important letter, the family that mattered to Wilder was only that small nuclear Ingalls/Quiner family that inhabited the Little House. Other family connections were not important, she told her daughter, and should be kept at the periphery of the novels, or out of them entirely. "Don't bring Aunt Docia, Uncle Henry and the cousins into the story more than necessary.... I suppose Aunt Docia and Uncle Henry meant as much to Pa and Ma as my sisters did to me, but at that time they meant nothing whatever to me."[2] Aunt Docia Ingalls Forbes was the sister of Wilder's father; Uncle Henry Quiner was her mother's brother. Yet they are of minimal importance in the Little House series and are not significantly characterized. Wilder ex-

---

1. Wilder, *Little House in the Big Woods*, illus. Garth Williams (New York: Harper & Bros., 1932, 1953), p. 2. All citations in this essay come from the 1953 uniform edition of the Little House series. Page numbers are hereafter given in the text.

2. Wilder to Lane, Sept. 26, 1938, in Wilder, *The Selected Letters of Laura Ingalls Wilder*, ed. William Anderson (New York: HarperCollins, 2106), pp. 181–82.

The only known image of the entire Charles Ingalls family was likely taken around 1892. From left are Caroline, Carrie, Laura, Charles, Grace, and Mary.
*South Dakota State Historical Society*

plained why to Lane: "in going to the frontier, one meets strangers and makes friends and enemies. . . . One doesn't move west with whole communities, not with all their 'uncles and their cousins and their aunts.'"[3] The reason for the Little House series' singularly intense focus on the Ingalls/Quiner nuclear family and its relative disinterest in other relatives, Wilder implied, was the *frontier* lifestyle of her family, with its many moves and sometime transience.

To understand more fully what it meant to grow up in such a frontier family, I turned to scholars who have studied such families. One of the most helpful was historian Lillian Schlissel. In *Far from Home*, she wrote, "a family on an American frontier . . . was a family separated from some part of itself. Frontier settlers were fragments of families."[4] She concluded that frontier histories show "the constant 'wash' of families who do not put down roots, who

3. Ibid., Aug. 17, 1938, p. 176.
4. Schlissel, Introduction to *Far from Home: Families of the Westward Journey*, by Schlissel, Byrd Gibbens, and Elizabeth Hampsten (New York: Schocken Books, 1989), p. xv.

choose to 'move on,'" as the Ingalls/Quiner family often did. "A family is a fragile assortment of human needs. In all our migrations, our families come apart. We leave a parent here, a sister or a brother there, somewhere else a child. The family continues as best it can, but it is less than, and different from, the family that arrived."[5]

According to Schlissel, frontier families inevitably experienced change and loss and alienating distance from those with whom they may once have shared the closeness of a sheltering family. The Little House, as constructed by Caroline and Charles Ingalls, was intended to protect their young daughters from the pain of such distance and loss. For the fictional Laura Ingalls and her sisters, it worked remarkably well. By the last book of the series, *These Happy Golden Years*, Laura is beginning to leave that Little House behind her. At fifteen, reluctant and terrified, she leaves home for her first teaching job. Desperately homesick, she confides to her younger sister Carrie that she hates teaching. "Maybe you'll get married. Ma did," Carrie says consolingly.

> "I don't want to," Laura said.... "I'd rather stay home than anything."
> "Always?" Carrie asked.
> "Yes, always," Laura said, and she meant it with her heart. (p. 36)

For this girl, confronted with the frightening prospect of a new frontier-style life as a transient teacher, boarding in various other people's houses, her dearest and most heartfelt desire is to "stay home" forever, enjoying the unchanging shelter of her family in their own Little House.

Marriage, Laura thinks, would mean leaving her beloved "home" behind, something she decidedly does not want. Yet, at the end of this last Little House book, Laura is married. Her wedding day ends the book, and Ma prepares a wedding dinner for the nuclear Ingalls/Quiner family and Laura's new husband, Almanzo Wilder. But Laura cannot enjoy the "delicious" celebratory meal, for, miserably, "at last she realized that she was going away from home, that never would she come back to this home to stay" (p. 283). By evening, however, when she has begun to explore her new house and her new estate, "Laura's heart was full of happiness. She knew she need never be homesick for the old home. It was so near that she could go to it whenever she wished, while she and Almanzo made the new home in their own little house" (p. 289). What Laura hopefully and finally imagines is that she will be able to evade the pain and loss of leaving "the old home" and her family of

---

5. Schlissel, "Families and Frontiers: A Reading for Our Time," ibid., pp. 237–38. Schlissel's earlier book, *Women's Diaries of the Westward Journey* (New York: Schocken Books, 1982), is also an invaluable source on the dynamics of frontier families.

*Helen Sewell, last page of* These Happy Golden Years, *1943*

origin behind, as frontier travelers did, and keep that home and family close and available while she and Almanzo simultaneously make "the new home in their own little house."

However, the last words of *These Happy Golden Years* tell us that this will not happen, as it did not in fact happen for the actual Laura and Almanzo Wilder. The original 1943 edition of this last Little House novel ended with these words (much dreaded by avid child-readers such as me): "The End of the Little House Books." These weighty final words tell another story: as a young adult, Laura has left the Little House behind her. And so have we.

Wilder's Little House was the necessary product of a frontier family lifestyle, marked by distance, transience, separation, and rapid change—as most American lives still are to some degree. Writing in 1989, Schlissel argued that the frontier family is still quintessentially American. In its "self-willed dislocations and discontinuities are the outlines of our own [contemporary] lives," which may help to explain why many American readers continue to identify powerfully with the story of Wilder' frontier family.[6] The Little House series is also a story told for children, and (as Wilder's publisher reminded her) there are some stories that our culture presumes that children "cannot" be told—stories of separation, loss, aging, and death, all of which inevitably occurred in the Ingalls/Quiner family history, as in most other family histories. Another reason why the Little House series has been so indispensably satisfying to generations of American readers, children and adults, is that it both protects us from such issues and acknowledges them, achieving a remarkable balance for its young readers. Wilder and her collaborating daughter also attempted to write for an adult audience, in both fiction and memoir, telling and retelling some of the stories from their own frontier family history that could not be fully told to children in the protected space of the series.

A quick glimpse at just a few generations confirms that Laura Ingalls Wilder did indeed grow up in a frontier family as defined by Schlissel and others. Both the Quiner and the Ingalls families experienced multiple moves, usually (though not always) in a westward direction. Wilder's maternal grandfather, Henry Newton Quiner, was born in 1807 in New Haven, Connecticut, and attended Yale University there. In 1831, he married Charlotte Tucker, born in 1809 in Roxbury, Massachusetts. The young Quiners moved west, living in Ohio and Indiana and then settling in Wisconsin, where their daughter Caroline, Wilder's Ma, was born in 1839. Henry Quiner, who worked as a trader with Wisconsin Indians, died in a shipwreck on Lake Michigan when Caroline was five. Her mother remained with her children in Wisconsin, where Caroline met Charles Ingalls, whom she married in 1860. Charles's father, Lansford Whiting Ingalls, was born in Quebec in 1812; he grew up in New York State and there, in 1832, married Laura Louise Colby, also born in the state in 1810. Sometime before 1850, Lansford and Laura Ingalls moved their growing family to Elgin, Illinois, joining relatives who had purchased land there. The rich, open prairies impressed Charles Ingalls as a boy; as an adult, he would search for such land in Kansas, Minnesota, and Dakota Territory. But Charles's father did not succeed financially in Illinois, and the family moved to Concord, Wisconsin, where Charles and Caroline met and married in 1860. Again, Lansford Ingalls did not find financial security, and when he could not pay the mortgage on his property, the family moved yet again.[7]

6. Schlissel, Introduction, p. xviii.

7. My major source for discerning the families' movements were the United States Census and other records, available on Ancestry.com. I also consulted William Anderson, *Laura Ingalls Wilder: A Biography* (New York: HarperCollins, 1992), p. 29, and John E. Miller, *Becoming Laura Ingalls Wilder: The Woman behind the Legend* (Columbia: University of Missouri Press, 1998), pp. 16–17.

Young Caroline Quiner Ingalls, recently married into the Ingalls family, wrote to her sister about this move: "Father Ingalls folks have gone up to the head waters of the Baraboo river.... They felt very bad about leaving their place and it was to[o] bad. They were to[o] old to be moving; but Pa did his best to save it but he could not. Peter and Eliza [their oldest son and his wife] have gone with them."[8] Eventually, the whole family made yet another westward move to Pepin, Wisconsin, near the Minnesota state line.

Charles and Caroline Ingalls were living near Pepin when their second daughter, Laura Ingalls, was born in 1867. Soon thereafter, they may have moved briefly to Missouri, then spent a year on the Osage Diminished Reserve in Kansas, where they managed to build a house and plant crops, but anxious and uncertain about their future in Kansas, they returned to Wisconsin. Three years later, they sold their Wisconsin farm (again) and moved west to Minnesota. When crop failures led to financial disasters, they moved to Iowa for a year as hotel-keepers, then, with four daughters, returned to Minnesota for almost two years before their final move to Dakota Territory. There they remained, near or in De Smet, for the rest of their lives. In the years before Wilder's marriage in 1885, the family continued to move around regularly—from the railroad camps to the surveyors' house to a store building in town, as well as in and out of the expanding shanty on their claim.

How many moves is that for Laura Ingalls Wilder's parents and grandparents? Seventeen? I have lost count. After their 1885 marriage, Laura and Almanzo Wilder spent four years unsuccessfully farming on Almanzo's claim, where their home burned, then left to live for a year with Almanzo's family in Minnesota. In 1891, with daughter Rose in tow, they moved to the backwoods of Florida, then returned the next year to join Laura's family in De Smet, and in 1894 made their final move to Wright County in the Missouri Ozarks. The young Wilders thus continued the pattern of the "frontier family" that had been established by at least three generations of Laura's family.

According to historian Mary P. Ryan, a frontier family is "an ephemeral, perhaps a paradoxical, institution," inhabiting a landscape "doomed to extinction probably within the space of a generation."[9] Wilder, as we saw, wrote to Lane that families like hers had to leave extended family members behind and form new (and often ephemeral) relationships. And the communities that such families formed were indeed often "doomed to extinction" or to

---

8. Caroline Ingalls to Martha Quiner Carpenter, Oct. 6, 1861, Wisconsin Historical Society, content.wisconsinhistory.org/cdm/ref/collection/tp/id/ 44380.

9. Ryan, *Cradle of the Middle Class: The Family in Oneida County, New York, 1790–1865* (Cambridge, UK: Cambridge University Press, 1981), p. 20.

rapid, disorienting change. In her earlier years in Missouri, Wilder wrote of De Smet, South Dakota, which she still considered her hometown, as a vanished place: "This little town has disappeared/It vanished with the years/A different town with the same name/In the same place appears." Past voices and faces are "bright" only in the poet's memory, for they are ephemeral: the "little town of memory" is "gone beyond recall/Its music fades away." That little town, which Laura Ingalls and her parents and sisters and husband-to-be helped to create in its earliest days, was near extinction because it was accessible only through memory, and memory fades "beyond recall."[10]

However, Wilder's first autobiographical Little House book, set in her birthplace, spotlighted what were apparently her memories of an Ingalls/Quiner family that seems not to be fragile, diminished, or changed but thriving and growing in frontier Wisconsin. A memorable central scene in *Little House in the Big Woods* depicts a large, extended family party, a sugaring-off dance at the log home of five-year-old Laura's Ingalls grandparents (pp. 133–55). The convivial crowd includes Pa's two pretty single sisters, his Civil War veteran brother, and other siblings, relatives, and friends—some of them probably from Ma's family of origin because three Quiner siblings married three Ingalls siblings. There are numerous babies and children, and more than one little girl is named "Laura Ingalls" after Grandma Ingalls. Grandpa, assisted by his sons, has harvested and boiled down the maple sap, and Grandma—although she takes time out to win a vigorous jigging contest with her son—presides at the stove, assisted by daughters and daughter-in-law Caroline, as the sap is transformed into maple syrup and sugar. Pa plays his fiddle and calls the dances, and Ma joins the dancers on the floor, while Laura watches raptly. She is caught up in the magic of this great family occasion, presided over by her grandparents, who appear fit and active and unhampered by any of the impediments of age.

This family seems stable and self-perpetuating, preserving its own history as Pa tells young Mary and Laura stories about Grandpa Ingalls's New York State boyhood and his later adventure with a Wisconsin panther. Wilder still remembered these stories in her sixties, and she wrote them into this first book, published in 1932. Yet, when a possible Ingalls relative wrote her in 1934 asking for family history, Wilder could offer no information beyond her own nuclear family of origin, and she replied: "My father was Charles Philip Ingalls and he was born in New York State, but I have no idea of the county.

---

10. Wilder, "Little Town of Memory," in *A Little House Reader: A Collection of Writings by Laura Ingalls Wilder*, ed. William Anderson (New York: HarperCollins, 1998), p. 166.

Neither do I remember what my Grandfather Ingalls was named.... My father's brothers married and there were numerous children, but I have not kept any trace of them and do not know how many or where they are."[11]

If Wilder's parents had stayed in Wisconsin near her relatives (many of whom remained there for the rest of their lives), she would almost certainly have kept in closer touch with her extended Ingalls/Quiner family, and her own nuclear family would not have been a frontier family as defined by Schlissel and Ryan. They became that when, as recounted at the beginning of *Little House on the Prairie*, they realized that the Big Woods was changing rapidly as a result of increased European-American settlement and would soon lose its frontier characteristics. Pa says, with regret, that wild animals will soon leave Wisconsin. "There were too many people in the Big Woods now.... The path that went by the little house had become a road. Almost every day Laura and Mary... stared in surprise at a wagon slowly creaking by on that road" (pp. 1–2). Pa proposes to move farther west, to a prairie where there are ample wild animals, no trees to impede farming, and "no settlers. Only Indians lived there" (p. 2). The "Indian territory" that Pa imagines is uninhabited by any non-Indian settlers except his own family, although, as we see in the novel, it soon becomes a quintessential frontier, marked by competing cultures, a rapidly changing environment, and transient families.[12]

Laura's nuclear family leaves Wisconsin for Kansas before dawn on a cold day in late winter. In the novel, the extended Ingalls/Quiner family assembles to see them off: "through the gray woods came lanterns with wagons and horses, bringing Grandpa and Grandma and aunts and uncles and cousins. ... Grandma and all the aunts hugged and kissed them and hugged and kissed them again, saying good-by" (pp. 4–5). Although some of them live at considerable distances, this family travels in the dark for hours, with young children, to bid Laura's family a brief farewell. And, for the fictional family of Caroline and Charles Ingalls, it is a permanent farewell; they will never return to Wisconsin again—and they will never again see many of these relatives, including the oldest family members, Grandpa and Grandma.

From Caroline Ingalls's 1861 letter to her sister, we see that she thought her

11. Wilder to Mrs. Dalphin, Feb. 6, 1934, in *Selected Letters*, pp. 72–73.

12. I am drawing on Annette Kolodny's revisionist definition of frontier as a locus of first cultural contact, "circumscribed by a particular physical terrain in the process of change *because* of the forms that contact takes, all of it inscribed by the collisions and interpenetrations of language.... [This is experienced by] a currently indigenous population and at least one group of newcomer 'intruders'" (Kolodny, "Letting Go Our Grand Obsessions: Notes toward a New Literary History of American Frontiers," *American Literature* 64 [Mar. 1992]: 3, 5).

in-laws, then aged forty-nine and fifty-one, were already "too old to be moving" yet again. In her mind, apparently, the peripatetic frontier lifestyle that she and her husband Charles were launching was only for the young. In the party scene in which Wilder depicted her Ingalls grandparents as vigorous and active, they would have actually been around sixty and sixty-two. Lansford Ingalls, Laura Ingalls Wilder's grandfather—whose name she could not remember—did not die until 1896, when he was eighty-four and his granddaughter Laura had already been living in Missouri for two years. Presumably, she would have received this news from her family in South Dakota (although almost none of that correspondence has survived).[13] By this time, Charles and Caroline Ingalls had left their prairie homestead and were settled permanently in the town of De Smet.

After the move to Missouri, Wilder returned only four times to her hometown and family home. She traveled by train in 1902, when she learned that her father was near death, and she was there for his death and burial at age sixty-six. She was not there for the death and burial of her mother in 1924 at age eighty-five or of her oldest sister Mary in 1928. Between 1931 and 1939, while the Little House books were being written, Laura and Almanzo made three trips by car to De Smet, attending "Old Settlers' Day" and visiting her two surviving sisters. However, according to William Anderson, "The people who filled Laura's life during her years in De Smet were largely lost to her after she moved to Missouri."[14] When the editor of the *De Smet News* sent the Wilders copies in 1941, Wilder thanked him, but she admitted that, although they found the newspapers "interesting . . . we do not find many names we remember."[15] Clearly, both the extended family and the frontier settlements that Wilder knew as a girl and young woman were now accessible only through memory, and as she had written years earlier in the poem "Little Town of Memory," even memory was fading and "beyond recall."

When I devoured and reread the Little House serial as a child, a young woman, and eventually a fledgling Wilder scholar, I did not notice two significant facts about those enchanting books. First, there are (almost) no old people in them.[16] And second, except for a few unnamed victims of weather-

13. Caroline Ingalls to Martha Quiner Carpenter, Oct. 6, 1861; Anderson, Introduction to Wilder, *Selected Letters*, pp. xvi, xviii.

14. Anderson, *Little House Reader*, p. 165.

15. Wilder to Sherwood, Aug. 20, 1941, p. 233.

16. John E. Miller's discussion of the demographics of De Smet in the 1880s and 1890s, when Laura Ingalls lived there, is interesting and pertinent. According to the 1880 census, "almost two-thirds (64.7 percent) were between twenty-one and forty years old. Males in their twenties outnumbered females two to one; for those in their thirties the ratio

related accidents, no one dies in the Little House books. Now, at a later stage in my own life, these facts leap out at me and raise compelling questions.

In *Pioneer Girl*, Wilder regularly referred to persons who were considered old in the various locations where the Ingalls family lived. In Walnut Grove, Minnesota, for example, she recalled "Old Mr & Mrs Pool, [who] with their grown daughter, Missouri [then about thirty-eight], lived in a queer little house near us.... Missouri did all the work, caring for her father and mother for they were old." Wilder also recounted one of her father's cases as justice of the peace in Walnut Grove. It involved Mr. Ray (around seventy), "a feeble, small, old man," and his wife (about sixty), "a tiny little white haird [*sic*] woman." During the first year in De Smet, she remembered, "an old railroader and his wife named Hunt with their son Jack, his wife and two babies camped back of our place and we became quite well acquainted." Even though she had encountered significant numbers of older persons in the various real communities where the Little House books are set, Wilder wrote almost none of them into the Little House series.[17]

Only twice, in the last two novels, does the series briefly acknowledge the

---

was four to one." Soon thereafter, these ratios changed significantly, "as more and larger families continued to arrive.... many individuals and families stayed only a short time in one place and then moved on to greener pastures" (Miller, *Laura Ingalls Wilder's Little Town: Where History and Literature Meet* [Lawrence: University Press of Kansas, 1994], pp. 121–22).

17. Wilder, *Pioneer Girl: The Annotated Autobiography*, ed. Pamela Smith Hill (Pierre: South Dakota Historical Society Press, 2014), pp. 127–28, 141, 194. The annotations in this book flesh out the communities where Wilder lived and confirm that numbers of older people lived there and were known to her. While few appear in the Little House series, there are some exceptions. One is the Congregationalist minister Edward Brown, cousin of John Brown of Kansas, who was sixty-five when he arrived in De Smet in 1880. In *Pioneer Girl*, Wilder introduced him as a "fierce looking old man," who was "rude and rough and unclean," with unkempt white whiskers. None of the Ingalls family liked him (pp. 192–93). She described Brown similarly in *Little Town on the Prairie*, where Laura is especially repelled by his "long white beard ... stained yellow as if with dribbling tobacco juice" (p. 208), but the word "old" is never used. Brown's preaching is alarmingly energetic. He is a recurring character, and in *These Happy Golden Years*, he marries Almanzo and Laura. A second old man, an Indian dressed in traditional American Indian style, appears both in *Pioneer Girl*, p. 203, and the Little House series, where, in *The Long Winter*, he announces to a group of men that the coming winter will be severe: "Then he tapped his breast with his forefinger. 'Old! Old! I have seen!' he said proudly'" (pp. 61–62). This man's age, assurance, and difference impress the assembled men, and in a new town that entirely lacks the experienced advice of longtime elder residents, the Indian assumes that role and, for Pa at least, fills an important need.

presence of multiple elders. Both scenes are set in the church, newly constructed in the growing town of De Smet. In *Little Town on the Prairie*, when the Ingalls family attends a crowded revival meeting, seating at the church seems to be determined by age, gender, and marital status: "Graybeards sat close around the pulpit, families were in the middle seats, and young men and boys filled the back seats" (pp. 275–76). Near the end of *These Happy Golden Years*, Laura, Mary, and Pa attend a Sunday service. Since the church is crowded and "they could not find three empty places together," Pa, although his beard is still brown, "went forward to sit with the graybeards in the amen corner" (p. 260). Clearly, old men are present in De Smet; there is no indication that Laura is surprised to see them. They have a designated place in the church, one of the new town's central institutions. But none of these "graybeards" is given a name or a role as a character in the series. And the presence of old women is never even mentioned.

Young Caroline Ingalls, as she was about to embark on a life of frontier moves herself, considered her in-laws "too old" to continue such a life. In *By the Shores of Silver Lake*, as the family prepares to spend their first, solitary winter near De Smet, Pa learns that one other man, [Horace G.] Woodworth, who is attempting the "prairie cure" for his tuberculosis, is also determined to stay through the winter. Pa and the last departing teamster persuade him to take the last train out and rejoin his family "in the East." Pa describes Woodworth to Ma and his daughters as "an old man. . . . so feeble. . . . skin and bones" and concludes, "The place for him is with his own folks" (pp. 151–52). This account of the frail old man makes a powerful impression on Laura, reminding her of how isolated and without resources the Dakota prairie is. "Thinking of that old man going out with the last teamster, Laura really knew how deserted the country was" (p. 152). Clearly, the Ingalls family agrees that it is no place for old people. Yet, by the next novel, *The Long Winter*, Woodworth (both the real man and the fictional character) has returned to De Smet as agent in the new railroad station, accompanied by his wife and four children. "The 'prairie cure' had truly almost cured his consumption of the lungs and he had come west again for more of it" (p. 82). When he returns, Woodworth, whose real-life counterpart was about fifty-three, is well enough to launch a new career as a railroad agent and is no longer referred to as an old man. Is "age" a matter of disability or illness, then, rather than of years?

Wilder and Lane may have avoided the subjects of aging and death because they feared they were not suitable or marketable for child readers. The fact that Wilder's chosen title for her fifth novel, "The Hard Winter," was vetoed by her publisher because it was "too depressing" for children indicates the constraints that she and Lane worked under while producing the books.[18] In her Detroit Book Fair speech, Wilder explained, "All I have told is true but it is not the whole truth. There were some stories I wanted to tell but would not be responsible for putting in a book for children, even though I knew them as a child." She went on to tell the horrific story of the murders allegedly committed by the Bender family in Kansas; when multiple bodies were found in their cellar, Pa joined a vigilante party to pursue the Benders. "It was late the next day when he came back and he never told us where he had been." In following years, whenever the search for the Benders was mentioned, "Pa always said in a strange tone of finality, 'They will never be found.'"[19] One of the typescript versions of *Pioneer Girl,* which was not aimed at child readers, elaborated on this story, adding that Laura as a small child overheard Pa telling Ma about the discovery of the bodies, including that of a little girl who appeared to have been buried alive: "I screamed, and Ma told Pa he should have known better." This story was the stuff of a recurrent nightmare for young Laura, in which she sometimes became the buried girl herself.[20] In her Book Fair speech, Wilder also mentioned the story of "the family of children frozen in the terrible blizzard on Plum Creek. I couldn't tell that either."[21]

In the Little House books, Ma is vigilant and protective about the stories she allows her daughters (and Wilder's young readers) to hear. In *Little House on the Prairie,* for example, she stops her neighbor, Mrs. Scott, when she begins to tell a detailed story of the "Minnesota massacre" of settlers by Indians. Laura's curiosity is piqued, but when she questions her mother later about massacres, Ma replies, "she could not explain that now; it was something that Laura would understand when she was older" (pp. 211–12). Death—and perhaps especially the death of children—is something from which children must be shielded as much as possible.

Yet, the three oldest Ingalls daughters were intimately introduced to death at home. The fourth Ingalls child (and only son), Charles Frederick, was born in November 1875, when the family was living on Plum Creek in Minnesota. The sisters were delighted with their "little brother.... We were very proud of him and always hurried home from school to see him," Wilder wrote in *Pioneer Girl.* The following summer, a plague of grasshoppers destroyed

---

18. George Bye to Lane, ca. June 3, 1940, James Oliver Brown Papers, Rare Book and Manuscript Library, Columbia University, New York, N.Y.

19. Wilder, Speech, Detroit Book Fair, Oct. 16, 1937, pp. 8, 11, Box 13, file 197, Laura Ingalls Wilder Series, Rose Wilder Lane Papers, Herbert Hoover Presidential Library, West Branch, Iowa. This speech is reproduced in this volume.

20. Wilder, *Pioneer Girl*, p. 354.

21. Wilder, Speech, p. 12. She told this story in *Pioneer Girl*, pp. 139–40.

Charles Ingalls's crops for a second year, and he decided that his family could not remain in such a "blasted country." They would move to Burr Oak, Iowa, and he and Caroline would work for friends who were opening a hotel there. On their way to Iowa, the family stopped to spend the rest of the summer in eastern Minnesota with close relatives—Peter Ingalls, Charles's brother, who had married Caroline's sister, Eliza, and their children.[22] While they were there, "Baby Freddy" sickened and died.

Wilder wrote this account of her brother's death, which she apparently witnessed at the age of nine: "Little Brother was not well and the Dr. came. I thought that would cure him as it had Ma when the Dr. came to see her. But little Brother got worse instead of better and one awful day he straightened out his little body and was dead." Charles Frederick, nine months old, died in August 1876 and was buried near the Minnesota home of Peter and Eliza Ingalls. The location of his grave is unknown. Up until Freddy's final illness, young Wilder had thought that doctors prevented death—as they had previously when members of her family had been ill. Freddy's death destroyed this innocent belief. Wilder's description of the child's death is the only specific image of the beloved baby brother in *Pioneer Girl*; clearly, it remained seared into Wilder's memory many decades later. Like the frontier families that Schlissel described, the Ingalls family was broken by this son's death. And they could not remain settled nearby, where they might tend and visit his grave—and his memory. Wilder's *Pioneer Girl* acknowledged their mourning: "We felt so badly to go on and leave Freddy, but in a little while we had to go on to Iowa to help keep the hotel. It was a cold miserable little journey."[23]

These experiences of death and mourning never find their way into the Little House books, although, given the high rate of infant mortality in the nineteenth-century United States and the difficulty and expense of getting medical care on the frontier, they must have been a part of many frontier children's lives.[24] They were among the stories that Wilder and Lane felt they "could not tell" in books for children. And the story of Freddy may have been especially painful for Wilder. She and Lane both gave birth to sons who died in infancy, so the Ingalls family's loss of an only son was echoed in two subsequent generations. Also, the Little House series omits the family's departure from the Plum Creek farm, the months during which Freddy died in eastern

22. Wilder, *Pioneer Girl*, p. 94.
23. Ibid., pp. 97, 99.
24. Paula Nelson explored these issues in her article, "'In the Midst of Life We Are in Death': Medical Care and Mortality in Early Canton," *South Dakota History* 33 (Fall 2003): 193–254.

Minnesota, the year in Burr Oak, and their return to Walnut Grove, where Charles Ingalls ran a butcher shop and did odd jobs before the family's final move to Dakota Territory. The last Ingalls daughter, Grace, was actually born in Burr Oak, but her birthplace is never acknowledged; she simply appears on the first page of *By the Shores of Silver Lake* to complete the Ingalls nuclear family. Childbirth is another scene that is never narrated in the series.

Another common family experience that is absent from the Little House books is the death of an elder relative. Three of Laura Ingalls Wilder's grandparents died during her lifetime, but there is no mention of these deaths in any of Wilder's published or unpublished writings that I have seen. Charles and Caroline Ingalls lived far from their parents for most of their adult lives, but the interrelated families kept in occasional touch through the "circulator," a letter passed on from family to family. In it, Caroline's mother, Charlotte Tucker Quiner Holbrook, wrote of her concern for her daughter's constantly moving family: "I wonder when they will get a stopping place? I shall be glad for their sake; they have had a hard time of it since they left Pepin."[25] When this concerned grandmother died in Wisconsin in 1884, Wilder was seventeen and still living in her parents' house. Caroline must have received the news of her mother's death and mourned this loss. Surely she shared this news and her sorrow with her oldest daughter still at home, Laura, who by then was working as a teacher and was no longer a child to be shielded. But no word of this significant family event occurs in the last Little House book, which is set in 1884–1885.

However, when Wilder herself received a telegram in Missouri in 1924 announcing her mother's death, she wrote about it for *The Missouri Ruralist*: "'Mother passed away this morning' was the message that came over the wires, and a darkness overshadowed the spring sunshine; a sadness crept into the birds' songs. Some of us have received such messages. Those who have not, one day will."[26] For the separated members of a frontier family, receiving such news and enduring the "darkness" and "sadness" that followed was a near-universal experience, and it was one that Wilder would endure again and again as she received news of the deaths of her three sisters with whom she had shared the Little House, as well as of other members of the Ingalls/Quiner/Wilder family.

In the Little House books, the one death that occurs in the Ingalls family is that of the family bulldog, Jack. In a sense, this episode stands in for other

---

25. Holbrook, quoted in Anderson, *Laura Ingalls Wilder*, p. 62.

26. Wilder, "Mother Passed Away," reprinted in Wilder, *Little House in the Ozarks*, ed. Stephen W. Hines (New York: Galahad Books, 1991), p. 315.

*Helen Sewell,* Little House on the Prairie, *1935*

events in the family history that Wilder must have felt she "couldn't tell." It occurs in Chapter 2 of *By the Shores of Silver Lake.* Jack has been an active, protective member of the Ingalls family since the first pages of the first book, traveling with them from Wisconsin to Indian Territory to the banks of Plum Creek, trotting beneath the covered wagon and serving as a vigilant and vigorous watchdog. Now Pa is preparing to travel to Dakota Territory for a new railroad job; Ma and the girls will follow later on the train. Always before Jack has been "eager and joyful" to travel. Laura urges him, "Jack, Jack! We're going west! Don't you want to go west again, Jack?" But now "he did not want to go, even in the wagon." Stroking him gently, Laura "could feel how very tired he was." His "fine hairs were gray now. First his nose had been gray and then his jaws, and now even his ears were no longer brown" (pp. 9–10). Although Jack's graying has been a gradual process, Laura is only now recognizing that the familiar and beloved dog has grown old. He exhibits the same symptoms of aging that a human might: rheumatism, wrinkles, gray hair, fatigue.

In the past weeks, twelve-year-old Laura has been busy and anxious with the responsibilities of an adult, nursing her sisters and mother while they were gravely ill with scarlet fever. She has neglected Jack, who has always been "especially Laura's own dog." Now, overcome with guilt and regret, she thinks, "Perhaps all that time he had been feeling lonely and forgotten." Expecting that Jack will depart in the wagon with Pa the next day, Laura gives him all the time and attention she can, feeding him, stroking him, and making his bed. "'Good Jack, good dog,' she told him" as he settled down for the night. In the morning, Jack does not answer Pa's call. "Only Jack's body, stiff and cold, lay curled there on the blanket. They buried it on the low slope above the wheat field.... Grass would grow there after they had all gone away to the west." Later in the morning, when Pa drives away, Laura mourns: "Jack was not standing beside Laura to watch Pa go. There was only emptiness to turn to instead of Jack's eyes looking up to say that he was there to take care of her" (pp. 12–13). Jack has been a cherished member of the nuclear Little House family. Now his grave must be left alone, untended—as the Ingalls family once left the grave of baby Freddy.

Jack has been one of Laura's elders—always there "to take care of her." Wilder, reporting in 1924 on the death of her own mother, wrote, "the world seems a lonesome place when mother has passed away."[27] Now, Laura feels that same lonesomeness and many of the other responses that one may have to the death of a loved elder: abandonment, guilt, and regret that she did not observe signs of aging and attend to the elder's changing needs—even though she had other pressing family duties. In *Little Town on the Prairie*, set some years later, Laura tries to explain to her parents why she still intensely dislikes Nellie Olson, whom she first met when they were little girls on Plum Creek. Nellie had made fun of Mary and her, was "impudent" to Ma and "'mean to Jack,' Laura said, and tears smarted in her eyes." Pa recognizes that his near-adult daughter is still mourning the family bulldog and replies soothingly, "'Never mind, . . . Jack was a good dog and he's gone to his reward'" (pp. 183–84).

The chapter about Jack's death in *Silver Lake* introduces Laura to death, grief, and mourning inside the Little House as a part of the process of maturation. As the chapter's title announces, Laura now considers herself "Grown Up." It ends with these words: "Laura knew then that she was not a little girl any more. Now she was alone; she must take care of herself. When you must do that, then you do it and you are grown up.... no one was there to depend on. Pa and Jack had gone, and Ma needed help to take care of [blind] Mary and the little girls, and somehow to get them all safely to the west on a train" (p. 14). At this point, Laura Ingalls's childhood ends.

The death of Jack was obviously a story that Wilder and Lane felt free to write about for children, perhaps because many child readers had already been, or soon would be, introduced to death through the loss of a family pet. For many readers—including me and many of the university students with

27. Ibid.

whom I read this book—the chapter is one of the most memorable and moving episodes in the series. Such readers may be surprised and disappointed to learn that the death of Jack is not a "true story." In *Pioneer Girl*, Wilder wrote that, as the Ingalls family prepared to return from Kansas to Wisconsin (when Wilder was only four years old), "Pa traded the horses Pet and Patty for some larger horses and because Jack wanted to stay with Pet and Patty as he always did Pa gave him to the man who had them."[28] Jack was only a part of the Ingalls household for the first four years of the real Laura's life, and (in Charles Ingalls's opinion, at least) Jack's first loyalty was to the horses, with which he "always" stayed, and not to the human family in the Little House. The story of Jack as it continues in *On the Banks of Plum Creek* and *By the Shores of Silver Lake* is entirely fiction, and the account of Jack's death may be the work of Lane.

One of the most vehement arguments between Wilder and Lane about the writing of the series concerned how to open *Silver Lake*. Wilder wanted to begin the book in the Dakota hotel lobby, where Ma and her daughters waited for Pa to come and drive them to the railroad camp that would be their first Dakota home. While waiting, Laura would fill in the sad events of the family's last months on Plum Creek in a dreamy narrative. Such a narrative would not be sad, Wilder argued, but would be "passed over lightly by the reader in the interest of the new adventure which is already begun." To begin the book with the family's recent illness, Mary's blindness, Pa's financial failure, and Jack's death would make "an unpleasant beginning, a tale of sickness and failure and death. We don't want to tell of Jack's dying. . . . Mary's sickness. . . . Pa's failure. . . . The readers must know all that but they should not be made to think about it."[29] Clearly, Wilder was again concerned about making a children's book "too depressing" and about dealing directly with Laura's feelings of grief and abandonment as she experiences the first (and only) narrated death in her family, feelings that were probably painful for Wilder herself to confront.

After a protracted debate with her daughter, Wilder finally surrendered. "Change the beginning of the story if you want," she wrote Lane. "Do anything you please with the damn stuff if you will fix it up.[30] Wilder probably collaborated with Lane on final revisions of the book's opening chapters, and it was she who insisted that the tragedy of Mary's blindness, which "added to Laura's age," must be an important part of the series, although Lane had

28. Wilder, *Pioneer Girl*, p. 22.
29. Wilder to Lane, Jan. 28, 1938, in *Selected Letters*, p. 153–54.
30. Ibid., n.d., p. 156.

advised her to omit it.[31] But it was clearly Lane who insisted that the book directly address the death of Jack as an important event in Laura's maturation, as well as the atmosphere of "sickness and failure" in which *Silver Lake* begins. Of course, that "sickness and failure" was a painful memory for Wilder, something she had lived through as her daughter had not. An experienced author of fiction for adults, Lane was able to contribute the story of Jack's death, which added an important and needed dimension to the Little House series.

For many of us, the presence and influence of old people, often grandparents, in our lives is epitomized in the stories they tell, which convey history, values, culture. As a member of a mobile frontier family, Laura Ingalls Wilder was separated from such family storytellers for most of her life. After her family left Wisconsin early in her childhood, she apparently heard stories only from her father, who told tales of his own past and present experiences and from his father's boyhood and adulthood. These stores contained no female characters, no girls like Laura herself. Nevertheless, she told her Detroit Book Fair audience, out of all their childhood, she and Mary "loved Pa's stories best. We never forgot them and I have always felt they were too good to be altogether lost."[32] When Wilder, with her daughter's help, finally found a way to write and publish those stories in *Little House in the Big Woods*, her father had been dead for three decades, and at sixty-five, she had begun to worry that her own memory was failing and that his stories might soon be lost. She told her daughter that she was alarmed about her memory's unreliability, "That's why the sooner I write my stuff the better."[33]

When Wilder and Lane first tried to market these stories for children, the manuscript they submitted to an editor acknowledged the tradition of the grandparent as elder storyteller. The first words of that manuscript were, "When Grandma was a little girl she lived in a little gray house made of logs." That sentence contained the two staples of the series to come: a little girl, who would provide the book's point of view, and a little house. For five paragraphs, the little girl is "Grandma," presumably an elder of the reader's own family. But then we are told, "Grandma's name was Laura," and from that point onward, "Grandma" disappeared from the twenty-two-page manuscript. Almost half of that manuscript consisted of the stories that Pa told to Laura and Mary, set off by handwritten subtitles such as "The Story of Grandma's Grandpa and the Panther." These were Charles Ingalls's mem-

31. Ibid., Jan. 26, 1938, p. 152.
32. Wilder, Speech, p. 2.
33. Wilder to Lane, Feb. 5, 1937, in *Selected Letters*, p. 109.

orable stories, and only in their titles did "Grandma" remain.[34] Such titles make them distant to a present-day child reader, for Grandma's Grandpa seems far in the past. What is more immediately interesting is the life of a little girl in a little house surrounded by big woods.

When that manuscript was published in 1932, Wilder and Lane had much revised and expanded it. "Grandma" is now entirely gone; the book begins, "Once upon a time, sixty years ago, a little girl lived in the Big Woods of Wisconsin, in a little gray house made of logs" (p. 1). After the time-honored storyteller's opening, "Once upon a time," this story is firmly placed in geography (Wisconsin woods) and in historical, biographical time. In 1932, "sixty years ago" would have meant 1872, the year in which the actual Laura Ingalls turned five, as she does in the book. The story has grown to 238 pages, exploring a year of the Ingalls family's life in detail. The four inset stories from the original manuscript remain, but "Grandma's" name no longer appears in the stories' titles. When Pa begins to tell the first of these inset tales, "The Story of Grandpa and the Panther," Laura now questions him:

> "Your Grandpa?" Laura asked.
> "No, Laura, your Grandpa. My father."
> "Oh," Laura said, and she wriggled closer against Pa's arm. She knew her Grandpa. He lived far away in the Big Woods, in a big log house. (p. 40)

Before Laura listens to the story, she places it in her time and place. By now, forty pages into the book, a child reader has already begun to forge a relationship with this engaging protagonist. If this story is about someone who is an important part of Laura's world, that reader is more likely to want to read it. And although Wilder and Lane expanded the original manuscript greatly, they did not add any more tales set in a distant past. Instead, the additional stories that Pa tells his wife and daughters come from his present experiences in the woods that surround the little house, and their immediacy and relevance is obvious.

In this first book, especially, we see Wilder negotiating between her desire to preserve her father's stories and her desire to tell the story of her own childhood and adolescence, which she had already written (but not yet published) in *Pioneer Girl*. Both Pa's stories *and* her own, she must have thought, were "too good to be lost." And now her mother and her sister Mary, the only two other persons who had fully shared both Pa's storytelling and Laura's life as a pioneer girl, were dead. Wilder was the only living person who could pre-

---

34. "Facsimile of 'Juvenile Pioneer Girl,'" in Wilder, *Pioneer Girl*, pp. 331–52.

serve those stories. In her sixties, she was of an age to be "Grandma" herself and to pass on history and values to future generations through storytelling. She had already done so with her daughter Rose, who had been the chosen first reader of *Pioneer Girl*, which contained a few bits that were clearly intended for a close family member and no one else. For example, in her account of 1875–1876, Wilder boxed off a paragraph in her handwritten text and labeled it "Private." It shared this information: "And then we caught the itch at school and couldn't touch the baby. Gosh how it did itch and Ma rubbed us with sulpher and grease and turned us before the fire to heat it in. We had an awful time."[35] Wilder did not want to share this account of an embarrassing and uncomfortable ailment that was associated with uncleanliness with a wider audience, but she wanted to tell—and perhaps to warn—her daughter about it. Lane was an active editor and promotor of *Pioneer Girl* and an attentive reader; she incorporated many incidents from the manuscript (unpublished during Lane's lifetime) into her fiction, with no acknowledgement of their source. Just as Wilder must have thought that Charles Ingalls's family stories were her legacy to preserve and retell as she thought best, Lane may have thought the same about the stories she heard (and sometimes solicited) from both Laura and Almanzo Wilder.

Despite her brief appearance in the first *Big Woods* manuscript as "Grandma," Wilder was never a (biological) grandmother herself. Rose Wilder Lane was the only grandchild in the Ingalls family; Laura's three sisters were all childless. Lane's only child had died at birth in 1910. So there were no young descendants to hear grandmotherly family stories from Wilder. In 1937, she tried to explain the origin of her series, which by then was half complete. "When to my surprise," she said, *Big Woods* "made such a success and children from all over the U.S. wrote to me begging for more stories, I began to think what a wonderful childhood I had had.... I had seen and lived it all—all the successive phases of the frontier.... I wanted the children now to understand more about the beginning of things[,] to know what is behind the things they see—what it is that made America as they know it. Then I thought of writing the story of my childhood in several volumes—a seven-volume historical novel for children."[36]

The novel project would allow Wilder to fulfill her role as a storytelling elder, transmitting history, culture, values, and "understanding" to an ever-expanding child audience. And, as the author of an unprecedented multi-volume historical novel for children, she was taking on a literary form more

35. Wilder, *Pioneer Girl*, p. 83.
36. Wilder, Speech, p. 3–4.

extended and demanding than any she had attempted before. As she completed it, she would be feeding her own burgeoning ambitions as a writer, which had been growing ever since she wrote (and carefully preserved) her first poems and composition as a teenager. Like Emily Dickinson, Laura Ingalls stitched her early poems into little books. On the paper cover of one, she invited readers: "When you open this book/Just take one good look." And on the back cover, she willingly revealed the fledgling author's name: "If you've read this book through/With all its jingles/I'll let you know that it's been filled,/By Laura E. Ingalls."[37] At sixty-five, when she would have been considered "old" in the prevailing culture of the 1930s, Laura Ingalls Wilder had achieved wide readership and name recognition in the United States, with an honored reputation that would continue to expand throughout her long life and beyond. In fact, she was the kind of active, successful, professional "old" woman who never appears in the Little House series.[38]

The Little House series is an act of creative, edited memory. In 1924, when Wilder wrote about her mother's death, she reflected: "only memories of her are left us—happy memories if we have not given ourselves any cause for regret. Memories! We go through life collecting them whether we will or not! Sometimes I wonder if they are our treasures in Heaven or the consuming fires of torment when we carry them with us as we, too, pass on."[39] Wilder clearly saw happy memories as a treasure, but if one had "cause for regret," memories could be a hellish torment, perhaps even extending after death. Did Wilder have regrets? She had not seen her mother for twenty-two years. She would not attend her mother's funeral to mourn with her three surviving sisters, all of whom had been more involved in Caroline Ingalls's care in her last years and had observed her aging more closely than Wilder could.

Although mother and daughter corresponded regularly in the thirty years after the young Wilders left De Smet, that correspondence has been almost entirely lost. The few surviving letters that I have seen from Caroline Ingalls to her daughter Laura do not suggest that she was able to express an immediate, intimate relationship on paper. This brief letter of thanks is an example: "Dear Laura[,] Your nice Christmas gifts received. Thank you for them. We

---

37. Quoted in Anderson, *Laura Ingalls Wilder*, p. 112.

38. The only possible example is the wife of the sixty-five-year-old minister, Reverend Brown, who "wrote for the church papers" (*These Happy Golden Years*, p. 97) and plays the organ at church (*Little Town on the Prairie*, p. 276). But there is no indication of Mrs. Brown's age.

39. Wilder, "Mother Passed Away," p. 315.

Caroline Ingalls (far left) posed with her sisters Eliza (middle) and Martha (far right) in the late 1800s. *Laura Ingalls Wilder Memorial Society*

are grateful indeed for the love that prompted."[40] I read this letter, however affectionate, as restrained, vague, and formulaic—and probably maddeningly nonspecific about the gifts that Wilder had laboriously mailed from Missouri to South Dakota. It suggests that much of the happy, often-unspoken, day-to-day mother-daughter intimacy of the frontier Little House family had been lost. For sister Mary Ingalls, however, it had not been. During Mary's seven years at the Iowa College for the Blind, she returned home for regular visits before her final return to her parents' home in 1889. After her father's death, she and her mother became inseparable. "I am feet for Ma, and Ma is eyes for

40. Caroline Ingalls to Wilder, Jan. 9, 1913, Archives, Laura Ingalls Wilder Memorial Society, De Smet, S.Dak.

me," Mary wrote.[41] This physical intimacy and interdependence obviously kept them close, and we may remember that, in the Little House books, Mary always had a special affinity with Ma, as Laura did with Pa. After the move to Missouri, Wilder's ties to her little House family were inevitably diminished, following Schlissel's model of the frontier family. And she may have felt the pain of regret, perhaps especially about her mother.

A year after Caroline Ingalls's death, Wilder wrote to her mother's surviving sister, Martha Quiner Carpenter, back in Wisconsin, requesting recipes, stories, and memories from "Aunt Martha's" childhood. She had wanted her sisters to collect such reminiscences from their mother, "but they never got around to it and Mother herself was not able. I wanted all the stories she could remember of the early days in Wisconsin when you all were children and young people. Now it is too late to ever get them from her." It would be wonderful to have such a family record, Wilder wrote, and the stories might also be useful to Lane and to her in their writing.[42]

Carpenter replied to her niece's letter with voluminous reminiscences, of which neither Wilder nor Lane apparently made much use. Anderson suggested that the letter to her aunt indicated Wilder's "first tentative resolve to write about frontier times"—a resolve that began by reaching out to a maternal family elder for stories.[43] Her father's family stories were Wilder's earliest and most cherished memories; she "never forgot them." Now that her mother was gone, she longed for the same link with her, and she wished for the intimacy of proximity with Aunt Martha: "if only you could talk to me," she wrote.[44] This letter is filled with both desire and regret.

By mid-point in the writing of her series, Wilder's creative engagement with her memories must have fulfilled many desires—for creative achievement, fame, and an admiring, receptive audience. She had also succeeded in writing about her mother and honoring her strengths in the early books—even though Caroline Ingalls is often silent compared with her voluble and much-romanticized husband. Pa's stories and songs are exuberantly audible; Ma's stories, while often unspoken, are powerfully conveyed through things and domestic practices. In *Big Woods*, for example, Laura receives her first doll as a Christmas gift. Wilder described the homemade rag doll in detail, and those details are a catalog of Ma's skills: selecting and combining fabrics, cutting, stitching, drawing, dying, knitting. Laura names the doll Charlotte.

41. Mary Ingalls, quoted in Anderson, *Little House Reader*, p. 15.
42. Wilder to Carpenter, June 22, 1925, in *Selected Letters*, p. 34.
43. Anderson, *Selected Letters*, p. 33.
44. Wilder to Carpenter, p. 34.

It is no accident, surely, that Charlotte is the name of her maternal grandmother, Charlotte Tucker Quiner Holbrook, who was a dressmaker. The name evokes a maternal tradition and a set of skills that produced a cherished gift for Laura. Just two months later, seven-year-old Mary makes a dress for Charlotte as a gift for Laura's fifth birthday—evidence that Ma is already teaching those skills to her eldest daughter. And three books later, in *Plum Creek*, when a thoughtless neighbor child abandons poor Charlotte in the icy mud, Ma restores the bedraggled doll, adding thawing, laundering, patching, starching, and ironing to her original set of doll-making skills. Charlotte is "as good as new. . . . clean and crisp, her red mouth smiled, her eyes shone black" (p. 236). Ma has demonstrated her powers to create and to recreate, restoring the most treasured possession in her daughter's world. Significantly, this scene takes place during one of Pa's long absences, when he is laboring for money to compensate for yet another crop failure and the girls are missing his male-centered stories and his music. Although Ma speaks few words in the scene, Charlotte is a story—a story about what a woman can do. Such stories—expressed in handmade objects such as a button lamp or a green pumpkin pie—celebrate Ma Ingalls.[45]

However, when Wilder tried to get started on *Silver Lake*, Ma was at perhaps her lowest point in the series. "Mary and Carrie and baby Grace and Ma had all had scarlet fever. . . . The doctor had come every day; Pa did not know how he could pay the bill. Far worst of all . . . Mary was blind." Ill herself, Ma has been unable to care for her family, and now her beloved firstborn has an incurable disability that will change and limit her life. When an unknown woman visitor approaches, Ma cannot summon any of her usual reliable coping strategies: "'Can you think of anything for dinner?' Ma asked. She meant for a company dinner" (pp. 1–2). These are the circumstances about which Wilder disagreed so vehemently with Lane. For years in this creative process, Wilder had been immersed in memory, and now as she contemplated this low point in her family's fortunes, those memories must have been painfully suffused with regret. According to Lane, her grandparents "never quite got over it. She [Mary] was their oldest, and so beautiful and so smart. They'd had great hopes for her," as had the whole family.[46] Such remembered regrets, as Wilder wrote at her mother's death, could be hellish. In 1937, she suggested

---

45. In *Constructing the Little House: Gender, Culture, and Laura Ingalls Wilder* (Amherst: University of Massachusetts Press, 1997), pp. 165–69, I provided a much more thorough discussion of this scene.

46. Rose Wilder Lane, "Grandpa's Fiddle," in Wilder and Lane, *A Little House Sampler*, ed. William T. Anderson (Lincoln: University of Nebraska Press, 1988), p. 61.

to Lane in a letter that her memories were causing her mental anguish: "I can't work on my book in the evening, because if I do, I can't sleep. My brain goes right on remembering and it's H——."[47]

In 1924, Wilder ended her brief essay about her mother's death with a strategy for creating "happy" memories: "glad or sad [memories] are with us forever. Let us make them carefully of all good things, rejoicing in the wonderful truth that while we are laying up for ourselves the very sweetest and best of happy memories, we are at the same time giving them to others."[48] Although Wilder told her Detroit Book Fair audience that she remembered her frontier childhood as "busy and happy," we may also see it—as her Grandmother Holbrook did—as a "hard time," marked by disaster, failure, constant starting over, loss, all the stresses of frontier life and the damage they could do to frontier families. What made such hard times into a "happy" childhood? The tight shelter of the Little House, the collaborative creation of Ma and Pa, and, in the series, the collaborative creation of Wilder and Lane as they chose from Wilder's *Pioneer Girl* memories, both happy and hellish, for the pages of the books. In the process, they did not hesitate to alter or invent memories as needed—as we saw, for example, with the story of Jack's death.

As Wilder's memories became the stuff of children's books, they were both edited and fictionalized to produce the artful and still-celebrated Little House novels. The de-emphasis or omission of deaths and aging elders in a series for children must have seemed necessary to both Wilder and Lane. But both of them were also aware that the stuff of Wilder's memories contained the potential for telling, or retelling, other stories for other audiences. This realization is apparent in the fiction that both women wrote for adult readers during the years when the Little House series was being written.

Lane's *Let the Hurricane Roar*, published in 1933, depended heavily on details from *Pioneer Girl* and possibly on stories she had heard from her grandparents (before the Wilders left De Smet when she was seven) and from her mother. The protagonists, Caroline and Charles, are based on the actual Charles and Caroline Ingalls, newlyweds from the "Big Woods," where they grew up in a relatively settled community with multiple generations, including old women and men, but with "little good land left." Charles and Caroline move to the West to establish their first frontier claim on the banks of "Wild Plum Creek," living in a dugout with a town nearby. Grasshoppers destroy Charles's first crop, and he must leave Caroline to find work to support them; Caroline is alone with the baby on the isolated claim during long weeks of

---

47. Wilder to Lane, Feb. 5, 1937, p. 110.
48. Wilder, "Mother Passed Away," p. 315.

blizzards. Charles's return ends the book. This story obviously draws on the Minnesota years that Wilder narrated in *Pioneer Girl*, which would later provide the basis for *On the Banks of Plum Creek*. But Lane altered that material in telling ways. First, she gave the book the female point of view of Caroline, who, as "Ma," is the most opaque character in the Little House series. Second, Lane's Caroline is only sixteen ("that child," a frontier woman calls her), and Charles is nineteen. These ages contradicted the Little House disapproval of early marriage (before the age of eighteen), which Wilder probably wanted to convey to child readers. They also contradicted the ages at which Lane's actual grandparents were married; Caroline was twenty and Charles twenty-four. Their first child, Mary, was not born until Caroline Ingalls was twenty-five, followed by Laura two years later. So the Little House books, beginning when Laura is five, portray Ma as a mature woman in her early thirties. But in Lane's novel, the young couple's baby is born on Caroline's seventeenth birthday, and he is a robust boy, the male descendant that three generations of Laura Ingalls Wilder's family did not produce.[49]

In this book, written in the depths of the Great Depression and at the onset of the New Deal, Lane expressed in occasional, highly didactic passages her own political philosophy and its emerging Libertarian principles. (Wilder's fiction, by contrast, was never explicitly political.) Lane clearly chose, and altered, her *Pioneer Girl* material so that she could show her female protagonist, who is still a quiet child at her marriage to a voluble, expansive, optimistic young man whom she reveres and adores, as she discovers her identity, voice, and powers as a free-standing individual. This approach allowed Lane to explore subjects that could not be explored through "Ma" in a series for children: childbirth, nursing, a mother's recognition of her child's individual will, and the sexual relationship of husband and wife, as well as Caroline's deepening understanding of her young husband's strengths and weaknesses as a vulnerable, fallible human being. According to Pamela Smith Hill, Caroline, as the lone adult in a prairie blizzard, becomes "the feminist ideal of a pioneer woman."[50] She rescues frozen cattle, ties a rope between house and barn so she can bring in hay for fuel—tasks that Pa, not Ma, accomplished in the Little House series—and keeps her child and herself safe, fed, and alive. Ultimately, she rescues Charles, who has lost his way in yet another blizzard, trying to find his way home to her. As the book ends, they gaze at their beaming baby son, who promises a prosperous post-frontier world: "a

49. Lane, *Let the Hurricane Roar* (New York: Longmans, Green & Co., 1993), pp. 5, 12, 20. *See also* Miller, *Becoming Laura Ingalls Wilder*, p. 21.

50. Hill, *Laura Ingalls Wilder: A Writer's Life* (Pierre: South Dakota Historical Society Press, 2007), p. 151.

light from the future was shining in the baby's face. The big white house [*not* a frontier Little House] was waiting for him, and the acres of wheat fields, the fast driving teams and swift buggies."[51] The Little House books never make such expansive promises of future prosperity.

Although they were living in adjacent houses on Rocky Ridge Farm and saw each other often, Lane did not tell her mother that she was writing and publishing a novel that made extensive use of family stories, many from *Pioneer Girl*. When Wilder learned of her daughter's use of these materials, she was reportedly extremely angry in the most serious recorded rift between the two.[52] At its center was a thorny question: who owns family stories? Does the answer to this question change when such stories have been written and then (in some cases) published? Are family stories shared property? Can they—and the profits that accrue from them—be inherited? Wilder had not written her parents' stories in *Pioneer Girl* until they were dead and she was their oldest surviving child, and she was still hoping to publish those stories in some format; in fact, *Big Woods* was already a publishing success by 1933. Lane, only grandchild and only daughter, would be the sole heir of her mother's Ingalls/Quiner family stories. But could she claim them now, with her mother still alive, and profit from them? (*Let the Hurricane Roar* was a bestseller, initially far more profitable than *Big Woods*.)

Or were family stories community property? Lane seems to have assumed so, as she simultaneously collaborated with her mother on the first Little House book and produced her own novel based on the same materials. But if she so assumed, why keep her novel a secret from her mother? Wilder came from a family and cultural tradition of collaborating women, who worked together on cooking, housework, furniture arrangement and rearrangement, and all kinds of sewing. In the Little House books, Ma teaches her girls to collaborate on such projects. For their first Dakota Christmas in *Silver Lake*, for example, they work together on gifts made from recycled materials. From the end of a worn blanket, Ma "cut bed shoes for Mary. Laura had made one, and Carrie the other, seaming and turning and finishing them neatly." From remnants of yarn, Laura and Mary knit striped mittens, one apiece, for Carrie. And, for "the most beautiful of all" the gifts, "they had all worked . . . to-

---

51. Lane, *Let the Hurricane Roar*, p. 152. Hill, *Laura Ingalls Wilder*, also noted the significance of this male child's gender, calling it a "poignant and revealing" change to Lane's "grandparents' story—and by extension, to her mother's and her own. Baby Charles . . . will someday inherit the future his parents envision for him" (p. 151).

52. Hill, *Laura Ingalls Wilder*, pp. 153–56, and William Holtz, *The Ghost in the Little House: A Life of Rose Wilder Lane* (Columbia: University of Missouri Press, 1993), pp. 239–40, provided contrasting accounts of this rift.

gether" on a tiny blue coat and hood for baby Grace, lining it with the downy skin of a swan shot by Pa (p. 176).

Collaboration has thus been an important part of these girls' female education in the Little House. But it has not always been easy, as the series also acknowledges. In *Little House on the Prairie,* when the fictional Laura and Mary are only six and eight, they each find a handful of pretty, glittering Indian beads. Ma proposes that they put them together and string them to make a necklace for baby Carrie. They agree, but not willingly, and Laura continues to resent having to contribute her individual treasures to a communal project. "Often after that Laura thought of those pretty beads and she was still naughty enough to want her beads for herself" (p. 181). Such possessiveness and resistance to a collaborative culture are "naughty," little Laura knows—but they are feelings that most children and adults know well, and which Wilder and Lane must both have been experiencing in the early 1930s. Wilder was beginning to formulate her plan for "writing the story of my childhood in several volumes," and Lane, buoyed by her first major success with a novel, "began sketching a plan for a massive, ten-volume work of fiction for which *Let the Hurricane Roar* would be the prelude."[53] Presumably, family stories would be a major source for both.

Wilder and Lane soon resumed their Little House collaboration, and their rift healed, at least partially. However, Lane, who had been living on her parents' farm (and contributing significantly to its support) since 1928, left the farm permanently in 1936 and did not return until her father's funeral in 1949. The collaboration continued by mail through the publication of the last Little House book in 1943. Lane never wrote her projected ten-volume novel, but she did write a second one, *Free Land,* based on family stories.[54] Her two family-inspired novels are widely considered her best fiction, and they produced regular royalties throughout her life.[55] In *Free Land*, Lane based her protagonist and primary point-of-view character, David Beaton, on her father, Almanzo Wilder. The novel begins on David's parents' prosperous family farm in Minnesota; young David takes a claim in Dakota and moves there with his new wife to begin life as a farmer.

Lane had already been much involved in the writing of her father's boyhood story, *Farmer Boy*, the second Little House novel. As she began this second "pioneer" novel of her own, Lane told her parents about the project and bombarded them—particularly Almanzo—with questions and quizzes

53. Holtz, *Ghost*, p. 240.
54. Lane, *Free Land* (New York: Longmans, Green & Co., 1938). Page numbers hereafter appear in the text.
55. Holtz, *Ghost*, p. 313.

about farming. They both complied and took an eager interest in the book's progress. Again, Lane drew on material from *Pioneer Girl*. For example, the memoir's story of a white settler's theft of a mummified Indian baby formed the basis for a long and highly dramatic episode that nearly provoked "another Minnesota massacre" (p. 112).[56] Like the alleged Bender family killings, also included in *Free Land*, this episode must have been another of the stories of death and danger (and cultural conflict) that Wilder felt she "could not tell" for children. Writing for adults, Lane felt free to include stories of death in a new prairie town. After a blizzard, David watches eight large boxes being loaded onto the train. A friend tells him "that the pine boxes contained a whole family, father, mother, and six children. . . . found frozen to death in their claim shanty" (p. 147). After another blizzard, David and his wife Mary attend the funeral of the first man buried in the town's new cemetery. During the outdoor service, as David holds his "apple-cheeked" and "laughing" year-old son, he thinks of his own death: "It was strange to know that some day new ropes would creak while men lowered another pine box into the earth, and David himself would be in it" (p. 235). Such close (and necessary) proximity of children and death is not acknowledged in the Little House books, in which there are no funerals.

Much of the stuff of Lane's 1938 novel—such as the vicissitudes of prairie farming and weather, the economics of railroad building, and the importance of horses to David and Mary—can be found in *Pioneer Girl* and is also prominent in the last four Little House books. Almanzo's homesteading sister, Eliza Jane, is a major character in *Free Land,* and she gets a fuller and more complex and sympathetic portrayal than in *Pioneer Girl* or *Little Town on the Prairie*, perhaps because Lane lived a year with her Aunt Eliza Jane in Louisiana while she finished high school there. Although her father and her Wilder grandparents are prominently portrayed in this novel, Lane also included a nuanced portrayal of her Ingalls grandparents as the Peters family. This middle-aged pioneer couple, with four children and yet another on the way, are living on the edge of poverty and disaster, but with hard work, cheer, and survival skills, they always manage to pull through. Like the Ingalls family, they have had to leave behind a claim in "Indian territory" and have also lived in Iowa. Mrs. Peters, "gentle and composed," with "gray streaks in her smooth brown hair and fine wrinkles across her patient forehead" (p. 23), strongly resembles Caroline Ingalls. Mr. Peters, like Charles Ingalls, must work in the eastern harvest to support his homesteading family. Lane described him as he returns: "The drive of harvest work in the east had worn

---

56. *See also* Wilder, *Pioneer Girl*, pp. 227, 229.

Mr. Peters down. He was thinner than ever, and footsore.... But he was in high spirits, his eyes an intense blue fire.... He went singing to get the oxen" (pp. 233-34). Here and elsewhere, Lane clearly based Mr. Peters on Pa Ingalls of *Pioneer Girl* and the Little House books. Lane emphasized the physical effects of aging and a hard life—gray hair, wrinkles, emaciation—on Mr. and Mrs. Peters, while the Little House books, with the exception of *The Long Winter*, are never explicit about such potentially alarming changes in Pa and Ma. And although David and Mary are close friends and neighbors with the Peters family, differences in social class are apparent and noted.

Perhaps Lane's most interesting revision of the family stories in *Free Land* is in David's wife. Almanzo Wilder's wife, of course, was Laura Ingalls, and we might expect Mary Beaton to resemble her. She does not. Mary comes from a neighboring Minnesota farm family, similarly prosperous; she and David have grown up together and are expected to marry. She is a loving, capable wife and mother, resembling the Caroline of *Let the Hurricane Roar*. But she is quite unlike the Laura of the Little House, who is mercurial, passionate, and fiercely loyal to her family of origin. The female character who has those qualities in abundance is the oldest Peters daughter, Nettie, who emerges from the slough grass when David is traveling in Dakota to file for his claim: "She was perhaps sixteen years old, and carried a rifle. Her hair, redder than a buckeye, hung in braids beside her cheeks ... and her thin face was as brown as an Indian's" (p. 23). Although the Little House Laura does not carry a gun or have red hair, this girl otherwise resembles Laura Ingalls as Almanzo first meets her in *The Long Winter*, when she and Carrie have gone on an unexpected errand to town in their everyday clothes and gotten lost in the tall grasses of the Big Slough.

David and Nettie bond immediately over horses, as do Laura and Almanzo. Like Laura, Nettie is hard-working, intelligent, and spirited; her ambition, like Laura's, is to become a schoolteacher so that she can help support her family. David, although newly engaged to Mary, is drawn to this girl in her worn and outgrown clothes. Her eyes are "filled with blue laughter. She was too thin, she was young, with a wildness in her, playful and awkward, like a colt's. Her mouth was fine and clear.... A man could not be blamed for knowing that some other man, some day, would kiss that mouth" (p. 24). During the Hard Winter, when David has sent Mary to stay with her parents until their first child is born and is staying with the Peters family, he and Nettie, holding hands on adjacent pallets, tentatively acknowledge a "bond, a loveliness, a special feeling between them." David "would not have anything different between him and Mary, his wife," he tries to tell Nettie. "'It's different, with you.... You're so—'" And she replies, "I know.... It's one of the things that don't happen" (p. 156). In constructing David, Nettie, and the Peters family, Lane made use of pieces of her family's stories, reassembling them to imagine an alternative world in which her father is happily married to a woman of his own class but is also powerfully drawn to an engaging girl/woman who greatly resembles her mother, Laura Ingalls, as she appears in the Little House books.

*Free Land* ends not with a portrait of a fractured, diminished frontier family, as we sometimes see in both *Pioneer Girl* and the Little House books, but with a reunion of three generations of the Beaton family. David's elderly parents come for an extended visit on his and Mary's homestead to inspect the property, get to know their two grandchildren, and give their approval of their son's homesteading project. As they get off the train, David recognizes the signs of his parents' aging for the first time; they are now "an elderly, stocky man" and "a plump, fussy, little elderly lady" (p. 325). David's father insists on helping him with haying and wheat harvesting, even though "his age was weighing down his steps, and he had a gold-headed cane which he often carried though protesting that he did not need one" (p. 327). His aging is portrayed as both comfortable and prosperous. Before leaving, David's father tells him of the division of property in his will and gives David a two-thousand-dollar advance on his inheritance to cover his debts on the homestead. In *Pioneer Girl* and the Little House books, no Ingalls or Quiner grandparents ever visit the Ingalls family or offer the financial assistance that is sometimes much needed. Almanzo Wilder's parents, however, did visit their son and his family during their early years on their Missouri farm and helped out with a (smaller) gift or legacy.[57] As she drew from her father's, as well as her mother's, family history for *Free Land*, Lane creatively expanded and altered her own legacy of family stories and avoided some of the constraints imposed by the Little House project in a novel (her best, in my opinion) for adult readers.

Laura Ingalls Wilder made a similar attempt in the 1930s. In 1937, she wrote to her editor: "For some time I have had in mind to try a story for grown-ups about the times I am writing of in the Little House books. I have the idea, but do not know if it will jell."[58] Such a manuscript, "The First Three Years and a Year of Grace," was among Wilder's papers that her daughter inherited after her death. Lane apparently never acknowledged the manuscript nor pursued publication of it; only after Lane's death in 1968 did her "adopted grandson," Roger Lea MacBride, seek to publish it. Retitled *The First Four Years*, this

---

57. Anderson, *Laura Ingalls Wilder*, p. 165.
58. Wilder to Louise Raymond, Dec. 13, 1937, in *Selected Letters*, p. 137.

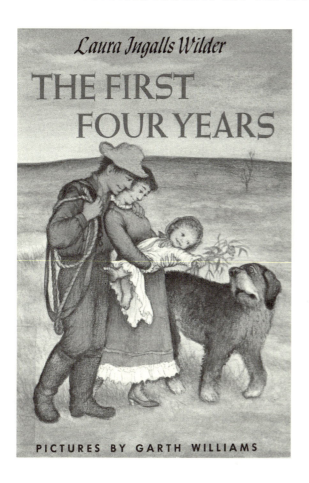

last book has ever since been marketed (erroneously, I think) as an addition to the Little House series and sold as the ninth volume in the boxed set of Little House books.

In *The First Four Years*, Wilder continued the story of Laura and Almanzo ("Manly") from the point where *These Happy Golden Years* ends. It begins with a brief and extremely romantic prologue, with "lovers . . . abroad in the still, sweet evenings." In the rose-scented prairie twilight, "a sweet contralto voice [presumably Laura's] rose softly" in a song that ends: "In the starlight, in the starlight,/We will wander gay and free."[59] Chapter 1 follows immediately, beginning with another view of the prairie: "It was a hot afternoon with

---

59. Wilder, *The First Four Years* (New York: Harper & Row, 1971), p. xx. Again, page numbers are hereafter given in the text. The song, "In the Starlight" (1843), with words by J. E. Carpenter, is the same one that Almanzo asks Laura to sing on the night he proposes to her in *These Happy Golden Years*, pp. 213–14. *See* Eugenia Garson, comp. and ed., *The Laura Ingalls Wilder Songbook: Favorite Songs from the "Little House" Books* (New York: Harper & Row, 1968), pp. 100–102.

a strong wind from the south," and such wind and heat "were to be expected: a natural part of life" (p. 1). No longer a "gay and free" evening for young lovers, it is a hot August workday, and Laura's fiancé is trying to persuade her to marry much earlier than planned in order to save money and so she will be on hand to help him with the coming harvest. The book veers immediately from romance to blunt practicality, and it offers two contrasting views of marriage. Laura now has doubts (which she never expressed in the last Little House book): "I've been thinking.... I don't want to marry a farmer. ... a farm is such a hard place for a woman.... Besides a farmer never has any money" (pp. 3–4). Almanzo proposes that they try farming (in which he has already heavily invested his time, work, and money) for three years, and if they have not "made a success" by then, "we will quit farming" (pp. 5–6). Laura consents.

At the end of *These Happy Golden Years,* Wilder signaled that her child readers would not be returning to the Little House in any additional books, and we are left wondering if Laura really can, as she wishes, have two homes, two iconic Little Houses, as a married woman. These are questions for an adult reader, and Wilder wrestled with them in *The First Four Years.* Despite the homesickness she anticipated, Laura does not return to her nearby former home during the first five months of her marriage, nor do her parents or sisters visit her and Almanzo in the small house he has built for them. Instead, Laura is immediately immersed in the unfamiliar rhythms of farm life—in fact, she must cook a large dinner for threshers with only a few hours' notice on the second day of her marriage. (Some culinary disasters ensue.) Almanzo was a "farmer boy," and his ambition has always been to farm. But Laura "had always been a pioneer girl rather than a farmer's daughter," and her frontier family was "always moving on to new places before the fields grew large" (p. 18). In characterizing her father for Lane, Wilder described him not as a farmer but as "a hunter and trapper, a musician and poet."[60] Life as a farmer's wife requires major adjustments for the Laura of *The First Four Years.*

Laura finds married life satisfying in the first months. The novel is never sexually explicit, but—as in the Little House books—Laura and Almanzo's sexual attraction and compatibility are implied in their mutual passion for horses. The "gay and free" times of this book's romantic prologue are suggested by the newlyweds' pony rides together, often "a twenty-mile ride over the open prairie before breakfast. It was a carefree, happy time, for two people thoroughly in sympathy can do pretty much as they like" (p. 27). Clearly, there is only one little house in Laura's new married life. "Laura was never

---

60. Wilder to Lane, Mar. 23, 1937, in *Selected Letters,* p. 121.

lonely. She loved her little house and the housework" (p. 44). Nevertheless, the first fall harvest is slim, and as debts and mortgages increase, so do Laura's worries. When they must mortgage Skip and Barnum, the horses that facilitated Laura and Almanzo's courtship in the series, the happy times of the new marriage seem threatened. Laura would "almost as soon have had a mortgage on Manly" (pp. 50, 52).

In early spring, Laura finds herself pregnant. No joy accompanies this discovery. For months, she suffers severe and constant nausea, but no one suggests that this should curtail her responsibilities as farm wife. Determined not to "shirk," Laura is soon "creeping around the house, doing what must be done.... As she went so miserably about her work ... she remembered a saying of her mother's: 'They that dance must pay the fiddler.' Well, she was paying, but she would do the work" (pp. 46–47). Ma of the Little House books, of course, also always did the work, apparently unhampered by her invisible pregnancies. For the first time in this novel, Laura remembers one of the maxims in which her mother often spoke, and her interpretation is that sexual pleasure has a price that she is now paying. She is too ill to drive with Almanzo over the greening spring prairie, "but when wild rose time came in June she was able to ride behind Skip and Barnum along the country roads where the prairie roses" fill the air with "their sweetness." On one drive, Laura proposes a name for their baby: "It will be a girl and we will call her Rose" (pp. 47–48). This scene briefly restores the romance of the novel's prologue and includes the coming child in it. But soon Laura, weak and "emaciated" because she cannot "retain her food for more than a few minutes" (p. 52), is worrying again about money and wishing they could afford to hire someone to do housework and cooking. Shortly thereafter, the entire wheat crop is lost to a hailstorm, and Laura, who has been dreading cooking for the now unneeded threshers, thinks of another of her mother's maxims: "As Ma used to say, 'There is no great loss without some small gain.' That she should think of so small a gain bothered Laura" (p. 56).

In the Little House books, which include some great losses, Ma specializes in small and saving gains. When the family is nearly without food in *The Long Winter*, for example, she brings out a hidden piece of a salt codfish and uses it to make gravy. "'Just the smell of it chirks a fellow up,' Pa said. 'Caroline, you are a wonder'" (p. 254). Even in extremity, Pa's praise (and the daughters' admiration) validates Ma's efforts and confirms that her smallest gain is a "wonder." But Laura, in her new role as farmer's wife, is impatient with a life of small gains. And her mother's maxims now seem joyless and trivial. When Laura goes into long and painful labor in December, we see Ma in her daughter's house for the first time; strangely, we have not seen her advising or assisting Laura during her pregnancy. Ma and a townswoman and doctor deliver baby Rose—a large gain, at last.

After a few days of care from Ma and a hired girl, Laura, Almanzo, and Rose are "left by themselves in the little house . . . with the sweep of the empty prairie all around it" (p. 72). Although the small new family is happy, their home now seems more isolated and lonely to Laura, and she longs for her "home folks" as she has not before. On Christmas, it is too cold and stormy to join the Ingalls family for their traditional celebration, but a few days later, the weather is better, and Laura and Almanzo take Rose, only three weeks old, for a visit. Her parents greet them with alarm: "'You're crazy!' Pa said. . . 'it is fifteen below.' . . . 'She might have smothered,' Ma added. . . . Laura had never thought it might be dangerous to take the baby out. . . . It seemed there was a good deal to taking care of babies" (pp. 74–75). The baby's presence narrows Laura's horizons even more and limits where she can go—just as in the Ingalls family, Pa ranged over great distances, but Ma remained with her daughters in or near the Little House. Laura and Almanzo both delight in their new daughter, and although Laura recognizes that they can make errors of judgment, they devise ways to reduce constrictions of parenthood that Ma accepts. Almanzo installs a sturdy box in their road-cart, and with Barnum hitched to the cart and little Rose sitting in the box, Laura "would drive away wherever she cared to go," usually "to see her Ma and the girls. At first Ma was afraid to have Rose travel that way, but soon she became used to it." With Rose safe in the cart, Laura "never had a moment's uneasiness," and she is reestablishing her Little House family connections and including her daughter in them. Manly approves; he "didn't care how often she went, just so she came home in time to get supper" (pp. 81–82). When Rose is a little older and is sleeping soundly in bed, her parents also reestablish their pattern of nighttime prairie rides: they "came to saddling the ponies and riding them . . . on the run for a half mile south and back, . . . a pause to see that Rose was still sleeping," then repeating this routine "until ponies and riders were both ready to stop" (p. 93).

The three-year farming experiment stretches to four years, and those years are full of disasters (all of which the actual Wilders experienced). More crops fail; more debts and mortgages accrue. Manly's original, proved-up claim is lost, and only his tree claim and the house on it remain. Laura and Almanzo contract diphtheria, and he is left permanently lame. Another child—a boy—is born and dies suddenly, "taken with spasms," three weeks later (p. 127). That same month, when Laura starts a fire of hay to cook supper, it rages out of control, the house burns, and—although Laura and Rose escape—almost all possessions are lost. On the last pages of the book, the little family is re-established in a flimsy tar-papered shanty "near the ruins of their house" (p. 131). Laura asks her husband, "Was farming a success?" Four years, and they are "making a fresh start with nothing" (pp. 132-33). Laura would be within her rights to declare this experiment a failure. But she does not.

*The First Four Years* is clearly an unfinished, unrevised experimental text. What has Wilder accomplished in it? She has begun to write stories that she could not include in a children's series, including death, pregnancy and childbirth, and a young woman's adjustments to the new circumstances and challenges of marriage and parenthood. In the Little House books and *Pioneer Girl*, Charles and Caroline Ingalls raised their daughters in mobile frontier circumstances, far from their own families of origin. But their daughter Laura, in this last book, launches her married life near her parents and must constantly negotiate what she wants to retain of her Little House childhood and how she will invent another kind of life for herself, her husband, and her child. In many ways, her story is like that of Persephone, which critic Marianne Hirsch proposed as the typical modernist mother/daughter plot. Persephone shuttles back and forth in a "repeated cycle" between her fruitful mother, Demeter, and her husband, alternating a passionate maternal attachment with "the anxieties which shape the heterosexual plot" of her marriage.[61] Thus, we see the newly married Laura keeping her distance from her parents' home as she explores the possibilities of her marriage, then being drawn powerfully back to it—and especially to her mother and sisters—when she becomes a mother herself. At moments of crisis—when she is recovering from burns after the fire or when Rose needs to be kept away from diphtheria—Laura and her daughter return to the original Little House for safety and healing. But after that respite, Manly, like Persephone's husband, always comes for her; he never stays at the Ingalls house. At the end of the last Little House book, the newly married Laura thinks she can both "make the new home" and keep the old. But, as *The First Four Years* confirms, she cannot.

At this novel's end, Laura identifies herself as "still the pioneer girl" who holds her pioneer ancestors' creed "that 'it is better farther on,'" which governed the movement of her frontier family throughout the Little House series. But she redefines that creed: "instead of farther on in space, it was farther on in time, over the horizon of the years ahead instead of the far horizon of the west" (p. 134). Almanzo understands; he is a farmer, committed to the temporal potential of a particular piece of land. Throughout this novel, he repeats his belief in the promise of time, "surely next year would be a good

---

61. Hirsch, *The Mother/Daughter Plot: Narrative, Psychoanalysis, Feminism* (Bloomington: Indiana University Press, 1989), pp. 102-4.

crop year" (p. 132). In the Little House series, young Laura shares her father's enthusiasm for the frontier possibilities "farther on" in space; they both long to go to Oregon. The real farmer in the Ingalls family is Ma. In *Little Town on the Prairie,* when she gets her first flock of young chickens (the traditional specialty of farm women)[62] and begins to teach her daughters how to raise them, she looks out over the planted fields of the Ingalls claim—still not proved up—and says to Laura with a deep satisfaction that Pa never expresses, "The place begins to look like a farm" (p. 61). Ma is like Demeter, the Greek goddess of agriculture, who never moves. Persephone must always go to her—and then leave her. Ma is the reason that the Ingalls family remains in De Smet, putting down roots there, just as the actual Almanzo and Laura Wilder remained on their Missouri farm together for fifty-five years. As *The First Four Years* ends and Laura commits to a farmer's life, she has become a "pioneer girl" in the style of her mother, not her father.

The *Pioneer Girl* manuscript offered both Wilder and Lane materials for a long shelf of books. We have seen how they picked and chose and revised and augmented and fictionalized those materials in their fiction. With the meticulously documented published edition of *Pioneer Girl* in hand, we can better recognize and understand the choices they made. Most of us would agree that the most stunning and durable success of both women's writing careers is the Little House series, which has been an important and indispensable part of so many American lives. Why do we need a constructed Little House where nobody dies, especially since *Pioneer Girl* reminds us of how many people did die or were lost or damaged or forgotten in the world where Laura Ingalls grew up? I think it is because we need to know how a fragile frontier family, on the road with limited resources and unlimited hard times, manages to create a portable safe space where children can grow into full and fruitful humanity, strong enough to deal with all the various and uncensored stories that life is going to thrust before them. Wilder and Lane knew those stories, and they wrote many of them. But their masterwork, the Little House, is always there, a cherished place where we can go if we need it. And we will.

---

62. Significantly, when Laura Ingalls Wilder began to attract attention and eventually a *Missouri Ruralist* readership as an outstanding Missouri farm woman, it was through her unusual success in raising chickens. Anderson, *Laura Ingalls Wilder,* p. 176.

# CONTRIBUTORS

WILLIAM ANDERSON had Norwegian ancestors who homesteaded in Dakota Territory in 1880, a century before he became active in developments at the Laura Ingalls Wilder Memorial Society in De Smet, South Dakota, and the Wilder Home and Museum in Mansfield, Missouri. Anderson's research on Ingalls and Wilder history has produced many books, including *Laura Ingalls Wilder Country*, *Laura Ingalls Wilder: A Biography*, and *The Selected Letters of Laura Ingalls Wilder*. Other historical and biographical works include *M Is for Mount Rushmore*, *The World of the Trapp Family*, and *River Boy: The Story of Mark Twain*. Anderson combines a career in writing, teaching, and speaking.

CAROLINE FRASER is the editor of the Library of America's two-volume edition of Laura Ingalls Wilder's Little House books and has written on Wilder and other topics for the *New Yorker*, *New York Review of Books*, *London Review of Books*, *Atlantic*, and other publications. She holds a Ph.D. in literature from Harvard University and is the author of two non-fiction works as well as the forthcoming historical biography, *Prairie Fires: The American Dreams of Laura Ingalls Wilder*. She lives in Santa Fe, New Mexico.

MICHAEL PATRICK HEARN is a freelance writer and independent scholar living in New York City. His many books include *The Annotated Wizard of Oz*, *The Annotated Christmas Carol*, *The Annotated Huckleberry Finn*, and *The Victorian Fairy Tale Book*. He has taught at Brooklyn College, Columbia University, Queens College, and Simmons College. Hearn has lectured throughout the United States and Europe and has curated several important exhibitions concerning children's books and their illustrators.

ELIZABETH JAMESON is a professor of history at the University of Calgary and a historian of women in the North American West. She is the co-editor (with Susan Armitage) of *The Women's West* and *Writing the Range: Race, Class, and Gender in the Women's West* and (with Sheila McManus) of *One Step over the Line: Toward a History of Women in the North American Wests*. She served as president of the Western History Association and of the Pacific Coast Branch-American Historical Association. She thanks the Herbert Hoover Presidential Library Association and the Imperial Oil-Lincoln McKay Chair in American Studies at the University of Calgary for supporting her work on the essay in this volume.

SALLIE KETCHAM is the author of *Laura Ingalls Wilder: American Writer on the Prairie* (Routledge, 2014) and two critically acclaimed books for children. She has been featured as an instructor and lecturer on the history of children's books at The Loft Literary Center in Minneapolis, Minnesota, and most recently as a presenter at the 2015 Laura Ingalls Wilder Legacy and Research Association Conference in Brookings, South Dakota.

NANCY TYSTAD KOUPAL is director and editor-in-chief of the Pioneer Girl Project and the South Dakota Historical Society Press. She received an M.A. in English from Morehead State University in Kentucky and did postgraduate work in American literature at the University of Wisconsin, Madison. She edited the journal *South Dakota History* for over thirty-five years and founded the South Dakota Historical Society Press in 1997. Koupal is also the editor and annotator of *Our Landlady* (Lincoln: University of Nebraska Press, 1996), a collection of L. Frank Baum's satirical newspaper columns.

AMY MATTSON LAUTERS, a Wisconsin native, grew up in close proximity to many of Laura Ingalls Wilder's little towns, and an early childhood acquaintance with Wilder's Wisconsin family fed a lifelong interest in the author. A former journalist and freelance web designer, Lauters earned a doctorate in mass communications with an emphasis in American Studies from the University of Minnesota in 2005. She has published two books: *The Rediscovered Writings of Rose Wilder Lane, Literary Journalist* (2007) and *More than a Farmer's Wife: Voices of American Farm Women, 1910–1960* (2009). She currently serves as the chair of the Department of Mass Media at Minnesota State University, Mankato.

JOHN E. MILLER is a historian from Brookings, South Dakota. He received his B.A. in history from the University of Missouri and his M.A. and Ph.D. degrees in history from the University of Wisconsin. Miller taught twentieth-century American history and other history courses at the University of Tulsa and at South Dakota State University for thirty years before becoming a full-time writer in 2003. Among his eight books are *Looking for History on Highway 14*, *Small-Town Dreams: Stories of Midwestern Boys Who Shaped America*, and three books on Laura Ingalls Wilder: *Laura Ingalls Wilder's Little Town: Where History and Literature Meet*; *Becoming Laura Ingalls Wilder: The Woman behind the Legend*; and *Laura Ingalls Wilder and Rose Wilder Lane: Authorship, Place, Time, and Culture*.

PAULA M. NELSON is professor emeritus in the Department of History at the University of Wisconsin-Platteville, where she taught for twenty-six years. Her research interests include agricultural settlement in the Great Plains and upper Midwest, rural life and culture, rural women's history, and small towns. Nelson is the author of *After the West Was Won* and *The Prairie Winnows Out Its Own*, books about homesteading and agriculture in West River South Dakota, and the editor of *Sunshine Always*, a book of courtship letters from Dakota territorial days. She has also written numerous articles, essays, and book reviews. Although Nelson lives in Platteville, Wisconsin, South Dakota is the home of her heart. She credits Laura Ingalls Wilder for her deep attachment to the prairie.

ANN ROMINES grew up in the Missouri Ozarks, about fifty miles from the Wilders' Rocky Ridge Farm, and meeting her favorite author, Laura Ingalls Wilder, at a bookstore signing event was a great moment in her childhood. Romines grew up to be a professor of American literature at George Washington University, with a special interest in American women's writing. She is the author and editor of several books, including *The Home Plot: Women, Writing, and Domestic Ritual*, *Willa Cather's Southern Connections*, and *At Willa Cather's Tables: The Cather Foundation Cookbook*, as well as numerous essays. In the 1990s, she spent several years immersed in Little House sites and archival materials, fulfilling a childhood dream. The resultant book, *Constructing the Little House: Gender, Culture, and Laura Ingalls Wilder*, received the Children's Literature Association's 1997 award for best scholarly book on children's literature. Romines retired from her university professorship in 2015 and is active in the work of the Willa Cather Foundation.

NOEL L. SILVERMAN is an attorney specializing in copyright and literary property for more than fifty years. He graduated magna cum laude from Brown University and Harvard Law School and has been active in the Copyright Society of the United States of America, Association of the Bar of the City of New York, and presently serves on the board of the Jazz Gallery, a New York nonprofit that provides opportunities to up-and-coming musicians. Silverman began representing Roger MacBride, who had inherited the rights to Laura Ingalls Wilder's works as well as those of Rose Wilder Lane, shortly after Lane's death in 1968. Following MacBride's death in 1995, his daughter Abigail assigned all of the copyrighted literary property she had inherited from her father to the Little House Heritage Trust, which Silverman has represented since that time.

LAURA INGALLS WILDER (1867–1957) finished her autobiography, *Pioneer Girl*, in 1930 when she was sixty-three years old. Throughout the 1930s and into the 1940s, she utilized her original manuscript to write a successful series of books for young readers. Her daughter, journalist Rose Wilder Lane, served as her editor and borrowed from her mother's life story to write two novels of her own. *Pioneer Girl*, which chronicles sixteen years of Wilder's pioneer youth, is where all the stories begin. Wilder died in Mansfield, Missouri, at ninety years of age on February 10, 1957.

# INDEX

Page numbers in italics refer to figures; those followed by n refer to notes.

Albert, Susan Wittig, 104–5
Alcott, Louisa May, 116, 122
Alfred A. Knopf publishers, and Little House series, 109, 110
American Civil Liberties Union, 66
American Indians: Dunn and, 161; Erdrich's *The Birchbark House* and, 132–33; in Little House series, 131–32, 210–11, 216–17, 222, 254–55; Turner's erasure from frontier, 239
American Library Association, Laura Ingalls Wilder Award, 127–28
Anderson, William, 1, *82*, 88–90, 98–101, 210, 272
anti-suffragists: arguments made by, 183, 185, 189, 192–95; critiques of, 191–92; rejection of equality as sameness, 194–95, 198

balance, Wilder on, 175
*Bambi* (Salten), 217, 218
Baum, L. Frank, 108, 111, 127
Beatty, Bessie, 22, 54, 55
Bender family murders, 38–40; in Detroit book fair speech, 11, 16–17, 47–48; in draft of *Little House on the Prairie*, 44; flight and pursuit following, 40, 40nn71, 73, *41*, 42–43; Lane's additions to story, 43–44, 46–47; Lane's use of, 37–38, 43–44, 121; Wilder's imperfect memory of, 121; Wilder's omission of, 16–17, 48, 121, 275; yellow press stories on, 40–43, 44

Berger, John, 222–23
Bettelheim, Bruno, 213, 221, 229–30
Biddle, Francis, 65
Bignell, Allan, 88, *89*
Bignell, Sheila, 87–92, *89*, 93
biographies, fictionalized, as genre: Lane and, 33–37, 114; Wilder's stories and, 119–20
*The Birchbark House* (Erdrich), 132–33
Bly, Nellie, 28–29
Bouchie (Brewster) family, 249–53
Boyle, Mildred, 123, 127
Boylston, Helen, 56
Brandt, Carl, 37, 109, 231, 231n1
Brewster (Bouchie) family, 249–53
Brown, D. K., 65–66
Brown, Edward, 273n17
Burr Oak, Iowa: employment in, 242–43, 242n22; Ingalls family in, 93, 147, 243–44, 276; omission from Little House stories, 121, 224, 241, 276–77
Bye, George T., 81, 100, 110, 129, 131, 231, 231n1
*By the Shores of Silver Lake* (Wilder): on Dakota homestead rush, 164; on death of Jack the bulldog, 278–81; Grace Ingalls birth in, 277; and historical fiction as genre, 120, 121; inclusion of adult-themed stories

{ 305 }

in, 248–49, 255; Lane's editing of, 280–81; old people in, 274; scarlet fever in, 287; style of, 116; technological change in, 235; Wilder and Lane's debate on opening of, 117, 280–81, 287; and women's work, 290–91

Cameron, Eleanor, 113, 116, 118
Campbell, Joseph, 213, 214–15
Carpenter, Martha Quiner (aunt), 226, 285, 286
Cather, Willa, 165, 165–67
Chaplin, Charlie, Lane biography of, 33–34, 114
characters in Little House series, 169–70
Charbo, Eileen, 85–86, 87
*Charlotte's Web* (White), 127, 131
Chesterton, G. K., 213
Chicago & North Western Railroad, 168–69
Childhoods of Famous Americans series (Bobbs-Merrill), 114
*Children's and Household Tales* (Grimm brothers), 213
Civil War, and sectional differences, 148
Clement, Margaret, 92–93
Commission on Country Life, 182
community: Caroline Ingalls and, 153, 240, 256–58, 260–61; Charles Ingalls and, 153, 241, 260–62; frontier tension between individualism and, 163, 167, 199, 263; human interdependence in Little House series, 140–41; Laura's discomfort in town, 260; and midwestern culture, 170–71; in *Pioneer Girl* (Wilder), 246–47; Wilder in Mansfield, Mo., 153, 171, 188. *See also* small towns
Conzen, Kathleen Neils, 150–51
*Country Gentleman* magazine, Wilder's writing for, 105
coverture concept, and women's role, 186
"Credo" (Lane), 233
Crevecoeur, Hector St. John de, 155–56

Dakota Territory: and Homestead Act of 1862, 162–64; Wilder and husband in, 21, 157; and woman suffrage movement, 5, 183. *See also* De Smet, S.Dak.
"Declaration of Sentiments" (Seneca Falls Convention), 189–90
De Smet, S.Dak.: Charles Ingalls in, 258–59, 261, 262; and community focus, 171; as frontier, 153, 163, 249, 272–73n16; Ingalls family in, 237, 246–48, 257–58; population of, 272n16; setbacks suffered by Wilder family in, 179, 237, 269, 298–99; as typical midwestern town, 168–69; Wilder as witness to, 167, 170, 270, 272. *See also The First Four Years*
*De Smet Leader*, 249
Detroit book fair (1937), 9, 10; Wilder's speech at, 9–19, 12, 47–49, 121, 145, 275, 281, 288
*The Discovery of Freedom* (Lane), 59, 68, 233
*Diverging Roads* (Lane), 54
Dunn, Harvey, 157–61, 158, 160

"Ed Monroe, Man-Hunter" (Lane), 31–32
Einstein, Albert, 212–13

*Elementary English*, articles on Wilder in, 86–88

fairy tales: American, characteristics of, 213–14; Bettelheim on, 229–30; deaths of animals in, 218; elements of in Little House series, 209–30; framing features of, 221–24; magic of nature in, 219–20; modern versions of, purging of dark elements from, 212–13; as oral tradition, and mnemonic prompts, 220; socializing function of, 221; underlying truth in, 212–13; Wilder's interest in, 223–24; woods in, 214–15, 227, 228, 229

*Far from Home* (Schlissel), 265–67

*Farmer Boy* (Wilder): decision to write, 14; Lane's work on, 291; payment for, 129; revisions of, 115

farm wives: Wilder as, 11, 103–5, 180; Wilder on life of, 200–202

Federal Bureau of Investigation (FBI): investigation of Lane, 59–67; Lane's criticism of, 60, *60*, 61, 63–67

Federated Women's Clubs, 191

Fellman, Anita Clair, 171n55, 211, 221

feminist scholars: on Little House series, 211; on stereotype of reluctant pioneer women, 251

Fern, Fanny, 42n80

Fiery, Marion, 109, 110, 226

*The First Four Years* (Wilder), 81, 95, 294–300, *295*

"The First Three Years and a Year of Grace" (Wilder), 81, 294. See also *The First Four Years*

Foner, Eric, 190

Forbes, Docia Ingalls (aunt), 264

Ford, Henry, Lane biography of, 33, 34, 114

Fraser, Caroline, 217, 221

*Free Land* (Lane), 58, 81, 110, 121, 137, 291–94

frontier: family and, 265–70; Frederick Jackson Turner on, 174–75, 214, 236, 238–39; Laura's views on, 258, 299–300; as locus of cultural contact, 271, 271n12; Ma Ingalls's views on, 256–58; myths of, 107–8, 212, 240, 262–63; and tension between individualism and community, 163, 167, 199; Wilder's views on, 13, 13n8, 17–18, 163; women on, 248–49

Garland, Hamlin, 108

*The Ghost in the Little House* (Holtz), 90, 104, 211

*Give Me Liberty* (Lane), 233

Goldberg, Rube, 31

*Golden Thoughts on Mother, Home, and Heaven* (1882), 177–79, *178*

*Good Housekeeping*: Lane's writing for, 57–58; rejection of *Pioneer Girl*, 109

Good Templars, 187, 188, 244

government: Lane on freedom from, 59, 63–64, 70, 72–75; Pa Ingalls's views on, 262; progressivism and, 180–81, 191; need for, 263; southern Midwest culture and, 153; Wilder's views on, 199, 211, 221, 232, 239, 263. *See also* Federal Bureau of Investigation; individualism; self-reliance

Grafton, Samuel, 59, 62, 64

grasshopper plague: in Lane's fiction, 288; Wilder on, 15, 257, 275–76

Great Dakota Boom, 162–63

Great Depression, and *Little House in the Big Woods*, 212
Greeley, Horace, 107
Grimm Brothers, 213

Harper & Brothers: brochure, 84–85, *85*; and *Little House in the Big Woods*, 110, 114–15, 227–28; Wilder's editors at, 124; Wilder's payment from, 129
Harper & Row: and historical accuracy of Wilder's novels, 85–86; Little House Publishing Program, 100–101; and *Pioneer Girl*, 99–100; and sales of Little House series, 129–31
HarperCollins, and *Pioneer Girl*, 100–101
Hearst, William Randolph, 23; background of, 24; Older and, 31; and Spanish-American War, 27–28; and yellow journalism, 24–26
Herbert Hoover Presidential Library: donation of Wilder-Lane documents to, 96–98; Wilder-Lane documents in, 1, 9, 52, 82
Hill, Pamela Smith: biography of Wilder, 101; on Lane's *Let the Hurricane Roar*, 289; and *Pioneer Girl: The Annotated Autobiography* project, 1, 2, 80, 101–2; on Wilder as novelist, 105
historians: and midwestern history, 148–49
Holbrook, Charlotte Tucker Quiner. *See* Quiner, Charlotte Tucker
Holtz, William V., 35, 90, 104, 211
Homestead Act (1862), 162; Wilder on, 239; women's right under, 251–53

homesteading: Cather on, 165–67; and midwestern culture, 162–67; Wilder on, 163–64
"A Homey Chat for Mothers" (Wilder), 202
Hoover, Herbert, Lane biography of, 36–37, 96
Hoover, J. Edgar, 61, 65–66

illustrations for Little House books, 122–27, *123*, *126*, 216, 227, 227–29, *234*, *278*. *See also* Boyle, Mildred; Sewell, Helen; Williams, Garth
individualism: community and, 163, 167, 199; Lane's belief in, 68, 70–75, 159n30; as theme in Little House series, 221; Turner on, 239; Wilder's belief in, 75, 159n30, 170–71, 199. *See also* self-reliance
industrialization, and women's role, 186
Ingalls, Caroline Lake Quiner (mother), *240*, *265*, *285*; as avid reader, 224; and Bender murders, 17; death of, 272, 277, 279, 282, 284, 288; desire to remain in community, 240, 260–61; income of, 260; lessons in unselfishness by, 203–4; and married life, 268–69; and Mary, 285–86; parents of, 268; in *Pioneer Girl* vs. Little House series, 256–58, 260–61; protection of children from unsuitable stories, 254, 275; resourcefulness of, 297; and socialization of Ingalls daughters, 173; and temperance movement, 187–88; Wilder and, 12, 13, 226, 284–86
Ingalls, Carrie (sister), 188, *259*, *265*
Ingalls, Charles Frederick (brother):

death of, 275–76; omission from novels, 121, 224, 276–77
Ingalls, Charles Philip (father), 252, 265; and Bender murders, 17, 43–44, 46, 47, 121, 275; and community, 241; death of, 260, 272; desire to follow frontier, 15, 107, 235, 240, 256–59, 261; De Smet lots purchased by, 167; efforts at farming, 157; marriage, 268; music and stories by, 11, 13, 18–19, 103–4, 281–82; parents of, 268–69; in *Pioneer Girl* vs. Little House series, 258–59, 261–62; and socialization of Ingalls daughters, 172–73; Wilder on, 11, 12–13, 17, 18–19, 202–3
Ingalls, Eliza (aunt), 276
Ingalls, Grace (sister), 188, 265
Ingalls, John J. (distant cousin), 27
Ingalls, Lansford Whiting (grandfather), 220, 268–69, 270, 272
Ingalls, Laura Louise Colby (grandmother), 268–69, 270, 272
Ingalls, Mary (sister), 265; awareness of Bender murders, 17; death of, 282; illness and blindness of, 121–22, 138, 173, 243, 257, 258, 287; at Iowa College for the Blind, 239, 239n17, 247; later life of, 285–86
Ingalls, Peter (uncle), 276
Ingalls family, 265; daughters of, 266–67, 283, 288, 300; economic insecurity of, 234–35, 263; extended family, 268–72, 277, 281; nuclear family, 264–67; peripatetic life of, 179, 269, 277; Wilder's idealization of, 49, 51, 253–54, 267–68
*The Ingalls Family from Plum Creek to Walnut Grove via Burr Oak* (Lichty), 93–94

"Intimate Immensity" (Rosenblum), 229
Irwin, Will, 24, 29, 36–37

Jack the bulldog, 278; death of, 277–80, 281
Jameson, Elizabeth, 179
journalism: ethics and schools, 28. *See also* yellow journalism

Kansas, Ingallses in, 84–86
Kaye, Frances W., 210–11
Kerber, Linda K., 185–86
Kiewit, Fred, 104, 129
*Kinder und Hausmärchen* (Grimm brothers), 213
Kirkus, Virginia, 49–50, 110, 112, 114–15, 122, 212
Koupal, Nancy Tystad: and *Pioneer Girl: The Annotated Autobiography* project, 2–3, 79, 101–2; on Wilder scholarship, 87

*Ladies Home Journal*, 57, 109, 114
*Ladies of the Press* (Ross), 55–56
Lane, Claire Gillette (son-in-law): career of, 31, 54–55; financial woes of, 22, 23; marriage to Rose Wilder, 20, 53, 54
Lane, Rose Wilder (daughter), 30, 63, 232; as avid reader, 224; and Bender murders, 37–38, 43–47, 121; on childhood, 231, 233; chronic depression of, 54, 57–58; death of, 93; death of parents and, 67; and family financial woes, 22–23, 80; FBI investigation of, 59–67; as journalist, 20–37, 51, 53–56; marriage, 20, 53–54; in Paris (1920s), 56–57; and Paterson, 45, 45n89; patho-

logical lying by, 50; as pioneering woman, 53–54; political opinions of, 58–59, 63–64, 171n55, 232–33, 239, 289; as professional writer, 14n9, 30, 33–37, 52–59, 67–68, 76, 80, 112, 114, 129, 290, 291; range of opinions on, 52; and scholarship on Wilder, 88, 90–92; stillborn son of, 35, 54, 276–77, 283; and stock market crash (1929), 57, 80, 109; use of mother's stories, 34–35, 81, 109, 110, 226, 283, 288–90, 292–94; and Wilder's early writing, 105–7, 109–10, 226; on Wilder's life, 10–11, 84, 188; and Wilder's plan for novel series, 14n9, 15n11; Wilder's works as influence on, 14n9, 58. *See also* Lane, Rose Wilder, works by

Lane, Rose Wilder, and Little House series: as editor, 19n15, 45–47, 47n82, 58, 84, 104, 109, 117–18, 129, 137–38, 225, 280–82; efforts to find publisher for, 109–10, 226; illustrations for, 124; insistence on truth of, 48–49, 50, 86, 87, 93, 209–10; knowledge of Wilder's plan for, 119–20; rumored authorship of, 104–5, 112, 137, 211

Lane, Rose Wilder, and *Pioneer Girl*: editing of, 37–38, 43–44, 109, 225–26, 232–33; effort to publish, 231n1; suppression of manuscript, 86; use of stories from, 34–35, 81, 109, 110, 226, 283, 288–90, 292–94

Lane, Rose Wilder, works by: "Credo," 233; *The Discovery of Freedom*, 59, 68, 233; *Diverging Roads*, 54; "Ed Monroe, Man-Hunter," 31–32; *Free Land*, 58, 81, 110, 121, 137, 291–94; *Give Me Liberty*, 233; *Let the Hurricane Roar*, 14n9, 58, 110, 137, 288–90; "What Is This–The Gestapo?," 60, 60, 65; "Yarbwoman," 57. *See also Woman's Day Book of American Needlework*

*Laura: The Life of Laura Ingalls Wilder* (Zochert), 94–96

*Laura Ingalls Wilder: A Biography* (Anderson), 97

*Laura Ingalls Wilder: A Writer's Life* (Hill), 101

"Laura Ingalls Wilder and the Little House Books" (Smith), 90

Laura Ingalls Wilder Award, 127–28

Laura Ingalls Wilder Home and Museum, 82; Hill and Koupal visit, 2, 102; preservation of documents by, 94, 96–98; Wilder manuscripts found in, 2, 3, 81. *See also* Lichty, Irene; Lichty, Lewis

Laura Ingalls Wilder Home Association: formation of, 81; Wilder manuscripts possessed by, 81–82

Lerner, Max, 167–68

*Let the Hurricane Roar* (Lane), 14n9, 58, 110, 137, 288–90

"Let Us Be Just" (Wilder), 202–3

Lewis, R. W. B., 167

Lewis, Sinclair, 172

Lichty, Irene, 82; booklet on Ingalls family life, 93–94; and defense of Wilder's reputation, 84, 90–93, 94; donation of documents to Hoover Presidential Library, 97; friendship with Wilder, 83; and scholarship on Wilder, 94–95; and Wilder Home and Museum, 81, 82–84, 94; and Wilder manuscripts, 82

Lichty, Lewis: booklet on Ingalls family life, 93–94; death of, 94; and defense of Wilder's reputation, 84, 92, 94; and Wilder Home and Museum, 81, 82–84

Lipson, Eden Ross, 133–34

"The Literary Apprenticeship of Laura Ingalls Wilder" (Anderson), 1

literary awards, Wilder and, 127–28

*Little House, Long Shadow* (Fellman), 211, 221

*The Little House Cookbook* (Walker), 92

Little House Heritage Trust, 2, 101, 135

*Little House in the Big Woods* (Wilder): "Dance at Grandpa's," 219, 270; efforts to publish, 109–10, 226; ending of, 230; erasure of American Indian presence in, 216–17, 254–55n56; extended family in, 270–71; fairy tale elements in, 209, 215–20, 222–23, 227, 228, 230; folklore details in, 226–27; "Grandma" as original narrator of, 281–82; illustrations in, 122, *123*, 125, *234*; killing of animals in, 217–19; Lane's editing of, 37–38, 109, 225–26; Laura's doll Charlotte in, 286–87; Laura's unjust spanking in, 202–3; limited editing by publisher, 112; literary influences on, 224–25; on Ma's skills, 286–87; moral lessons in, 113; and public's desire for more books, 13; racism in, 131–32, 220; reviews of, 115; storytelling in, 282; style of, 110–12; technological change in, 235; timing of release and, 107–8, 212; Wilder's reason for writing, 9, 13; Wilder's revisions of, 108–10, 131, 281–82; wolves in, 216; woods in, 214–15, 227, 228

*Little House on the Prairie* (TV series), 94; as adaptation, 131; political overtones of, 50–51

*Little House on the Prairie* (Wilder): Bender family murders and, 44, 47; and displacement of American Indians, 161, 210–11; and historical fiction as genre, 120; racism in, 131; reviews of, 115; Wilder's research for, 118–19; writing of, 14

Little House series: appeal of, 133–34, 138–41, 233–34; books in, 104; dangers of childhood in, 254–55; decline in Ingalls family security, 234–35; efforts to ban, 210–11; as first novel series for children, 13–14, 115–16; Laura's maturation in, 279; literary awards and, 127; midwestern culture portrayed in, 172–73, 175; models for, 116; motion picture rights, 129; outsiders as threat in, 255–56, 260; Pa's fiddle as literary device in, 11n7, 220; and political messages, 171n55; politicized debate on, 211; sales of, 128–31; shielding of children in, 254–55; style of, 45, 105, 112–13; 115–6, 118, 128, 137; television rights for, 131; third person narrator in, 113–14; translations of, 128; use in schools, 128; Wilder's motives for, 13–14, 14n9, 21–22, 103–4, 107, 281–82, 283–84; Wilder's plan for, 11, 14–15, 48; and women's work, 290–91; values taught in, 133–34, 159, 221. *See also* Lane, Rose Wilder, and Little House series: as editor; truth of Little House series; *other specific subjects*

*Little Town on the Prairie* (Wilder): and death of Jack the bulldog, 279; events removed from, 247–48; and familiarity of midwestern small towns, 169, 172; illustrations in, 123; Laura's dislike of town in, 260; old people in, 274; racism in, 131–32; Wilder's plan for, 15; Wilder's revisions of, 132

*Little Women* (Alcott), 116, 122

Loftus, Daniel, 171, 262

London, Jack, Lane biography of, 35–36, 114

*The Long Winter* (Wilder): and decline in Ingalls family security, 235; heroic optimism in, 224; and historical fiction as genre, 120; economic forces in, 235; old people in, 274; and *Pioneer Girl*, 169–70; resonance with South Dakotans, 1; title of, 124, 274–75; Wilder's conflicts with Lane over, 117; Wilder's plan for, 15; Wilder's research for, 118–19

Lurie, Alison, 213–14

MacBride, Abigail, and Pioneer Girl Project, 101, 135–36

MacBride, Roger Lea, 97; death of, 101, 135; and donation of documents to Hoover Presidential Library, 96–98; and *The First Four Years*, 294–300, *295*; and historical accuracy of Wilder's novels, 93; and *Pioneer Girl*, 95, 99–101; and scholarship on Wilder, 94–95

*McCall's* magazine: Lane's writing for, 58; Wilder's writing for, 105, 200–202, *201*

*Main Street* (Lewis), 172

*The Making of Herbert Hoover* (Lane), 36–37, 96

Manifest Destiny: and pioneer spirit, 107, 161; Wilder's reinterpretation of, 210, 212; and Wilder's shaping of Little House series, 241

Mansfield, Mo.: culture of, 153–55; Wilders' social life in, 153, 188. *See also* Laura Ingalls Wilder Home and Museum; Rocky Ridge Farm

Man-Suffrage Association, 192

Masters, George and Maggie, 169–70, 246–47

Masters, Mattie, 245–46

Masters, Will, 243, 244–45

Masters, William and Emmeline, 243, 244, 245

Midwest: boundaries of, 149, 149–50n7; culture of, 155–61, 176; homesteading and, 155, 162–67, 176; small towns and, 155, 167–72, 176; values in, 172–73, 175–76; Wilder's portrayal of, 158–60, 166–67

midwesterner(s): and influence of place on identity, 146–47, 147n4; self-image of, 150–51; as term, 149; Wilder as, 145–46, 150, 176

Miller, John E., 188, 210–11, 272

mirages, 17–18

Missouri: regional identity of, 150n7; Wilder family move to, 21, 157, 269. *See also* Mansfield, Mo.

*Missouri Ruralist*, Wilder's writing for, 80, 105, 147, 180, *181*; on balance in one's life, 175; on Christian treatment of neighbors, 154; on farm wife's skills, 163; on home influence on children, 204; on impact of World War I, 198–99; on improving small town life, 172n59; on Laura's unjust spanking, 202–3; length of tenure, 180; on life choices, 185, 204; on mother's death, 277, 279, 284, 288; popularity of, 180; on selfishness, 203–4; *The Small Farm Home*, 21; on tension between community and individualism, 198–99; tone of, 221; on unchanging fundamental values, 184–85; and Wilder as farm wife, 180; Wilder's interest in fairy tales and, 223–24; and Wilder's status as writer, 80; on woman suffrage movement, 195–98; women's farm life as central concern of, 199–200; on women's role, 177, 184, 194n36, 198

Montgomery, L. M., 116

Mortensen, Louise Hovde, 86–87

*Mother, Home, and Heaven* (1882), 177–79, *178*

motherhood, in *The First Four Years*, 297–98

*My Ántonia* (Cather), 166–67

Newbery Medal, 127

New Deal, 181, 232, 263, 289

newspaper and journal articles by Wilder, 20–21; instruction on from daughter, 20, 23–24, 37, 51. See also *Missouri Ruralist*

*New York Journal*, 24–28

*New York Ledger*, 42, 42n80

*New York World*, 24–28

Nineteenth Amendment, 183

Nordstrom, Ursula, 99, 124, 125, 127, 131

Older, Cora, 31

Older, Fremont, 30–31, 55–56

*On the Banks of Plum Creek* (Wilder): and decline in Ingalls family security, 235; illustrations in, 123, 125; on Jack the bulldog, 280; Laura's dislike of town in, 260; Laura's independent agency in, 255; on Ma's skills, 287; story of frozen children in, 17n13; Wilder's writing of, 14–15

*On the Way Home* (Wilder), 95

Ozarks: culture of, 147, 152; Wilder moves to, 21. See also Mansfield, Mo.; Rocky Ridge Farm

Panama-Pacific International Exposition (1915), 20

Panic of 1873, 190

parents, 202–3

Paterson, Isabel, 45–46, 45n89

Persephone, as mother/daughter plot, 299

perseverance: as characteristic of fairy tale hero, 224; of Ingalls family, 138–40; as message of Little House series, 159

*Pioneer Girl* (Wilder): audience for, 81, 283; on deaths of children, 17n13, 247; early scholarship on, 90–92, 93–95; efforts to publish, 37, 81, 98–101, 109–10, 231, 231n; factual errors in, 236; on girls' exposure to violent people, 241–51, 253; on happiness of frontier life, 163; happy ending of, 237; lack of deep reflection in, 203; Lane's editing of, 37–38, 43–44, 109, 225–26, 232–33; Lane's suppression of, 86; Lane's use of stories from, 34–35, 81, 109, 110, 226, 283, 288–90, 292–94; manuscripts of, 2, 3, 81, 95–96, 231n1, 242n20, 246, 247; reworking of, 37–39, 43–44, 51, 81, 109,

115–16, 121, 224–26, 232–33, 236–38, 241–51, 253–59, 261–63, 272–80, 288; as start of Wilder's success, 75; Wilder Home and Museum protection of, 84, 90–93, 94; and women's rights issue, 5, 183–84, 193–94; writing of, 37, 80, 109

*Pioneer Girl: The Annotated Autobiography* (Wilder; Hill ed.): development of, 1–3, 101–2; high quality of, 79–80; inclusion of "Bender" narrative in, 38; introduction to, 80, 105; maps and photographs in, 136; as source material, 231–32, 235–36; and Wilder's legacy, 136–37, 210

Pioneer Girl Project, 101–2

pioneers: Lane on, 14n9; Wilder on, 13. *See also* frontier; homesteading

place, influence on identity, 146–47, 147n5

politics: Lane's political opinions, 58–59, 63–64, 171n55, 232–33, 239, 289; of *Little House on the Prairie* TV series, 50–51; and Little House series, 87, 171n55, 211, 232–33, 239, 247, 262–63; Wilder's political opinions, 153, 171n55, 181–82, 184, 188, 211, 232, 239. *See also* individualism; self-reliance

Populist movement, Wilder and, 181

prairie: Wilder's portrait of, 156–61

Preemption Act (1841), 162

Progressivism: goals of, 191; Wilder and, 180–82, 199; and woman suffrage, 191–92

Pulitzer, Joseph, 24–25, 28

Quiner, Caroline Lake (mother). *See* Ingalls, Caroline Lake Quiner

Quiner, Charlotte Tucker (grandmother), 268–69, 277, 287

Quiner, Eliza (aunt), *285*

Quiner, Henry (uncle), 264

Quiner, Henry Newton (grandfather), 268–69

Quiner, Martha (aunt). *See* Carpenter, Martha Quiner

racism: in Little House books, 131–32, 210–11, 216–17, 220; in Mansfield, Mo., 154

railroads, and midwestern small towns, 168–69

Raymond, Ida Louise, 9, 49, 115, 124

Reconstruction, 190

Red Cross, 37, 182

regional differences (U.S.): blurriness of, 147n3; history of, 148

republican motherhood, and role of women, 185–86

Rocky Ridge Farm (Mansfield, Mo.), 189; donation to Laura Ingalls Wilder Home Association, 81; fans' visits to Wilder at, 83; *Pioneer Girl* manuscripts at, 2, *3*, 81; and Wilders' financial woes, 21–22, 22–23, 80, 237; Wilders' move to, 180, 237; Wilder's writing desk at, 140. *See also* Laura Ingalls Wilder Home and Museum; Mansfield, Mo.

Roosevelt, Eleanor, 61

Roosevelt, Franklin D., 181

Rosenblum, Dolores, 211, 229

"The Rose Years" series, 100

Ross, Betsy, 70, 74–75

*St. Louis Star Farmer*, Wilder's writing for, 105

San Francisco: Lane's journalism ca-

reer in, 20, 22, 23, 30–35, 37, 55–56, 223
*San Francisco Bulletin*: Claire Lane at, 54; Lane at, 22, 23, 30–35, 37, 55–56; Wilder's writing for, 105, 223
*San Francisco Call*: Lane at, 20, 24, 29, 56; Older at, 31, 56
*San Francisco Examiner*, 24
*Saturday Evening Post*, Lane's writing for, 58, 81, 232–33
Schlissel, Lillian, 265–66, 267
scholarship on Wilder: and historical accuracy of Wilder's novels, 87–96; origin and growth of, 86–87; Wilder-Lane documents at Hoover Presidential Library and, 96–98
Second Great Awakening, and women's role, 187
*The Selected Letters of Laura Ingalls Wilder* (Anderson, ed.), 210
self-reliance: in Lane's *Woman's Day Book of American Needlework*, 68, 70–75; in Little House series, 170–71, 171n55, 216, 221, 235, 241, 254; Turner on, 239; Wilder's belief in, 75. *See also* individualism
Seneca Falls Convention, 189–90
settlers: Wilder on, 117–18. *See also* homesteading; pioneers
Sewell, Helen, 122–23, *123*, 127, 227, 227–28, *228*, *234*, 278
*Shepherd of the Hills* (Wright), 154–55
Sherwood, Aubrey, 88, *97*, 119
"Significance of the Frontier in American History" (Turner), 238–39, 238n14
Silverman, Noel: interview with, 136–41; and Pioneer Girl Project, 101, 135–36
"The Small Farm Home" (Wilder), 21

small-town culture: Cather on, 166; importance in Wilder's life, 168; writers critical of, 171–72
small towns: and midwestern culture, 155, 167–72; Wilder's positive view of, 172, 172n59. *See also* De Smet, S.Dak.
Smith, Art, Lane "autobiography" of, 33
sob sisters, yellow journalism and, 24, 31
South Dakota, Dunn paintings of, 157–61, *158*, *160*. *See also* De Smet, S.Dak.
South Dakota Historical Society Press, and *Pioneer Girl* publication, 2–3, 79–80, 101–2, 136
Spanish-American War, yellow journalism and, 27–28
Stanton, Elizabeth Cady, 190
Steadman family, 242, 242n22, 243, 244
stock market crash (1929), and Wilder family, 57, 80, 109
*Stuart Little* (White), 124

Tarbell, Ida, 28–29
telegraphy, Lane's career in, 43, 53–54
television. *See Little House on the Prairie* (TV series)
temperance movement, 187–88
*These Happy Golden Years* (Wilder): adult-themed stories in, 249–51; events removed from, 247; fairy tale elements in, 212; final page of, 267, *267*; on Laura's reluctance to leave family, 266–67; old people in, 274; romantic fiction conventions and, 237; Wilder's research for, 118–19; Wilder's retirement following, 129; and women's rights issue, 5, 184

Thompson, Dorothy, 55, 56
truth: controversy surrounding, in Wilder series, 49–50; 84–96; and fictionalized biography, 114; and historical novel as genre, 119–22; as part of appeal, 133; *Pioneer Girl* as challenge to, 84; Wilder's conception of, 32, 48–49, 118–19, 159, 210. *See also* fairy tales: elements of in Little House series; *Pioneer Girl*: reworking of
"The Truth of the Little House Books" (Zochert), 94–95
Turner, Frederick Jackson, 148, *174*, 174–75, 214, 236, 238–40

uniform edition of Little House series, 85–86, 124, 233–34
*The Uses of Enchantment* (Bettelheim), 229–30

values: in Little House series, 133–34, 159, 221; in midwestern culture, 172–73, 175–76; taught by Wilder to daughter, 52, 53, 74, 75–76; Wilder on nature of, 184–85. *See also* individualism; self-reliance
*The Virginian* (Wister), 107–8
voluntary societies, and women's role, 187

Walnut Grove, Minn.: children frozen in blizzard, 17, 37n66, 247; girls' exposure to violent people in, 244–45; Ingalls family employment in, 42, 164, 243, 259, 262, 277; Ingalls family religious practice in, 153; Ingalls family return to, 93–94, 234, 243
*West from Home: Letters of Laura Ingalls Wilder to Almanzo Wilder, San Francisco, 1915*, 23
"What Is This–The Gestapo?" (Lane), 60, *60*, 65
*When Dreams Come True* (Zipes), 219
White, E. B., 124, 127, 131
"Whom Will You Marry?" (Wilder), 200–202, *201*
Wiggin, Kate Douglas, 116
Wilder, Almanzo (husband), *189*; copy of *Mother, Home, and Heaven* given to Wilder, 177–79, *178*; cultural changes witnessed by, 14; disability of, 21–22; favorite authors of, 224–25; illness and death of, 67, 83, 129; marriage of, 104; name, origin of, 14; political opinions of, 181; trip in snowstorm to fetch grain, 171, 262; on value of common sense, 133; in Wilder's *The First Four Years*, 294–300, *295*
Wilder, Eliza Jane (sister-in-law), 292
Wilder, Laura Ingalls, *130*, *139*, *146*, *189*, *265*; on appeal of Little House series, 134; as avid reader, 224; birth of, 269; death of, 67; education of, 104; and family financial woes, 80; and family stories, ownership of, 290; grandchildren, lack of, 283; life of, as representation of period of history, 13, 106–8, 145, 283; many roles of, 103–5, 145; political opinions of, 153, 171n55, 181–82, 184, 188, 211, 232, 239; religious beliefs of, 153, 184; as shrewd negotiator, 129; son, death of, 179, 237, 276–77, 298; on upsetting memories, 287–88; values transferred to daughter by, 52, 53, 74, 75–76; Williams's

illustrations and, 125; and women's work, 290–91; as writer, 103–7, 119–20, 137–38, 140, 223, 225, 284, 286. *See also* Little House series; individual titles

Wilder family: move to Missouri, 21, 157, 269; stock market crash (1929) and, 57, 80, 109. *See also* De Smet, S.Dak., Wilder family in; Mansfield, Mo.; Rocky Ridge Farm

wilderness, lost, Wilder's yearning for, 217

*A Wilder Rose* (Albert), 104–5

Williams, Garth, 124–27, *126*, 216, 228–29, 233

Wilson, Woodrow, and progressivism, 180–82

Wister, Owen, 107–8

Woman's Christian Temperance Union (WCTU), 187–88, 191

*Woman's Day* (magazine): Lane as writer for, 58–59, 67–68, 76; and values of self-reliance and individualism, 75; women writers published in, 67–68

*Woman's Day Book of American Needlework* (Lane), 67–75, *69*; on American values of individualism and self-reliance, 68, 70–75; on needlework as expression of the maker, 69–70; popularity of, 68; on poverty, 72–73; on women's contribution to culture, 70

woman suffrage movement: in Dakota Territory, 5, 183; history of, 182–83, 187, 189–91; natural rights arguments for, 189–90; Progressive movement and, 191–92; Wilder's views on, 183–84, 185, 192, 193–94, 195–98; women's political engagement in, 205–6. *See also* anti-suffragists

women: in cities, 200; on frontier, 238–39, 239–40; in journalism, 28–29, 55–56; in workforce, 198–99, 205. *See also* Lane, Rose Wilder: as journalist

women's rights, Wilder on, 183–84

women's role: anti-suffragists on, 192–93; history of (U.S.), 185–87; middle-class view of, 177–79; temperance movement and, 187–88; Wilder on, 177, 179, 184, 185, 194n36, 198, 200–202, *201*, 204–5

*The Wonderful Wizard of Oz* (Baum), 108, 111, 127

World War I: and expansion of federal power, 181; and women, 196–99

Wright, Harold Bell, 154–55

"Yarbwoman" (Lane), 57

yellow journalism: attraction of new readers by, 28–29; Bender murders and, 40–43, 44; characteristics of, 26–27; history of, 24–28, *25*; Lane's career in, 24, 27, 29, 31–37, 55; and progressivism, 26

Yellow Kid (comic-strip character), *25*, 25

Zipes, Jack, 218, 221–22, 230

Zochert, Donald, 94–96